*The entire subject
of Psychoanalysis—
complete, clear,
comprehensive*

This is *the* classic book on psychoanalysis by Sigmund Freud. The one book on this momentous subject that makes it possible for everyone to understand and benefit from the great discoveries Dr. Freud made.

Here are twenty-eight lectures, frank, lucid and conversational, that describe both the methods of psychoanalysis and its results—the exposition of The Psychology of Errors, the famous Technique of Dream Interpretation and The General Theory of Neuroses. These lectures prepared especially for laymen are Freud's clearest and most comprehensive statement of his world-famous theory.

Not to read this is to miss an essential part of modern-day life—and one of the most fascinating books ever written.

A GENERAL INTRODUCTION TO PSYCHOANALYSIS
was originally published by
the Liveright Publishing Corporation.

A General Introduction to

PSYCHOANALYSIS

BY SIGMUND FREUD, M.D., LL.D.

Authorized English Translation of the Revised Edition by
JOAN RIVIERE

With a Preface by ERNEST JONES, M.D.
*President of the International Psycho-Analytical Association
and* G. STANLEY HALL
Former President, Clark University

PUBLISHED BY POCKET BOOKS NEW YORK

A GENERAL INTRODUCTION TO PSYCHOANALYSIS

Boni & Liveright edition published 1924

POCKET BOOK edition published February, 1953

26th printing.......................March, 1975

Standard Book Number: 671-80032-9.

Printed in the U.S.A.

I. Preface to American Edition

Few, especially in this country, realize that while Freudian themes have rarely found a place on the programs of the American Psychological Association, they have attracted great and growing attention and found frequent elaboration by students of literature, history, biography, sociology, morals and æsthetics, anthropology, education, and religion. They have given the world a new conception of both infancy and adolescence, and shed much new light upon characterology; given us a new and clearer view of sleep, dreams, reveries, and revealed hitherto unknown mental mechanisms common to normal and pathological states and processes, showing that the law of causation extends to the most incoherent acts and even verbigerations in insanity; gone far to clear up the *terra incognita* of hysteria; taught us to recognize morbid symptoms, often neurotic and psychotic in their germ; revealed the operations of the primitive mind so overlaid and repressed that we had almost lost sight of them; fashioned and used the key of symbolism to unlock many mysticisms of the past; and in addition to all this, affected thousands of cures, established a new prophylaxis, and suggested new tests for character, disposition, and ability, in all combining the practical and theoretic to a degree salutary as it is rare.

These twenty-eight lectures to laymen are elementary and

almost conversational. Freud sets forth with a frankness almost startling the difficulties and limitations of psychoanalysis, and also describes its main methods and results as only a master and originator of a new school of thought can do. These discourses are at the same time simple and almost confidential, and they trace and sum up the results of thirty years of devoted and painstaking research. While they are not at all controversial, we incidentally see in a clearer light the distinctions between the master and some of his distinguished pupils. A text like this is the most opportune and will naturally more or less supersede all other introductions to the general subject of psychoanalysis. It presents the author in a new light, as an effective and successful popularizer, and is certain to be welcomed not only by the large and growing number of students of psychoanalysis in this country but by the yet larger number of those who wish to begin its study here and elsewhere.

The impartial student of Sigmund Freud need not agree with all his conclusions, and indeed, like the present writer, may be unable to make sex so all-dominating a factor in the psychic life of the past and present as Freud deems it to be, to recognize the fact that he is the most original and creative mind in psychology of our generation. Despite the frightful handicap of the *odium sexicum,* far more formidable today than the *odium theologicum,* involving as it has done for him lack of academic recognition and even more or less social ostracism, his views have attracted and inspired a brilliant group of minds not only in psychiatry but in many other fields, who have altogether given the world of culture more new and pregnant *aperçus* than those which have come from any other source within the wide domain of humanism.

A former student and disciple of Wundt, who recognizes to the full his inestimable services to our science, cannot avoid making certain comparisons. Wundt has had for decades the prestige of a most advantageous academic chair. He founded the first laboratory for experimental psychology, which attracted many of the most gifted and mature students from all lands. By his development of the doctrine of apperception he took psychology forever beyond the old associationism which had ceased to be fruitful. He also established the independence of psychology from physiology, and by his encyclopedic and always thronged lectures, to say nothing of his more or less esoteric seminary, he materially advanced every branch of mental science and extended its influence over the whole wide domain of folklore, mores, language, and primitive religion. His best texts will long constitute a thesaurus which every psychologist must know.

Again, like Freud, he inspired students who went beyond him (the Wurzburgers and introspectionists) whose method and results he could not follow. His limitations have grown more and more manifest. He has little use for the unconscious or the abnormal, and for the most part he has lived and wrought in a preevolutionary age and always and everywhere underestimated the genetic standpoint. He never transcends the conventional limits in dealing, as he so rarely does, with sex. Nor does he contribute much likely to be of permanent value in any part of the wide domain of affectivity. We cannot forbear to express the hope that Freud will not repeat Wundt's error in making too abrupt a break with his more advanced pupils like Adler or the Zurich group. It is rather precisely just the topics that Wundt neglects that Freud makes his chief corner-stones, viz., the unconscious, the abnormal, sex, and affectivity generally, with many genetic, especially ontogenetic, but also phylogenetic factors. The Wundtian influence has been great in the past, while Freud has a great present and a yet greater future.

In one thing Freud agrees with the introspectionists, viz., in deliberately neglecting the "physiological factor" and building on purely psychological foundations, although for Freud psychology is mainly unconscious, while for the introspectionists it is pure consciousness. Neither he nor his disciples have yet recognized the aid proffered them by students of the autonomic system or by the distinctions between the epicritic and protopathic functions and organs of the cerebrum, although these will doubtless come to have their due

place as we know more of the nature and processes of the unconscious mind.

If psychologists of the normal have hitherto been too little
disposed to recognize the precious contributions to psychology
made by the cruel experiments of Nature in mental diseases,
we think that the psychoanalysts, who work predominantly
in this field, have been somewhat too ready to apply their
findings to the operations of the normal mind; but we are
optimistic enough to believe that in the end both these errors
will vanish and that in the great synthesis of the future that
now seems to impend our science will be made vastly richer
and deeper on the theoretical side and also far more practical
than it has ever been before.

G. STANLEY HALL

Clark University.

II. PREFACE TO ENGLISH EDITION

AMONG THE MANY DIFFICULTIES CONFRONTING THOSE WHO wish to acquire a knowledge of psycho-analysis, not the least has been the absence of a suitable text-book with which they could begin their studies. They have hitherto had their choice among three classes of book, against each of which some objection could be urged from the point of view of the beginner. They could pick their way through the heterogeneous collection of papers, such as those published by Freud, Brill, Ferenczi, and myself, which were not arranged on any coherent plan and were also for the greater part addressed to those already having some knowledge of the subject Or they could struggle with more systematic volumes, such as those by Hitschmann and Barbara Low, which suffer from condensation because of the difficulty of having to compress so much into a small space. Or, finally, it might be their fate to come across one of the numerous books, which need not be mentioned by name, that purport to give an adequate account of psycho-analysis, but whose authors have neglected the necessary preliminary of acquiring a proper knowledge of the subject themselves. The gap in the literature of psycho-analysis has now been filled by the writer most competent of all to do it—namely, Professor Freud himself, and the world of clinical psychology must be grateful to him for the effort it must have cost to write such a book in the midst of his other multitudinous duties. In the future we can unhesitatingly deal with the question so often asked, and say: This is the book with which to begin a study of psycho-analysis.

Even here, however, the reader should be warned that it is necessary to add a few modifications to the statement that the present volume is a complete text-book of psycho-analysis. The circumstances of its inception forbid its being so regarded. The book consists of three separate courses of lectures delivered at the University of Vienna in two winter sessions, 1915–1917. The first two of these presuppose absolutely no knowledge of the subject, and the style in which they were delivered constitute them an ideal introduction to the subject. But in the third Semester Professor Freud, doubtless assuming that those of his audience who had pursued their studies so far would by then have widened their reading otherwise, decided to treat them no longer as mere beginners, and so felt himself free to deal more technically with the more difficult subject-matter of the third course—the psycho-analysis of neurotic affections. The result is that the second half of the book is of a much more advanced nature than the first, a fact which, it is true, has the advantage that the author was able here and there to communicate some of his latest conclusions on obscure points. Every student of psycho-analysis, therefore, however advanced, will be able to learn much from this volume.

One must also remark that the book does not convey an adequate impression of the extensive bearing that psycho-analysis has on other humanistic studies than those here dealt with. Apart from a few hints scattered here and there, there is little indication of the extent to which psycho-analysis has already been applied, to sociology, to the study of racial development, and above all, to the psychology of the normal man. The book is definitely confined to its three topics of psychopathology of everyday life, dreams, and neuroses, these having been chosen as constituting the most suitable subject-matter with which to effect the author's purpose—namely, to introduce students to psycho-analysis.

An American translation of the book has already appeared, but, apart from its deficiencies of style, it contained so many serious falsities in translation—a passage, for instance, to the effect that *delusions* cannot be influenced is translated in such a way as to commit Professor Freud, of all people, to the statement that *obsessions* cannot be cured—that it was decided to issue a fresh translation. This has been carried out with scrupulous care by Mrs. Riviere, aided by drafts carried out by Miss Cecil M. Baines of the eleven lectures in Part II. I have compared the whole book with the original, and have discussed doubtful and difficult points with Professor Freud and Mrs. Riviere. Mrs. Riviere's English translation will be its own recommendation: I can give the reader the assurance that it is a faithful and exact rendering.

ERNEST JONES

CONTENTS

13

Introductory Note

THESE LECTURES WERE BROUGHT OUT FOR THE FIRST TIME IN English in 1920 by Horace Liveright, Inc., with an introductory preface by G. Stanley Hall. No translator was named. Two years later another translation made by Joan Riviere was published in London by G. Allen & Unwin. It is obviously undesirable to have the original German text presented to the English-reading public in more than one version. I therefore feel called upon to express my gratitude to the American publishers for their acceptance of the Riviere translation for their new edition.

FREUD

Vienna, November 1934.

PART I

FIRST LECTURE

INTRODUCTION

I DO NOT KNOW WHAT KNOWLEDGE ANY OF YOU MAY ALREADY have of psychoanalysis, either from reading or from hearsay. But having regard to the title of my lectures—Introductory Lectures on Psychoanalysis—I am bound to proceed as though you knew nothing of the subject and needed instruction, even in its first elements.

One thing, at least, I may pre-suppose that you know—namely, that psychoanalysis is a method of medical treatment for those suffering from nervous disorders; and I can give you at once an illustration of the way in which psychoanalytic procedure differs from, and often even reverses, what is customary in other branches of medicine. Usually, when we introduce a patient to a new form of treatment we minimize its difficulties and give him confident assurances of its success. This is, in my opinion, perfectly justifiable, for we thereby increase the probability of success. But when we undertake to treat a neurotic psychoanalytically we proceed otherwise. We explain to him the difficulties of the method, its long duration, the trials and sacrifices which will be required of him; and, as to the result, we tell him that we can make no definite promises, that success depends upon his endeavours, upon his understanding, his adaptability and his perseverance. We have, of course, good reasons, into which you will perhaps gain some insight later on, for adopting this apparently perverse attitude.

Now forgive me if I begin by treating you in the same way as I do my neurotic patients, for I shall positively advise you against coming to hear me a second time. And with this intention I shall explain to you how of necessity you can obtain from me only an incomplete knowledge of psychoanalysis and also what difficulties stand in the way of your forming an independent judgment on the subject. For I shall show you how the whole trend of your training and your accustomed modes of thought must inevitably have made you hostile to psychoanalysis, and also how much you would have to overcome in your own minds in order to master this instinctive opposition. I naturally cannot foretell what degree of understanding of psychoanalysis you may gain from my lectures, but I can at least assure you that by attending them you will not have learnt how to conduct a psychoanalytic investigation, nor how to carry out a psychoanalytic treatment. And further, if any one of you should feel dissatisfied with a merely cursory acquaintance with psychoanalysis and should wish to form a permanent connection with it, I shall not merely discourage him, but I shall actually warn him against it. For as things are at the present time, not only would the choice of such a career put an end to all chances of academic success, but, upon taking up work as a practitioner, such a man would find himself in a community which misunderstood his aims and intentions, regarded him with suspicion and hostility, and let loose upon him all the latent evil impulses harboured within it. Perhaps you can infer from the accompaniments of the war now raging in Europe what a countless host that is to reckon with.

However, there are always some people to whom the possibility of a new addition to knowledge will prove an attraction strong enough to survive all such inconveniences. If there are any such among you who will appear at my second lecture in spite of my words of warning they will be welcome. But all of you have a right to know what these inherent difficulties of psychoanalysis are to which I have alluded.

First of all, there is the problem of the teaching and exposition of the subject. In your medical studies you have been accustomed to use your eyes. You see the anatomical specimen, the precipitate of the chemical reaction, the contraction of the muscle as the result of the stimulation of its nerves. Later you come into contact with the patients; you learn the symptoms of disease by the evidence of your senses; the results of pathological processes can be demonstrated to you, and in many cases even the exciting cause of them in an isolated form. On the surgical side you are witnesses of the measures by which the patient is helped, and are permitted to attempt them yourselves. Even in psychiatry, demonstration of patients, of their altered expression, speech and behaviour, yields a series of observations which leave a deep impression on your minds. Thus a teacher of medicine acts for the most part as an exponent and guide, leading you as it were through a museum, while you gain in this way a direct relationship to what is displayed to you and believe yourselves to have been convinced by your own experience of the existence of the new facts.

But in psychoanalysis, unfortunately, all this is different. In psychoanalytic treatment nothing happens but an exchange of words between the patient and the physician. The patient talks, tells of his past experiences and present impressions, complains, and expresses his wishes and his emotions. The physician listens, attempts to direct the patient's thought-processes, reminds him, forces his attention in certain directions, gives him explanations and observes the reactions of understanding or denial thus evoked. The patient's unenlightened relatives—people of a kind to be impressed only by something visible and tangible, preferably by the sort of 'action' that may be seen at a cinema—never omit to express their doubts of how "mere talk can possibly cure anybody." Their reasoning is of course as illogical as it is inconsistent. For they are the same people who are always convinced that the sufferings of neurotics are purely "in their own imagination." Words and magic were in the beginning one and the same thing, and even to-day words retain much of their magical power. By words one of us can give to another the greatest happiness or bring about utter despair; by words the teacher imparts his knowledge to the student; by words the orator sweeps his audience with him and determines its judgements and decisions. Words call forth emotions and are universally the means by which we influence our fellow-creatures. Therefore let us not despise the use of words in psycho-therapy and let us be content if we may overhear the words which pass between the analyst and the patient.

But even that is impossible. The dialogue which constitutes the analysis will admit of no audience; the process cannot be demonstrated. One could, of course, exhibit a neurasthenic or hysterical patient to students at a psychiatric lecture. He would relate his case and his symptoms, but nothing more. He will make the communications necessary to the analysis only under the conditions of a special affective relationship to the physician; in the presence of a single person to whom he was indifferent he would become mute. For these communications relate to all his most private thoughts and feelings, all that which as a socially independent person he must hide from others, all that which, being foreign to his own conception of himself, he tries to conceal even from himself.

It is impossible, therefore, for you to be actually present during a psychoanalytic treatment; you can only be told about it, and can learn psychoanalysis, in the strictest sense of the word, only by hearsay. This tuition at second hand, so to say, puts you in a very unusual and difficult position as regards forming your own judgement on the subject, which will therefore largely depend on the reliance you can place on your informant.

Now imagine for a moment that you were present at a lecture in history instead of in psychiatry, and that the lecturer was dealing with the life and conquests of Alexander the Great. What reason would you have to believe what he told you? The situation would appear at first sight even more unsatisfactory than in the case of psychoanalysis, for the professor of history had no more part in Alexander's campaigns than you yourselves; the psychoanalyst at least informs you of matters in which he himself has played a part. But then we come to the question of what evidence there is to support the historian. He can refer you to the accounts of early writers who were either contemporaries or who lived not long after the events in question, such as Diodorus, Plutarch, Arrian, and others; he can lay before you reproductions of the preserved coins and statues of the king, and pass round a photograph of the mosaic at Pompeii representing the battle at Issus. Yet, stictly speaking, all these documents only prove that the existence of Alexander and the reality of his deeds were already believed in by former generations of men, and your criticism might begin anew at this point. And then you would find that not everything reported of Alexander is worthy of belief or sufficiently authenticated in detail, but I can hardly suppose that you would leave the lecture-room in doubt altogether as to the reality of Alexander the Great. Your conclusions would be principally determined by two considerations: first, that the lecturer could have no conceivable motive for attempting to persuade you of something which he did not himself believe to be true, and secondly, that all the available authorities agree more or less in their accounts of the facts. In questioning the accuracy of the early writers you would apply these tests again, the possible motives of the authors and the agreement to be found between them. The result of such tests would certainly be convincing in the case of Alexander, probably less so in regard to figures like Moses and Nimrod. Later on you will perceive clearly enough what doubts can be raised against the credibility of an exponent of psychoanalysis.

Now you will have a right to ask the question: If no objective evidence for psychoanalysis exists and no possibility of demonstrating the process, how is it possible to study it at all or to convince oneself of its truth? The study of it is indeed not an easy matter, nor are there many people who have thoroughly learned it; still, there is, of course, some way of learning it. Psychoanalysis is learnt first of all on oneself, through the study of one's own personality. This is not exactly what is meant by introspection, but it may be so described for want of a better word. There is a whole series of very common and well-known mental phenomena which can be taken as material for self-analysis when one has acquired some knowledge of the method. In this way one may obtain the required conviction of the reality of the processes which psychoanalysis describes, and of the truth of its conceptions, although progress on these lines is not without its limitations. One gets much further by submitting oneself to analysis by a skilled analyst, undergoing the working of the analysis in one's own person and using the opportunity to observe the finer details of the technique which the analyst employs. This, eminently the best way, is of course only practicable for individuals and cannot be used in a class of students.

The second difficulty you will find in connection with psychoanalysis is not, on the other hand, inherent in it, but is one for which I must hold you yourselves responsible, at least in so far as your medical studies have influenced you. Your training will have induced in you an attitude of mind very far removed from the psychoanalytical one. You have been trained to establish the functions and disturbances of the organism on an anatomical basis, to explain them in terms of chemistry and physics, and to regard them from a biological point of view; but no part of your interest has ever been directed to the mental aspects of life, in which, after all, the development of the marvellously complicated organism culminates. For this reason a psychological attitude of mind is still foreign to you, and you are accustomed to regard it with suspicion, to deny it a scientific status, and to leave it to the general public, poets, mystics, and philosophers. Now this limitation in you is undoubtedly detrimental to your medical efficiency; for on meeting a patient it is the mental aspects with which one first comes into contact, as in most human relationships, and I am afraid you will pay the penalty of having to yield a part of the curative influence at which you aim to the quacks, mystics, and faith-healers whom you despise.

I quite acknowledge that there is an excuse for this defect in your previous training. There is no auxiliary philosophical science that might be of service to you in your profession. Neither speculative philosophy nor descriptive psychology,

nor even the so-called experimental psychology which is
studied in connection with the physiology of the sense-organs,
as they are taught in the schools, can tell you anything useful
of the relations existing between mind and body, or can give
you a key to comprehension of a possible disorder of the
mental functions. It is true that the psychiatric branch of
medicine occupies itself with describing the different forms of
recognizable mental disturbances and grouping them in clinical
pictures, but in their best moments psychiatrists themselves are
doubtful whether their purely descriptive formulations deserve
to be called science. The origin, mechanism, and interrelation
of the symptoms which make up these clinical pictures are undiscovered: either they cannot be correlated with any demonstrable changes in the brain, or only with such changes as in
no way explain them. These mental disturbances are open to
therapeutic influence only when they can be identified as secondary effects of some organic disease.

This is the lacuna which psychoanalysis is striving to fill. It
hopes to provide psychiatry with the missing psychological
foundation, to discover the common ground on which a cor-
relation of bodily and mental disorder becomes comprehensible. To this end it must dissociate itself from every foreign
preconception, whether anatomical, chemical, or physiological,
and must work throughout with conceptions of a purely psychological order, and for this very reason I fear that it will appear strange to you at first.

For the next difficulty I shall not hold you, your training or
your mental attitude, responsible. There are two tenets of
psychoanalysis which offend the whole world and excite its
resentment; the one conflicts with intellectual, the other with
moral and æsthetic prejudices. Let us not underestimate these
prejudices; they are powerful things, residues of valuable,
even necessary, stages in human evolution. They are maintained by emotional forces, and the fight against them is a
hard one.

The first of these displeasing propositions of psychoanalysis
is this: that mental processes are essentially unconscious, and
that those which are conscious are merely isolated acts and

parts of the whole psychic entity. Now I must ask you to remember that, on the contrary, we are accustomed to identify
the mental with the conscious. Consciousness appears to us as
positively the characteristic that defines mental life, and we
regard psychology as the study of the content of consciousness. This even appears so evident that any contradiction of
it seems obvious nonsense to us, and yet it is impossible for
psychoanalysis to avoid this contradiction, or to accept the
identity between the conscious and the psychic. The psychoanalytical definition of the mind is that it comprises processes
of the nature of feeling, thinking, and wishing, and it maintains that there are such things as unconscious thinking and
unconscious wishing. But in doing so psychoanalysis has for-
feited at the outset the sympathy of the sober and scientifically
minded, and incurred the suspicion of being a fantastic cult
occupied with dark and unfathomable mysteries.[1] You yourselves must find it difficult to understand why I should stigmatize an abstract proposition, such as "The psychic is the
conscious," as a prejudice; nor can you guess yet what evolutionary process could have led to the denial of the unconscious, if it does indeed exist, nor what advantage could have
been achieved by this denial. It seems like an empty wrangle
over words to argue whether mental life is to be regarded as
co-extensive with consciousness or whether it may be said to
stretch beyond this limit, and yet I can assure you that the
acceptance of unconscious mental processes represents a decisive step towards a new orientation in the world and in
science.

As little can you suspect how close is the connection between this first bold step on the part of psychoanalysis and
the second to which I am now coming. For this next proposition, which we put forward as one of the discoveries of psychoanalysis, consists in the assertion that impulses, which can
only be described as sexual in both the narrower and the
wider sense, play a peculiarly large part, never before sufficiently appreciated, in the causation of nervous and mental

[1][Literally: "that wishes to build in the dark and fish in murky
waters."—Tr.]

disorders. Nay, more, that these sexual impulses have contributed invaluably to the highest cultural, artistic, and social achievements of the human mind.

In my opinion, it is the aversion from this conclusion of psychoanalytic investigation that is the most significant source of the opposition it has encountered. Are you curious to know how we ourselves account for this? We believe that civilization has been built up, under the pressure of the struggle for existence, by sacrifices in gratification of the primitive impulses, and that it is to a great extent for ever being re-created, as each individual, successively joining the community, repeats the sacrifice of his instinctive pleasures for the common good. The sexual are amongst the most important of the instinctive forces thus utilized: they are in this way sublimated, that is to say, their energy is turned aside from its sexual goal and diverted towards other ends, no longer sexual and socially more valuable. But the structure thus built up is insecure, for the sexual impulses are with difficulty controlled; in each individual who takes up his part in the work of civilization there is a danger that a rebellion of the sexual impulses may occur, against this diversion of their energy. Society can conceive of no more powerful menace to its culture than would arise from the liberation of the sexual impulses and a return of them to their original goal. Therefore society dislikes this sensitive place in its development being touched upon; that the power of the sexual instinct should be recognized, and the significance of the individual's sexual life revealed, is very far from its interests; with a view to discipline it has rather taken the course of diverting attention away from this whole field. For this reason, the revelations of psychoanalysis are not tolerated by it, and it would greatly prefer to brand them as æsthetically offensive, morally reprehensible, or dangerous. But since such objections are not valid arguments against conclusions which claim to represent the objective results of scientific investigation, the opposition must be translated into intellectual terms before it can be expressed. It is a characteristic of human nature to be inclined to regard anything which is disagreeable as untrue, and then without much difficulty to find arguments against it. So society pronounces the unacceptable to be untrue, disputes the results of psychoanalysis with logical and concrete arguments, arising, however, in affective sources, and clings to them with all the strength of prejudice against every attempt at refutation.

But we, on the other hand, claim to have yielded to no tendency in propounding this objectionable theory. Our intention has been solely to give recognition to the facts as we found them in the course of painstaking researches. And we now claim the right to reject unconditionally any such introduction of practical considerations into the field of scientific investigation, even before we have determined whether the apprehension which attempts to force these considerations upon us is justified or not.

These, now, are some of the difficulties which confront you at the outset when you begin to take an interest in psychoanalysis. It is probably more than enough for a beginning. If you can overcome their discouraging effect, we will proceed further.

Second Lecture

The Psychology of Errors

We shall now begin, not with postulates, but with an investigation. For this purpose we shall select certain phenomena which are very frequent, very familiar and much overlooked, and which have nothing to do with illness, since they may be observed in every healthy person. I refer to the errors that everyone commits: as when anyone wishes to say a certain thing but uses the wrong word ('slip of the tongue')[1]; or when the same sort of mistake is made in writing ('slip of the pen')[2], in which case one may or may not notice it; or when anyone reads in print or writing something other than what is actually before him ('misreading')[3]; or when anyone mishears[4] what is said to him, naturally when there is no question of any disease of the auditory sense-organ. Another series of such phenomena are those based on forgetting[5] something temporarily, though not permanently; as, for instance, when anyone cannot think of a name which he knows quite well and is always able to recognize whenever he sees it; or when anyone forgets to carry out some intention, which he afterwards remembers, and has therefore forgotten only for a certain time. This element of transitoriness is lacking in a third

[1] In German—*Versprechen*.   [2] *Verschreiben.*
[3] *Verlesen.*   [4] *Verhören.*
[5] *Vergessen.*

class, of which mislaying[1] things so that they cannot be found
is an example. This is a kind of forgetfulness which we regard
differently from the usual kind; one is amazed or annoyed at
it, instead of finding it comprehensible. Allied to this are
certain *mistakes*, in which the temporary element is again
noticeable, as when one believes something for a time which
both before and afterwards one knows to be untrue, and a
number of similar manifestations which we know under
various names.

Some inner relation between all these kinds of occurrences
is indicated in German, by the use of the prefix *"ver"* which is
common to all the words designating them.[2] These words almost all refer to acts of an unimportant kind, generally temporary and without much significance in life. It is only rarely
that anything of the kind, such as the loss of some object, attains any practical importance. For this reason little attention
is paid to such happenings and they arouse little feeling.

I am now going to ask you to consider these phenomena.
But you will object, with annoyance: "There are so many
tremendous puzzles both in the wide world and in the narrower life of the soul, so many mysteries in the field of mental
disorder which demand and deserve explanation, that it really
seems frivolous to waste labour and interest on these trifles.
If you could explain to us how it is possible for anyone with
sound sight and hearing, in broad daylight, to see and hear
things which do not exist, or how anyone can suddenly believe
that his nearest and dearest are persecuting him, or can justify
with the most ingenious arguments a delusion which would
seem nonsensical to any child, then we might be willing to
take psychoanalysis seriously. But if psychoanalysis cannot
occupy us with anything more interesting than the question
why a speaker uses a wrong word or why a *Hausfrau* mislays
her keys and similar trivialities, then we shall find something
better to do with our time and our interest."

My reply is: Patience! Your criticism is not on the right

[1] *Verlegen.*

[2] [The equivalent English prefix is "mis-," but is not so widely
employed.—Tr.]

track. It is true that psychoanalysis cannot boast that it has never occupied itself with trifles. On the contrary, the material of its observations is usually those commonplace occurrences which have been cast aside as all too insignificant by other sciences, the refuse, so to speak, of the phenomenal world. But in your criticism are you not confounding the magnitude of a problem with the conspicuous nature of its manifestations? Is it not possible, under certain conditions and at certain times, for very important things to betray themselves in very slight indications? I could easily cite many instances of this. What slight signs, for instance, convey to the young men in my audience that they have gained a lady's favour? Do they expect an explicit declaration, a passionate embrace, or are they not content with a glance which is almost imperceptible to others, a fleeting gesture, a handshake prolonged by a second? Or suppose you are a detective engaged in the investigation of a murder, do you actually expect to find that the murderer will leave his photograph with name and address on the scene of the crime? Are you not perforce content with slighter and less certain traces of the person you seek? So let us not under-value small signs: perhaps from them it may be possible to come upon the tracks of greater things. Besides, I think as you do that the larger problems of the world and of science have the first claim on our interest. But on the whole it avails little to form a definite resolution to devote oneself to the investigation of this or that great problem. One is then often at a loss how to set about the next step. In scientific work it is more profitable to take up whatever lies before one whenever a path towards its exploration presents itself. And then, if one carries it through thoroughly, without prejudice or pre-conceptions, one may, with good fortune and by virtue of the interrelationship linking each thing to every other (hence, also, the small to the great), find, even in the course of such humble labour, a road to the study of the great problems.

It is from this point of view that I hope to enlist your interest in considering the apparently trivial errors made by normal people. I propose now that we question someone who has no knowledge of psychoanalysis as to how he explains these occurrences.

His first answer is sure to be: "Oh, they are not worth any explanation; they are little accidents." What does the man mean by this? Does he mean to maintain that there are any occurrences so small that they fail to come within the causal sequence of things, that they might as well be other than they are? Anyone thus breaking away from the determination of natural phenomena, at any single point, has thrown over the whole scientific outlook on the world (*Weltanschauung*). One may point out to him how much more consistent is the religious outlook on the world, which emphatically assures us that "not one sparrow shall fall to the ground" except God wills it. I think our friend would not be willing to follow his first answer to its logical conclusion; he would give way and say that if he were to study these things he would soon find some explanation of them. It must be a matter of slight functional disturbances, of inaccuracies of mental performance, the conditions of which could be discovered. A man who otherwise speaks correctly may make a slip of the tongue, (1) when he is tired or unwell, (2) when he is excited, or (3) when his attention is concentrated on something else. It is easy to confirm this. Slips of the tongue do indeed occur most frequently when one is tired, or has a headache, or feels an attack of migraine coming on. Forgetting proper names very often occurs in these circumstances; many people are habitually warned of the onset of an attack of migraine by the inability to recall proper names. In excitement, too, one mixes up words or even things, one performs actions erroneously[1]; and the forgetting of intentions, as well as a number of other undesigned acts, comes to the fore when one is distracted, in other words, when the attention is concentrated on other things. A familiar instance of such distraction is the professor in *Fliegende Blätter* who forgets his umbrella and takes the wrong hat, because he is thinking of the problems which are to be the subject of his next book. We all know from our own experience how one can forget to carry out intentions or

[1] In German—*Vergreifen.*

promises when something has happened in the interval that absorbs one very deeply.

This seems so entirely comprehensible and also irrefutable. It is perhaps not very interesting or not so much so as we expected. Let us look at this explanation of errors more closely. The various conditions which have been cited as necessary for the occurrence of these phenomena are not all similar in kind. Illness and disorders of the circulation afford a physiological basis for an affection of the normal functions; excitement, tiredness, and distraction are conditions of a different kind which could be described as psycho-physiological. These last could easily be converted into a theory. Fatigue, as well as distraction, and perhaps also general excitement, cause a dissipation of the attention from which it may follow that the act in question has insufficient attention devoted to it. It can then very easily be disturbed and inexactly performed. Slight illness or a change in the distribution of blood in the central organ of the nervous system can have the same effect, by these conditions affecting the determining factor, the distribution of attention, in a similar way. In all cases it would be a question of the effects of a disturbance of the attention from organic or psychical causes.

But all this doesn't seem to promise much of interest for a psychoanalytic investigation. We might feel tempted to give up the topic. To be sure, a closer inspection of the facts shows that they are not all in accord with the 'attention' theory of errors of this sort, or at least that not everything can be directly deduced from it. We find that such errors and such forgetfulness also take place when people are not fatigued or excited, but are in every way in their normal condition, unless, just because of the errors, we were subsequently to attribute to them a condition of excitement which they themselves did not acknowledge. Nor can the matter be quite so simple as that the successful performance of an act will be ensured by an intensification of attention, or endangered by a diminution of it. For a great number of actions may be carried out in a purely automatic way with very little attention and yet quite successfully. In walking, a man may perhaps scarcely know where he is going but keep to the right road and stop at his destination without having gone astray. At least, this is what usually happens. A practised pianist strikes the right notes without thinking of them. He may of course also make an occasional mistake, but if automatic playing increased the danger of errors the virtuoso, whose constant practice has made his playing entirely automatic, would be the most exposed to this danger. Yet we see, on the contrary, that many acts are most successfully carried out when they are not the objects of particularly concentrated attention, and that mistakes may occur just on occasions when one is most eager to be accurate, that is, when a distraction of the necessary attention is most certainly not present. One could then say that this is the effect of the 'excitement,' but we do not understand why the excitement does not rather intensify the concentration on the end so much desired. So that if in an important speech anyone says the opposite of what he intends, it can hardly be explained according to the psycho-physiological or the attention theory.

There are also many other minor features in connection with these errors which we do not understand and which are not rendered more comprehensible by these explanations. For instance, when one has temporarily forgotten a name one is annoyed, one is determined to recall it and cannot desist from the attempt. Why is it that despite this annoyance the person so often cannot succeed, as he wishes, in directing his attention to the word which, as he says, is "on the tip of his tongue," and which he instantly recognizes when it is supplied to him? Or, to take another example, there are cases in which the errors multiply, link themselves together or act as substitutes for one another. The first time, one forgets an appointment; the next time, after having made a special resolution not to forget it, one discovers that one has made a mistake in the day or hour. Or one tries by devious ways to remember a forgotten word, and in the course of so doing loses track of a second name which would have been of use in finding the first. If one then pursues the second name, a third gets lost, and so on. It is notorious that the same thing happens with misprints, which are of course errors on the part of the compositor. A stubborn error of this sort is said once to have crept into a Social-Democratic newspaper, where, in the account of a festivity, the following words were printed: "Amongst those present was His Highness, the Clown Prince." The next day a correction was attempted. The paper apologized and said: "The sentence should of course have read, 'the Crow-Prince.'" Again, in a war-correspondent's account of meeting a famous general whose infirmities were pretty well known, a reference to the general was printed as "this battle-scared veteran." Next day an apology appeared which read "the words of course should have been 'the bottle-scarred veteran!'"[1] We like to attribute these occurrences to a devil in the type-setting machine or to some malevolent goblin—figurative expressions which at least imply something more than a psycho-physiological theory of the misprint.

I do not know if you are aware of the fact that slips of the tongue can be provoked, called forth by suggestion, as it were. An anecdote will serve to illustrate this. Once when a novice on the stage was entrusted with the important part in *The Maid of Orleans* of announcing to the King: "The Constable sends back his sword," the principal player, during the rehearsal, played the joke of several times repeating to the timid beginner, instead of the text, the following: "The *Komfortabel* sends back his steed."[2] At the performance the unfortunate actor actually made his début with this perverse announcement, though he had been amply warned against so doing, or perhaps just because he had been.

All these little characteristics of errors are not much illuminated by the theory of diverted attention. But that does not necessarily prove the theory wrong. There may be something missing, a link, by the addition of which the theory

[1] [English example.—Tr.]

[2] [*Komfortabel* is a slang Viennese expression for a one-horse cab. An English example of this is as follows: In a play during a scene of a funeral procession the actor was made to say, "Stand back, my Lord, and let the *parson cough!*" instead of "the coffin pass."—Tr.]

might be made completely satisfactory. But many of the errors themselves can be considered from another aspect.

Let us select slips of the tongue, as the type of error best suited to our purpose. We might equally well choose slips of the pen or of reading. Now we must first remind ourselves that, so far, we have only enquired when and under what conditions the wrong word is said, and have received an answer on that point only. Interest may be directed elsewhere, though, and the question raised why just this particular slip is made and no other: one can consider the nature of the mistake. You will see that so long as this question remains unanswered, and the *effect* of the mistake is not explained, the phenomenon remains a pure accident on the psychological side, even if a physiological explanation has been found for it. When it happens that I make a mistake in a word I could obviously do this in an infinite number of ways, in place of the right word substitute any one of a thousand others, or make innumerable distortions of the right word. Now, is there anything which forces upon me in a specific instance just this one special slip, out of all those which are possible, or does that remain accidental and arbitrary, and can nothing rational be found in answer to this question?

Two authors, Meringer and Mayer (a philologist and a psychiatrist) did indeed in 1895 make an attempt to approach the problem of slips of the tongue from this side. They collected examples and first treated them from a purely descriptive standpoint. This of course does not yet furnish any explanation, but it may lead the way to one. They differentiated the distortions which the intended phrase suffered through the slip into: interchanges (in the positions of words, syllables or letters), anticipations, perseverations, compoundings (contaminations), and substitutions. I will give you examples of these authors' main categories. As an instance of an interchange (in the position of words) someone might say "The Milo of Venus" instead of "The Venus of Milo." The well-known slip of the hotel-boy who, knocking at the bishop's door, nervously replied to the question "Who is it?" "The Lord, my boy!" is another example of such an interchange in

the position of words.[1] In the typical Spoonerism the position
of certain letters is interchanged, as when the preacher said:
"How often do we feel a half-warmed fish within us!"[1] It is a
case of anticipation if any one says: "The thought lies
heartily . . ." instead of: "The thought lies heavily on my
heart." A perseveration is illustrated by the well-known ill-
fated toast,   "Gentlemen, I call upon (*auf*) you to
(*auf*) hiccough (= *auf*zustossen)

                                    to the health of our Chief."
(drink) (= *an*zustossen)

And when a member of the House of Commons referred to
another as the "honourable member for Central *Hell*," instead
of "Hull," it was a case of perseveration; as also when a
soldier said to a friend "I wish there were a thousand of our
men *mortified* on that hill, Bill," instead of "fortified." In one
case the *ell* sound has perseverated from the previous words
"member for Centra*l*," and in the other the *m* sound in "*m*en"
has perseverated to form "*m*ortified."[1] These three types of slip
are not very common. You will find those cases much more
frequent in which the slip happens by a compounding or contraction, as for example when a gentleman asks a lady if he
may *insort* her on her way (*begleit-digen*); this contraction is
made up of *begleiten* = to escort, and *beleidigen* = to insult.
(And by the way, a young man addressing a lady in this way
will not have much success with her.) A substitution takes
place when a poor woman says she has an "incurable *infernal*
disease,"[1] or in Mrs. Malaprop's mind when she says, for instance, "few gentlemen know how to value the *ineffectual*
qualities in a woman."[1]

The explanation which the two authors attempt to formulate as the basis of their collection of examples is peculiarly
inadequate. They hold that the sounds and syllables of a word
have different values and that the innervation of the sounds
of higher value can interfere with those of lower value. They
obviously base this conclusion on the cases of anticipation
and perseveration which are not at all frequent; in other forms of
slips of the tongue the question of such sound priorities, even

[1][English examples.—TR.]

if they exist, does not enter at all; for the most frequent type of slip is that in which instead of a certain word one says another which resembles it, and this resemblance is considered by many people sufficient explanation of it. For instance, a professor may say in his opening lecture, "I am not inclined (*geneigt* instead of *geeignet* = fitted) to estimate the merits of my predecessor." Or another professor says, "In the case of the female genital, in spite of the *tempting* . . . I mean, the *attempted* . . ." (*Versuchungen* instead of *Versuche*).

The commonest and also the most noticeable form of slip of the tongue, however, is that of saying the exact opposite of what one meant to say. These cases are quite outside the effect of any relations between sounds or confusion due to similarity, and in default one may therefore turn to the fact that opposites have a strong conceptual connection with one another and are psychologically very closely associated. There are well-known examples of this sort. For instance, the President of our Parliament once opened the session with the words "Gentlemen, I declare a quorum present and herewith declare the session *closed.*"

Any other common association may work in a way as insidious as the association of opposites and may on occasion lead to results as inopportune. So there is a story to the effect that, at a festivity in honour of the marriage of a child of H. Helmholtz with a child of the well-known inventor and captain of industry, W. Siemens, the famous physiologist Dubois-Reymond was asked to speak. He concluded his doubtless brilliant speech with the toast "Success to the new partnership, Siemens and *Halske!*" which was of course the name of the old firm. The association of the two names must have been as familiar to a resident in Berlin as "Cross & Blackwell" to a Londoner.

So the effect of word-associations must be taken into account, as well as that of sound-values and similarities between words. But even that is not enough. In one type of case, before we can arrive at an adequate explanation of the slip we must consider some phrase which had been said, or perhaps

only thought, previously. Again, that is, a case of perseveration, as Meringer insists, but arising in a more distant source.
—I must confess that altogether I have the impression that we
are further than ever from comprehension of slips of the
tongue.

However, I hope I am not mistaken in thinking that in the
course of our examination of the above examples an impression
has formed itself in us which may be of a kind to repay
further attention. We were considering the general conditions
under which slips of the tongue occur and then the influences
which determine the kind of distortion effected in the slip,
but so far we have not examined at all the result of the slip
itself, as an object of interest without regard to its origin. If
we bring ourselves to do this we shall in the end have to
assert courageously that in some of the examples the slip
itself makes sense. Now what does it mean when we say "it
makes sense"? Well, it means that the result of the slip may
perhaps have a right to be regarded in itself as a valid mental
process following out its own purpose, and as an expression
having content and meaning. Hitherto we have only spoken
of errors, but now it appears as if the error could sometimes
be quite a proper act, except that it has intruded itself in the
place of one more expected or intended.

In certain cases the sense belonging to the slip itself appears
obvious and unmistakable. When the President in his opening speech closes the session of Parliament, a knowledge of
the circumstances under which the slip was made inclines us
to see a meaning in it. He expects no good result from the
session and would be glad to be able to disperse forthwith;
there is no difficulty in discovering the meaning, or interpreting the sense, of this slip. Or when a lady, appearing to com-
pliment another, says "I am sure *you* must have *thrown* this
delightful hat together" instead of "sewn it together" (*aufge-
patzt* instead of *aufgeputzt*), no scientific theories in the world
can prevent us from seeing in her slip the thought that the
hat is an amateur production. Or when a lady who is well
known for her determined character says: "My husband asked
his doctor what sort of diet ought to be provided for him.

But the doctor said he needed no special diet, he could eat and drink whatever *I* choose," the slip appears clearly as the unmistakable expression of a consistent scheme.

Now supposing it should turn out that not only a few cases of slips of the tongue and errors in general, but the great majority of them, have a meaning, then the meaning of the error, to which we have hitherto paid no attention, would become the point of greatest interest to us and would justifiably drive all other points of view into the background. All physiological and psycho-physiological conditions could then be ignored and attention could be devoted to the purely psychological investigation of the *sense,* that is, the meaning, the intention, in the errors. With this in view, therefore, we shall soon consider further material.

Before undertaking this, however, I should like to invite you to follow up another clue with me. It often happens that a poet makes use of a slip of the tongue or some other error as a means of artistic expression. This fact in itself proves that he thinks the error, for instance, a slip of the tongue, has a meaning; for he constructs it intentionally. It could hardly happen that a poet accidentally made a slip of the pen and then allowed his slip of the pen to stand as a slip of the tongue of the character. He wishes to reveal something by means of the slip and we may well enquire what that may be—whether perhaps he wishes to indicate that the person in question is distracted or over-tired, or is expecting a headache. Of course we should not exaggerate the importance of it if poets do make use of slips to express their meaning. Slips might be in reality without meaning, accidents in the mental world, or only occasionally have a meaning, and poets would still be entitled to refine them by infusing sense into them for their own purposes. However, it would not be surprising if more were to be learned from poets about slips of the tongue than from philologists and psychiatrists.

There is an example of a slip of this kind in Schiller's *Wallenstein* (Piccolomini, Act I, Scene 5). In the foregoing scene, young Max Piccolomini had taken up Duke Wallenstein's cause ardently, and had been passionately describing the blessings of peace, which he had become aware of in the course of a journey accompanying Wallenstein's beautiful daughter to the camp. As he leaves the stage, his father (Octavio) and the courtier Questenberg are plunged in consternation. The fifth scene continues:—

QUESTENBERG. Alas! and stands it so?
  Friend, do we let him go
  In this delusion? let him go from us?
  Not call him back at once, not
  Open his eyes here and now?

OCTAVIO (*recovering himself out of deep thought*).
  He has now opened *mine*
  And I see more than pleases me.
QUESTENBERG. What is it?
OCTAVIO. A curse upon this journey!
QUESTENBERG. But why so? What is it?
OCTAVIO. Come, come, friend! I must up
  And follow the ill-omened clue at once
  And see with mine own eyes—come with me now!
QUESTENBERG. What now? Where go you then?
OCTAVIO (*hastily*). To her, herself!
QUESTENBERG. To . . .
OCTAVIO (*corrects himself*). To the Duke! Come, let us go

Octavio meant to say: "To him, to the Duke," but his tongue slips and he betrays (to us, at least) by the words *"to her"* that he has clearly recognized the influence at work behind the famous young warrior's rhapsodies in favour of peace.

A still more impressive example was found by O. Rank in Shakespeare. It occurs in the *Merchant of Venice,* in the famous scene in which the fortunate suitor makes his choice among the three caskets; and I can perhaps not do better than read to you now Rank's short account of it.

"A slip of the tongue which occurs in Shakespeare's *Merchant of Venice* (Act III, Sc. 2) is exceedingly fine in the poetic feeling it shows and in the brilliant way in which it is

applied technically. Like the slip in Wallenstein quoted by
Freud in his *Psycho-pathology of Everyday Life*, it shows
that the poets well understand the mechanism and meaning
of such slips and assume that the audience will also understand them. Portia, who by her father's wish has been bound
to the choice of a husband by lot, has so far escaped all the
unwelcome suitors by the lack of fortune. Having at last
found in Bassanio the suitor to whom she is inclined, she fears
that he too will choose the wrong casket. She would like to
tell him that even so he may rest assured of her love, but she
is prevented by her oath. In this inner conflict the poet makes
her say to her chosen suitor:

> *I pray you tarry; pause a day or two,*
> *Before you hazard: for, in choosing wrong,*
> *I lose your company; therefore, forbear awhile:*
> *There's something tells me (but it is not love)*
> *I would not lose you . . .*
> > *. . . I could teach you*
> *How to choose right, but then I am forsworn;*
> *So will I never be; so may you miss me;*
> *But if you do you'll make me wish a sin,*
> *That I had been forsworn. Beshrew your eyes,*
> *They have o'erlooked me, and divided me;*
> *One half of me is yours, the other half yours,—*
> *Mine own, I would say; but if mine, then yours,*
> *And so all yours.*

Just that which she only meant to indicate subtly to him
because she should really have concealed it from him altogether, namely, that even before the lot she was his and
loved him, this the poet with exquisite fineness of psychological feeling causes to come to expression in her slip; and is
able, by this artistic device, to relieve the unbearable uncertainty of the lover as well as the suspense of the audience as
to the issue of the choice."

And notice, at the end, how subtly Portia reconciles the
two declarations which are contained in the slip, how she

resolves the contradiction between them, and finally even justifies the slip.

> . . . but if mine, then yours,
> And so all yours.

It has happened that other thinkers outside the field of medicine have disclosed by an observation the meaning of some error and so anticipated our efforts in this direction. You all know the witty satirist Lichtenberg (1742–1799) of whom Goethe said: "Where he makes a joke, a problem lies concealed." And occasionally the solution of the problem is revealed in the joke. Lichtenberg writes in his witty and satirical *Notes,* "He always read 'Agamemnon' for 'angenommen' (verb meaning 'to take for granted'), so deeply versed was he in Homer." This really contains the whole theory of slips in reading.

At the next lecture we will see whether we can agree with the poets in their conception of the meaning of psychological errors.

THIRD LECTURE

THE PSYCHOLOGY OF ERRORS (*continuation*)

AT THE LAST LECTURE IT OCCURRED TO US TO CONSIDER THE error by itself alone, apart from its relation to the intended act with which it had interfered, and we perceived that in certain cases it seemed to betray a meaning of its own. We said to ourselves that if this conclusion, that the error has its own meaning, could be established on a larger scale, that meaning would soon prove more interesting to us than the investigation of the conditions under which errors arise.

Let us once more agree upon what we understand by the "meaning" of a mental process. This is nothing else but the intention which it serves and its place in a mental sequence. In most of the cases we examined we could substitute for the word "meaning" the words "intention" and "tendency." Now was it only a deceptive appearance, or a poetic glorification of the error, that led us to believe that we could see an intention in it?

Let us still keep to the examples of slips of the tongue and review a larger number of such manifestations. We then find whole categories of cases in which the intention, the meaning, of the slip is quite obvious, particularly so in those instances in which the opposite of what was intended is said. The President says in his opening speech: "I declare the session *closed*." That is surely not ambiguous. The meaning and intention of this slip is that he wants to close the session. One might well say, "he said so himself"; we only take him at his word. Please do not interrupt me with the objection that this is impossible, that we know quite well that he wished to open the session, not to close it, and that he himself whom we have just recognized as the best judge of his intention will affirm that he meant to open it. In doing so you forget that we agreed to consider the error by itself; its relation to the intention which it disturbs will be discussed later. *You* would be guilty of an error in logic, by which you would conveniently dispose of the whole problem under discussion, which in English is called "begging the question."

In other cases, where the form of the slip is not exactly the opposite of what is intended, a contradictory sense may still often come to expression. "I am not *inclined* (*geneigt*) to appreciate my predecessor's merits." "Inclined" is not the opposite of "in a position to" (*geeignet*), but it is an open confession of a thought in sharpest contradiction to the speaker's duty to meet the situation gracefully.

In still other cases the slip simply adds a second meaning to the intended. The sentence then sounds like a contraction, an abbreviation, a condensation of several sentences into one. Thus the determined lady who said: "He may eat and drink whatever *I* choose." That is as if she had said: "He can eat and drink what he chooses, but what does it matter what he chooses? It is for me to do the choosing!" Slips of the tongue often give this impression of abbreviation; for instance, when a professor of anatomy at the end of his lecture on the nasal cavities asks whether his class has thoroughly understood it and, after a general reply in the affirmative, goes on to say: "I can hardly believe that that is so, since persons who can thoroughly understand the nasal cavities can be counted, even in a city of millions, on *one finger* . . . I mean, on the fingers of one hand." The abbreviated sentence has its own meaning: it says that there is only one person who understands the subject.

In contrast to these types in which the slip plainly discloses its meaning are others in which the slip of the tongue conveys nothing intelligible, and therefore directly controverts our expectations. The mis-pronunciation by mistake of proper names, or the enunciation of meaningless sounds, is such a frequent occurrence that this alone would appear to dispose at once of the question whether all errors have a meaning. Yet closer inspection of such examples discloses the fact that it is easily possible to understand such distortions; indeed, that the difference between these unintelligible cases and the previous more comprehensible ones is not so very great.

The owner of a horse, on being asked how it was, replied: "O, it may *stad*—it may *take* another month."[1] Asked what he really meant to say, he answered that he was thinking it was a *sad* business, and the words "sad" and "take" together gave rise to *stad*. (Meringer and Mayer.)

Another man was relating some objectionable incidents and went on: "and then certain facts were *refilled*."[2] He explained that he meant to say these facts were "filthy." "Revealed" and "filthy" together combine to form *refilled*. (Meringer and Mayer.)

You will recall the case of the young man who offered to "insort" an unknown lady. We took the liberty of resolving this word into "insult" and "escort," and were quite convinced of this interpretation without requiring proof of it.[3] From these examples you can see that even these more obscure cases can be explained as the concurrence, or *interference*, of two different intentions of speech with one another; the differences arise only in that in the first type of slip the one intention has entirely excluded the other, as when the opposite is said; while in the second type the one intention only succeeds in distorting or modifying the other, from which arise combinations of a more or less senseless appearance.

We believe that we have now discovered the secret of a

[1]"Ja, das draut" = das *dauert* . . . eine *traurige* Geschichte.

[2]"Dann aber sind Tatsachen zum *Vorschwein* gekommen" = *Vorchein* . . . *Schweinerei*.

[3][The two words *"begleiten"* and *"beleidigen"* are a good deal more obvious in the German *"begleidigen"* than in the translation. TR.]

large number of slips of the tongue. If we keep this clear in mind we shall be able to comprehend still further groups hitherto entirely mysterious. Although, for instance, in a case of distortion of a name we cannot suppose that it is always a matter of a contest between two similar but different names, yet the second intention is easily perceived. Distortions of names are common enough apart from slips of the tongue; they are attempts to liken the name to something derogatory or degrading, a common form of abuse, which educated persons soon learn to avoid but nevertheless do not willingly give up. It may be dressed up as a joke, although one of a very low order. To quote one gross and ugly example of such a distortion of a name, the name of the President of the French Republic, *Poincaré*, has lately been transformed into *"Schweinskarré."* It is not going much further to assume that some such abusive intention may also be behind distortions of names produced by a slip of the tongue. In pursuing our idea, similar explanations suggest themselves for cases of slips where the effect is comic or absurd. In the case of the member of parliament who referred to the "honourable member for Central Hell," the sober atmosphere of the House is unexpectedly disturbed by the intrusion of a word that calls up a ludicrous and unflattering image; we are bound to conclude from the analogy with certain offensive and abusive expressions that an impulse has interposed here, to this effect: "You needn't be taken in. I don't mean a word of this. To hell with the fellow!" The same applies to slips of the tongue which transform quite harmless words into obscene and indecent ones.[1]

We are familiar with this tendency in certain people intentionally to convert harmless words into indecent ones for the sake of the amusement obtained; it passes for wit, and in fact when one hears of a case one at once asks whether it was intended as a joke or occurred unintentionally as a slip of the tongue.

[1][Two untranslatable examples are given in the text, *apopos* for *à propos* and *Eischeissweibchen* for *Eiweissscheibchen*. (Meringer and Mayer.)—TR.]

Well, we seem to have solved the riddle of errors with comparatively little trouble! They are not accidents; they are serious mental acts; they have their meaning; they arise through the concurrence—perhaps better, the mutual interference—of two different intentions. But now I can well understand that you want to overwhelm me with a flood of questions and doubts, which must be answered and resolved before we can enjoy this first result of our efforts. I certainly do not want to press any hasty conclusions upon you. Let us coolly consider everything in turn.

What would you like to say? Whether I think that this explanation accounts for all cases of slips of the tongue or only for a certain number? Whether this conception can be extended to the many other types of errors, to misreading, slips of the pen, forgetting, wrongly performed actions, mislaying things and so on? What part the factors of fatigue, excitement, absent-mindedness and distraction of attention play in regard to the mental nature of errors? Besides this, it is clearly seen that of the two competing meanings in the slip one is always manifest, but not always the other. How is one to arrive at the latter? And if one believes that one has guessed it, how is one to find proof that this is not merely a probability but the only true meaning? Is there anything else you wish to ask? If not, then I myself will continue. I will remind you that we are not really greatly concerned with errors in themselves, but that we wished to learn from a study of them something of value from the point of view of psychoanalysis. Therefore I will put this question: What sort of purposes or tendencies are these which thus interfere with other intentions, and what is the relation between the interfering tendency and the other? Thus, as soon as we have found the answer to the riddle, our efforts begin again.

Very well then; is this the explanation of all cases of slips of the tongue? I am very much inclined to think so, and for this reason, because whenever one examines an instance of it this type of solution may be found. Still, one cannot prove that a slip of the tongue cannot come to pass without the agency of this mechanism. It may be so: for our purposes it is a matter of indifference, theoretically; for the conclusions which we wish to draw by way of an introduction to psychoanalysis remain valid, even if only a small proportion of the total incidence of slips of the tongue comes under our explanation, and this is certainly not so. The next question, whether this explanation extends to other forms of errors, may be answered by way of anticipation in the affirmative. You can convince yourselves of it when we turn to consider examples of slips of the pen, of wrongly performed acts, and so on. I propose, however, for technical reasons that we should postpone doing this until we have investigated the slip of the tongue itself more thoroughly.

The question what significance those factors, which some writers have placed in the foreground, can now have for us—such factors as disturbances of the circulation, fatigue, excitement, distraction, disturbances of attention—demands a more exhaustive reply if we assume the mental mechanism of slips described above. You will notice that we do not deny these factors. Indeed, in general it doesn't often happen that psychoanalysis contests anything which is maintained in other quarters; as a rule, psychoanalysis only adds something new to what has been said; and it does certainly happen on occasion that what has hitherto been overlooked, and is now supplied by psychoanalysis, is the most essential part of the matter. The influence of such physiological predispositions as arise in slight illness, circulatory disturbances and conditions of fatigue, upon the occurrence of slips of the tongue is to be admitted without more ado; everyday personal experience may convince you of it. But how little is explained by this admission! Above all, these are not necessary conditions of errors. Slips of the tongue may just as well occur in perfect health and normal conditions. These bodily factors, therefore, are merely contributory; they only favour and facilitate the peculiar mental mechanism which produces slips of the tongue. I once used an illustration for this state of things which I will repeat here, as I know of no better. Just suppose that on some dark night I am walking in a lonely neighbourhood and am assaulted by a rogue who seizes my watch and money, whereupon, since I could not see the robber's face clearly, I make my complaint at the police-station in these words: "Loneliness and darkness have just robbed me of my valuables." The police officer might reply to me: "You seem to carry your support of the extreme mechanistic point of view too far for the facts. Suppose we put the case thus: Under cover of darkness and encouraged by the loneliness of the spot, some unknown thief has made away with your valuables. It appears to me that the essential thing to be done is to look about for the thief. Perhaps we shall then be able to take the plunder from him again."

Psycho-physiological factors such as excitement, absent-mindedness, distraction of attention, obviously provide very little in the way of explanation. They are mere phrases; they are screens, and we should not be deterred from looking behind them. The question is rather what has here called forth the excitement or the particular diversion of attention. The influence of sound-values, resemblances between words, and common associations connecting certain words, must also be recognized as important. They facilitate the slip by pointing out a path for it to take. But if there is a path before me does it necessarily follow that I must go along it? I also require a motive to determining my choice and, further, some force to propel me forward. These sound-values and word associations are, therefore, just like the bodily conditions, the facilitating causes of slips of the tongue, and cannot provide the real explanation of them. Consider for a moment the enormous majority of cases in which the words I am using in my speech are not deranged on account of sound-resemblance to other words, intimate associations with opposite meanings, or with expressions in common use. It yet remains to suppose, with the philosopher Wundt, that a slip of the tongue arises when the tendency to associations gains an ascendance over the original intention owing to bodily fatigue. This would be quite plausible if experience did not controvert it by the fact that in a number of cases the bodily, and in another large group the associative, predisposing causes are absent.

Particularly interesting to me, however, is your next question, namely, by what means the two mutually disturbing tendencies may be ascertained. You probably do not suspect how portentous this question is. You will agree that one of these tendencies, the one which is interfered with, is always unmistakable; the person who commits the slip knows it and acknowledges it. Doubt and hesitation only arise in regard to the other, what we have called the interfering tendency. Now we have already heard, and you will certainly not have forgotten, that in a certain number of cases this other tendency is equally plain. It is evident in the result of the slip if only we have the courage to let the slip speak for itself. The President who said the opposite of what he meant—it is clear that he wishes to open the session, but equally clear that he would also like to close it. That is so plain that it needs no interpreting. But in the other cases, in which the interfering tendency merely distorts the original without itself coming to full expression,—how can the interfering tendency be detected in the distortion?

In one group of cases by a very safe and simple method, by the same method, that is, by which we establish the tendency that is interfered with. We enquire of the speaker, who tells us then and there; after making the slip he restores the word he originally intended. "O, it may *stad*—no, it may *take* another month." Well, the interfering tendency may be likewise supplied by him. We say, "Now why did you first say stad?" He replies, "I meant to say it was a sad business"; and in the other case in which "refilled" was said, the speaker informs you that he first meant to say it was a filthy business, but controlled himself and substituted another expression. The discovery of the disturbing tendency is here as definitely established as that of the disturbed tendency. It is not without intention that I have selected as examples cases which owe neither their origin nor their explanation to me or to any supporter of mine. Still, in both these cases, a certain intervention was necessary in order to produce the explanation. One had to ask the speaker why he made the slip, what explanation he could give. Without that he might have passed it by without seeking to explain it. Being asked, however, he gave as his answer the first idea that occurred to him. And see now, this little intervention and the result of it constitute already a psychoanalysis, a prototype of every psychoanalytic investigation that we may undertake further.

Now, should I be too suspicious if I were to surmise that, at the very moment at which psychoanalysis begins to dawn upon you, a resistance to it instantly raises itself within your mind? Are you not eager to object that information supplied by the person enquired of, who committed the slip, is not completely reliable evidence. He naturally wishes, you think, to meet your request to explain his slip, and so he says the first thing that he can think of, if it will do at all. There is no proof that that is actually how the slip arose. It may have been so, but it may just as well have been otherwise. Something else also might have occurred to him that would have met the case as well or even better.

It is remarkable how little respect you have, in your hearts, for a mental fact! Imagine that someone had undertaken a chemical analysis of a certain substance and had ascertained that one ingredient of it is of a certain weight, so and so many milligrams. From this weight, thus arrived at, certain conclusions may be drawn. Do you think now it would ever occur to a chemist to discredit these conclusions on the ground that the isolated substance might as well have had some other weight? Everyone recognizes the fact that it actually had this weight and no other, and builds further conclusions confidently on that fact. But when it is a question of a mental fact, that it *was* such an idea and no other that occurred to the person when questioned, you will not accept that as valid, but say that something else might as well have occurred to him! The truth is that you have an illusion of a psychic freedom within you which you do not want to give up. I regret to say that on this point I find myself in sharpest opposition to your views.

Now you will break off here only to take up your resistance at another point. You will continue: "We understand that it lies in the peculiar technique of psychoanalysis to bring the person analysed to give the solution of its problems. Let us take another example, that in which the after-dinner speaker calls upon the company to *hiccough* to the health of their guest. The interfering tendency is, you say, in this case to ridicule; this it is which opposes the intention to do honour. But this is a mere interpretation on your part, based on observations made independently of the slip. If in this case you were to question the perpetrator of the slip he would not confirm your view that he intended an insult; on the contrary, he would vehemently deny it. Why do you not abandon your undemonstrable interpretation in the face of this flat denial?"

Yes, this time you have lighted upon something formidable. I can picture to myself that unknown speaker; he is probably an assistant of the guest of honour, perhaps already a junior lecturer himself, a young man with the brightest prospects. I will press him and ask whether he is sure he did not perceive some feeling in himself antagonistic to the demand that he should pay honour to his chief. A nice fuss there is! He becomes impatient and suddenly bursts out at me: "Look here, enough of this cross-examination, or I'll make myself disagreeable! You will ruin my career with your suspicions. I simply said *"aufstossen"* instead of *"anstossen,"* because I'd already said *"auf"* twice before it. It's the thing that Meringer calls a perseveration, and there's nothing else to be read into it. Do you understand me? That's enough." H'm, this is a startling reaction, a truly energetic repudiation. I see that there is nothing more to be done with the young man, but I think to myself that he betrays a strong personal interest in making out that his slip has no meaning. You will perhaps agree too that he has no right to become so uncivil over a purely theoretical investigation, but after all, you will think, he must know what he wanted to say and what not.

O, so he must? That is perhaps still open to question.

Now you think you have me in a trap. "So that is your technique," I hear you say. "When the person who commits a slip gives an explanation which fits your views then you declare him to be the final authority on the subject. He says so himself! But if what he says does not suit your book, then

you suddenly assert that what he says does not count, one
need not believe it."

Certainly that is so. But I can give you another instance of
a similarly monstrous procedure. When an accused man confesses to a deed the judge believes him, but when he denies
it the judge does not believe him. Were it otherwise the law
could not be administered, and in spite of occasional mis-
carriages you will admit that the system, on the whole, works
well.

"Well, but are you a judge, and is the person who commits
a slip to be accused before you? Is a slip of the tongue a
crime?"

Perhaps we need not reject even this comparison. But see
now to what deep-seated differences our attempt to investigate the apparently harmless problems of errors has brought
us, differences which at this stage we do not know in the least
how to reconcile. I suggest that we should make a temporary
compromise on the basis of the analogy with the judge and
the prisoner. You shall grant me that the meaning of an error
admits of no doubt when the subject of the analysis acknowledges it himself. I, in turn, will admit that a direct proof for
the suspected meaning cannot be obtained if the subject refuses us the information, and, of course, this applies also when
the subject is not present to give us the information. As also
in legal proceedings, we are then thrown back upon indications in order to form a decision, the truth of which is sometimes more and sometimes less probable. At law, for practical
reasons, guilt has to be declared also on circumstantial evidence. There is no such necessity here; but neither are we
bound to refrain from considering such evidence. It is a mistake to believe that a science consists in nothing but conclusively proved propositions, and it is unjust to demand that
it should. It is a demand only made by those who feel a craving for authority in some form and a need to replace the religious catechism by something else, even if it be a scientific
one. Science in its catechism has but few apodictic precepts;
it consists mainly of statements which it has developed to
varying degrees of probability. The capacity to be conten

with these approximations to certainty and the ability to carry on constructive work despite the lack of final confirmation are actually a mark of the scientific habit of mind.

But where shall we find a starting-point for our interpretations, and the indications for our proof, in cases where the subject under analysis says nothing to explain the meaning of the error? From various sources. First, by analogy with similar phenomena not produced by error, as when we maintain that the distortion of a name by mistake has the same intention to ridicule behind it as intentional distortion of names. And then, from the mental situation in which the error arose, from our knowledge of the character of the person who commits it, and of the feelings active in him before the error, to which it may be a response. As a rule what happens is that we find the meaning of the error according to general principles; and this, to begin with, is only a conjecture, a tentative solution, proof being discovered later by an examination of the mental situation. Sometimes it is necessary to await further developments, which have been, so to speak, foreshadowed by the error, before we can find confirmation of our conjecture.

I cannot easily give you evidence of this if I have to limit myself to the field of slips of the tongue, although even here I have a few good examples. The young man who offered to "insort" the lady is in fact very shy; the lady whose husband may eat and drink what *she* likes I know to be one of those managing women who rule the household with a rod of iron. Or take the following case: At a general meeting of a club a young member made a violent attack in a speech, in the course of which he spoke of the officers of the society as *"Lenders* of the Committee,"* which appears to be a substitute for *Members* of the Committee.[1] We should conjecture that against his attack some interfering tendency was active which was itself in some way connected with the idea of *lending*. As a matter of fact an informant tells us that the speaker is in constant money difficulties and was actually attempting to raise money at the time. So the interfering tendency really is to be translated into the thought: "Be more moderate in your op-

[1] *Vor*schussmitglieder instead of *Aus*schussmitglieder.

position: these are the people whom you want to lend you money."

If I diverge into the field of other kinds of errors I can give you a wide selection of examples of such circumstantial evidence.

If anyone forgets an otherwise familiar proper name and has difficulty in retaining it in his memory—even with an effort —it is not hard to guess that he has something against the owner of the name and does not like to think of him; consider in the light of this the following notes on the mental situation in which an error of this kind was made.

A Mr. Y. fell in love with a lady, who did not return the feeling and shortly after married a Mr. X. Although Mr. Y. had already known Mr. X. for some time, and even had business relations with him, he forgets his name over and over again, so that he frequently has to ask someone the man's name when it is necessary to write to him.[1] Obviously Mr. Y. wants to obliterate all knowledge of his fortunate rival. "Never thought of shall he be."

Another example: a lady inquires of a doctor about a common acquaintance, calling her by her maiden name. She has forgotten the married name. She admits that she strongly objected to the marriage and dislikes the husband intensely.[2]

Later we shall have much to say in other connections in regard to the forgetting of names; at the moment we are chiefly interested in the 'mental situation' in which the lapse of memory occurs.

The forgetting of resolutions can in general be referred to an opposing current of feeling which is against carrying out the intention. It is not only we psychoanalysts who hold this view, however; it is the ordinary attitude of everyone in their daily affairs, which they only deny in theory. The protégé whose patron apologizes for having forgotten his request is not pacified by such an apology. He thinks immediately: "It's evidently nothing to him; he promised, but he doesn't mean to do it." Forgetting is therefore criticized even in life, in certain connections, and the difference between the popular and the

[1] From C. G. Jung.   [2] From A. A. Brill.

psychoanalytic conception of these errors seems to be dispelled. Imagine a hostess receiving a guest with the words:
"What, is it to-day you were coming? I quite forgot that I
had asked you for to-day"; or a young man confessing to his
beloved that he had forgotten all about the appointment
they had arranged on the last occasion. He will never admit
it; he will rather invent on the spur of the moment the most
wildly improbable hindrances which prevented his coming
and made it impossible for him to communicate with her from
that day to this. We all know that in military service the
excuse of having forgotten is worthless and saves no one from
punishment; the system is recognized as justifiable. Here
everyone is suddenly agreed that a certain mistake has a meaning and what that meaning is. Why are they not consistent
enough to extend their insight to other errors and then openly
acknowledge it? There is naturally also an answer to this.

If the meaning of forgetting resolutions is so little open to
doubt in the minds of people in general you will be the less
surprised to find that writers employ such mistakes in a
similar sense. Those of you who have seen or read Shaw's
Cæsar and Cleopatra will recall that Cæsar, when departing
in the last scene, is pursued by the feeling that there was
something else he intended to do which he had now forgotten.
At last it turns out what it is: to say farewell to Cleopatra. By
this small device the author attempts to ascribe to the great
Cæsar a feeling of superiority which he did not possess and
to which he did not at all aspire. You can learn from historical
sources that Cæsar arranged for Cleopatra to follow him to
Rome and that she was living there with her little Cæsarion
when Cæsar was murdered, whereupon she fled the city.

The cases of forgetting resolutions are as a rule so clear that
they are of little use for our purpose, which is to discover in
the mental situation indications of the meaning of the error.
Let us turn, therefore, to a particularly ambiguous and obscure
form of error, that of losing and mislaying objects. It will certainly seem incredible to you that the person himself could
have any purpose in losing things, which is often such a
painful accident. But there are innumerable instances of this

kind: A young man loses a pencil to which he was much attached. A few days before he had had a letter from his brother-in-law which concluded with these words: "I have neither time nor inclination at present to encourage you in your frivolity and idleness."[1] Now the pencil was a present from this brother-in-law. Had it not been for this coincidence we could not of course have maintained that the loss involved any intention to get rid of the gift. Similar cases are very numerous. One loses objects when one has quarrelled with the giver and no longer wants to be reminded of him, or again, when one has tired of them and wants an excuse to provide oneself with something different and better. Dropping, breaking, and destroying things of course serve a similar purpose in regard to the object. Can it be considered accidental when, just before his birthday, a child loses and damages his possessions, for instance, his watch and his schoolbag?

Anyone who has experienced often enough the annoyance of not being able to find something which he has himself put away will certainly be unwilling to believe that he could have had any intention in so doing. And yet cases are not at all rare in which the circumstances attendant on the act of mislaying point to a tendency to put the object aside temporarily or permanently. Perhaps the best example of this kind is the following.

A young man told me this story: "A few years ago there were misunderstandings between me and my wife; I thought her too cold, and though I willingly acknowledged her excellent qualities we lived together without affection. One day, on coming in from a walk, she brought me a book which she had bought me because she thought it would interest me. I thanked her for her little attention, promised to read the book, put it among my things and never could find it again. Months passed by and occasionally I thought of this derelict book and tried in vain to find it. About six months later my dear mother, who lived some distance away, fell ill. My wife left our house to go and nurse her mother-in-law, who became seriously ill, giving my wife an opportunity of showing her best qualities.

[1] From B. Dattner.

One evening I came home full of enthusiasm and gratitude towards my wife. I walked up to my writing desk and opened a certain drawer in it, without a definite intention but with a kind of somnambulistic sureness, and there before me lay the lost book which I had so often looked for."

With the disappearance of the motive the inability to find the mislaid object also came to an end.

I could multiply this collection of examples indefinitely; but I will not do so now. In my *Psycho-pathology of Everyday Life* (first published in 1901) you will find plenty of examples for the study of errors.[1] All these examples demonstrate the same thing over and over again; they make it probable to you that mistakes have a meaning and they show you how the meaning can be guessed or confirmed from the attendant circumstances. I restrict myself rather to-day, because our intention here was limited to studying these phenomena with a view to obtaining an introduction to psychoanalysis. There are only two groups of occurrences into which I must still go, the accumulated and combined errors, and the confirmation of our interpretations by subsequent events.

Accumulated and combined errors are certainly the finest flowers of the species. If we were only concerned to prove that errors had a meaning, we should have limited ourselves to them at the outset, for the meaning in them is unmistakable, even to the dullest intelligence, and strong enough to impress the most critical judgment. The repetition of the occurrences betrays a persistence which is hardly ever an attribute of chance, but which fits well with the idea of design. Further, the exchanging of one kind of mistake for another shows us what is the most important and essential element in the error; and that is, not its form, or the means of which it makes use, but the *tendency* which makes use of it and can achieve its end in the most various ways. Thus I will give you a case of repeated forgetting: Ernest Jones relates that he once allowed a letter to lie on his writing desk for several days for some unknown reason. At last he decided to post it, but received it

[1] Also in the writings of A. Maeder (*French*), A. A. Brill and Ernest Jones (*English*), and J. Stärcke (*Dutch*) and others.

back from the dead-letter office, for he had forgotten to address it. After he had addressed it he took it to post but this time without a stamp. At this point he finally had to admit to himself his objection to sending the letter at all.

In another case, taking up a thing by mistake is combined with mislaying it. A lady travelled to Rome with her brother-in-law, a famous artist. The visitor was much fêted by the Germans living in Rome and received, among other things, a present of an antique gold medal. The lady was vexed because her brother-in-law did not appreciate the fine specimen highly enough. After her sister had arrived she returned home and discovered, upon unpacking, that she had brought the medal with her—how, she did not know. She wrote at once to her brother-in-law telling him that she would send the stolen property back to him the next day. But the next day the medal was so cleverly mislaid that it could not be discovered and could not be returned, and then it began to dawn upon the lady what her "absent-mindedness" had meant, namely, that she wanted to keep the work of art for herself.[1]

I have already given you an example of a combination of forgetfulness with an error, in the case in which someone forgets an appointment, and a second time, with the firm intention of not forgetting it again, appears at an hour which is not the appointed one. A quite analogous case was told me from his own experience by a friend who pursues literary as well as scientific interests. He said: "Some years ago I accepted election to the Council of a certain literary society because I hoped that the society might at some time be useful to me in getting a play of mine produced; and, although not much interested, I attended the meetings regularly every Friday. A few months ago I received an assurance that my play would be produced at a theatre in F. and since then it has invariably happened that I *forget* to attend the meetings of the society. When I read your writings on this subject, I reproached myself with my meanness in staying away now that these people can no longer be of use to me and determined on no account to forget on the following Friday. I kept reminding myself of

[1] From R. Reitler.

my resolution until I carried it out and stood at the door of the meeting-room. To my amazement it was closed and the meeting was already over! I had made a mistake in the day of the week and it was then Saturday!"

It would be tempting to collect more of these examples, but I will pass on and, instead, let you glance at those cases in which interpretation has to wait for confirmation in the future.

The main condition in these cases is, as we might expect, that the mental situation at the time is unknown or cannot be ascertained. At the moment, therefore, our interpretation is no more than a supposition to which we ourselves would not ascribe too much weight. Later, however, something happens which shows us how well justified our previous interpretation was. I was once the guest of a young married couple and heard the young wife laughingly describe her latest experience, how the day after the return from the honeymoon she had called for her sister and gone shopping with her as in former times, while her husband went to his business. Suddenly she noticed a man on the other side of the street and, nudging her sister, said, "Look, there goes Mr. K." She had forgotten that this man had been her husband for some weeks. A shudder went over me as I heard the story, but I dared not draw the inference. Several years later the little incident came back to my mind after this marriage had come to a most unhappy end.

Maeder tells a story of a lady who had forgotten to try on her wedding-dress the day before the wedding, to the despair of the dressmaker, and remembered it only late in the evening. He connects it with the fact that soon after the marriage she was divorced by her husband. I know a woman now divorced from her husband who, in managing her money-affairs, frequently signed documents with her maiden name, many years before she really resumed it. I know of other women who lost their wedding-rings on the honeymoon and know, too, that the course of the marriage lent meaning to this accident. And now one striking example more, with a better ending. It is told of a famous German chemist that his marriage never took place because he forgot the hour of the ceremony and went to the laboratory instead of to the church. He was wise enough to let the matter rest with one attempt, and died unmarried at a ripe age.

Perhaps the idea has also come to you that in these examples mistakes seem to have replaced the omens or portents of the ancients. And indeed, certain kinds of portents were nothing but errors, for instance, when anyone stumbled or fell down. It is true that another group of omens bore the character of objective events rather than of subjective acts. But you would not believe how difficult it is sometimes to decide whether a specific instance belongs to the first category or to the second. The act knows so often how to disguise itself as a passive experience.

Every one of us who can look back over a fairly long experience of life would probably say that he might have spared himself many disappointments and painful surprises, if he had had the courage and resolution to interpret as omens the little mistakes which he noticed in his intercourse with others, and to regard them as signs of tendencies still in the background. For the most part one does not dare to do this; one has an impression that one would become superstitious again by a circuitous scientific path. And then, not all omens come true, and our theories will show you how it is that they need not all come true.

Fourth Lecture

The Psychology of Errors (*conclusion*)

THAT ERRORS HAVE A MEANING WE MAY CERTAINLY SET DOWN as established by our efforts up to this point, and may take this conclusion as a basis for our further investigations. Let me once more emphasize the fact that we do not maintain—and for our purposes do not need to maintain—that every single mistake which occurs has a meaning, although I think that probable. It is enough for us to prove that such a meaning is relatively frequent in the various forms of errors. In this respect, by the way, the various forms show certain differences. Some cases of slips of the tongue, slips of the pen, and so on, may be the effect of a purely physiological cause, though I cannot believe this possible of those errors which depend upon forgetfulness (forgetting of names or intentions, mislaying, and so on); losing possessions is in all probability to be recognized as unintentional in some cases; altogether our conceptions are only to a certain extent applicable to the mistakes which occur in daily life. These limitations should be borne in mind by you when we proceed on the assumption that errors are mental acts arising from the mutual interference of two intentions.

This is the first result of our psychoanalysis. Hitherto psychology has known nothing of such interferences or of the possibility that they could occasion manifestations of this kind. We have widened the domain of mental phenomena to a very considerable extent and have won for psychology phenomena which were never before accredited to it.

Let us dwell for a moment on the proposition that errors are "mental acts." Does this mean any more than our former statement, that they have a meaning? I do not think so; on the contrary, it is a more indefinite statement and one more open to misunderstanding. Everything that can be observed in mental life will be designated at one time or another as a mental phenomenon. It depends, however, whether the particular mental phenomenon is directly due to bodily, organic or material agencies, in which case it does not fall to psychology for investigation; or whether it arose directly from other mental processes, behind which at some point the succession of organic agencies then begins. We have in mind the latter state of things when we describe a phenomenon as a mental process, and it is therefore more expedient to put our statement in this form: The phenomenon has meaning; and by meaning we understand significance, intention, tendency and a position in a sequence of mental concatenations.

There is another group of occurrences which is very closely related to errors but for which this name is not suitable. We call them 'accidental' and symptomatic acts. They also appear to be unmotivated, insignificant and unimportant but, in addition to this, they have very clearly the feature of superfluity. They are, on the one hand, distinguishable from errors by the absence of any second intention to which they are opposed and which they disturb; on the other hand, they merge without any definite line of demarcation into the gestures and movements which we regard as expressions of the emotions. To this class of accidental performances belong all those apparently purposeless acts which we carry out, as though in play, with clothing, parts of the body, objects within reach; also the omission of such acts; and again the tunes which we hum to ourselves. I maintain that all such performances have meaning and are explicable in the same way as are errors, that they are slight indications of other more important mental processes, and are genuine mental acts. I propose, however, not to linger over this further extension of the field of mental phenomena, but to return to the errors; for by a consideration of them problems of importance in the enquiry into psychoanalysis can be worked out much more clearly.

Undoubtedly, the most interesting questions which we formulated while considering errors, and have not yet answered, are the following: We said that errors result from the mutual interference of two different intentions, of which one may be called the intention interfered with, and the other the interfering tendency. The intentions interfered with give rise to no further questions, but concerning the others we wish to know, first, what kind of intentions these are that arise as disturbers of others, and secondly, what are the relations between the interfering tendencies and those which suffer the interference?

Allow me to take slips of the tongue again as representative of the whole series, and to answer the second question before the first.

The interfering tendency in the slip of the tongue may be connected in meaning with the intention interfered with, in which case the former contains a contradiction of the latter, or corrects, or supplements it. Or, in other more obscure and more interesting cases, the interfering tendency may have no connection whatever in meaning with the intention interfered with.

Evidence for the first of these two relationships can be found without difficulty in the examples already studied and in others similar to them. In almost all cases of slips of the tongue where the opposite of what is meant is said the interfering tendency expresses the opposite meaning to that of the intention interfered with, and the slip is the expression of the conflict between two incompatible impulses. "I declare the meeting open, but would prefer to have closed it" is the meaning of the President's slip. A political paper which had been accused of corruption defends itself in an article meant to culminate with the words: "Our readers will testify that we have always laboured for the public benefit in the most *disinterested* manner." But the editor entrusted with the composition of the defence wrote "in the most *interested* manner." That is

to say, he thinks, "I have to write this stuff, but I know
better." A representative of the people, urging that the Kaiser
should be told the truth *"rückhaltslos"* (unreservedly) hears
an inner voice terrified at his boldness, and by a slip of the
tongue transforms *rückhaltslos* into *"rückgratslos"* (without
backbone, ineffectually).

In the examples already given, which produce an impression of contraction and abbreviation, the process represents a
correction, addition, or continuation, in which a second tendency manifests itself alongside the first. "Things were then
revealed, but better say it straight out, they were filthy, therefore,—things were then *refilled*." "The people who understand
this subject may be counted on the fingers of one hand, but
no, there is really only one person who understands it, very
well then,—can be counted on *one finger*." Or, "my husband
can eat and drink what he likes, but you know, *I* don't permit
him to like this and that; so then,—he may eat and drink what
I like." In all these cases the slip arises from the content of the
intention interfered with, or is directly connected with it.

The other kind of relationship between the two interfering
tendencies seems strange. If the interfering tendency has nothing to do with the content of the one interfered with, whence
comes it then, and how does it happen to make itself manifest
just at that point? Observation, which alone can supply the
answer to this, shows that the interfering tendency proceeds
from a train of thought which has occupied the person shortly
before and then reveals itself in this way as an after-effect, irrespective of whether or not it has already been expressed in
speech. It is really therefore to be described as a perseveration, though not necessarily a perseveration of spoken words.
An associative connection between the interfering tendency
and that interfered with is not lacking here either, though it
is not found in the content but is artificially established, sometimes with considerable "forcing" of the connections.

Here is a simple example of this which I observed myself.
Once in the beautiful Dolomites I met two Viennese ladies
who were starting for a walking-tour. I accompanied them
part of the way and we discussed the pleasures, but also the

trials, of this way of life. One of the ladies admitted that spending the day like this entailed much discomfort. "It certainly is very unpleasant to tramp all day in the sun till one's blouse . . . and things are soaked through." In this sentence she had to overcome a slight hesitation at one point. Then she continued: "But then, when one gets *nach Hose* and can change . . ." (*Hose* means *drawers:* the lady meant to say *nach Hause* which means *home*). We did not analyse this slip, but I am sure you will easily understand it. The lady's intention had been to enumerate a more complete list of her clothes, "blouse, chemise and drawers." From motives of propriety, mention of the drawers (*Hose*) was omitted; but in the next sentence, the content of which is quite independent, the unuttered word came to light as a distortion of the word it resembled in sound, *home* (*Hause*).

Now we can turn at last to the main question which has been so long postponed, namely, what kind of tendencies these are which bring themselves to expression in this unusual way by interfering with other intentions. They are evidently very various, yet our aim is to find some element common to them all. If we examine a series of examples for this purpose we shall soon find that they fall into three groups. To the *first* group belong the cases in which the interfering tendency is known to the speaker and, moreover, was felt by him before the slip. Thus, in the case of the slip "refilled," the speaker not only admitted that he had criticized the events in question as "filthy," but further, that he had had the intention, which he subsequently reversed, of expressing this opinion in words. A *second* group is formed by other cases in which the interfering tendency is likewise recognized by the speaker as his own, but he is not aware that it was active in him before the slip. He therefore accepts our interpretation, but remains to some extent surprised by it. Examples of this attitude are probably more easily found in other errors than in slips of the tongue. In the *third* group the interpretation of the interfering tendency is energetically repudiated by the speaker; not only does he dispute that it was active in him before the slip, but he will maintain that it is altogether entirely alien to him. Recall the case about hiccoughing and the positively discourteous rebuff which I brought upon myself by detecting the interfering tendency. You know that in our attitude towards these cases you and I are still far from an agreement. I should make nothing of the after-dinner speaker's denial and hold fast to my interpretation unwaveringly, while you, I imagine, are still impressed by his vehemence and are wondering whether one should not forego the interpretation of such errors and let them pass for purely physiological acts, as in the days before analysis. I can imagine what it is that alarms you. My interpretation includes the assumption that tendencies of which a speaker knows nothing can express themselves through him and that I can deduce them from various indications. You hesitate before a conclusion so novel and so pregnant with consequences. I understand that, and admit that up to a point you are justified. But let one thing be clear: if you intend to carry to its logical conclusion the conception of errors which has been confirmed by so many examples, you must decide to make this startling assumption. If you cannot do this, you will have to abandon again the understanding of errors which you had only just begun to obtain.

Let us pause a moment on that which unites the three groups and is common to the three mechanisms of a slip of the tongue. Fortunately this common element is unmistakable. In the first two groups the interfering tendency is admitted by the speaker; in the first, there is the additional fact that it showed itself immediately before the slip. But in both cases *it has been forced back.*[1] *The speaker had determined not to*

---

[1] [German: *Zurückdrängen* = to force back. This word is stronger than *unterdrücken* = to press under, which we translate by suppress (not a technical term); *zurückdrängen* contains already the *drängen* of *verdrängen*, the technical word used by Freud to denote the strongest pressure of all, *repression*. In the examples discussed here, the agency withholding the intention from expression may be either conscious or unconscious (groups one, two, and three, according to the degree of unconsciousness); Freud does not use *verdrängen* = "repression," the technical word for *unconscious* agency only, here, but one very near to it in sense.—Tr.]

convert the idea into speech and then it happens that he makes a slip of the tongue; that is to say, the tendency which is debarred from expression asserts itself against his will and gains utterance, either by altering the expression of the intention permitted by him, or by mingling with it, or actually by setting itself in place of it. This then is the mechanism of a slip of the tongue.

For my own part I can bring the process in the third group also into perfect harmony with the mechanism here described. I need only assume that these three groups are differentiated by the varying degrees to which the forcing back of an intention is effective. In the first group, the intention is present and makes itself perceptible before the words are spoken; not until then does it suffer the rejection for which it indemnifies itself in the slip. In the second group the rejection reaches further back; the intention is no longer perceptible even before the speech. It is remarkable that this does not hinder it in the least from being the active cause of the slip! But this state of things simplifies the explanation of the process in the third group. I shall be bold enough to assume that a tendency can still express itself by an error though it has been debarred from expression for a long time, perhaps for a very long time, has not made itself perceptible at all, and can therefore be directly repudiated by the speaker. But leaving aside the problem of the third group, you must conclude from the other cases that *a suppression (Unterdrückung) of a previous intention to say something is the indispensable condition for the occurrence of a slip of the tongue.*

We may now claim to have made further progress in the understanding of errors. We not only know them to be mental phenomena in which meaning and purpose are recognizable, not only know that they arise from the mutual interference of two different intentions, but in addition we know that, for one of these intentions to be able to express itself by interfering with another, it must itself have been subject to some hindrance against its operation. It must first be itself interfered with, before it can interfere with others. Naturally this does not give us a complete explanation of the phenomena which we call errors. We see at once further questions arising, and in general we suspect that as we progress towards comprehension the more numerous will be the occasions for new questions. We might ask, for instance, why the matter does not proceed much more simply. If the intention to restrain a certain tendency instead of carrying it into effect is present in the mind, then this restraint ought to succeed, so that nothing whatever of the tendency gains expression, or else it might fail so that the restrained tendency achieves full expression. But errors are *compromise*-formations; they express part-success and part-failure for each of the two intentions; the threatened intention is neither entirely suppressed nor, apart from some instances, does it force itself through intact. We can imagine that special conditions must be present for the occurrence of such interference (or compromise)-formations, but we cannot even conjecture of what kind they may be. Nor do I think that we could discover these unknown circumstances by penetrating further into the study of errors. It will be necessary first to examine thoroughly yet other obscure fields of mental life: only the analogies to be met with there can give us courage to form those assumptions which are requisite for a more searching elucidation of errors. And one other point! To work from slight indications, as we constantly do in this field, is not without its dangers. There is a mental disorder called combinatory paranoia in which the practice of utilizing such small indications is carried beyond all limits, and I naturally do not contend that the conclusions which are built up on such a basis are throughout correct. Only by the breadth of our observations, by the accumulation of similar impressions from the most varied forms of mental life, can we guard against this danger.

So now we will leave the analysis of errors. But there is one more thing which I might impress upon you: to keep in mind, as a model, the method by which we have studied these phenomena. You can perceive from these examples what the aim of our psychology is. Our purpose is not merely to describe and classify the phenomena, but to conceive them as brought about by the play of forces in the mind, as expressions of tendencies striving towards a goal, which work together or against one another. We are endeavouring to attain a *dynamic conception* of mental phenomena. In this conception, the trends we merely infer are more prominent than the phenomena we perceive.

So we will probe no further into errors; but we may still take a fleeting glimpse over the breadth of this whole field, in the course of which we shall both meet with things already known and come upon the tracks of others that are new. In so doing, we will keep to the division into three groups made at the beginning of our study: slips of the tongue, with the co-ordinate forms of slips of the pen, misreading, mis-hearing; of forgetting with its subdivisions according to the object forgotten (proper names, foreign words, resolutions, impressions); and of mislaying, mistaking, and losing objects. Mistakes, in so far as they concern us, are to be grouped partly under the head of forgetting, partly under acts erroneously performed (picking up the wrong objects, etc.).

We have already treated slips of the tongue in great detail yet there is still something to add. There are certain small affective manifestations related to slips of the tongue which are not entirely without interest. No one likes to think he has made a slip of the tongue; one often fails to hear it when made by oneself, but never when made by someone else. Slips of the tongue are in a certain sense infectious; it is not at all easy to speak of them without making them oneself. It is not hard to detect the motivation of even the most trifling forms of them, although these do not throw any particular light on hidden mental processes. If, for instance, anyone pronounces a long vowel as a short one, in consequence of a disturbance over the word, no matter how motivated, he will as a result soon after lengthen a short vowel and commit a new slip in compensation for the first. The same thing occurs if anyone pronounces a diphthong indistinctly and carelessly, for instance, "ew" or "oy" as "i"; he tries to correct it by changing a subsequent "i" into "ew" or "oy." Some consideration relating to the hearer seems to be behind this behaviour, as though he were not to be allowed to think that the speaker is indifferent how he treats his mother-tongue. The second, compensating distortion actually has the purpose of drawing the hearer's attention to the first and assuring him that it has not escaped the speaker either. The most frequent, insignificant, and simple forms of slips consist in contractions and anticipations in inconspicuous parts of the speech. In a long sentence, for instance, slips of the tongue would be of the kind in which the last word intended influences the sound of an earlier word. This gives an impression of a certain impatience to be done with the sentence, and in general it points to a certain resistance against the communication of this sentence, or the speech altogether. From this we come to border-line cases, in which the differences between the psychoanalytical and the ordinary physiological conception of slips of the tongue become merged. We assume that in these cases a disturbing tendency is opposing the intended speech; but it can only betray its presence and not what its own purpose is. The interference which it causes follows some sound-influence or associative connection and may be regarded as a distraction of attention away from the intended speech. But neither in this distraction of attention, nor in the associative tendency which has been activated, lies the essence of the occurrence; the essence lies rather in the hint the occurrence gives of the presence of some other intention interfering with the intended speech, the nature of which cannot in this case be discovered from its effects, as is possible in all the more pronounced cases of slips of the tongue.

Slips of the pen, to which I now turn, are so like slips of the tongue in their mechanism that no new points of view are to be expected from them. Perhaps a small addition to our knowledge from this group will content us. Those very common little slips of the pen, contractions, anticipations of later words, particularly of the last words, point to a general distaste for writing and to an impatience to be done; more pronounced effects in slips of the pen allow the nature and intention of the interference to be recognized. In general, if one finds a slip of the pen in a letter one knows that the writer's mind was not working smoothly at the moment; what was the matter one cannot always establish. Slips of the pen are frequently as little noticed by those who make them as slips of the tongue. The following observation is striking in this connection. There are, of course, some persons who have the habit of always re-reading every letter they write before sending it. Others do not do this; but if the latter make an exception and re-read a letter they then always have an opportunity of finding and correcting a striking slip of the pen. How is this to be explained? It almost looks as if such people knew that they had made a slip in writing the letter. Are we really to believe that this is so?

There is an interesting problem connected with the practical significance of slips of the pen. You may recall the case of the murderer H. who managed, by asserting himself to be a bacteriologist, to obtain cultures of highly dangerous disease-germs from scientific institutions, but used them for the purpose of doing away in this most modern fashion with people connected with him. This man once complained to the authorities of one of these institutions about the ineffectiveness of the cultures sent him, but committed a slip of the pen and, instead of the words "in my experiments on mice and guinea-pigs (*Mäusen und Meerschweinchen*)", the words "in my experiments on people (*Menschen*)" were plainly legible. This slip even attracted the attention of the doctors at the institute but, so far as I know, they drew no conclusion from it. Now, what do you think? Would it not have been better if the doctors had taken the slip of the pen as a confession and started an investigation so that the murderer's proceedings might have been arrested in time? In this case, does not ignorance of our conception of errors result in neglect which, in actuality, may be very important? Well, I know that such a slip of the pen would certainly rouse great suspicion in me; but there is an important objection against regarding it as a confession. The matter is not so simple. The slip of the pen is certainly an indication but, alone, it would not have justified an enquiry. It does indeed betray that the man is occupied with the thought of infecting human beings; but it does not show with certainty whether this thought is a definite plan to do harm or a mere phantasy of no practical importance. It is even possible that a person making such a slip will deny, with the soundest subjective justification, the existence of such a phantasy in himself, and will reject the idea as a thing utterly alien to him. Later, when we come to consider the difference between psychical reality and material reality you will be better able to appreciate these possibilities. But this again is a case in which an error was found subsequently to have unsuspected significance.

Misreading brings us to a mental situation which is clearly different from that of slips of the tongue or the pen. One of the two conflicting tendencies is here replaced by a sensory excitation and is perhaps therefore less tenacious. What one is reading is not a product of one's own mind, as is that which one is going to write. In the large majority of cases, therefore, misreading consists in complete substitution. A different word is substituted for the word to be read, without there necessarily being any connection in the content between the text and the effect of the mistake, and usually by means of a resemblance between the words. Lichtenberg's example of this, *"Agamemnon"* instead of *"agenommen,"* is the best of this group. To discover the interfering tendency which causes the mistake one may put aside the original text altogether; the analytic investigation may begin with two questions: What is the first idea occurring in free association to the effect of the misreading (the substitute), and in what circumstances did the misreading occur? Occasionally a knowledge of the latter is sufficient in itself to explain the misreading, as, for instance, when someone wandering about a strange town, driven by urgent needs, reads the word *"Closethaus"* on a large sign on the first storey. He has just time to wonder that the board has been fixed at that height when he discovers that the word on it is actually *"Corsethaus."* In other cases where there is a lack of connection in content between the text and the slip a thorough analysis is necessary, which cannot be accomplished without practice in psychoanalytic technique and confidence in it. But it is not usually so difficult to come by the explanation of a case of misreading. In the example *"Agamemnon,"*

the substituted word betrays without further difficulty the line
of thought from which the disturbance arose. In this time of
war, for instance, it is very common for one to read everywhere names of towns, generals, and military expressions,
which are continually in one's ears, wherever one sees a word
at all resembling them. Whatever interests and occupies the
mind takes the place of what is alien and as yet uninteresting.
The shadows of thoughts in the mind dim the new perceptions.

Another kind of misreading is possible, in which the text itself arouses the disturbing tendency, whereupon it is usually
changed into its opposite. Someone is required to read something which he dislikes, and analysis convinces him that a
strong wish to reject what is read is responsible for the alteration.

In the first-mentioned, more frequent cases of misreading
two factors to which we ascribed great importance in the
mechanism of errors are inconspicuous; these are the conflict
between two tendencies and the forcing back of one of them
which compensates itself by producing the error. Not that
anything contradictory of this occurs in misreading, but nevertheless the importunity of the train of thought tending to the
mistake is far more conspicuous than the restraint which it
may have previously undergone. Just these two factors are
most clearly observable in the different situations in which
errors occur through forgetfulness.

The forgetting of resolutions has positively but one meaning; the interpretation of it, as we have heard, is not denied
even by the layman. The tendency interfering with the resolution is always an opposing one, an unwillingness, concerning
which it only remains to enquire why it does not come to expression in a different and less disguised form; for the existence of this opposing tendency is beyond doubt. Sometimes it
is possible, too, to infer something of the motives which necessitate the concealment of this antipathy; one sees that it would
certainly have been condemned if it declared its opposition
openly, whereas by craft, in the error, it always achieves its
end. When an important change in the mental situation occurs

between the formation of the resolution and its execution, in consequence of which the execution would no longer be required, then if it were forgotten the occurrence could no longer come within the category of errors. There would be nothing to wonder at in the error, for one recognizes that it would have been superfluous to remember the resolution; it had been either permanently or temporarily cancelled. Forgetting to carry out a resolution can only be called an error when there is no reason to believe that any such cancellation has occurred.

Cases of forgetting to carry out resolutions are usually so uniform and transparent, that they are of no interest for our researches. There are two points, nevertheless, at which something new can be learnt by studying this type of error. We have said that forgetting and not executing a resolution indicate an antagonistic tendency in opposition to it. This is certainly true, but our own investigations show that this "counter-will" may be of two kinds, either immediate or mediate. What is meant by the latter is best explained by one or two examples. When the patron forgets to say a good word for his protégé to some third person, it may happen because he is actually not much interested in the protégé and therefore has no great inclination to do it. This, in any case, will be the protégé's view of the patron's omission. But the matter may be more complicated. The antipathy against executing the resolution may come from some other source in the patron and be directed to some other point. It need have nothing at all to do with the protégé, but is perhaps directed against the third person to whom the recommendation was to be made. Here again, you see, what objections there are against applying our interpretations practically. In spite of having correctly interpreted the error, the protégé is in danger of becoming too suspicious and of doing his patron a grave injustice. Again, if someone forgets an appointment which he had promised and was resolved to attend, the commonest cause is certainly a direct disinclination to meet the other person. But analysis might produce evidence that the interfering tendency was concerned, not with the person, but with the place of meeting, which was avoided on account of some painful memory associated with it. Or if one forgets to post a letter the opposing tendency may be concerned with the contents of the letter; but this does not exclude the possibility that the letter in itself is harmless and becomes the subject of a counter-tendency only because something in it reminds the writer of another letter, written previously, which did in fact afford a direct basis for antipathy. It may then be said that the antipathy has been *transferred* from the earlier letter, where it was justified, to the present one where it actually has no object. So you see that restraint and caution must be exercised in applying our quite well-founded interpretations; that which is psychologically equivalent may in actuality have many meanings.

That such things should be must seem very strange to you. Perhaps you will be inclined to assume that the "indirect" counter-will is enough to characterize the incident as pathological. But I can assure you that it is also found within the boundaries of health and normality. And further, do not misunderstand me; this is in no sense a confession on my part that our analytic interpretations are not to be relied on. I have said that forgetting to execute a plan may bear many meanings, but this is so only in those cases where no analysis is undertaken and which we have to interpret according to our general principles. If an analysis of the person in the case is carried out it can always be established with sufficient certainty whether the antipathy is a direct one, or what its source is otherwise.

The following is a second point: when we find proof in a large majority of cases that the forgetting of an intention proceeds from a counter-will, we gain courage to extend this solution to another group of cases in which the person analysed does not confirm, but denies, the presence of the counter-will inferred by us. Take as an example of this such exceedingly frequent occurrences as forgetting to return borrowed books or to pay bills or debts. We will be so bold as to suggest, to the person in question, that there is an intention in his mind of keeping the books and not paying the debts, whereupon he will deny this intention but will not be able to give us any other explanation of his conduct. We then insist that he has this intention but is not aware of it; it is enough for us, though, that it betrays itself by the effect of the forgetting. He may then repeat that he had merely forgotten about it. You will recognize the situation as one in which we have already been placed once before. If we intend to carry through, to their logical conclusions, the interpretations of errors which have been proved justified in so many cases, we shall be unavoidably impelled to the assumption that tendencies exist in human beings which can effect results without their knowing of them. With this, however, we place ourselves in opposition to all views prevailing in life and in psychology.

Forgetting proper names, and foreign names and words, can be traced in the same way to a counter-tendency aiming either directly or indirectly against the name in question. I have already given you several examples of such direct antipathy. Indirect causation is particularly frequent here and careful analysis is generally required to elucidate it. Thus, for instance, in the present time of war which forces us to forego so many of our former pleasures, our ability to recall proper names suffers severely by connections of the most far-fetched kind. It happened to me lately to be unable to remember the name of the harmless Moravian town of Bisenz; and analysis showed that I was guilty of no direct antagonism in the matter, but that the resemblance to the name of the Palazzo Bisenzi in Orvieto, where I had spent many happy times in the past, was responsible. As a motive of the tendency opposing the recollection of this name, we here for the first time encounter a principle which will later on reveal itself to be of quite prodigious importance in the causation of neurotic symptoms: namely, the aversion on the part of memory against recalling anything connected with painful feelings that would revive the pain if it were recalled. In this tendency towards *avoidance of pain* from recollection or other mental processes, this flight of the mind from that which is unpleasant, we may perceive the ultimate purpose at work behind not merely the forgetting of names, but also many other errors, omissions, and mistakes.

The forgetting of names seems, however, to be especially facilitated psycho-physiologically, and therefore does occur on occasions where the intervention of an unpleasantness-motive cannot be established. When anyone has a tendency to forget names, it can be confirmed by analytic investigation that names escape, not merely because he does not like them or because they remind him of something disagreeable, but also because the particular name belongs to some other chain of associations of a more intimate nature. The name is anchored there, as it were, and is refused to the other associations activated at the moment. If you recall the devices of memory systems you will realize with some surprise that the same associations which are there artificially introduced, in order to save names from being forgotten, are also responsible for their being forgotten. The most conspicuous example of this is afforded by proper names of persons, which naturally possess quite different values for different people. For instance, take a first name, such as Theodore. For some of you it will have no particular significance; for others it will be the name of father, brother, friend, or your own name. Analytic experience will show you that the former among you will be in no danger of forgetting that some stranger bears this name; whereas the latter will be continually inclined to grudge to strangers a name which to them seems reserved for an intimate relationship. Now let us assume that this inhibition due to associations may coincide with the operation of the "pain"-principle, and in addition with an indirect mechanism; you will then be able to form a commensurate idea of the complexity, in causation, of such temporary forgetting of names. An adequate analysis that does justice to the facts will, however, completely disclose all these complications.

The forgetting of impressions and experiences shows the working of the tendency to ward off from memory that which is unpleasant much more clearly and invariably than the forgetting of names. It does not of course belong in its entirety to the category of errors, but only in so far as it appears to us remarkable and unjustified, judged by the standard of general experience; as, for instance, where recent or important impressions are forgotten, or where one memory is forgotten out of an otherwise well-remembered sequence. How and why we have the capacity of forgetting in general, particularly how we are able to forget experiences which have certainly left the deepest impression on us, such as the events of our childhood, is quite a different problem, in which the defence against painful associations plays a certain part but is far from explaining everything. That unwelcome impressions are easily forgotten is an indubitable fact. Various psychologists have remarked it; and the great Darwin was so well aware of it that he made a golden rule for himself of writing down with particular care observations which seemed unfavourable to his theory, having become convinced that just these would be inclined to slip out of recollection.

Those who hear for the first time of this principle of defence against unpleasant memory by forgetfulness seldom fail to raise the objection that, on the contrary, in their experience it is just that which is painful which it is hard to forget, since it always comes back to mind to torture the person against his will—as, for example, the recollection of grievances or humiliations. This fact is quite correct, but the objection is not sound. It is important to begin early to reckon with the fact that the mind is an arena, a sort of tumbling-ground, for the struggles of antagonistic impulses; or, to express it in non-dynamic terms, that the mind is made up of contradictions and pairs of opposites. Evidence of one particular tendency does not in the least preclude its opposite; there is room for both of them. The material questions are: How do these opposites stand to one another and what effects proceed from one of them and what from the other?

Losing and mislaying objects is of especial interest on account of the numerous meanings it may have, and the multiplicity of the tendencies in the service of which these errors may be employed. What is common to all the cases is the wish to lose something; what varies in them is the reason for the wish and the aim of it. One loses something if it has become damaged; if one has an impulse to replace it with a better; if one has ceased to care for it; if it came from someone with whom unpleasantness has arisen; or if it was acquired in circumstances that one no longer wishes to think of. Letting things fall, spoiling, or breaking things, serves the same tendency. In social life it is said that unwelcome and illegitimate children are found to be far more often weakly than those conceived in happier circumstances. This result does not imply that the crude methods of the so-called baby-farmers have been employed; some degree of carelessness in the supervision of the child should be quite enough. The preservation, or otherwise, of objects may well follow the same lines as that of children.

Then too it may happen that a thing will become destined to be lost without its having shed any of its value—that is, when there is an impulse to sacrifice something to fate in order to avert some other dreaded loss. According to the findings of analysis, such conjurings of fate are still very common among us, so that our losses are often voluntary sacrifices. Losing may equally well serve the impulses of spite or of self-punishment; in short, the more remote forms of motivation behind the impulse to do away with something by losing cannot easily be exhausted.

Mistaking of objects, or erroneous performance of actions, like other errors, is often made use of to fulfil a wish which should be denied; the intention masquerades as a lucky chance. Thus, as once happened to a friend, one has to take a train, most unwillingly, in order to pay a visit in the suburbs and then, in changing trains at a connection, gets by mistake into one which is returning to town; or, on a journey someone might greatly like to make a halt at some stopping-place, which cannot be done owing to fixed engagements elsewhere, whereupon he mistakes or misses the connection, so that the desired delay is forced upon him. Or, as happened to one of my patients whom I had forbidden to telephone to the lady he was in love with, he "by mistake" and "thoughtlessly" gave the wrong number when he meant to telephone to me, so that he was suddenly connected with her. The following account by an engineer is a pretty example of the conditions under which damage to material objects may be done, and also demonstrates the practical significance of directly faulty actions.

"Some time ago I worked with several colleagues in the laboratory of a High School on a series of complicated experiments in elasticity, a piece of work we had undertaken voluntarily; it was beginning to take up more time, however, than we had anticipated. One day, as I went into the laboratory with my friend F., he remarked how annoying it was to him to lose so much time to-day as he had so much to do at home; I could not help agreeing with him and said half-jokingly, referring to an occasion the week before: 'Let us hope the machine will break down again so that we can stop work and go home early.' In arranging the work it happened that F. was given the regulation of the valve of the press; that is to say, he was, by cautiously opening the valve, to let the liquid pressure out of the accumulator slowly into the cylinder of the hydraulic press. The man who was conducting the experiment stood by the pressure gauge, and, when the right pressure was reached, called out loudly, 'Stop.' At this command F. seized the valve and turned with all his might—to the left! (All valves without exception close to the right.) Thereby the whole pressure in the accumulator suddenly came into the press, a strain for which the connecting-pipes are not designed, so that one of them instantly burst—quite a harmless accident, but one which forced us, nevertheless, to cease work for the day and go home. It is characteristic, by the way, that not long after, when we were discussing the affair, my friend F. had no recollection whatever of my remark, which I recalled with certainty."

So with this in mind you may begin to suspect that it is not always a mere chance which makes the hands of your servants such dangerous enemies to your household effects. And you may also raise the question whether it is always an accident when one injures oneself or exposes oneself to danger—ideas which you may put to the test by analysis when you have an opportunity.

This is far from being all that could be said about errors. There is still much to be enquired into and discussed. But I shall be satisfied if you have been shaken somewhat in your previous beliefs by our investigations, so far as they have gone, and if you have gained a certain readiness to accept new ones. For the rest, I must be content to leave you with certain problems still unsolved. We cannot prove all our principles by the study of errors, nor are we indeed by any means solely dependent on this material. The great value of errors for our purpose lies in this, that they are such common occurrences, may easily be observed in oneself, and are not at all contingent upon illness. I should like to mention one more of your unanswered questions before concluding: "If, as we see from so many examples, people come so close to understanding errors and so often act as if they perceived their meaning, how is it possible that they should so generally consider them accidental, senseless, and meaningless, and so energetically oppose the psychoanalytic explanation of them?"

You are right: this is indeed striking and requires an explanation. But I will not give it to you; I will rather guide you slowly towards the connections by which the explanation will be forced upon you without any aid from me.

PART II

DREAMS

FIFTH LECTURE

DIFFICULTIES AND PRELIMINARY APPROACH TO THE SUBJECT

ONE DAY THE DISCOVERY WAS MADE THAT THE SYMPTOMS OF disease in certain nervous patients have meaning.[1] It was upon this discovery that the psychoanalytic method of treatment was based. In this treatment it happened that patients in speaking of their symptoms also mentioned their dreams, whereupon the suspicion arose that these dreams too had meaning.

However, we will not pursue this historical path, but will strike off in the opposite direction. Our aim is to demonstrate the meaning of dreams, in preparation for the study of the neuroses. There are good grounds for this reversal of procedure, since the study of dreams is not merely the best preparation for that of the neuroses, but a dream is itself a neurotic symptom and, moreover, one which possesses for us the incalculable advantage of occurring in all healthy people. Indeed, if all human beings were healthy and would only dream, we could gather almost all the knowledge from their dreams which we have gained from studying the neuroses.

So dreams become the object of psychoanalytic research—another of these ordinary, under-rated occurrences, apparently of no practical value, like "errors," and sharing with them

[1] By Joseph Breuer, in the years 1880–1882. Cf. my Lectures on Psycho-Analysis delivered in the United States in 1909.

the characteristic of occurring in healthy persons. But in other respects the conditions of work are rather less favourable. Errors had only been neglected by science, people had not troubled their heads much about them, but at least it was no disgrace to occupy oneself with them. True, people said, there are things more important but still something may possibly come of it. To occupy oneself with dreams, however, is not merely unpractical and superfluous, but positively scandalous: it carries with it the taint of the unscientific and arouses the suspicion of personal leanings towards mysticism. The idea of a medical student troubling himself about dreams when there is so much in neuropathology and psychiatry itself that is more serious—tumours as large as apples compressing the organ of the mind, hæmorrhages, chronic inflammatory conditions in which the alterations in the tissues can be demonstrated under the microscope! No, dreams are far too unworthy and trivial to be objects of scientific research.

There is yet another factor involved which, in itself, sets at defiance all the requirements of exact investigation. In investigating dreams even the object of research, the dream itself, is indefinite. A delusion, for example, presents clear and definite outlines. "I am the Emperor of China," says your patient plainly. But a dream? For the most part it cannot be related at all. When a man tells a dream, has he any guarantee that he has told it correctly, and not perhaps altered it in the telling or been forced to invent part of it on account of the vagueness of his recollection? Most dreams cannot be remembered at all and are forgotten except for some tiny fragments. And is a scientific psychology or a method of treatment for the sick to be founded upon material such as this?

A certain element of exaggeration in a criticism may arouse our suspicions. The arguments brought against the dream as an object of scientific research are clearly extreme. We have met with the objection of triviality already in "errors," and have told ourselves that great things may be revealed even by small indications. As to the indistinctness of dreams, that is a characteristic like any other—we cannot dictate to things their characteristics; besides, there are also dreams which are

clear and well-defined. Further, there are other objects of
psychiatric investigation which suffer in the same way from
the quality of indefiniteness, e.g. the obsessive ideas of many
cases, with which nevertheless many psychiatrists of repute
and standing have occupied themselves. I will recall the last
case of the kind which came before me in medical practice.
The patient, a woman, presented her case in these words:
"I have a certain feeling, as if I had injured, or had meant to
injure, some living creature—perhaps a child—no, no, a dog
rather, as if perhaps I had pushed it off a bridge—or done
something else." Any disadvantage resulting from the uncertain recollection of dreams may be remedied by deciding that
exactly what the dreamer tells is to count as the dream, and
by ignoring all that he may have forgotten or altered in the
process of recollection. Finally, one cannot maintain in so
sweeping a fashion that dreams are unimportant things. We
know from our own experience that the mood in which we
awake from a dream may last throughout the day, and cases
have been observed by medical men in which mental disorder
began with a dream, the delusion which had its source in
this dream persisting; further, it is told of historical persons
that impulses to momentous deeds sprang from their dreams.
We may therefore ask: what is the real cause of the disdain
in which dreams are held in scientific circles? In my opinion
it is the reaction from the over-estimation of them in earlier
times. It is well known that it is no easy matter to reconstruct
the past, but we may assume with certainty (you will forgive
my jest) that as early as three thousand years ago and more
our ancestors dreamt in the same way as we do. So far as we
know, all ancient peoples attached great significance to dreams
and regarded them as of practical value; they obtained from
them auguries of the future and looked for portents in them.
For the Greeks and other Orientals, it was at times as un-
thinkable to undertake a campaign without a dream-interpreter as it would be to-day without air-scouts for intelligence.
When Alexander the Great set out on his campaign of conquest the most famous interpreters of dreams were in his
following. The city of Tyre, still at that time on an island,

offered so stout a resistance to the king that he entertained
the idea of abandoning the siege; then one night he dreamed
of a satyr dancing in triumph, and when he related this dream
to his interpreters they informed him that it foretold his victory over the city; he gave the order to attack and took Tyre
by storm. Among the Etruscans and Romans other methods of
foretelling the future were employed, but during the whole
of the Græco-Roman period the interpretation of dreams was
practised and held in high esteem. Of the literature on this
subject the principal work at any rate has come down to us,
namely, the book of Artemidorus of Daldis, who is said to
have lived at the time of the Emperor Hadrian. How it happened that the art of dream-interpretation declined later and
dreams fell into disrepute, I cannot tell you. The progress of
learning cannot have had very much to do with it, for in the
darkness of the middle ages things far more absurd than the
ancient practice of the interpretation of dreams were faithfully retained. The fact remains that the interest in dreams
gradually sank to the level of superstition and could hold its
own only amongst the uneducated. In our day, there survive,
as a final degradation of the art of dream-interpretation, the
attempts to find out from dreams numbers destined to draw
prizes in games of chance. On the other hand, exact science
of the present day has repeatedly concerned itself with the
dream, but always with the sole object of illustrating *physiological* theories. By medical men, naturally, a dream was never
regarded as a mental process but as the mental expression of
physical stimuli. Binz in 1876 pronounced the dream to be
"a physical process, always useless and in many cases actually
morbid, a process above which the conception of the world-
soul and of immortality stands as high as does the blue sky
above the most low-lying, weed-grown stretch of sand." Maury
compares dreams with the spasmodic jerkings of St. Vitus'
dance, contrasted with the co-ordinated movements of the
normal human being; in an old comparison a parallel is drawn
between the content of a dream and the sounds which would
be produced if "someone ignorant of music let his ten fingers
wander over the keys of an instrument."

"Interpretation" means discovering a hidden meaning, but there can be no question of attempting this while such an attitude is maintained towards the dream-performance. Look up the description of dreams given in the writings of Wundt, Jodl and other recent philosophers: they are content with the bare enumeration of the divergences of the dream-life from waking thought with a view to depreciating the dreams: they emphasize the lack of connection in the associations, the suspended exercise of the critical faculty, the elimination of all knowledge, and other indications of diminished functioning. The single valuable contribution to our knowledge about dreams for which we are indebted to exact science relates to the influence upon the dream-content of physical stimuli operating during sleep. We have the work of a Norwegian author who died recently—J. Mourly Vold—two large volumes on experimental investigation of dreams (translated into German in 1910 and 1912), which are concerned almost entirely with the results obtained by change in the position of the limbs. These investigations have been held up to us as models of exact research in the subject of dreams. Now can you imagine what would be the comment of exact science on learning that we intend to try to find out the *meaning* of dreams? The comment that has perhaps been made already! However, we will not allow ourselves to be appalled at the thought. If it was possible for errors to have an underlying meaning, it is possible that dreams have one too; and errors have, in very many cases, a meaning which has eluded the researches of exact science. Let us adopt the assumption of the ancients and of simple folk, and follow in the footsteps of the dream-interpreters of old.

First of all, we must take our bearings in this enterprise, and make a survey of the field of dreams. What exactly is a dream? It is difficult to define it in a single phrase. Yet we need not seek after a definition, when all we need is to refer to something familiar to everyone. Still we ought to pick out the essential features in dreams. How are we to discover these features? The boundaries of the region we are entering comprise such vast differences, differences whichever way we turn. That which we can show to be common to all dreams is probably what is essential.

Well then—the first common characteristic of all dreams would be that we are asleep at the time. Obviously, the dream is the life of the mind during sleep, a life bearing certain resemblances to our waking life and, at the same time, differing from it widely. That, indeed, was Aristotle's definition. Perhaps dream and sleep stand in yet closer relationship to each other. We can be waked by a dream; we often have a dream when we wake spontaneously or when we are forcibly roused from sleep. Dreams seem thus to be an intermediate condition between sleeping and waking. Hence, our attention is directed to sleep itself: what then is sleep?

That is a physiological or biological problem concerning which much is still in dispute. We can come to no decisive answer, but I think we may attempt to define one psychological characteristic of sleep. Sleep is a condition in which I refuse to have anything to do with the outer world and have withdrawn my interest from it. I go to sleep by retreating from the outside world and warding off the stimuli proceeding from it. Again, when I am tired by that world I go to sleep. I say to it as I fall asleep: "Leave me in peace, for I want to sleep." The child says just the opposite: "I won't go to sleep yet; I'm not tired, I want more things to happen to me!" Thus the biological object of sleep seems to be recuperation, its psychological characteristic the suspension of interest in the outer world. Our relationship with the world which we entered so unwillingly seems to be endurable only with intermission; hence we withdraw again periodically into the condition prior to our entrance into the world: that is to say, into intra-uterine existence. At any rate, we try to bring about quite similar conditions—warmth, darkness and absence of stimulus—characteristic of that state. Some of us still roll ourselves tightly up into a ball resembling the intra-uterine position. It looks as if we grownups do not belong wholly to the world, but only by two-thirds; one-third of us has never yet been born at all. Every time we wake in the morning it is as if we were newly born. We do, in fact, speak of the condition of waking from sleep in these very words: we feel "as if we were newly born,"—and in this we are probably quite mistaken in our idea of the general sensations of the new-born infant; it may be assumed on the contrary that it feels extremely uncomfortable. Again, in speaking of birth we speak of "seeing the light of day."

If this is the nature of sleep, then dreams do not come into its scheme at all, but seem rather to be an unwelcome supplement to it; and we do indeed believe that dreamless sleep is the best, the only proper sleep. There should be no mental activity during sleep; if any such activity bestirs itself, then in so far have we failed to reach the true pre-natal condition of peace; we have not been able to avoid altogether some remnants of mental activity, and the act of dreaming would represent these remnants. In that event it really does seem that dreams do not need to have meaning. With errors it was different, for they were at least activities manifested in waking life; but if I sleep and have altogether suspended mental activity, with the exception of certain remnants which I have not been able to suppress, there is no necessity whatever that they should have any meaning. In fact, I cannot even make use of any such meaning, seeing that the rest of my mind is asleep. It can really then be a matter of spasmodic reactions only, of such mental phenomena only as have their origin in physical stimulation. Hence, dreams must be remnants of the mental activity of waking life disturbing sleep, and we might as well make up our minds forthwith to abandon a theme so unsuited to the purposes of psychoanalysis.

Superfluous as dreams may be, however, they do exist nevertheless, and we can try to account for their existence to ourselves. Why does not mental life go off to sleep? Probably because there is something that will not leave the mind in peace; stimuli are acting upon it and to these it is bound to react. Dreams therefore are the mode of reaction of the mind to stimuli acting upon it during sleep. We note here a possibility of access to comprehension of dreams. We can now endeavour to find out, in various dreams, what are the stimuli seeking to disturb sleep, the reaction to which takes the form of dreams. By doing this we should have worked out the first characteristic common to all dreams.

Is there any other common characteristic? Yes, there is another, unmistakable, and yet much harder to lay hold of and describe. The character of mental processes during sleep is quite different from that of waking processes. In dreams we go through many experiences, which we fully believe in, whereas in reality we are perhaps only experiencing the single disturbing stimulus. For the most part our experiences take the form of visual images; there may be feeling as well, thoughts, too, mixed up with them, and the other senses may be drawn in; but for the most part dreams consist of visual images. Part of the difficulty of reciting a dream comes from the fact that we have to translate these images into words. "I could draw it," the dreamer often says to us, "but I do not know how to put it into words." Now this is not exactly a diminution in the mental capacity, as seen in a contrast between a feeble-minded person and a man of genius. The difference is rather a qualitative one, but it is difficult to say precisely wherein it lies. G. T. Fechner once suggested that the stage whereon the drama of the dream (within the mind) is played out is other than that of the life of waking ideas. That is a saying which we really do not understand, nor do we know what it is meant to convey to us, but it does actually reproduce the impression of strangeness which most dreams make upon us. Again, the comparison of the act of dreaming with the performances of an unskilled hand in music breaks down here, for the piano will certainly respond with the same notes, though not with melodies, to a chance touch on its keys. We will keep this second common characteristic of dreams carefully in view, even though we may not understand it.

Are there any other qualities common to all dreams? I can think of none, but can see differences only, whichever way I look, differences too in every respect—in apparent duration, definiteness, the part played by affects, persistence in the mind, and so forth. This is really not what we should naturally expect in the case of a compulsive attempt, at once meagre

and spasmodic, to ward off a stimulus. As regards the length
of dreams, some are very short, containing only one image,
or very few, or a single thought, possibly even a single word;
others are peculiarly rich in content, enact entire romances
and seem to last a very long time. There are dreams as distinct as actual experiences, so distinct that for some time after
waking we do not realize that they were dreams at all; others,
which are ineffably faint, shadowy and blurred; in one and
the same dream, even, there may be some parts of extraordinary vividness alternating with others so indistinct as to be
almost wholly elusive. Again, dreams may be quite consistent
or at any rate coherent, or even witty or fantastically beautiful; others again are confused, apparently imbecile, absurd
or often absolutely mad. There are dreams which leave us
quite cold, others in which every affect makes itself felt—
pain to the point of tears, terror so intense as to wake us,
amazement, delight, and so on. Most dreams are forgotten
soon after waking; or they persist throughout the day, the
recollection becoming fainter and more imperfect as the
day goes on; others remain so vivid (as, for example, the
dreams of childhood) that thirty years later we remember
them as clearly as though they were part of a recent experience. Dreams, like people, may make their appearance once
and never come back; or the same person may dream the
same thing repeatedly, either in the same form or with slight
alterations. In short, these scraps of mental activity at night-
time have at command an immense repertory, can in fact
create everything that by day the mind is capable of—only, it
is never the same.

One might attempt to account for these diversities in dream
by assuming that they correspond to different intermediate
states between sleeping and waking, different levels of imperfect sleep. Very well; but then in proportion as the mind
approached the waking state there should be not merely an
increase in the value, content, and distinctness of the dream-
performance, but also a growing perception that it *is* a dream;
and it ought not to happen that side by side with a clear and
sensible element in the dream there is one which is nonsensical

or indistinct, followed again by a good piece of work. It is certain that the mind could not vary its depth of sleep so rapidly as that. This explanation therefore does not help; there is in fact no short cut to an answer.

For the present we will leave the "meaning" of the dream out of question, and try instead, by starting from the common element in dreams, to clear a path to a better understanding of their nature. From the relationship of dreams to sleep we have drawn the conclusion that dreams are the reaction to a stimulus disturbing sleep. As we have heard, this is also the single point at which exact experimental psychology can come to our aid; it affords proof of the fact that stimuli brought to bear during sleep make their appearance in dreams. Many investigations have been made on these lines, culminating in those of Mourly Vold whom I mentioned earlier; we have all, too, been in a position to confirm their results by occasional observations of our own. I will choose some of the earlier experiments to tell you. Maury had tests of this kind carried out upon himself. Whilst dreaming, he was made to smell some eau de Cologne, whereupon he dreamt he was in Cairo, in the shop of Johann Maria Farina, and this was followed by some crazy adventures. Again, someone gave his neck a gentle pinch, and he dreamt of the application of a blister and of a doctor who had treated him when he was a child. Again, they let a drop of water fall on his forehead and he was immediately in Italy, perspiring freely and drinking the white wine of Orvieto.

The striking feature about these dreams produced under experimental conditions will perhaps become still clearer to us in another series of "stimulus"-dreams. These are three dreams of which we have an account by a clever observer, Hildebrandt, and all three are reactions to the sound of an alarum-clock:

"I am going for a walk on a spring morning, and I saunter through fields just beginning to grow green, till I come to a neighbouring village, where I see the inhabitants in holiday attire making their way in large numbers to the church, their hymn-books in their hands. Of course! it is Sunday and the morning service is just about to begin. I decide to take part in it, but first as I am rather overheated I think I will cool down in the churchyard which surrounds the church. Whilst reading some of the epitaphs there I hear the bell-ringer go up into the tower, where I now notice, high up, the little village bell which will give the signal for the beginning of the service. For some time yet it remains motionless, then it begins to swing, and suddenly the strokes ring out, clear and piercing—so clear and piercing that they put an end to my sleep. But the sound of the bell comes from the alarum-clock."

Here is another combination of images. "It is a bright winter day, and the roads are deep in snow. I have promised to take part in a sleighing expedition, but I have to wait a long time before I am told that the sleigh is at the door. Now follow the preparations for getting in, the fur rug is spread out and the foot-muff fetched and finally I am in my place. But there is still a delay while the horses wait for the signal to start. Then the reins are jerked and the little bells, shaken violently, begin their familiar janizary music, so loudly that in a moment the web of the dream is rent. Again it is nothing but the shrill sound of the alarum-clock."

Now for the third example! "I see a kitchen-maid with dozens of piled-up plates going along the passage to the dining-room. It seems to me that the pyramid of china in her arms is in danger of overbalancing. I call out a warning: 'Take care, your whole load will fall to the ground.' Of course I receive the usual answer: that they are accustomed to carrying china in that way, and so on; meanwhile I follow her as she goes with anxious looks. I thought so—the next thing is a stumble on the threshold, the crockery falls, crashing and clattering in a hundred pieces on the ground. But—I soon become aware that that interminably prolonged sound is no real crash, but a regular ringing—and this ringing is due merely to the alarum-clock, as I realize at last on awakening."

These dreams are very pretty, perfectly sensible, and by

no means so incoherent as dreams usually are. We have no
quarrel with them on those grounds. The thing common to
them all is that in each case the situation arises from a noise,
which the dreamer on waking recognizes as that of the alarum-
clock. Hence we see here how a dream is produced, but we
find out something more. In the dream there is no recognition of the clock, which does not even appear in it, but for the
noise of the clock another noise is substituted; the stimulus
which disturbs sleep is interpreted, but interpreted differently
in each instance. Now why is this? There is no answer; it appears to be mere caprice. But to understand the dream we
should be able to account for its choice of just this noise and
no other to interpret the stimulus given by the alarum-clock.
In analogous fashion we must object to Maury's experiments
that, although it is clear that the stimulus brought to bear
on the sleeper does appear in the dream, yet his experiments don't explain why it appears exactly in that form,
which is one that does not seem explicable by the nature of
the stimulus disturbing sleep. And further, in Maury's experiments there was mostly a mass of other dream-material attached to the direct result of the stimulus, for example, the
crazy adventures in the eau de Cologne dream, for which we
are at a loss to account.

Now will you reflect that the class of dreams which wake
one up affords the best opportunity for establishing the influence of external disturbing stimuli. In most other cases it
will be more difficult. We do not wake up out of all dreams,
and if in the morning we remember a dream of the night
before, how are we to assign it to a disturbing stimulus operating perhaps during the night? I once succeeded in subsequently establishing the occurrence of a sound-stimulus of this
sort, but only, of course, because of peculiar circumstances.
I woke up one morning at a place in the Tyrolese mountains
knowing that I had dreamt that the Pope was dead. I could
not explain the dream to myself, but later my wife asked
me: "Did you hear quite early this morning the dreadful
noise of bells breaking out in all the churches and chapels?"
No, I had heard nothing, my sleep is too sound, but thanks

to her telling me this I understood my dream. How often may such causes of stimulus as this induce dreams in the sleeper without his ever hearing of them afterwards? Possibly very often: and possibly not. If we can get no information of any stimulus we cannot be convinced on the point. And apart from this we have given up trying to arrive at an estimation of the sleep-disturbing external stimuli, since we know that they only explain a fragment of the dream and not the whole dream-reaction.

We need not on that account give up this theory altogether; there is still another possible way of following it out. Obviously it is a matter of indifference what disturbs sleep and causes the mind to dream. If it cannot always be something external acting as a stimulus to one of the senses, it is possible that, instead, a stimulus operates from the internal organs—a so-called somatic stimulus. This supposition lies very close, and moreover it corresponds to the view popularly held with regard to the origin of dreams, for it is a common saying that they come from the stomach. Unfortunately, here again we must suppose that in very many cases information respecting a somatic stimulus operating during the night would no longer be forthcoming after waking, so that it would be incapable of proof. But we will not overlook the fact that many trustworthy experiences support the idea that dreams may be derived from somatic stimuli; on the whole it is indubitable that the condition of the internal organs can influence dreams. The relation of the content of many dreams to distention of the bladder or to a condition of excitation of the sex-organs is so plain that it cannot be mistaken. From these obvious cases we pass to others, in which, to judge by the content of the dream, we are at least justified in suspecting that some such somatic stimuli have been at work, since there is something in this content which can be regarded as elaboration, representation, or interpretation of these stimuli. Scherner, the investigator of dreams (1861), emphatically supported the view which traces the origin of dreams to organic stimuli, and contributed some excellent examples towards it. For instance, he sees in a dream "two rows of beautiful boys, with fair hair and delicate complexions, confronting each other pugnaciously, joining in combat, seizing hold of one another, and again letting go their hold, only to take up the former position and go through the whole process again"; his interpretation of the two rows of boys as the teeth is in itself plausible and seems to receive full confirmation when after this scene the dreamer "pulls a long tooth from his jaw." Again, the interpretation of "long, narrow, winding passages" as being suggested by a stimulus originating in the intestine seems sound and corroborates Scherner's assertion that dreams primarily endeavour to represent, by like objects, the organ from which the stimulus proceeds.

We must therefore be prepared to admit that internal stimuli can play the same rôle in dreams as external ones. Unfortunately, evaluation of this factor is open to the same objections. In a great number of instances the attribution of dreams to somatic stimuli must remain uncertain or incapable of proof; not all dreams, but only a certain number of them, rouse the suspicion that stimuli from internal organs have something to do with their origin; and lastly, the internal somatic stimulus will suffice no more than the external sensory stimulus to explain any other part of the dream than the direct reaction to it. The origin of all the rest of the dream remains obscure.

Now, however, let us direct our attention to a certain peculiarity of the dream-life which appears when we study the operation of these stimuli. The dream does not merely reproduce the stimulus, but elaborates it, plays upon it, fits it into a context, or replaces it by something else. This is a side of the dream-work which is bound to be of interest to us because possibly it may lead us nearer to the true nature of dreams. The scope of a man's production is not necessarily limited to the circumstance which immediately gives rise to it. For instance, Shakespeare's *Macbeth* was written as an occasional drama on the accession of the king who first united in his person the crowns of the three kingdoms. But does this historical occasion cover the whole content of the drama, or explain its grandeur and its mystery? Perhaps in the same way the external and internal stimuli operating upon the sleeper are merely the occasion of the dream and afford us no insight into its true nature.

The other element common to all dreams, their peculiarity in mental life, is on the one hand very difficult to grasp and on the other seems to afford no clue for further inquiry. Our experiences in dreams for the most part take the form of visual images. Can these be explained by the stimuli? Is it really the stimulus that we experience? If so, why is the experience visual, when it can only be in the very rarest instance that any stimulus has operated upon our eyesight? Or, can it be shown that when we dream of speech any conversation or sounds resembling conversation reached our ears during sleep? I venture to discard such a possibility without any hesitation whatever.

If we cannot get any further with the common characteristics of dreams as a starting-point, let us try beginning with their differences. Dreams are often meaningless, confused, and absurd, yet there are some which are sensible, sober, and reasonable. Let us see whether these latter sensible dreams can help to elucidate those which are meaningless. I will tell you the latest reasonable dream which was told to me, the dream of a young man: "I went for a walk in the Kärntnerstrasse and there I met Mr. X.; after accompanying him for a short time I went into a restaurant. Two ladies and a gentleman came and sat down at my table. At first I was annoyed and refused to look at them, but presently I glanced across at them and found that they were quite nice." The dreamer's comment on this was that the evening before he had actually been walking in the Kärntnerstrasse, which is the way he usually goes, and that he had met Mr. X. there. The other part of the dream was not a direct reminiscence, but only bore a certain resemblance to an occurrence of some time previously. Or here we have another prosaic dream, that of a lady. Her husband says to her: "Don't you think we ought to have the piano tuned?" and she replies: "It is not worth it, for the hammers need fresh leather anyhow." This dream repeats a conversation which took place in almost the same words between herself and her husband the day before the dream. What then do we learn from these two prosaic dreams? Merely that there occur in them recollections of daily life or of matters connected with it. Even that would be something if it could be asserted of all dreams without exception. But that is out of the question; this characteristic too belongs only to a minority of dreams. In most dreams we find no connection with the day before, and no light is thrown from this quarter upon meaningless and absurd dreams. All we know is that we have met with a new problem. Not only do we want to know what a dream is saying, but if as in our examples that is quite plain, we want to know further from what cause and to what end we repeat in dreams this which is known to us and has recently happened to us.

I think you would be as tired as I of continuing the kind of attempts we have made up to this point. It only shows that all the interest in the world will not help us with a problem unless we have also an idea of some path to adopt in order to arrive at a solution. Till now we have not found this path. Experimental psychology has contributed nothing but some (certainly very valuable) information about the significance of stimuli in the production of dreams. Of philosophy we have nothing to expect, unless it be a lofty repetition of the reproach that our object is intellectually contemptible; while from the occult sciences we surely do not choose to borrow. History and the verdict of the people tell us that dreams are full of meaning and importance, and of prophetic significance; but that is hard to accept and certainly does not lend itself to proof. So then our first endeavours are completely baffled.

But unexpectedly there comes a hint from a direction in which we have not hitherto looked. Colloquial speech, which is certainly no matter of chance but the deposit, as it were, of ancient knowledge—a thing which must not indeed be made too much of—our speech, I say, recognizes the existence of something to which, strangely enough, it gives the name of "day-dreams." Day-dreams are phantasies (products of phantasy); they are very common phenomena, are observable in

healthy as well as in sick persons, and they also can easily
be studied by the subject himself. The most striking thing
about these 'phantastic' creations is that they have received
the name of "day-dreams," for they have nothing in common
with the two universal characteristics of dreams. Their name
contradicts any relationship to the condition of sleep and, as
regards the second universal characteristic, no experience or
hallucination takes place in them, we simply imagine something; we recognize that they are the work of phantasy, that
we are not seeing but thinking. These day-dreams appear
before puberty, often indeed in late childhood, and persist
until maturity is reached when they are either given up or
retained as long as life lasts. The content of these phantasies
is dictated by a very transparent motivation. They are scenes
and events which gratify either the egoistic cravings of ambition or thirst for power, or the erotic desires of the subject. In
young men, ambitious phantasies predominate; in women,
whose ambition centres on success in love, erotic phantasies;
but the erotic requirement can often enough in men too be
detected in the background, all their heroic deeds and successes are really only intended to win the admiration and
favour of women. In other respects these day-dreams show
great diversity and their fate varies. All of them are either
given up after a short time and replaced by a new one, or
retained, spun out into long stories, and adapted to changing
circumstances in life. They march with the times; and they
receive as it were "date-stamps" upon them which show the
influence of new situations. They form the raw material of
poetic production; for the writer by transforming, disguising,
or curtailing them creates out of his day-dreams the situations
which he embodies in his stories, novels, and dramas. The
hero of a day-dream is, however, always the subject himself,
either directly imagined in the part or transparently identified
with someone else.

Perhaps day-dreams are so called on account of their similar
relation to reality, as an indication that their content is no
more to be accepted as real than is that of dreams. But it is
possible that they share the name of dreams because of some

mental characteristic of the dream which we do not yet know but after which we are seeking. On the other hand, it is possible that we are altogether wrong in regarding this similarity of name as significant. That is a question which can only be answered later.

SIXTH LECTURE

PRELIMINARY HYPOTHESES AND TECHNIQUE OF INTERPRETATION

WE THUS REALIZE OUR NEED OF A NEW WAY OF APPROACH, A definite method, if we are to make any advance in our researches into dreams. I will now offer an obvious suggestion: let us accept as the basis of the whole of our further enquiry the following hypothesis—that dreams are not a somatic, but a mental, phenomenon. You know what this means; but what is our justification in making this assumption? We have none, but on the other hand there is nothing to prevent us. The position is this: if the dream is a somatic phenomenon it does not concern us; it can only be of interest to us on the hypothesis that it is a mental phenomenon. So we will assume that this hypothesis is true, in order to see what happens if we do so. The results of our work will determine whether we may adhere to the assumption, and uphold it in its turn as an inference fairly drawn. Now what exactly is the object of this enquiry of ours, or to what are we directing our efforts? Our object is that of all scientific endeavour—namely, to achieve an understanding of the phenomena, to establish a connection between them, and, in the last resort, wherever it is possible to increase our power over them.

So we continue our work on the assumption that dreams are a mental phenomenon. In that event, they are a performance and an utterance on the part of the dreamer, but of a kind that conveys nothing to us, and which we do not understand. Now supposing that I give utterance to something that you do not understand, what do you do? You ask me to explain, do you not? Why may not we do the same—*ask the dreamer the meaning of the dream?*

Remember, we have already found ourselves in a similar position. It was when we were enquiring into certain errors, and the instance we took was a slip of the tongue. Someone had said: "Then certain things were *re-filled*," and thereupon we asked—no, fortunately it was not *we* who asked, but other people who had nothing to do with psychoanalysis—*they* asked what he meant by this enigmatic expression. He answered at once that what he had intended to say was: "That was a filthy business," but had checked himself and substituted the milder words: "Things were revealed there." I explained to you then that this enquiry was the model for every psychoanalytic investigation, and you understand now that psychoanalytic technique endeavours as far as possible to let the persons being analysed give the answer to their own problems. The dreamer himself then should interpret his dream for us.

That is not so simple with dreams, however, as we all know. Where errors were concerned, this method proved possible in many cases; there were others where the person questioned refused to say anything and even indignantly repudiated the answer suggested to him. With dreams, instances of the first type are entirely lacking; the dreamer always says he knows nothing about it. He cannot very well repudiate our interpretation, since we have none to offer him. Shall we have to give up our attempt then? Since *he* knowns nothing, and *we* know nothing, and a third person can surely know nothing either, there cannot be any prospect of finding the answer. Well, if you like, give up the attempt. But if you are not so minded, you can accompany me. For I assure you that it is not only quite possible, but highly probable, that the dreamer really does know the meaning of his dream; *only he does not know that he knows, and therefore thinks that he does not.*

At this point you will probably call my attention to the fact that I am again introducing an assumption, the second in quite a short context, and that by so doing I greatly detract from the force of my claim to a trustworthy method of procedure. Given the hypothesis that dreams are a mental phenomenon, and given further the hypothesis that there are in the minds of men certain things which they know without knowing that they know them—and so forth! You have only to keep in view the intrinsic improbability of both these hypotheses, and you may with an easy mind abandon all interest in the conclusions to be drawn from them.

Well, I have not brought you here either to delude you or to conceal anything from you. True, I announced that I would give a course of lectures entitled Introductory Lectures on Psychoanalysis; but it was no part of my purpose to play the oracle, professing to show you an easy sequence of facts, whilst carefully concealing all difficulties, filling up gaps, and glossing over doubtful points, so that you might comfortably enjoy the belief that you have learnt something new. No, it is the very fact that you are beginners that makes me anxious to show you our science as it is, with all its excrescences and crudities, the claims that it makes and the criticism to which it may give rise. I know indeed that it is the same in every science and that, especially in the beginnings, it cannot be otherwise. I know too that, in teaching other sciences, an effort is made at first to hide these difficulties and imperfections from the learner. But that cannot be done in psychoanalysis. So I really have set up two hypotheses, the one within the other; and anyone who finds it all too laborious, or too uncertain, or who is used to higher degrees of certainty, or to more refined deductions, need go no further with me. Only I should advise him to leave psychological problems altogether alone, for it is to be feared that this is a field in which he will find no access to such exact and sure paths as he is prepared to tread. And further, it is quite superfluous for any science which can offer a real contribution to knowledge to strive to make itself heard and to win adherents. Its reception must depend upon its results, and it can afford to wait until these have compelled attention.

But I may warn those of you who are not to be deterred in this way that my two assumptions are not of equal importance. The first, that dreams are a mental phenomenon, is the hypothesis which we hope to prove by the results of our work. The second has already been proved in a different field, and I am merely taking the liberty of transferring it thence to our problems.

Where, and in what connection, is it supposed to have been proved that a man can possess knowledge without knowing that he does so, which is the assumption we are making of the dreamer? Surely that would be a remarkable and surprising fact, which would change our conception of mental life and would have no need of concealment. Incidentally, it would be a fact belied in the very statement of it, which yet intends to be literally true—a contradiction in terms. There is not, however, any attempt at concealment. We cannot blame the fact for people's ignorance of it, or lack of interest in it, any more than we ourselves are to blame because all these psychological problems have been passed in judgement by persons who have held aloof from all the observations and experiments which alone can be conclusive.

The proof to which I refer was found in the sphere of hypnotic phenomena. In the year 1889 I was present at the remarkably impressive demonstrations by Liébault and Bernheim, in Nancy, and there I witnessed the following experiment. A man was placed in a condition of somnambulism, and then made to go through all sorts of hallucinatory experiences. On being wakened, he seemed at first to know nothing at all of what had taken place during his hypnotic sleep. Bernheim then asked him in so many words to tell him what had happened while he was under hypnosis. The man declared that he could not remember anything. Bernheim, however, insisted upon it, pressed him, and assured him that he did know and that he must remember, and lo and behold! the man wavered, began to reflect, and remembered in a shadowy fashion first one of the occurrences which had been suggested to him, then something else, his recollection growing increasingly clear and complete until finally it was brought to light without a single

gap. Now, since in the end he had the knowledge without
having learnt anything from any other quarter in the mean-
time, we are justified in concluding that these recollections
were in his mind from the outset. They were merely inaccessible to him; he did not know that he knew them but believed
that he did not know. In fact, his case was exactly similar to
what we assume the dreamer's to be.

I hope you are duly surprised that this fact is already established and that you will ask me: "Why did you not refer to
this proof before, when we were considering errors and came
to the point of ascribing to a man who had made a slip of the
tongue intentions behind his speech, of which he knew nothing, and which he denied? If it is possible for a man to believe
that he knows nothing of experiences of which nevertheless he
does possess the recollection, it seems no longer improbable
that there should be other mental processes going on within
him about which also he knows nothing. We should certainly
have been impressed by this argument and should have been
in a better position to understand about errors." Certainly, I
might have brought forward this proof then, but I reserved it
for a later occasion when there would be more need for it.
Some of the errors explained themselves, others suggested to
us that in order to understand the connection between the
phenomena it would be advisable to postulate the existence of
mental processes of which the person is entirely ignorant.
With dreams we are compelled to seek our explanations elsewhere, and besides, I am counting on your being more ready
to accept in this connection a proof from the field of hypnosis.
The condition in which we perform errors must seem to you
normal and, as such, to bear no similarity to that of hypnosis.
On the other hand there exists a clear relationship between
the hypnotic state and sleep, the essential condition of dreaming. Hypnosis is actually called artificial sleep; we say to the
people whom we hypnotize: "Sleep," and the suggestions
made to them are comparable to the dreams of natural sleep.
The mental situation is really analogous in the two cases. In
natural sleep we withdraw our interest from the whole outer
world; so also in hypnotic sleep, with the exception of the one

person who has hypnotized us and with whom we remain in rapport. Again, the so-called "nurse's sleep" in which the nurse remains in rapport with the child and can be awakened only by him is a normal counterpart of hypnotic sleep. So it does not seem so very audacious to carry over to natural sleep something which is a condition in hypnosis. The assumption that some knowledge about his dream exists in the dreamer and that this knowledge is merely inaccessible to him, so that he himself does not believe he has it, is not a wild invention. Incidentally, we observe here that a third way of approaching the study of dreams is thus opened out for us; we may approach it by the avenue of sleep-disturbing stimuli, by that of day-dreams, and now by that of the dreams suggested during hypnosis.

Now perhaps we shall return to our task with greater confidence. We see it is very probable that the dreamer knows something about his dream; the problem is how to make it possible for him to get at his knowledge and impart it to us. We do not expect him immediately to tell us what his dream means, but we do think he will be able to discover its source, from what circle of thoughts and interests it is derived. With errors, you will remember the man was asked how the slip of the tongue "re-filled" had come about and his first association gave us the explanation. The technique we employ in the case of dreams is very simple and is modelled on this example. Here again we shall ask the dreamer how he came to have the dream, and his next words must be regarded as giving the explanation in this case also. It makes no difference to us therefore, whether he thinks that he does or does not know anything about it, and we treat both cases alike.

This technique is certainly very simple, nevertheless I am afraid it will provoke most strenuous opposition in you. You will say: "Another assumption, the third! And the most improbable of all! When I ask the dreamer what ideas come to him about the dream, do you mean to say that his very first association will give the desired explanation? But surely he might have no association at all, or heaven only knows what the association might be. We cannot imagine upon what grounds such an expectation is based. It really implies too much trust in Providence, and this at a point where rather more exercise of the critical faculty would better meet the case. Besides, a dream is not like a single slip of the tongue but is made up of many elements. That being so, upon which association is one to rely?"

You are right in all the unessentials. It is true that a dream differs from a slip of the tongue in the matter of its many elements as well as in other points. We must take account of that in our technique. So I suggest to you that we divide the dream up into its various elements, and examine each element separately; then we shall have re-established the analogy with a slip of the tongue. Again, you are right in saying that the dreamer when questioned on the single elements of the dream may reply that he has no ideas about them. There are cases in which we accept this answer, and later I will tell you which these are; curiously enough, they are cases about which we ourselves may have certain definite ideas. But in general, when the dreamer declares that he has no ideas, we shall contradict him, press him to answer, assure him that he must have some idea and—shall find we are right. He will produce an association, any one, it does not matter to us what it is. He will be especially ready with information which we may term historical. He will say: "That is something which happened yesterday" (as in the instance of the two "prosaic" dreams quoted above) or: "That reminds me of something which happened recently," and in this way we shall come to notice that dreams are much more often connected with impressions of the day before than we thought at first. Finally, with the dream as his starting-point, he will recall events which happened less recently, and at last even some which lie very far back in the past.

In regard to the main issue, however, you are wrong. When you think it arbitrary to assume that the first association of the dreamer must give us just what we are looking for, or at any rate lead to it, and further, that the association is much more likely to be quite capricious and to have no connection with what we are looking for, and that it only shows my blind trust in Providence if I expect anything else—then you make a very great mistake. I have already taken the liberty of pointing out to you that there is within you a deeply rooted belief in psychic freedom and choice, that this belief is quite un-scientific, and that it must give ground before the claims of a determinism which governs even mental life. I ask you to have some respect for the *fact* that that one association, and noth-ing else, occurs to the dreamer when he is questioned. Nor am I setting up one belief against another. It can be proved that the association thus given is not a matter of choice, not in-determinate, and that it is not unconnected with what we are looking for. Indeed, I have recently learnt—not that I attach too much importance to the fact—that experimental psychol-ogy itself has brought forward similar proofs.

Because of the importance of the matter I ask you to pay special attention to this. When I ask a man to say what comes to his mind about any given element in a dream, I require him to give himself up to the process of FREE ASSOCIATION *which follows when he keeps in mind the original idea.* This neces-sitates a peculiar attitude of the attention, something quite different from reflection, indeed, precluding it. Many people adopt this attitude without any difficulty, but others when they attempt to do so display an incredible inaptitude. There is a still higher degree of freedom in association which ap-pears when I dispense with any particular stimulus-idea and perhaps only describe the kind and species of association that I want; for example, ask someone to let a proper name or a number occur to him. An association of this sort should, one would say, be even more subject to choice and unaccountable than the kind used in our technique. Nevertheless, it can be shown that in every instance it will be strictly determined by important inner attitudes of mind, which are unknown to us at the moment when they operate, just as much unknown as are the disturbing tendencies which cause errors, and those tend-encies which bring about so-called "chance" actions.

I myself and many after me have repeatedly made an ex-amination of names and numbers called up without any par-ticular idea as a starting-point; some of these experiments

have been published. The method is this: a train of associations is stirred up by the name which occurred, and these associations, as you see, are no longer quite free, but are attached just so far as the associations to the different elements
of the dream are attached; this train of associations is then
kept up until the thoughts arising from the impulse have been
exhausted. By that time, however, you will have explained the
motivation and significance of the free association with a
name. The experiments yield the same result again and again;
the information they give us often includes a wealth of material and necessitates going far afield into its ramifications. The
associations to numbers that arise spontaneously are perhaps
the most demonstrative; they follow upon one another so
swiftly and make for a hidden goal with such astounding certainty that one is really quite taken aback. I will give you just
one example of a name-analysis of this sort, because it happens
to be one which does not involve the handling of a great mass
of material.

Once, when I was treating a young man, I happened to say
something on this subject and to assert that in spite of our apparent freedom of choice in such matters we cannot, in point
of fact, think of any name which cannot be shown to be narrowly determined by the immediate circumstances, the idiosyncrasies, of the person experimented with and his situation
at the moment. As he was inclined to be sceptical, I proposed
that he should make the experiment himself then and there. I
knew that he had usually numerous relationships of all sorts
with women and girls, so I told him that I thought he would
have an exceptionally large number to choose from if he were
to let the name of a woman occur to him. He agreed. To my
surprise, or rather perhaps to his own, he did not overwhelm
me with an avalanche of women's names, but remained silent
for a time, and then confessed that the only name which came
into his mind at all was "Albine." "How curious! What do you
connect with this name? How many Albines do you know?"
Strangely enough, he knew no one of the name of Albine, and
he found no associations to the name. One might infer that
the analysis had failed; but no, it was already complete, and

no further association was required. The man himself was unusually fair in colouring, and whilst talking to him in analysis
I had often jokingly called him an *albino;* moreover, we were
just in the midst of tracing the *feminine* element in his nature.
So it was he himself who was this female albino, the "woman"
who interested him most at the moment.

In the same way, the tunes which suddenly come into a
man's head can be shown to be conditioned by some train of
thought to which they belong, and which for some reason is
occupying his mind without his knowing anything about it. It
is easy to show that the connection with the tune is to be
sought either in the words which belong to it or in the source
from which it comes: I must, however, make this reservation,
that I do not maintain this in the case of really musical people
of whom I happen to have had no experience; in them the
musical value of the tune may account for its suddenly emerging into consciousness. The first case is certainly much more
common; I know of a young man who for some time was absolutely haunted by the tune (a charming one, I admit) of the
song of Paris in *Helen of Troy,* until his attention was drawn
in analysis to the fact that at that time an "Ida" and a "Helen"
were rivals in his interest.

If then the associations which arise quite freely are determined in this way and belong to some definite context, we are
surely justified in concluding that associations attached to one
single stimulus-idea must be equally narrowly conditioned.
Examination shows as a fact that they are not only attached
in the first place to the stimulus-idea which we have provided
for them, but that they are also dependent, in the second
place, on circles of thoughts and interests of strong affective
value (*complexes,* as we call them) of whose influence at the
time nothing is known, that is to say, on unconscious activities.

Associations attached in this way have been made the subject of very instructive experiments, which have played a
notable part in the history of psycho-analysis. Wundt's school
originated the so-called 'association-experiment,' in which the
subject of the experiment is bidden to reply to a given
'stimulus-word' as quickly as possible with whatever 'reaction-

word' occurs to him. The following points may then be noted: the interval which elapses between the utterance of the stimulus-word and of the reaction-word, the nature of the latter, and possibly any mistake which comes in when the same experiment is repeated later, and so on. The Zurich School, under the leadership of Bleuler and Jung, arrived at the explanation of the reactions to the association-experiment by asking the person experimented upon to throw light upon any associations which seemed at all remarkable, by means of subsequent associations. In this way it became clear that these unusual reactions were most strictly determined by the complexes of the person concerned. By this discovery Bleuler and Jung built the first bridge between experimental psychology and psychoanalysis.

Having heard this you may possibly say: "We admit now that free associations are subject to determination and not a matter of choice, as we thought at first, and we admit this also in the case of associations to the elements of dreams. But it is not this that we are bothering about. You maintain that the association to each element in the dream is determined by some mental background to this particular element, a background of which we know nothing. We cannot see that there is any proof of this. Naturally we expect that the association to the dream-element will be shown to be conditioned by one of the complexes of the dreamer, but what good is that to us? That does not help us to understand the dream; it merely leads to some knowledge of these so-called complexes, as did the association-experiment; but what have these to do with the dream?"

You are right, but you are overlooking an important point, the very thing which deterred me from choosing the association-experiment as a starting-point for this discussion. In this experiment the stimulus-word, the single thing which determines the reaction, is chosen by us at will, and the reaction stands as intermediary between this stimulus-word and the complex aroused in the person experimented upon. In the dream, the stimulus-word is replaced by something derived from the mental life of the dreamer, from sources unknown to him, and hence may very probably be itself a 'derivative of a complex.' It is not, therefore, altogether fantastic to suppose that the further associations connected with the elements of the dream are determined by no other complex than that which has produced the particular element itself, and that they will lead to the discovery of that complex.

Let me give you another instance which may serve to show that, in the case of dreams, the facts bear out our expectations. The forgetting of proper names is really an excellent prototype of what happens in dream-analysis, only that in the former case one person alone is concerned, while in the interpretation of dreams there are two. When I forget a name temporarily, I am still certain that I know it, and by way of a détour through Bernheim's experiment, we are now in a position to achieve a similar certainty in the case of the dreamer. Now this name which I have forgotten, and yet really know, eludes me. Experience soon teaches me that no amount of thinking about it, even with effort, is any use. I can, however, always think of another or of several other names instead of the forgotten one. When such a substitute name occurs to me spontaneously, only then is the similarity between this situation and that of dream-analysis evident. The dream-element also is not what I am really looking for; it is only a substitute for something else, for the real thing which I do not know and am trying to discover by means of dream-analysis. Again the difference is that when I forget a name I know perfectly well that the substitute is not the right one, whereas we only arrived at this conception of the dream-element by a laborious process of investigation. Now there also is a way in which, when we forget a name, we can by starting from the substitute, arrive at the real thing eluding our consciousness at the moment, i.e. the forgotten name. If I turn my attention to these substitute names and let further associations to them come into my mind, I arrive after a short or a long way round at the name I have forgotten, and in so doing I discover that the substitutes I have spontaneously produced had a definite connection with, and were determined by, the forgotten name.

I will give you an instance of an analysis of this sort: one day I found that I could not call to mind the name of the small country on the Riviera, of which Monte Carlo is the capital. It was most annoying, but so it was. I delved into all my knowledge about the country; I thought of Prince Albert of the House of Lusignan, of his marriages, of his passion for deep-sea exploration—in fact of everything I could summon up, but all to no purpose. So I gave up trying to think and, instead of the name I had lost, let substitute names come into my mind. They came quickly: Monte Carlo itself, then Piedmont, Albania, Montevideo, Colico. Albania was the first to attract my attention; it was immediately replaced by Montenegro, probably because of the contrast between black and white. Then I noticed that four of the substitute names have the same syllable "mon," and immediately I recalled the forgotten word and cried out "Monaco." You see the substitutes really originated in the forgotten name; the four first came from the first syllable and the last gave the sequence of the syllables and the whole of the final syllable. Incidentally, I could quite easily find out what had made me forget the name for the time being. Monaco is the Italian name for Munich, and it was some thoughts connected with this town which had acted as an inhibition.

Now that is a very pretty example, but it is too simple. In other cases you might have to take a longer succession of associations to the substitute name, and then the analogy to dream-analysis would be clearer. I have had experiences of that sort, too. A stranger once invited me to drink some Italian wine with him, and in the inn he found he had forgotten the name of the wine which he had meant to order on account of his very pleasant recollections of it. A number of dissimilar substitute names occurred to him, and from these I was able to infer that the thought of someone called Hedwig had made him forget the name of the wine. Sure enough, not only did he tell me that there had been a Hedwig with him on the occasion when he first tasted the wine, but this discovery brought back to him the name he wanted. He was now happily married, and "Hedwig" belonged to earlier days which he did not care to recall.

What is possible in the case of forgotten names must be also possible in the interpretation of dreams: starting from the substitute, we must be able to arrive at the real object of our search by means of a train of associations; and further, arguing from what happens with forgotten names, we may assume that the associations to the dream-element will have been determined not only by that element but also by the real thought which is not in consciousness. If we could do this, we should have gone some way towards justifying our technique.

SEVENTH LECTURE

MANIFEST CONTENT AND LATENT THOUGHTS

YOU SEE THAT OUR STUDY OF ERRORS HAS NOT BEEN FRUITLESS.
Thanks to our exertions in that direction, we have—reasoning
from the hypotheses with which you are familiar—secured two
results: a conception of the nature of the dream-element and
a technique of dream-interpretation. The conception of the
dream-element is as follows: it is not in itself a primary and
essential thing, a 'thought proper,' but a substitute for something else unknown to the person concerned, just as is the underlying intention of the error, a substitute for something the
knowledge of which is indeed possessed by the dreamer but
is inaccessible to him We hope to be able to carry over the
same conception on to the dream as a whole, which consists of
a number of such elements. Our method is to allow other substitute-ideas, from which we are able to divine that which lies
hidden, to emerge into consciousness by means of free association to the said elements.

I am now going to propose that we introduce an alteration
in our nomenclature in order to make our terminology more
flexible. Instead of using the words "hidden," "inaccessible,"
or "proper," let us give a more precise description and say "inaccessible to the consciousness of the dreamer" or "unconscious." By that we mean nothing more than was implied in
the case of the forgotten word, or the underlying intention

responsible for the error; that is to say, *unconscious at the moment*. It follows that in contradistinction we may call the dream-elements themselves, and those substitute-ideas arrived at by the process of association, *conscious*. No theoretical implication is so far contained in these terms; no exception can be taken to the use of the word "unconscious" as a description at once applicable and easy to understand.[1]

Now, transferring our conception from the single element to the dream as a whole, it follows that the latter is the distorted substitute for something else, something unconscious, and that the task of dream-interpretation is to discover these unconscious thoughts. Hence are derived three important rules which should be observed in the work of dream-interpretation:

1. We are not to trouble about the surface meaning of the dream, whether it be reasonable or absurd, clear or confused; in no case does it constitute the unconscious thoughts we are seeking. (An obvious limitation of this rule will force itself upon us later.)

2. We are to confine our work to calling up substitute-ideas for every element and not to ponder over them and try to see whether they contain something which fits in, nor to trouble ourselves about how far they are taking us from the dream-element.

3. We must wait until the hidden unconscious thoughts which we are seeking appear of their own accord, just as in the case of the missing word "Monaco" in the experiment which I decribed.

Now we understand also how entirely indifferent it is whether we remember much or little of our dreams, above all

---

[1] [It should be noted that in using the word "unconscious" to translate the German *"unbewusst"* we are deflecting it from its customary English sense, which is "absence of awareness," such as in the phrase "he lay unconscious," "a stone is unconscious," etc. *Unbewusst* is rather "unconscious'd," i.e. something of which the subject is not aware. Of it two statements may therefore be predicated. not only that it is not conscious in itself or of itself, but also that the subject is not conscious of its existence.—TR.]

whether we remember them accurately or not. The dream as remembered is not the real thing at all, but *a distorted substitute* which, by calling up other substitute-ideas, provides us with a means of approaching the thought proper, of bringing into consciousness the unconscious thoughts underlying the dream. If our recollection was at fault, all that has happened is that a further distortion of the substitute has taken place, and this distortion itself cannot be without motivation.

We can interpret our own dreams as well as those of others; indeed, we learn more from our own and the process carries more conviction. Now if we experiment in this direction, we notice that something is working against us. Associations come, it is true, but we do not admit them all; we are moved to criticize and to select. We say to ourselves of one association: "No, that does not fit in—it is irrelevant," and of another: "That is too absurd," and of a third: "That is quite beside the point"; and then we can observe further that in making such objections we stifle, and in the end actually banish, the associations before they have become quite clear. So on the one hand we tend to hold too closely to the initial idea, that is, the dream-element itself, and on the other, by allowing ourselves to select, we vitiate the results of the process of free association. If we are not attempting the interpretation by ourselves, but are allowing someone else to interpret, we shall clearly perceive another motive impelling us to this selection, forbidden as we know it to be. We find ourselves thinking at times: "No, this association is too unpleasant; I cannot, or will not, tell it to him."

Clearly these objections threaten to spoil the success of our work. We must guard against them when we are interpreting our own dreams by resolving firmly not to yield to them, and, in interpreting those of someone else, by laying down the hard and fast rule that he must not withhold any association, even if one of the four objections I have named rises up against it, namely, that it is too unimportant, too absurd, too irrelevant or too unpleasant to speak of. He promises to keep this rule, and we may well feel annoyed when we find how badly he fulfils his promise later on. At first we account for this by imagining that in spite of our authoritative assurance he is not convinced that the process of free association will be justified by its results; and perhaps our next idea will be to win him over first to our theory, by giving him books to read or sending him to lectures so that he may be converted to our views on the subject. But we shall be saved from any such false steps by observing that the same critical objections against certain associations arise even in ourselves, whom we surely cannot suspect of doubt, and can only subsequently, on second thoughts as it were, be overcome.

Instead of being annoyed at the dreamer's disobedience, we can turn this experience to good account as a means of learning something new, something which is the more important the more unprepared we were for it. We realize that the work of dream-interpretation is encountering opposition by a *resistance* which expresses itself in this very form of critical objections. This resistance is independent of the theoretical conviction of the dreamer. We learn even more than this. Experience shows that a critical objection of this nature is never justified. On the contrary, the associations which people wish to suppress in this way prove *without exception* to be the most important, to be decisive for the discovery of the unconscious thought. When an association is accompanied by an objection of this sort it positively calls for special notice.

This resistance is something entirely new; a phenomenon which we have found by following out our hypotheses, although it was not included in them. We are not altogether agreeably surprised by this new factor which we have to reckon with, for we suspect already that it will not make our work any easier: it might almost tempt us to give up the effort with dreams altogether. To take such a trivial subject and then to have so much trouble, instead of spinning along smoothly with our technique! But we might on the other hand find these difficulties fascinating and be led to suspect that the work will be worth the trouble. Resistances invariably confront us when we try to penetrate to the hidden unconscious thought from the substitute offered by the dream-element. We may suppose, therefore, that something very significant must be concealed behind the substitute; for, if not, why should we meet with such difficulties, the purpose of which is to keep up the concealment? When a child will not open his clenched fist to show what is in it, we may be quite certain that it is something which he ought not to have.

As soon as we introduce into our subject the dynamic conception of resistance, we must bear in mind that this factor is something quantitatively variable. There are greater and lesser resistances, and we are prepared to find these differences showing themselves in the course of our work. Perhaps we can connect with this another experience also met with in the process of dream-interpretation. I mean that sometimes only a few associations—perhaps not more than one—suffice to lead us from the dream-element to the unconscious thought behind it, whilst on other occasions long chains of associations are necessary and many critical objections have to be overcome. We shall probably think that the number of associations necessary varies with the varying strength of the resistances, and very likely we shall be right. If there is only a slight resistance, the substitute is not far removed from the unconscious thought; a strong resistance on the other hand causes great distortions of the latter, and thereby entails a long journey back from the substitute to the unconscious thought itself.

Perhaps this would be a good moment to select a dream and try our technique upon it, to see whether the expectations we have entertained are realized. Very well, but what dream shall we choose? You do not know how difficult it is for me to decide, nor can I make it clear to you yet what the difficulties are. Obviously there must be dreams in which on the whole there is very little distortion, and one would think it would be best to begin with these. But which are the least distorted dreams? Those which make good sense and are not confused, of which I have already given you two examples? In assuming this, we should make a great mistake, for examination shows that these dreams have undergone an exceptionally high degree of distortion. Supposing then that I make no special condition but take any dream at random, you would probably be very much disappointed. We might have to observe and record such a vast number of associations to the single dream-elements that it would be quite impossible to gain any clear view of the work as a whole. If we write the dream down and compare with it all the associations which it produces, we are likely to find that they have multiplied the length of the text of the dream many times. So the most practical method would seem to be that of selecting for analysis several short dreams, each of which can at least convey some idea to us or confirm some supposition. This will be the course we shall decide to take, unless experience gives us a hint where we ought really to look for slightly distorted dreams.

But I can suggest another means of simplifying matters, one which lies right before us. Instead of attempting the interpretation of whole dreams, let us confine ourselves to single dream-elements and find out by taking a series of examples how the application of our technique explains them:—

(a) A lady related that as a child she very often dreamt that *God had a pointed paper cap on his head.* How are you going to understand that without the help of the dreamer? It sounds quite nonsensical; but the absurdity disappears when the lady says that as a little girl she used to have a cap like that put on her head at table, because she wouldn't give up looking at the plates of her brothers and sisters to see whether any of them had been given more than she. Evidently the cap was meant to serve the purpose of blinkers; this piece of historical information was given, by the way, without any difficulty The interpretation of this element and, with it, of the whole short dream becomes easy enough with the help of a further association of the dreamer's: "As I had been told that God knew everything and saw everything, the dream could only mean that I knew and saw everything as God did, even when they tried to prevent me." This example is perhaps too simple.

(b) A sceptical patient had a longer dream, in which certain people were telling her about my book on *Wit* and praising it very highly. Then something else came in about a *canal;* it might have been another book in which the word canal oc-

curred, or something else to do with a canal . . . she did not know . . . it was quite vague.

Now you will certainly be inclined to suppose that the *canal* in the dream will defy interpretation on account of its vagueness. You are right in expecting difficulty, but the difficulty is not caused by the vagueness; on the contrary, the difficulty in interpretation is caused by something else, by the same thing that makes the element vague. The dreamer had no association to the word "canal"; naturally I did not know what to say either. Shortly afterwards, to be accurate, on the next day, she told me that an association had occurred to her which *perhaps* had something to do with it. It was in fact a witty remark which some one had told her. On board ship between Dover and Calais a well-known author was talking to an Englishman who in some particular context quoted the words: "Du sublime au ridicule il n'y a qu'un pas." The author answered: "Oui, le Pas-de-Calais," meaning that he regarded France as sublime and England as ridiculous. Of course, the Pas-de-Calais is a *canal*—that is to say, the Canal la Manche—the English Channel. Now, you ask, do I think that this association had anything to do with the dream? Certainly I think so: it gives the true meaning of the puzzling dream-element. Or are you inclined to doubt that the joke already existed before the dream and was the unconscious thought behind the element "canal," and to maintain that it was a subsequent invention? The association reveals the scepticism disguised under the obtrusive admiration, and resistance was no doubt the cause both of the association being so long in occurring to her, and of the corresponding dream-element being so vague. Observe here the relation between the dream-element and the unconscious thought underlying it: it is, as it were, a fragment of the thought, an allusion to it; by being isolated in that way it became quite incomprehensible.

(*c*) A patient had a fairly long dream, part of which was as follows: *Several members of his family were seated at a table of a particular shape . . .* etc. This table reminded the dreamer that he had seen one of the same sort when he was visiting a certain family. From that his thoughts ran on thus:

in this family the relation between father and son was a peculiar one, and the patient presently added that his own relations with his father were, as a matter of fact, of the same nature. So the table was introduced into the dream to indicate this parallelism.

It happened that this dreamer had long been familiar with the demands of dream-interpretation; otherwise he might have taken exception to the idea of investigating so trivial a detail as the shape of a table. We do literally deny that anything in the dream is a matter of chance or of indifference, and it is precisely by enquiring into such trivial and (apparently) unmotivated details that we expect to arrive at our conclusion. You may perhaps still be surprised that the dream-work should happen to choose the table, in order to express the thought "Our relationship is just like theirs." But even this is explicable when you learn that the family in question was named "Tischler." (Tisch = table.) In making his relations sit at this table the dreamer's meaning was that they too were "Tischler."[1] And notice another thing: that in relating dream-interpretations of this sort one is forced into indiscretion. There you have one of the difficulties I alluded to in the matter of choosing examples. I could easily have given you another example instead of this one, but probably I should have avoided this indiscretion only to commit another in its place.

This seems to me a good point at which to introduce two new terms which we might have used already. Let us call the dream as related *the manifest dream-content*, and the hidden meaning, which we should come by in following out the associations, *the latent dream-thoughts*. Then we must consider the relation between the manifest content and the latent thoughts, as shown in the above examples. There are many varieties of these relations. In examples (a) and (b) the manifest dream-element is also an integral part of the latent thoughts, but only a fragment of them. A small piece of a great, composite, mental structure in the unconscious dream-thoughts has made its way into the manifest dream also, in the

[1][Lit.: "Tablers."—TR.]

form of a fragment or in other cases as an allusion, like a catch-word or an abbreviation in a telegraphic code. The interpretation has to complete the whole to which this scrap or illusion belongs, which it did most successfully in example (b). One method of the distorting process in which the dreamwork consists is therefore that of substituting for something else a fragment or an illusion. In example (c) we notice, moreover, another possible relation between manifest content and latent thought, a relation which is even more plainly and distinctly expressed in the following examples:—

(d) *The dreamer was pulling a certain lady of his acquaintance out of a ditch.* He himself found the meaning of this dream-element by means of the first association. It meant: he "picked her out," preferred her.[1]

(e) Another man dreamt *that his brother was digging up his garden all over again.* The first association was to deep-trenching for vegetables, the second gave the meaning. The brother was *retrenching.* (Retrenching his expenses.)[2]

(f) *The dreamer was climbing a mountain from which he had a remarkably wide view.* This sounds most reasonable; perhaps no interpretation is called for and we have only to find out what recollection is referred to in the dream, and what had aroused it. No, you are mistaken; it comes out that this dream needed interpretation just as much as any other, more confused. For the dreamer remembers nothing about mountain-climbing himself; instead, it occurs to him that an acquaintance is publishing a *Rundschau* (Review), on the subject of our relations with the most distant parts of the earth: hence, the latent thought is one in which the dreamer identifies himself with the *"reviewer"* (lit. one who takes a survey).

Here you come across a new type of relation between the manifest and the latent element in dreams. The former is not so much a distortion of the latter as a representation—a plastic, concrete piece of imagery, originating in the sound of a word.

[1] [This example has been altered in translation to bring in the play upon words in English.—TR.]

[2] [See note on preceding example.—TR.]

It is true that this amounts in effect to a distortion, for we have long forgotten from what concrete image the word sprang, and hence fail to recognize it when that image is substituted for it. When you consider that the manifest dream consists of visual images in by far the greatest number of cases, and less frequently of thoughts and words, you will easily realize that this kind of relation between the manifest and the latent has a special significance in the structure of dreams. You see too that in this way it becomes possible for a long series of abstract thoughts to create substitute-images in the manifest dream which do indeed serve the purpose of concealment. This is how our picture-puzzles are made up. The source of the semblance of wit which goes with this type of representation is a special question which we need not touch on here.

There is a fourth kind of relation between the manifest and the latent elements which I will say nothing about until the time comes for it in my account of our technique. Even then I shall not have given you a full list of these possible relations, but we shall have sufficient for our purpose.

Now do you think you can summon up courage to venture on the interpretation of a whole dream? Let us see whether we are adequately equipped for the task. I shall not, of course, choose one of the most obscure, but all the same it shall be one which shows the characteristics of dreams in a well-marked form.

A young woman who had already been married for a number of years dreamt as follows: *She was at the theatre with her husband, and one side of the stalls was quite empty. Her husband told her that Elise L. and her fiancé also wanted to come, but could only get bad seats, three for a florin and a half, and of course they could not take those. She replied that in her opinion they did not lose much by that.*

The first thing stated by the dreamer is that the occasion giving rise to the dream is alluded to in the manifest content: her husband had really told her that Elise L., an acquaintance of about her own age, had become engaged, and the dream is the reaction to this piece of news. We know already that in many dreams it is easy to point to some such occasion occurring on the day before, and that this is often traced by the dreamer without any difficulty. This dreamer supplies us with further information of the same sort about other elements in the manifest dream. To what did she trace the detail of one side of the stalls being empty? It was an allusion to a real occurrence of the week before, when she had meant to go to a certain play and had therefore booked seats *early*, so early that she had to pay extra for the tickets. On entering the theatre it was evident that her anxiety had been quite superfluous, for one side of the stalls was almost empty. It would have been time enough if she had bought the tickets on the actual day of the performance and her husband did not fail to tease her about having been in *too great a hurry*. Next, what about the one florin and a half (1 fl. 50)? This was traced to quite another context which had nothing to do with the former, but it again refers to some news received on the previous day. Her sister-in-law had had a present of 150 florins from her husband and had rushed off *in a hurry*, like a silly goose, to a jeweller's shop and spent it all on a piece of jewellery. What about the number three? She knew nothing about that unless this idea could be counted an association, that the engaged girl, Elise L., was only three months younger than she herself who had been married ten years. And the absurdity of taking three tickets for two people? She had nothing to say to this and refused to give any more associations or information whatever.

Nevertheless, her few associations have provided us with so much material that it is possible to discover the latent dream-thoughts. We are struck by the fact that in her statements references to time are noticeable at several points, which form a common basis for the different parts of this material. She had got the theatre tickets *too soon*, taken them in *too great a hurry*, so that she had to pay extra for them; in the same way her sister-in-law had *hurried* off to the jeweller's with her money to buy an ornament with it, as though she might *miss something*. If the strongly emphasized points: *"too early," "too great a hurry,"* are connected with the occasion for the dream (namely, the news that her friend, only three months *younger* than herself, had now found a good husband after all) and with the criticism expressed in her asperity about her sister-in-law, that it was *folly* to be so precipitate, there occurs to us almost spontaneously the following construction of the latent dream-thoughts, for which the manifest dream is a highly distorted substitute:

"It was really *foolish* of me to be in such a hurry to marry! Elise's example shows me that I too could have found a husband later on." (The over-haste is represented by her own conduct in buying the tickets and that of her sister-in-law in buying the jewellery. Going to the theatre is substituted for getting married.) This would be the main thought; perhaps we may go on, though with less certainty because the analysis in these passages ought not to be unsupported by statements of the dreamer: "And I might have had one a hundred times better for the money!" (150 florins is 100 times more than one florin and a half.) If we may substitute the dowry for the money, it would mean that the husband is bought with the dowry: both the jewellery and the bad seats would stand for the husband. It would be still more desirable if we could see some connection between the element "three tickets" and a husband; but our knowledge does not as yet extend to this. We have only found out that the dream expresses *depreciation* of her own husband and regret at having *married so early*.

In my opinion we shall be more surprised and confused by the result of this our first attempt at dream-interpretation than satisfied with it. Too many ideas force themselves upon us at once, more than as yet we can master. We see already that we shall not come·to the end of what the interpretation of this dream can teach us. Let us immediately single out those points in which we can definitely see some new knowledge.

In the first place: we note that in the latent thoughts the chief emphasis falls upon the element of hurry; in the manifest dream that is exactly a feature about which we find nothing. Without analysis we could have had no suspicion that this thought entered in at all. It seems possible, therefore, that precisely the main point round which the unconscious thoughts centre does not appear in the manifest dream at all. This fact must radically change the impression made upon us by the whole dream. In the second place: in the dream there is a nonsensical combination of ideas (three for one florin and a half); in the dream-thoughts we detect the opinion: "It was folly (to marry so early)." Can one reject the conclusion that this thought, "It was *folly*," is represented by the introduction into the manifest dream of an *absurd* element? In the third place: comparison shows us that the relation between manifest and latent elements is no simple one, certainly not of such a kind that a manifest always replaces a latent element. The relation between the two is of the nature of a relation between two different groups, so that a manifest element can represent several latent thoughts or a latent thought be replaced by several manifest elements.

As regards the meaning of the dream and the dreamer's attitude towards it, here again we might find many surprising things to say. The lady certainly admitted the interpretation, but she wondered at it; she had not been aware that she had such disparaging thoughts of her husband; she did not even know why she should so disparage him. So there is still much that is incomprehensible about it. I really think that as yet we are not properly equipped for interpreting a dream and that we need further instruction and preparation first.

EIGHTH LECTURE

CHILDREN'S DREAMS

WE HAD THE IMPRESSION THAT WE HAD ADVANCED TOO rapidly; let us therefore retrace our steps a little. Before we made our last experiment in which we tried to overcome the difficulty of dream-distortion by means of our technique, we said that it would be best to circumvent it by confining our attention to dreams in which distortion is absent or occurs only to a very slight extent, if there are any such dreams. In doing this, we are again departing from the actual course of development of our knowledge; for in reality it was only after consistently applying our method of interpretation, and after exhaustive analysis of dreams in which distortion occurred, that we became aware of the existence of those in which it is lacking.

The dreams we are looking for are met with in children: short, clear, coherent, and easy to understand, they are free from ambiguity and yet are unmistakable dreams. You must not think, however, that all dreams in children are of this type. Distortion in dreams begins to appear very early in childhood, and there are on record dreams of children between five and eight years old which already show all the characteristics of the dreams of later life. But, if you confine yourselves to those occurring in the period between the dawn of recognizable mental activity and the fourth or fifth year of life, you will discover a series which we should characterize as infantile, and, in the later years of childhood, you may find single dreams of the same type; indeed, even in grown-up people under certain conditions dreams appear which in no way differ from the typically infantile.

Now from these children's dreams it is possible to obtain without any difficulty trustworthy information about the essential nature of dreams, which we hope will prove to be decisive and universally valid.

1. In order to understand these dreams there is no need for any analysis nor for the employment of any technique. It is not necessary to question the child who relates his dream. But we must know something about his life; in every instance there is some experience from the previous day which explains the dream. The dream is the mind's reaction in sleep to the experience of the previous day.

Let us consider some examples in order to base our further conclusions upon them:

(a) A boy of a year and ten months old had to present someone with a basket of cherries as a birthday gift. He plainly did it very unwillingly, although he had been promised some of them for himself. The next morning he told his dream: "Hermann eaten all the cherries."

(b) A little girl of three and a quarter years went for the first time for a trip on the lake. When they came to land, she did not wish to leave the boat and cried bitterly; the time on the water had evidently gone too quickly for her. Next morning she said: "Last night I was sailing on the lake." We may probably infer that this trip lasted longer.

(c) A boy five and a quarter years old was taken on an excursion to the Escherntal near Hallstatt. He had heard that Hallstatt lay at the foot of the Dachstein and had shown great interest in that mountain. From the lodgings in Aussee there was a fine view of the Dachstein, and with a telescope it was possible to make out the Simony Hut on top. The child had repeatedly endeavoured to see the hut through the telescope, but nobody knew whether he had succeeded. The excursion began in a mood of joyful expectation. Whenever a new mountain came into sight, the little boy asked: "Is that the Dachstein?" Every time his question was answered in the negative he grew more out of spirits and presently became silent and refused to climb a little way up to the waterfall with the others. He was thought to be overtired, but the next morning he said quite happily: "Last night I dreamt that we were in the Simony Hut." So it was with this expectation that he had taken part in the excursion. The only detail he gave was one he had heard before: "You have to climb up steps for six hours."

These three dreams will be enough to give us all the information we need at this point.

2. We see that these childhood dreams are not meaningless; they are complete, comprehensible mental acts. Remember the medical verdict about dreams, which I told you, and the comparison with unskilled fingers wandering over the keys of the piano. You cannot fail to notice how sharply this conception is contradicted by the children's dreams I have quoted. Now it would surely be most extraordinary if a child were able to achieve the performance of complete mental acts during sleep, and the grown-up person in the same situation contented himself with spasmodic reactions. Besides. we have every reason for attributing better and deeper sleep to a child.

3. In these dreams there is no distortion and therefore they need no interpretation: the manifest and the latent content is here identical. From this we conclude that *distortion is not essential to the nature of the dream*. I expect that this statement will take a weight off your minds. Nevertheless, closer consideration forces us to admit that even in these dreams distortion is present, though in a very slight degree, that there is a certain difference between the manifest content and the latent dream-thought.

4 The child's dream is a reaction to an experience of the previous day, which has left behind a regret, a longing, or an unsatisfied wish. *In the dream we have the direct, undisguised fulfilment of this wish.* Now consider our discussion as to the part played by the external or internal somatic

stimuli as disturbers of sleep and begetters of dreams. We learnt certain quite definite facts on this point, but this explanation only held good in a small number of dreams. In these children's dreams there is nothing to indicate the influence of such somatic stimuli; we can make no mistake about it, for the dreams are perfectly comprehensible and each can easily be grasped as a whole. But we need not on that account give up our notion of the stimulus as causing the dream. We can only ask why we forget from the outset that there are *mental* as well as bodily sleep-disturbing stimuli; surely we know that it is these which are mainly responsible for disturbing the sleep of the grown-up person, in that they hinder him from bringing about in himself the mental condition essential for sleep, i.e. the withdrawal of interest from the outside world. He wishes not to have any interruption in his life; he would prefer to continue working at whatever occupies him, and that is the reason why he does not sleep. The mental stimulus which disturbs sleep is therefore for a child the unsatisfied wish, and his reaction to this is a dream.

5. This takes us by a very short step to a conclusion about the function of dreams. If dreams are the reaction to a mental stimulus their value must lie in effecting a discharge of the excitation so that the stimulus is removed and sleep can continue. We do not yet know how this discharge through the dream is effected dynamically, but we notice already that dreams are not disturbers of sleep (the accusation commonly brought against them), but are guardians and deliverers of it from disturbing influences. True, we are apt to think we should have slept better if we had not dreamed, but there we are wrong: the truth is that without the help of the dream we should not have slept at all, and we owe it to the dream that we slept as well as we did. It could not help disturbing us a little, just as a policeman often cannot avoid making a noise when driving off disturbers of the peace who would wake us.

6. That dreams are brought about by a wish and that the content of the dream expresses this wish is one main characteristic of dreams. The other equally constant feature is

that the dream does not merely give expression to a thought, but represents this wish as fulfilled, in the form of an hallucinatory experience. "I should like to sail on the lake," runs the wish which gives rise to the dream; the content of the dream itself is: "I am sailing on the lake." So that even in these simple dreams belonging to childhood there is still a difference between the latent and the manifest dream, and still a distortion of the latent dream-thought, *in the translation of the thought into an experience*. In interpreting a dream, we must first of all undo this process of alteration. If this is to be regarded as one of the most universal characteristics of all dreams, we then know how to translate the dream-fragment I quoted before: "I see my brother digging" does not mean "my brother *is* retrenching," but "I wish my brother would retrench, he *is to* retrench." Of the two universal characteristics here mentioned the second is obviously more likely to be acknowledged without opposition than the first.

It is only by extensive investigations that we can make sure that what produces the dream must always be a *wish* and cannot sometimes be a preoccupation, a purpose, or reproach; but the other characteristic remains unaffected, namely, that the dream does not merely reproduce this stimulus, but, by a kind of living it through, removes it, sets it aside, relieves it.

7. In connection with these characteristics of dreams we may take up again our comparison between dreams and errors. In the latter we distinguished between a disturbing tendency and one which is disturbed, the error being a compromise between the two. Dreams fall into the same category; the disturbed tendency can only, of course, be the tendency to sleep, while the disturbing tendency resolves itself into the mental stimulus which we may call the wish (clamouring for gratification), since at present we know of no other mental stimulus disturbing sleep. Here again the dream is the result of a compromise; we sleep, and yet we experience the satisfaction of a wish; we gratify a wish and at the same time continue to sleep. Each achieves part-success and part-failure.

8. You will remember that at one point we hoped to find a path to an understanding of the problems presented by

dreams in the fact that certain very transparent phantasy-
formations are called "day-dreams." Now these day-dreams
are literally wish-fulfilments, fulfilments of ambitious or erotic
wishes, which we recognize as such; they are, however, carried
out in thought, and, however vividly imagined, they never
take the form of hallucinatory experiences. Here, therefore,
the less certain of the two main characteristics of the dream
is retained, whereas the other, to which the condition of sleep
is essential and which cannot be realized in waking life, is
entirely lacking. So in language we find a hint that a wish-
fulfilment is a main characteristic of dreams. And further, if
the experience we have in dreams is only another form of
imaginative representation, a form which becomes possible
under the peculiar conditions of the sleeping state—"a nocturnal day-dream," as we might call it—we understand at
once how it is that the process of dream-formation can
abrogate the stimulus operating at night and can bring gratification; for day-dreaming also is a mode of activity closely
linked up with gratification, which is in fact the only reason
why people practise it.

Again, there are other linguistic expressions, besides this,
which imply the same thing. We are familiar with the prov-
erbs: "The pig dreams of acorns and the goose of maize."
"What do chickens dream of? Of millet." The proverb, you
see, goes even lower in the scale than we do, beyond the
child to the animal, and asserts that the content of dreams is
the satisfaction of a want. And there are many phrases which
seem to point to the same thing: we say "as beautiful as a
dream." "I should never have dreamt of such a thing." "I
never imagined that in my wildest dreams." Here colloquial
speech is clearly partial in its judgement. Of course there
are also anxiety-dreams and dreams the content of which is
painful or indifferent, but these have not given rise to any
special phrases. We do indeed speak of "bad" dreams, but by
a "dream" pure and simple common usage always understands
some sort of exquisite wish-fulfilment. Nor is there any
proverb which attempts to assert that pigs or geese dream
of being slaughtered!

138 A GENERAL INTRODUCTION TO PSYCHOANALYSIS

It is, of course, inconceivable that this wish-fulfilling character of dreams should have escaped the notice of writers on the subject. On the contrary, they have very often remarked upon it; but it has not occurred to any of them to recognize this characteristic as universal, and to take it as the key to the explanation of dreams. We can easily imagine what may have deterred them, and later we will discuss the question.

Now see how much information we have gained, and that with hardly any trouble, from our study of children's dreams! We have learnt that the function of dreams is to protect sleep; that they arise out of two conflicting tendencies, of which the one, the desire for sleep, remains constant, whilst the other endeavours to satisfy some mental stimulus; that dreams are proved to be mental acts, rich in meaning; that they have two main characteristics, i.e., they are wish-fulfilments and hallucinatory experiences. And meanwhile we could almost have forgotten that we were studying psychoanalysis. Apart from the connection we have made between dreams and errors our work has not borne any specific stamp. Any psychologist knowing nothing of the assumptions of psychoanalysis could have given this explanation of children's dreams. Why has no one done so?

If only all dreams were of the infantile type the problem would be solved and our task already achieved, and that without questioning the dreamer, referring to the unconscious or having recourse to the process of free association. Clearly it is in this direction that we must continue our work. We have already repeatedly found that characteristics alleged to be universally valid have afterwards proved to hold good only for a certain kind and a limited number of dreams. So the question we now have to decide is whether the common characteristics revealed by children's dreams are any more stable than these, and whether they hold also for those dreams whose meaning is not obvious and in whose manifest content we can recognize no reference to a wish remaining from the day before Our idea is that these other dreams have undergone a good deal of distortion and on that account we

must refrain from immediate judgment. We suspect too that
to unravel this distortion we shall need the help of psychoanalytic technique, which we could dispense with while learning, as we have just now done, the meaning of children's
dreams.

There is yet one other class of dreams at least in which
no distortion is present and which, like children's dreams, we
easily recognize to be wish-fulfilments. These are dreams
which are occasioned all through life by imperative physical
needs—hunger, thirst, sexual desire—and are wish-fulfilments
in the sense of being reactions to internal somatic stimuli.
Thus I have on record the dream of a little girl, one year and
seven months old, which consisted of a kind of menu, together
with her name (Anna F . . . , strawberries, bilberries, egg,
pap), the dream being a reaction to a day of fasting, enforced
on account of indigestion due to eating the fruit which appeared twice in the dream. At the same time her grandmother
—their combined ages totalled seventy—was obliged, owing to
a floating kidney, to go without food for a day and dreamt
that night that she had been invited out and had had the
most tempting delicacies set before her. Observations on
prisoners who are left to go hungry, and on people who suffer
privations whilst travelling or on expeditions, show that in
these circumstances they regularly dream about the satisfaction of their wants. Thus Otto Nordenskjöld in his book on
the Antarctic (1904) tells us of the band of men in whose
company he spent the winter (Vol. I, p. 336): "Our dreams
showed very clearly the direction our thoughts were taking.
Never had we dreamt so frequently and so vividly as at that
time. Even those of our comrades who usually dreamt but
rarely had now long stories to tell in the mornings when we
exchanged our latest experiences in this realm of phantasy.
All the dreams were about that outside world now so far
away, but often they included a reference to our condition at
the time . . . eating and drinking were, incidentally, the
pivot on which our dreams most often turned. One of us, who
was particularly good at going out to large dinners in his
sleep, was delighted when he could tell us in the morning

that he had had a three-course dinner. Another dreamt of tobacco, whole mountains of tobacco; another of a ship which came full sail over the water, at last clear of ice. Yet another dream deserves mention: the postman came with the letters and gave a long explanation of why they were so late; he said he had made a mistake in delivering them, and had had great trouble in getting them back again. Of course, things even more impossible occupied our minds in sleep, but the lack of imagination in almost all the dreams which I dreamt myself or heard the others tell was quite striking. It would certainly be of great psychological interest if we had a record of all these dreams. You can imagine how we longed for sleep, when it offered each one of us all that he most eagerly desired." Another quotation, this time from Du Prel: "Mungo Park, when nearly dying of thirst on a journey in Africa, dreamt continually of the well-watered hills and valleys of his home. So Trenck, tormented with hunger in the redoubt at Magdebourg, saw himself in his dream surrounded by sumptuous meals; and George Back, who took part in Franklin's first expedition, when on the point of dying of hunger owing to their terrible privations, dreamt regularly of abundant food to eat."

Anyone who has made himself thirsty at night by eating highly seasoned dishes at supper is likely to dream of drinking. Of course it is not possible to relieve acute hunger or thirst by dreaming; in that case we awake thirsty and are obliged to drink real water. The service of the dream is here of little practical account, but it is none the less clear that it was called up for the purpose of protecting sleep from the stimulus impelling us to wake up and act. Where the intensity of the desire is less, 'satisfaction'-dreams do often answer the purpose.

In the same way, when the stimulus is that of sexual desire the dream provides satisfaction, but of a kind which shows peculiarities worthy of mention. Since it is a characteristic of the sexual impulse that it is a degree less dependent on its object than are hunger and thirst, the satisfaction in a pollution-dream can be real; and, in consequence of certain difficulties in the relation to the object (which will be discussed later), it particularly often happens that the real satisfaction is yet connected with a vague or distorted dream-content. This peculiarity of pollution-dreams makes them, as O. Rank has observed, suitable objects for the study of dream-distortion. Moreover, with adults, dreams of desire usually contain besides the satisfaction something else, springing from a purely mental source and requiring interpretation if it is to be understood.

We do not maintain, by the way, that wish-fulfilment dreams of the infantile type occur in adults solely as reactions to the imperative desires I have mentioned. We are equally familiar with short clear dreams of this type, occasioned by certain dominating situations and unquestionably produced by mental stimuli. For example, there are 'impatience'-dreams in which someone making preparations for a journey, for a theatrical performance in which he is specially interested, or for a lecture or a visit, has his expectations prematurely realized in a dream, and finds himself the night before the actual experience already at his journey's end, at the theatre, or talking to the friend he is going to visit. Or again, there is the 'comfort'-dream, rightly so-called, in which someone who wants to go on sleeping dreams that he has already got up, that he is washing, or is at school, while all the time he is really continuing his sleep, meaning that he would rather dream of getting up than do so in reality. In these dreams the desire for sleep, which we have recognized as regularly participating in dream-formation, expresses itself plainly and appears as their actual originator. The need for sleep ranks itself quite rightly with the other great physical needs.

I would refer you at this point to the reproduction of a picture by Schwind in the Schack Gallery at Munich and would ask you to notice how correctly the artist has realized the way in which a dream arises out of a dominating situation. The picture is called *The Prisoner's Dream*, and the subject of the dream must undoubtedly be his escape. It is a happy thought that the prisoner is to escape by the window, for it is through the window that the ray of light has entered and roused him from sleep. The gnomes standing one above the other no doubt represent the successive positions he would have to assume in climbing up to the window; and, if I am not mistaken and do not attribute too much intentional design to the artist, the features of the gnome at the top, who is filing the grating through (the very thing the prisoner himself would like to do), resemble the man's own.

I have said that in all dreams, other than those of children and such as conform to the infantile type, we encounter the obstacle of distortion. We cannot immediately say whether they too are wish-fulfilments, as we are inclined to suppose, nor can we guess from their manifest content in what mental stimulus they originate, or prove that they, like the others, endeavour to remove or relieve the stimulus. They must, in fact, be interpreted, i.e. translated; the process of distortion must be reversed, and the manifest content replaced by the latent thought, before we can make any definite pronouncement whether what we have found out about infantile dreams may claim to hold good for all dreams alike.

NINTH LECTURE

THE DREAM-CENSORSHIP

OUR STUDY OF CHILDREN'S DREAMS HAS TAUGHT US HOW DREAMS originate, what their essential character is, and what their function. Dreams are the means of removing, by hallucinatory satisfaction, mental stimuli that disturb sleep. It is true that with the dreams of adults we have been able to explain one group only, those which we termed dreams of the infantile type. We do not yet know how it may be with the others, neither do we understand them. The result we have arrived at already is one, however, of which the significance is not to be under-estimated. Every time that we fully understand a dream it proves to be a wish-fulfilment; and this coincidence cannot be accidental or unimportant.

Dreams of another type are assumed by us to be distorted substitutes for an unknown content, which first of all has to be traced; we have various grounds for this assumption, amongst others the analogy to our conception of errors. Our next task is to investigate and understand this *dream-distortion*.

It is dream-distortion which makes dreams seem strange and incomprehensible. There are several things we want to know about it: first, whence it comes (its dynamics), secondly, what it does, and finally, how it does it. Further, we can say that distortion is the production of the *dream-work*. Let us describe the dream-work and trace out the forces in it.

Now let me tell you a dream recorded by a lady well-known in psychoanalytical circles[1], who said that the dreamer was an elderly woman, highly cultivated and held in great esteem. The dream was not analysed and our informant observed that for psychoanalysts it needed no interpreting. Nor did the dreamer herself interpret it, but she criticized it and condemned it in such a way as though she knew what it meant. "Imagine," she said, "such abominable nonsense being dreamt by a woman of fifty, whose only thought day and night is concern for her child."

I will now tell you the dream, which is about "love service in war-time."[2] 'She went to the First Military Hospital and said to the sentinel at the gate that she must speak to the physician-in-chief (giving a name which she did not know), as she wished to offer herself for service in the hospital. In saying this, she emphasized the word service in such a way that the sergeant at once perceived that she was speaking of "love service." As she was an old lady, he let her pass after some hesitation, but instead of finding the chief physician, she came to a large gloomy room, where a number of officers and army doctors were standing or sitting around a long table. She turned to a staff doctor and told him her proposal; he soon understood her meaning. The words she said in her dream were: "I and countless other women and girls of Vienna are ready for the soldiers, officers or men, to . . ." This ended in a murmur. She saw, however, by the half-embarrassed, half-malicious expressions of the officers that all of them grasped her meaning. The lady continued: "I know our decision sounds odd, but we are in bitter earnest. The soldier on the battlefield is not asked whether he wishes to die or not." There followed a minute of painful silence; then the staff doctor put his arm round her waist and said: "Madam, supposing it really came to this, that . . . (murmur)." She withdrew herself from his arm, thinking: "They are all alike," and replied: "Good heavens, I am an old woman

[1] Frau Dr. von Hug-Hellmuth.

[2] [*Liebesdienst* = "love service," a popular expression adapted from "military service."—Tr.]

and perhaps it won't happen to me. And one condition must be observed: age must be taken into account, so that an old woman and a young lad may not . . . (murmur); that would be horrible." The staff doctor said: "I quite understand"; but some of the officers, amongst them one who as a young man had made love to her, laughed loudly, and the lady asked to be taken to the physician-in-chief, whom she knew, so that everything might be put straight. It then struck her, to her great consternation, that she did not know his name. The staff doctor, however, with the utmost respect and courtesy, showed her the way to the second floor, up a very narrow iron spiral staircase leading direct from the room where they were to the upper storeys. As she went up, she heard an officer say: "That is a tremendous decision, no matter whether she is young or old; all honour to her!" With the feeling that she was simply doing her duty, she went up an endless staircase.'

This dream was repeated twice within a few weeks, with alterations here and there which, as the lady remarked, were quite unimportant and entirely meaningless.

The way in which this dream progresses corresponds to the course of a day-dream; there are only a few places where an interruption occurs, and many individual points in its content might have been cleared up by enquiry: this, however, as you know, was not undertaken. But the most striking and to us the most interesting thing about it is the occurrence of many gaps, not in the recollection, but in the content. In three places the latter is, as it were, blotted out; where these gaps occur the speeches are interrupted by a *murmur*. As we did not analyse the dream, we have, strictly speaking, no right to say anything about its meaning; but there are certain indications from which we may draw conclusions, e.g. the words "love service"; and, above all, the broken speeches immediately preceding the murmurs require completion of a kind which admits of only one construction. If we do so complete them a phantasy results, in which the content is that the dreamer is ready at the call of duty to offer herself to gratify the sexual needs of the troops, irrespective of rank.

This is certainly shocking, a model of a shamelessly libidinous phantasy, but—the dream says nothing about this. Just where the context demands this confession, there is in the manifest dream an indistinct murmur: something has been lost or suppressed.

I hope you recognize how obvious is the inference that it is just the shocking nature of these passages which has led to their suppression. Now where will you find a parallel to what has taken place here? In these times you have not far to seek. Take up any political paper and you will find that here and there in the text something is omitted and in its place the blank white of the paper meets your eye: you know that this is the work of the press censor. Where these blank spaces occur, there originally stood something of which the authorities at the censorship disapproved and which has been deleted on that account. You probably think it a pity, for that must have been the most interesting part, the "cream" of the news.

On other occasions the censorship has not dealt with the sentence in its completed form; for the writer, forseeing which passages were likely to be objected to by the censor, has forestalled him by softening them down, making some slight modification or contenting himself with hints and allusions to what he really wants to write. In this case there are no blanks, but from the roundabout and obscure mode of expression you can detect the fact that, at the time of writing, the author had the censorship in mind.

Now keeping to this parallel we say that those speeches in the dream which were omitted or disguised by a murmur have also been sacrificed to some form of censorship. We actually use the term DREAM-CENSORSHIP, and ascribe part of the distortion to its agency. Wherever there are gaps in the manifest dream we know that the censorship is responsible; and indeed we should go further and recognize that wherever, amongst other more clearly defined elements, one appears which is fainter, more indefinite or more dubious in recollection, it is evidence of the work of the censorship. It is, however, seldom that it takes a form so undisguised, so naïve, as we might say, as it does in the case of the dream about "love service;" far more often the censorship makes itself felt in the second way I mentioned: by effecting modifications, hints, and allusions in place of the true meaning.

There is a third way in which the dream-censorship works, to which the ordinances of the press censorship supply no parallel; but it happens that I can demonstrate to you this particular mode of activity on the part of the dream-censorship in the only dream hitherto analysed by us. You will remember the dream of the "three bad theatre-tickets, costing one florin and a half." In the latent thoughts underlying this dream, the element "too great a hurry, too early" was in the foreground; the meaning was: "It was folly to marry so *early*, it was foolish also to take the tickets so *early*, it was ridiculous of the sister-in-law to spend her money so *hurriedly* on a piece of jewellery." Nothing of this central element of the dream-thoughts appeared in the manifest content, where everything was focussed on going to the theatre and taking tickets. By this displacement of the accent and regrouping of the dream-elements, the manifest content was made so unlike the latent thoughts that nobody would suspect the presence of the latter behind the former. This *displacement of accent* is one of the principal means employed in distortion, and it is this which gives the dream that character of strangeness which makes the dreamer himself reluctant to recognize it as the product of his own mind.

Omission, modification, regrouping of material—these then are the modes of the dream-censorship's activity and the means employed in distortion. The censorship itself is the originator, or one of the originators, of distortion, the subject of our present enquiry. Modification and alteration in arrangement are commonly included under the term '*displacement.*'

After these remarks on the activities of the dream-censorship, let us turn our attention to its dynamics. I hope you are not taking the expression "censorship" in too anthropomorphic a sense, picturing to yourselves the censor as a stern little manikin or a spirit, who lives in a little chamber of the brain and there discharges the duties of his office; and neither must you localize it too exactly, so that you imagine a "brain-centre" whence there emanates a censorial influence, liable to cease with the injury or disappearance of that centre. For the present we may regard it merely as a useful term by which to express a dynamic relationship. This need not hinder us from asking what sort of tendencies exercise this influence and is it exercised upon; and further, we must not be surprised to discover that we have already come across the censorship, perhaps without recognizing it.

Indeed this has actually happened. Remember a surprising experience we had when we began to apply our method of free association: we discovered that our efforts to penetrate from the dream-element to the unconscious thought proper for which the former is a substitute encountered a certain *resistance*. The strength of this resistance, we said, varies, being sometimes enormous and at other times very slight. In the latter case we need only a few connecting-links for the work of interpretation; but where there is great resistance we are compelled to go through long chains of associations, which carry us far from the initial idea, and on the way we have to overcome all the difficulties of professedly critical objections to associations arising. That which we encountered as resistance in the work of interpretation we now meet again as the censorship in the dream-work: the resistance is simply the censorship objectified; it proves to us that the power of the censorship is not exhausted in effecting distortion, being thereby extinguished, but that the censorship remains as a permanent institution, the object of which is to maintain the distortion when once it has been achieved. Moreover, just as the strength of the resistance encountered during interpretation varies with each element, so too the degree of distortion effected by the censorship is different for each element of a whole dream. A comparison of the manifest and the latent dream shows that certain latent elements are completely eliminated, others more or less modified, and others again appear in the manifest dream-content unaltered or perhaps even intensified.

Our purpose, however, was to find out which are the tendencies exercising the censorship and upon which tend-

encies it is exercised. Now this question, which is fundamental
for the understanding of dreams and perhaps of human life
altogether, is easy to answer when we survey the series of
dreams which we have succeeded in interpreting. The tendencies which exercise the censorship are those which are
acknowledged by the waking judgement of the dreamer and
with which he feels himself to be at one. You may be sure
that when you repudiate any correctly found interpretation
of a dream of your own, you do so from the same motives
as cause the censorship to be exercised and distortion effected,
and make interpretation necessary. Consider the dream of our
lady of fifty: her dream, although it had not been interpreted,
struck her as shocking and she would have been even more
outraged if Dr. von Hug-Hellmuth had told her something
of its unmistakable meaning; it was just this attitude of condemnation which caused the offensive passages in the dream
to be replaced by a murmur.

Those tendencies against which the dream-censorship is
directed must next be described from the point of view of
this inner critical standard. When we do this, we can only
say that they are invariably of an objectionable nature, offensive from the ethical, æsthetic or social point of view, things
about which we do not dare to think at all, or think of only
with abhorrence. Above all are these censored wishes, which
in dreams are expressed in a distorted fashion, manifestations
of a boundless and ruthless egoism; for the dreamer's own
ego makes its appearance in every dream, and plays the
principal part, even if it knows how to disguise itself completely as far as the manifest content is concerned. This *sacro
egoismo* of dreams is certainly not unconnected with the attitude of mind essential to sleep: the withdrawal of interest
from the whole outside world.

The ego which has discarded all ethical bonds feels itself
at one with all the demands of the sexual impulse, those
which have long been condemned by our æsthetic training
and those which are contrary to all the restraints imposed by
morality. The striving for pleasure—the libido, as we say,—
chooses its objects unchecked by any inhibition, preferring

indeed those which are forbidden: not merely the wife of another man, but, above all, the incestuous objects of choice which by common consent humanity holds sacred—the mother and the sister of men, the father and the brother of women. (Even the dream of our fifty-year-old lady is an incestuous one, the libido being unmistakably directed towards the son.) Desires which we believe alien to human nature show themselves powerful enough to give rise to dreams. Hate, too, rages unrestrainedly; wishes for revenge, and death-wishes, against those who in life are nearest and dearest—parents, brothers and sisters, husband or wife, the dreamer's own children—are by no means uncommon. These censored wishes seem to rise up from a veritable hell; when we know their meaning, it seems to us in our waking moments as if no censorship of them could be severe enough. Dreams themselves, however, are not to blame for this evil content; you surely have not forgotten that their harmless, nay, useful, function is to protect sleep from disturbance. Depravity does not lie in the nature of dreams; in fact, you know that there are dreams which can be recognized as gratifying justifiable desires and urgent bodily needs. It is true that there is no distortion in these dreams, but then there is no need for it, they can perform their function without offending the ethical and æsthetic tendencies of the ego. Remember, too, that the degree of distortion is proportionate to two factors: on the one hand, the more shocking the wish that must be censored, the greater will be the distortion; but it is also great in proportion as the demands of the censorship are severe. Hence in a strictly brought up and prudish young girl, a rigid censorship will distort dream-excitations which we medical men would have recognized as permissible and harmless libidinous desires, and which the dreamer herself would judge in the same way ten years later.

Besides, we are still not nearly far enough advanced to allow ourselves to be outraged at the result of our work of interpretation. I think we still do not understand it properly; but first of all it is incumbent upon us to secure it against certain possible attacks. It is not at all difficult to detect weak points in it. Our interpretations were based on hypotheses which we adopted earlier: that there really is some meaning in dreams; that the idea of mental processes being unconscious for a time, which was first arrived at through hypnotic sleep, may be applied also to normal sleep; and that all associations are subject to determination. Now if, reasoning from these hypotheses, we had obtained plausible results in our dream-interpretation we should have been justified in concluding that these hypotheses were correct. But what if these discoveries are of the kind I have described? In that case, surely it seems natural to say: "These results are impossible, absurd, at the very least highly improbable, so there must have been something wrong about the hypotheses. Either the dream is after all not a mental phenomenon, or there is nothing which is unconscious in our normal condition, or there is a flaw somewhere in our technique. Is it not simpler and more satisfactory to assume this than to accept all the abominable conclusions which we profess to have deduced from our hypotheses?"

Both! it is both simpler and more satisfactory, but not on that account necessarily more correct. Let us give ourselves time: the matter is not yet ripe for judgement. First of all, we can make the case against our interpretations even stronger. The fact that our results are so unpleasant and repellent would not perhaps weigh so very heavily with us; a stronger argument is the emphatic and well-grounded repudiation by dreamers of the wish-tendencies which we try to foist upon them after interpreting their dreams. "What," says one, "you want to prove to me from my dream that I grudge the money I have spent on my sister's dowry and my brother's education? But it is out of the question; I spend my whole time working for my brothers and sisters and my only interest in life is to do my duty by them, as, being the eldest, I promised our dead mother I would." Or a woman says: "I am supposed to wish that my husband were dead? Really that is outrageous nonsense! Not only is our married life very happy, though perhaps you won't believe that, but if he died I should lose everything I possess in the world." Or someone else will reply: "Do you mean to suggest that I entertain sexual desires towards my sister? The thing is ludicrous; she is nothing to me; we get on badly with one another, and for years I have not exchanged a word with her." We still might not be much impressed if these dreamers neither admitted nor denied the tendencies attributed to them; we might say that these are just the things of which they are quite unconscious. But when they detect in their own minds the exact opposite of such a wish as is interpreted to them, and when they can prove to us by their whole conduct in life that the contrary desire predominates, surely we must be nonplussed. Is it not about time now for us to discard our whole work of dream-interpretation as something which has led to a *reductio ad absurdum?*

No, not even now. Even this stronger argument falls to pieces when subjected to a critical attack. Assuming that unconscious tendencies do exist in mental life, the fact that the opposite tendencies predominate in conscious life goes to prove nothing. Perhaps there is room in the mind for opposite tendencies, for contradictions, existing side by side; indeed, possibly the very predominance of the one tendency conditions the unconscious nature of the opposite. So the first objections raised only amount to the statement that the results of dream-interpretation are not simple and are very disagreeable. To the first charge we may reply that, however much enamoured of simplicity you may be, you cannot thereby solve one of the problems of dreams; you have to make up your mind at the outset to accept the fact of complicated relations. And, as regards the second point, you are manifestly wrong in taking the fact that something pleases or repels yourself as the motive for a scientific judgement. What does it matter if you do find the results of dream-interpretation unpleasant, or even mortifying and repulsive? *Ça n'empêche pas d'exister*—as I, when a young doctor, heard my chief, Charcot, say in a similar case. We must be humble and put sympathies and antipathies honourably in the background if we would learn to know reality in this world. If a physicist could prove to you that organic life on the earth was bound to become extinct before long, would you venture to say to him also: "That cannot be so; I dislike the prospect too much." I think you would say nothing, until another physicist came along and convicted the first of a mistake in his premises or his calculations. If you repudiate whatever is distasteful to you, you are repeating the mechanism of a dream structure rather than understanding and mastering it.

Perhaps, then, you will undertake to overlook the offensive nature of the censored dream-wishes and will fall back upon the argument that it is surely very improbable that we ought to concede so large a part in the human constitution to what is evil. But do your own experiences justify you in this statement? I will say nothing of how you may appear in your own eyes, but have you met with so much goodwill in your superiors and rivals, so much chivalry in your enemies and so little envy amongst your acquaintances, that you feel it incumbent on you to protest against the idea of the part played by egoistic baseness in human nature? Do you not know how uncontrolled and unreliable the average human being is in all that concerns sexual life? Or are you ignorant of the fact that all the excesses and aberrations of which we dream at night are crimes actually committed every day by men who are wide awake? What does psychoanalysis do in this connection but confirm the old saying of Plato that the good are those who content themselves with dreaming of what others, the wicked, actually do?

And now look away from individuals to the great war still devastating Europe: think of the colossal brutality, cruelty and mendacity which is now allowed to spread itself over the civilized world. Do you really believe that a handful of unprincipled place-hunters and corrupters of men would have succeeded in letting loose all this latent evil, if the millions of their followers were not also guilty? Will you venture, even in these circumstances, to break a lance for the exclusion of evil from the mental constitution of humanity?

You will accuse me of taking a one-sided view of war, and tell me that it has also called out all that is finest and most noble in mankind, heroism, self-sacrifice, and public spirit. That is true; but do not now commit the injustice, from which psychoanalysis has so often suffered, of reproaching it that it denies one thing because it affirms another. It is no part of our intention to deny the nobility in human nature, nor have we ever done anything to disparage its value. On the contrary, I show you not only the evil wishes which are censored but also the censorship which suppresses them and makes them unrecognizable. We dwell upon the evil in human beings with the greater emphasis only because others deny it, thereby making the mental life of mankind not indeed better, but incomprehensible. If we give up the one-sided ethical valuation then, we are sure to find the truer formula for the relation of evil to good in human nature.

Here the matters rests. We need not give up the results of our work of dream-interpretation, even though we cannot fail to find them strange. Perhaps later we shall be able to come nearer to understanding them by another path. For the present let us hold fast to this: dream-distortion is due to the censorship exercised, by certain recognized tendencies of the ego, over desires of an offensive character which stir in us at night during sleep. Obviously, when we ask ourselves why it is just at night that they appear and what is the origin of these reprehensible wishes, we find that there is still much to investigate and many questions to answer.

It would, however, be wrong if we neglected to give due prominence at this point to another result of these investigations. The dream-wishes which would disturb our sleep are unknown to us; we first learn about them by dream-interpretation; they are therefore to be designated "unconscious at the moment" in the sense in which we have used the term. But we must recognize that they are also more than unconscious at the moment; for the dreamer denies them, as we have so frequently found, even after he has learnt of them through the interpretation of his dream. Here we have a repetition of the case which we first met with when interpreting the slip of the tongue "hiccough," where the after-dinner speaker indignantly assured us that neither then nor at any time had he been conscious of any feeling of disrespect towards his chief. We ventured even then to doubt the value of this assertion and assumed instead that the speaker was permanently ignorant of the existence of this feeling within him. We meet with the same situation every time we interpret a dream in which there is a high degree of distortion, and this lends an added significance to our conception. We are now prepared to assume that there are processes and tendencies in mental life, of which we know nothing; have known nothing; have, for a very long time, perhaps even never, known anything about at all. This gives the term *unconscious* a fresh meaning for us: the qualification "at the moment" or "temporary" is seen to be no essential attribute, the term may also mean *permanently unconscious,* not merely "latent at the moment." You see that later on we shall have to discuss this point further.

TENTH LECTURE

SYMBOLISM IN DREAMS

WE HAVE FOUND OUT THAT THE DISTORTION IN DREAMS WHICH hinders our understanding of them is due to the activities of a censorship, directed against the unacceptable, unconscious wish-impulses. But of course we have not asserted that the censorship is the only factor responsible for the distortion, and as a matter of fact a further study of dreams leads to the discovery that there are yet other causes contributing to this effect; that is as much as to say, if the censorship were eliminated we should nevertheless be unable to understand dreams, nor would the manifest dream be identical with the latent dream-thoughts.

This other cause of the obscurity of dreams, this additional contribution to distortion, is revealed by our becoming aware of a gap in our technique. I have already admitted to you that there are occasions when persons being analysed really have no associations to single elements in their dreams. To be sure, this does not happen as often as they declare that it does; in very many instances the association may yet be elicited by perseverance; but still there remains a certain number of cases where association fails altogether or, if something is finally extorted, it is not what we need. If this happens during psychoanalytic treatment it has a certain significance which does not concern us here; but it also occurs in the course of interpretation of dreams in normal people, or when we are interpreting our own. When we are convinced in such circumstances that no amount of pressing is of any use, we finally discover that this unwelcome contingency regularly presents itself where special dream-elements are in question; and we begin to recognize the operation of some new principle, whereas at first we thought we had only come across an exceptional case in which our technique had failed.

In this way it comes about that we try to interpret these "silent" elements, and attempt to translate them by drawing upon our own resources. It cannot fail to strike us that we arrive at a satisfactory meaning in every instance in which we venture on this substitution, whereas the dream remains meaningless and disconnected as long as we do not resolve to use this method. The accumulation of many exactly similar instances then affords us the required certainty, our experiment having been tried at first with considerable diffidence.

I am presenting all this somewhat in outline, but that is surely allowable for purposes of instruction, nor is it falsified by so doing, but merely made simpler.

We arrive in this way at constant translations for a series of dream-elements, just as in popular books on dreams we find such translations for everything that occurs in dreams. You will not have forgotten that when we employ the method of free association such constant substitutions for dream-elements never make their appearance.

Now you will at once say that this mode of interpretation seems to you far more uncertain and open to criticism than even the former method of free association. But there is still something more to be said: when we have collected from actual experience a sufficient number of such constant translations, we eventually realize that we could actually have filled in these portions of the interpretation from our own knowledge, and that they really could have been understood without using the dreamer's associations. How it is that we are bound to know their meaning is a matter which will be dealt with in the second half of our discussion.

We call a constant relation of this kind between a dream-element and its translation a *symbolic* one, and the dream-element itself a *symbol* of the unconscious dream-thought. You will remember that some time ago, when we were examining the different relations which may exist between dream-elements and the thoughts proper underlying them, I distinguished three relations: substitution of the part for the whole, allusion, and imagery. I told you then that there was a fourth possible relation, but I did not tell you what it was. This fourth relation is the symbolic, which I am now introducing; there are connected with it certain very interesting points for discussion, to which we will turn attention before setting forth our special observations on this subject. Symbolism is perhaps the most remarkable part of our theory of dreams.

First of all: since the relation between a symbol and the idea symbolized is an invariable one, the latter being as it were a translation of the former, symbolism does in some measure realize the ideal of both ancient and popular dream-interpretation, one from which we have moved very far in our technique. Symbols make it possible for us in certain circumstances to interpret a dream without questioning the dreamer, who indeed in any case can tell us nothing about the symbols. If the symbols commonly appearing in dreams are known, and also the personality of the dreamer, the conditions under which he lives, and the impressions in his mind after which his dream occurred, we are often in a position to interpret it straightaway; to translate it at sight, as it were. Such a feat flatters the vanity of the interpreter and impresses the dreamer; it is in pleasing contrast to the laborious method of questioning the latter. But do not let this lead you away: it is no part of our task to perform tricks nor is that method of interpretation which is based on a knowledge of symbolism one which can replace, or even compare with, that of free association. It is complementary to this latter, and the results it yields are only useful when applied in connection with the latter. As regards our knowledge of the dreamer's mental situation, moreover, you must reflect that you have not only to interpret dreams of people whom you know well; that, as a rule, you know nothing of the events of the previous day which stimu-

lated the dream; and that the associations of the person analysed are the very source from which we obtain our knowledge of what we call the mental situation.

Further, it is especially remarkable, particularly with reference to certain considerations upon which we shall touch
later, that the most strenuous opposition has manifested itself
again here, over this question of the existence of a symbolic
relation between the dream and the unconscious. Even persons of judgement and standing, who in other respects have
gone a long way with psychoanalysis, have renounced their
adherence at this point. This behaviour is the more remarkable
when we remember two things: first, that symbolism is not
peculiar to dreams, nor exclusively characteristic of them; and,
in the second place, that the use of symbolism in dreams was
not one of the discoveries of psycho-analysis, although this
science has certainly not been wanting in surprising discoveries. If we must ascribe priority in this field to anyone in
modern times, the discoverer must be recognized in the philosopher K. A. Scherner (1861); psychoanalysis has confirmed
his discovery, although modifying it in certain important respects.

Now you will wish to hear something about the nature of
dream-symbolism and will want some examples. I will gladly
tell you what I know, but I confess that our knowledge is less
full than we could wish.

The symbolic relation is essentially that of a comparison,
but not any kind of comparison. We must suspect that this
comparison is subject to particular conditions, although we
cannot say what these conditions are. Not everything with
which an object or an occurrence can be compared appears in
dreams as symbolic of it, and, on the other hand, dreams do
not employ symbolism for anything and everything, but only
for particular elements of latent dream-thoughts; there are
thus limitations in both directions. We must admit also that
we cannot at present assign quite definite limits to our conception of a symbol; for it tends to merge into substitution,
representation, etc., and even approaches closely to allusion.
In one set of symbols the underlying comparison may be

easily apparent, but there are others in which we have to look
about for the common factor, the *tertium comparationis* contained in the supposed comparison. Further reflection may
then reveal it to us, or on the other hand it may remain
definitely hidden from us. Again, if the symbol is really a comparison, it is remarkable that this comparison is not exposed
by the process of free association, and also that the dreamer
knows nothing about it, but makes use of it unawares; nay,
more, that he is actually unwilling to recognize it when it is
brought to his notice. So you see that the symbolic relation is
a comparison of a quite peculiar kind, the nature of which is
as yet not fully clear to us. Perhaps some indication will be
found later which will throw some light upon this unknown
quantity.

The number of things which are represented symbolically
in dreams is not great. The human body as a whole, parents,
children, brothers and sisters, birth, death, nakedness—and
one thing more. The only typical, that is to say, regularly occurring, representation of the human form as a whole is that
of a *house,* as was recognized by Scherner, who even wanted
to attribute to this symbol an overwhelming significance which
is not really due to it. People have dreams of climbing down
the front of a house, with feelings sometimes of pleasure and
sometimes of dread. When the walls are quite smooth, the
house means a man; when there are ledges and balconies
which can be caught hold of, a woman. Parents appear in
dreams as *emperor* and *empress, king* and *queen* or other
exalted personages; in this respect the dream attitude is highly
dutiful. Children and brothers and sisters are less tenderly
treated, being symbolized by *little animals* or *vermin.* Birth is
almost invariably represented by some reference to *water:*
either we are falling into water or clambering out of it, saving
someone from it or being saved by them, i.e. the relation between mother and child is symbolized. For dying we have setting out upon a *journey* or *travelling* by train, while the state
of death is indicated by various obscure and, as it were, timid
allusions; *clothes* and *uniforms* stand for nakedness. You see

that here the dividing line between the symbolic and the allusive kinds of representation tends to disappear.

In comparison with the poverty of this enumeration, it cannot fail to strike us that objects and matters belonging to another range of ideas are represented by a remarkably rich symbolism. I am speaking of what pertains to the sexual life—the genitals, sexual processes and intercourse. An overwhelming majority of symbols in dreams are sexual symbols. A curious disproportion arises thus, for the matters dealt with are few in number, whereas the symbols for them are extraordinarily numerous, so that each of these few things can be expressed by many symbols practically equivalent. When they are interpreted, therefore, the result of this peculiarity gives universal offense, for, in contrast to the multifarious forms of its representation in dreams, the interpretation of the symbols is very monotonous. This is displeasing to everyone who comes to know of it: but how can we help it?

As this is the first time in the course of these lectures that I have touched upon the sexual life, I owe you some explanation of the manner in which I propose to treat this subject. Psychoanalysis sees no occasion for concealments or indirect allusions, and does not think it necessary to be ashamed of concerning itself with material so important; it is of opinion that it is right and proper to call everything by its true name, hoping in this way the more easily to avoid disturbing suggestions. The fact that I am speaking to a mixed audience can make no difference in this. No science can be treated *in usum delphini*, or in a manner adapted to school-girls; the women present, by appearing in this lecture-room, have tacitly expressed their desire to be regarded on the same footing as the men.

The male genital organ is symbolically represented in dreams in many different ways, with most of which the common idea underlying the comparison is easily apparent. In the first place, the sacred number *three* is symbolic of the whole male genitalia. Its more conspicuous and, to both sexes, more interesting part, the penis, is symbolized primarily by objects which resemble it in form, being long and upstanding, such as *sticks, umbrellas, poles, trees* and the like; also by objects which, like the thing symbolized, have the property of penetrating, and consequently of injuring, the body,—that is to say, pointed weapons of all sorts: *knives, daggers, lances, sabres;* fire-arms are similarly used: *guns, pistols and revolvers,* these last being a very appropriate symbol on account of their shape. In the anxiety-dreams of young girls, pursuit by a man armed with a knife or rifle plays a great part. This is perhaps the most frequently occurring dream-symbol: you can now easily translate it for yourselves. The substitution of the male organ by objects from which water flows is again easily comprehensible: *taps, water-cans,* or *springs;* and by other objects which are capable of elongation, such as *pulley lamps, pencils which slide in and out of a sheath,* and so on. *Pencils, penholders, nail-files, hammers* and other *implements* are undoubtedly male sexual symbols, based on an idea of the male organ which is equally easily perceived.

The peculiar property of this member of being able to raise itself upright in defiance of the law of gravity, part of the phenomenon of erection, leads to symbolic representation by means of *balloons, aeroplanes,* and, just recently, *Zeppelins.* But dreams have another, much more impressive, way of symbolizing erection; they make the organ of sex into the essential part of the whole person, so that the *dreamer himself flies.* Do not be upset by hearing that dreams of flying, which we all know and which are often so beautiful, must be interpreted as dreams of general sexual excitement, dreams of erection. One psychoanalytic investigator, P. Federn, has established the truth of this interpretation beyond doubt; but, besides this, Mourly Vold, a man highly praised for his sober judgement, who carried out the experiments with artificial postures of the arms and legs, and whose theories were really widely removed from those of psychoanalysis (indeed he may have known nothing about it), was led by his own investigations to the same conclusion. Nor must you think to object to this on the ground that women can also have dreams of flying; you should rather remind yourselves that the purpose of dreams is wish-fulfilment, and that the wish to be a man is frequently met with in women, whether they are conscious of it or not. Further, no one familiar with anatomy will be misled by supposing that it is impossible for a woman to realize this wish by sensations similar to those of a man, for the woman's sexual organs include a small one which resembles the penis, and this little organ, the clitoris, does actually play during childhood and in the years before sexual intercourse the same part as the large male organ.

Male sexual symbols less easy to understand are certain *reptiles and fishes:* above all, the famous symbol of the *serpent.* Why *hats and cloaks* are used in the same way is certainly difficult to divine, but their symbolic meaning is quite unquestionable. Finally, it may be asked whether the representation of the male organ by some other member, such as the *hand* or the *foot,* may be termed symbolic. I think the context in which this is wont to occur, and the female counterparts with which we meet, force this conclusion upon us.

The female genitalia are symbolically represented by all such objects as share with them the property of enclosing a space or are capable of acting as receptacles: such as *pits, hollows and caves,* and also *jars and bottles,* and *boxes* of all sorts and sizes, *chests, coffers, pockets,* and so forth. *Ships* too come into this category. Many symbols refer rather to the uterus than to the other genital organs: thus *cupboards, stoves* and, above all, *rooms.* Room symbolism here links up with that of houses, whilst *doors and gates* represent the genital opening. Moreover, material of different kinds is a symbol of woman,—*wood, paper,* and objects made of these, such as *tables* and *books.* From the animal world, *snails and mussels* at any rate must be cited as unmistakable female symbols; of the parts of the body, the *mouth* as a representation of the genital opening, and, amongst buildings, *churches and chapels* are symbols of a woman. You see that all these symbols are not equally easy to understand.

The breasts must be included amongst the organs of sex; these, as well as the larger hemispheres of the female body, are represented by *apples, peaches and fruit* in general. The pubic hair in both sexes is indicated in dreams by *woods and thickets.* The complicated topography of the female sexual organs accounts for their often being represented by a *landscape* with rocks, woods and water, whilst the imposing mechanism of the male sexual apparatus lends it to symbolization by all kinds of complicated and indescribable *machinery*.

Yet another noteworthy symbol of the female genital organ is a *jewel case,* whilst "jewel" and "treasure" are used also in dreams to represent the beloved person,[1] and *sweetmeats* frequently stand for sexual pleasures. Gratification derived from a person's own genitals is indicated by any kind of *play,* including playing the piano. The symbolic representation of onanism by *sliding or gliding* and also by *pulling off a branch* is very typical. A particularly remarkable dream-symbol is the *falling out* or *extraction of teeth;* the primary significance of this is certainly castration as a punishment for onanism. Special representations of sexual intercourse are less frequent in dreams than we should expect after all this, but we may mention in this connection rhythmical activities such as *dancing, riding* and *climbing,* and also *experiencing some violence,* e.g. being run over. To these may be added certain manual occupations, and of course being threatened with weapons.

You must not imagine that these symbols are either employed or translated quite simply: on all sides we meet with what we do not expect. For instance, it seems hardly credible that there is often no sharp discrimination of the different sexes in these symbolic representations. Many symbols stand for sexual organs in general, whether male or female: for instance, a *little* child, or a *little* son or daughter. At another time a symbol which is generally a male one may be used to denote the female sexual organ, or vice versa. This is incomprehensible until we have acquired some knowledge of the development of conceptions about sexuality amongst human beings. In many cases this ambiguity of the symbols may be apparent rather than real; and moreover, the most striking amongst them, such as weapons, pockets and chests, are never used bisexually in this way.

I will now give a brief account, beginning with the symbols

[1][Cf. sweetheart, sweetest.—TR.]

themselves instead of with the objects symbolized, to show you from what spheres the sexual symbols have for the most part been derived, and I will add a few remarks relating particularly to those in which the attribute in common with the thing symbolized is hard to detect. An instance of an obscure symbol of this kind is the *hat*, or perhaps head-coverings in general; this usually has a masculine significance, though occasionally a feminine one. In the same way a *cloak* betokens a man, though perhaps sometimes without special reference to the organs of sex. It is open to you to ask why this should be so. A *tie*, being an object which hangs down and is not worn by women is clearly a male symbol, whilst *underlinen* and *linen* in general stands for the female. *Clothes and uniforms,* as we have heard, represent nakedness or the human form; *shoes and slippers* symbolize the female genital organs. *Tables and wood* we have mentioned as being puzzling, but nevertheless certain, female symbols; the *act of mounting* ladders, steep places or stairs is indubitably symbolic of sexual intercourse. On closer reflection we shall notice that the rhythmic character of this climbing is the point in common between the two, and perhaps also the accompanying increase in excitation —the shortening of the breath as the climber ascends.

We have already recognized that *landscapes* represent the female sexual organs; mountains and rocks are symbols of the male organ; *gardens,* a frequently occurring symbol of the female genitalia. *Fruit* stands for the breasts, not for a child. *Wild animals* denote human beings whose senses are excited, and, hence, evil impulses or passions. *Blossoms and flowers* represent the female sexual organs, more particularly, in virginity. In this connection you will recollect that the blossoms are really the sexual organs of plants.

We already know how rooms are used symbolically. This representation may be extended, so that *windows and doors* (entrances and exits from rooms) come to mean the openings of the body; the fact of rooms being *open or closed* also accords with this symbolism: the *key*, which opens them, is certainly a male symbol.

This is some material for a study of dream-symbolism. It is

not complete, and could be both extended and made deeper. However, I think it will seem to you more than enough; perhaps you may dislike it. You will ask: "Do I then really live in the midst of sexual symbols? Are all the objects round me, all the clothes I wear, all the things I handle, always sexual symbols and nothing else?" There really is good reason for surprised questions, and the first of these would be: How do we profess to arrive at the meaning of these dream-symbols, about which the dreamer himself can give us little or no information.

My answer is that we derive our knowledge from widely different sources: from fairy tales and myths, jokes and witticisms, from folklore, i.e. from what we know of the manners and customs, sayings and songs, of different peoples, and from poetic and colloquial usage of language. Everywhere in these various fields the same symbolism occurs, and in many of them we can understand it without being taught anything about it. If we consider these various sources individually, we shall find so many parallels to dream-symbolism that we are bound to be convinced of the correctness of our interpretations.

The human body is, we said, according to Scherner frequently symbolized in dreams by a house; by an extension of this symbolism, windows, doors and gates stand for the entrances to cavities in the body, and the façades may either be smooth or may have balconies and ledges to hold on to. The same symbolism is met with in colloquialisms; for instance, we speak of "a thatch of hair," or a "tile hat," or say of someone that he is not right "in the upper storey."[1] In anatomy, too, we speak of the openings of the body as its "portals."[2]

---

[1] [In German, an old acquaintance is often addressed as "old house" (*altes Haus*); the expression "giving him one on the roof" (*einem eins aufs Dachl geben*) corresponds to "hitting him over the head."]

[2] [The *portal* vein carries nourishment from the bowels to the body *via* the liver. The *pylorus* (from πνλη = gate) is the entrance to the small intestine. In German, the apertures of the body are called *Leibespforten* (gates of the body).—Tr.]

We may at first find it surprising that parents appear in our dreams as kings and emperors and their consorts, but we have a parallel to this in fairy tales. Does it not begin to dawn upon us that the many fairy tales which begin with the words "Once upon a time there were a king and queen" simply mean: "Once upon a time there were a father and mother"? In family life the children are sometimes spoken of jestingly as princes, and the eldest son as the crown prince. The king himself is called the father of his people.[1] Again, in some parts, little children are often playfully spoken of as little animals, e.g. in Cornwall, as "little toad," or in Germany as "little worm," and, in sympathizing with a child, Germans say "poor little worm."

Now let us return to the house symbolism. When in our dreams we make use of the projections of houses as supports, does that not suggest a well-known, popular German saying, with reference to a woman with a markedly developed bust: "She has something for one to hold on to" (*Die hat etwas zum Anhalten*), whilst another colloquialism in the same connection is: "She has plenty of wood in front of her house" (*Die hat viel Holz vor dem Hause*), as though our interpretation were to be borne out by this when we say that wood is a female maternal symbol.

There is still something to be said on the subject of wood. It is not easy to see why wood should have come to represent a woman or mother, but here a comparison of different languages may be useful to us. The German word *Holz* (wood) is said to be derived from the same root as the Greek ὕλη, which means stuff, raw material. This would be an instance of a process which is by no means rare, in that a general name for material has come finally to be applied to a particular material only. Now, in the Atlantic Ocean, there is an island named Madeira, and this name was given to it by the Portuguese when they discovered it, because at that time it was covered with dense forests; for in Portuguese the word for wood is *madeira*. But you cannot fail to notice that this

[1][Cf. the Russian expression, "Little father."—Tr.]

madeira is merely a modified form of the Latin *materia*, which again signifies material in general. Now *materia* is derived from *mater* = mother, and the material out of which anything is made may be conceived of as giving birth to it. So, in the symbolic use of wood to represent woman or mother, we have a survival of this old idea.

Birth is regularly expressed by some connection with water: we are plunging into or emerging from water, that is to say, we give birth or are being born. Now let us not forget that this symbol has a twofold reference to the actual facts of evolution. Not only are all land mammals, from which the human race itself has sprung, descended from creatures inhabiting the water—this is the more remote of the two considerations—but also every single mammal, every human being, has passed the first phase of existence in water—that is to say, as an embryo in the amniotic fluid of the mother's womb —and thus, at birth, emerged from water. I do not maintain that the dreamer knows this; on the other hand, I contend that there is no need for him to know it. He probably knows something else from having been told it as a child, but even this, I will maintain, has contributed nothing to symbol-formation. The child is told in the nursery that the stork brings the babies, but then where does it get them? Out of a pond or a well—again, out of the water. One of my patients who had been told this as a child (a little count, as he was then) afterwards disappeared for a whole afternoon, and was at last found lying at the edge of the castle lake, with his little face bent over the clear water, eagerly gazing to see whether he could catch sight of the babies at the bottom of the water.

In the myths of the births of heroes, a comparative study of which has been made by O. Rank—the earliest is that of King Sargon of Akkad, about 2800 B.C.—exposure in water and rescue from it play a major part. Rank perceived that this symbolizes birth in a manner analogous to that employed in dreams. When anyone in his dream rescues somebody from the water, he makes that person into his mother, or at any rate *a* mother, and in mythology, whoever rescues a child from water confesses herself to be its real mother. There is a well-

known joke in which an intelligent Jewish boy, when asked
who was the mother of Moses, answers immediately: "The
Princess." He is told: "No, she only took him out of the
water." "That's what *she* said," he replies, showing that he
had hit upon the right interpretation of the myth.

Going away on a journey stands in dreams for dying;
similarly, it is the custom in the nursery, when a child asks
questions as to the whereabouts of someone who has died and
whom he misses, to tell him that that person has "gone away."
Here again, I deprecate the idea that the dream-symbol has
its origin in this evasive reply to the child. The poet uses the
same symbol when he speaks of the other side as "the undiscovered country from whose bourne *no traveller* returns."
Again, in everyday speech it is quite usual to speak of the
"last journey," and everyone who is acquainted with ancient
rites knows how seriously the idea of a journey into the land
of the dead was taken, for instance, in ancient Egyptian belief. In many cases the "Book of the Dead" survives, which
was given to the mummy, like a Baedeker, to take with him
on the last journey. Since burial-grounds have been placed at
a distance from the houses of the living, the last journey of the
dead has indeed become a reality.

Nor does sexual symbolism belong only to dreams. You will
all know the expression "a baggage" as applied contemptu-
ously to a woman, but perhaps people do not know that they
are using a genital symbol. In the New Testament we read:
"The woman is the weaker *vessel*." The sacred writings of the
Jews, the style of which so closely approaches that of poetry,
are full of expressions symbolic of sex, which have not always
been correctly interpreted and the exegesis of which, e.g. in
the Song of Solomon, has led to many misunderstandings.[1] In
later Hebrew literature the woman is very frequently represented by a house, the door standing for the genital opening,
thus a man complains, when he finds a woman no longer a
virgin, that "he has found the door open." The symbol "table"
for a woman also occurs in this literature; the woman says of

[1][Cf. "I am a wall and my breasts like towers: then was I in his
eyes as one that found favour." Cant. viii. 10.—Tr.]

her husband "I spread the table for him, but he overturned it." Lame children are said to owe their infirmity to the fact that the man "overturned the table." I quote here from a treatise by L. Levy in Brünn: *Sexual Symbolism in the Bible and the Talmud.*

That ships in dreams signify women is a belief in which we are supported by the etymologists, who assert that "ship" (*Schiff*) was originally the name of an earthen vessel and is the same word as *Schaff* (a tub or wooden vessel). That an oven stands for a woman or the mother's womb is an interpretation confirmed by the Greek story of Periander of Corinth and his wife Melissa. According to the version of Herodotus, the tyrant adjured the shade of his wife, whom he had loved passionately but had murdered out of jealousy, to tell him something about herself, whereupon the dead woman identified herself by reminding him that he, Periander, "had put his bread into a cold oven," thus expressing in a disguised form a circumstance of which everyone else was ignorant. In the *Anthropophyteia,* edited by F. S. Kraus, a work which is an indispensable textbook on everything concerning the sexual life of different peoples, we read that in a certain part of Germany people say of a woman who is delivered of a child that "her oven has fallen to pieces." The kindling of fire and everything connected with this is permeated through and through with sexual symbolism, the flame always standing for the male organ, and the fireplace or the hearth for the womb of the woman.

If you have chanced to wonder at the frequency with which landscapes are used in dreams to symbolize the female sexual organs, you may learn from mythologists how large a part has been played in the ideas and cults of ancient times by "Mother Earth" and how the whole conception of agriculture was determined by this symbolism. The fact that in dreams a room represents a woman you may be inclined to trace to the German colloquialism by which *Frauenzimmer* (*lit.* "woman's room") is used for *Frau,* that is to say, the human person is represented by the place assigned for her occupation. Similarly we speak of the Porte, meaning thereby the Sultan and his government, and the name of the ancient Egyptian ruler, Pharaoh, merely means "great court." (In the ancient Orient the courts between the double gates of the city were places of assembly, like the market-place in classical times.) But I think this derivation is too superficial, and it strikes me as more probable that the room came to symbolize woman on account of its property of enclosing within it the human being. We have already met with the house in this sense; from mythology and poetry we may take towns, citadels, castles and fortresses to be further symbols for women. It would be easy to decide the point by reference to the dreams of people who neither speak nor understand German. Of late years I have mainly treated foreign patients, and I think I recollect that in their dreams rooms stand in the same way for women, even though there is no word analogous to our *Frauenzimmer* in their language. There are other indications that symbolism may transcend the boundaries of language, a fact already maintained by the old dream-investigator, Schubert, in 1862. Nevertheless, none of my patients were wholly ignorant of German, so that I must leave this question to be decided by those analysts who can collect instances in other countries from persons who speak only one language.[1]

Amongst the symbols for the male sexual organ, there is scarcely one which does not appear in jests, or in vulgar or poetic phrases, especially in the old classical poets. Here, however, we meet not only with such symbols as occur in dreams but also with new ones, e.g. the *implements* employed in various kinds of work, first and foremost, the *plough*. Moreover, when we come to male symbols, we trench on very extensive and much-contested ground, which, in order not to waste time, we will avoid. I should just like to devote a few remarks to the one symbol which stands, as it were, by itself; I refer to the number *three*. Whether this number does not in all probability owe its sacred character to its symbolic significance is a question which we must leave undecided, but it seems certain that many tripartite natural objects, e.g. the clover-leaf, are used in coats-of-arms and as emblems on ac-

[1][This is certainly so with English patients.—TR.]

count of their symbolism. The so-called "French" lily with its three parts and, again, the "trisceles," that curious coat-of-arms of two such widely separated islands as Sicily and the Isle of Man (a figure consisting of three bent legs projecting from a central point), are supposed to be merely disguised forms of the male sexual organ, images of which were believed in ancient times to be the most powerful means of warding off evil influences (*apotropaea*); connected with this is the fact that the lucky "charms" of our own time may all be easily recognized as genital or sexual symbols. Let us consider a collection of such charms in the form of tiny silver pendants: a four-leaved clover, a pig, a mushroom, a horseshoe, a ladder and a chimney-sweep. The four-leaved clover has taken the place of that with three leaves, which was really more appropriate for the purposes of symbolism; the pig is an ancient symbol of fruitfulness; the mushroom undoubtedly symbolizes the penis, there are mushrooms which derive their name from their unmistakable resemblance to that organ (*Phallus impudicus*); the horseshoe reproduces the contour of the female genital opening; while the chimney-sweep with his ladder belongs to this company because his occupation is one which is vulgarly compared with sexual intercourse. (Cf. *Anthropophyteia.*) We have learnt to recognize his ladder in dreams as a sexual symbol: expressions in language show what a completely sexual significance the word *steigen*, to mount, has, as in the phrases: *Den Frauen nachsteigen* (to run after women) and *ein alter Steiger* (an old roué). So, in French, where the word for "step" is *la marche*, we find the quite analogous expression for an old rake: *un vieux marcheur*. Probably the fact that with many of the larger animals sexual intercourse necessitates a mounting or "climbing upon" the female has something to do with this association of ideas.

Pulling off a branch to symbolize onanism is not only in agreement with vulgar descriptions of that act, but also has far-reaching parallels in mythology. But especially remarkable is the representation of onanism, or rather of castration as the punishment for onanism, by the falling-out or extraction of teeth; for we find in folk-lore a counterpart to this which could only be known to very few dreamers. I think that there can be no doubt that circumcision, a practice common to so many peoples, is an equivalent and replacement of castration. And recently we have learnt that certain aboriginal tribes in Australia practice circumcision as a rite to mark the attaining of puberty (at the celebration of the boy's coming of age), whilst other tribes living quite near have substituted for this practice that of knocking out a tooth.

I will end my account with these examples. They are only examples; we know more about this subject and you can imagine how much richer and more interesting a collection of this sort might be made, not by dilettanti like ourselves, but by real experts in mythology, anthropology, philology, and folk-lore. We are forced to certain conclusions, which cannot be exhaustive, but nevertheless will give us plenty to think about.

In the first place, we are confronted with the fact that the dreamer has at his command a symbolic mode of expression of which he knows nothing, and does not even recognize, in his waking life. This is as amazing as if you made the discovery that your housemaid understood Sanscrit, though you know that she was born in a Bohemian village and had never learnt that language. It is not easy to bring this fact into line with our views on psychology. We can only say that the dreamer's knowledge of symbolism is unconscious and belongs to his unconscious mental life, but even this assumption does not help us much. Up till now we have only had to assume the existence of unconscious tendencies which are temporarily or permanently unknown to us; but now the question is a bigger one and we have actually to believe in unconscious knowledge, thought-relations, and comparisons between different objects, in virtue of which one idea can constantly be substituted for another. These comparisons are not instituted afresh every time, but are ready to hand, perfect for all time; this we infer from their identity in different persons, even probably in spite of linguistic differences.

Whence is our knowledge of this symbolism derived? The usages of speech cover only a small part of it, whilst the manifold parallels in other fields are for the most part unknown to the dreamer; we ourselves had to collate them laboriously in the first instance.

In the second place, these symbolic relations are not peculiar to the dreamer or to the dream-work by which they are expressed; for we have discovered that the same symbolism is employed in myths and fairy tales, in popular sayings and songs, in colloquial speech and poetic phantasy. The province of symbolism is extraordinarily wide: dream-symbolism is only a small part of it; it would not even be expedient to attack the whole problem from the side of dreams. Many of the symbols commonly occurring elsewhere either do not appear in dreams at all or appear very seldom; on the other hand, many of the dream-symbols are not met with in every other department, but, as you have seen, only here and there. We get the impression that here we have to do with an ancient but obsolete mode of expression, of which different fragments have survived in different fields, one here only, another there only, a third in various spheres perhaps in slightly different forms. At this point I am reminded of the phantasy of a very interesting insane patient, who had imagined a "primordial language" (*Grundsprache*) of which all these symbols were survivals.

In the third place, it must strike you that the symbolism occurring in the other fields I have named is by no means confined to sexual themes, whereas in dreams the symbols are almost exclusively used to represent sexual objects and relations. This again is hard to account for. Are we to suppose that symbols originally of sexual significance were later employed differently and that perhaps the decline from symbolic to other modes of representation is connected with this? It is obviously impossible to answer these questions by dealing only with dream-symbolism; all we can do is to hold fast to the supposition that there is a specially close relation between true symbols and sexuality.

An important clue in this connection has recently been given to us in the view expressed by a philologist (H. Sperber, of Upsala, who works independently of psycho-analysis), that sexual needs have had the largest share in the origin and development of language. He says that the first sounds uttered were a means of communication, and of summoning the sexual partner, and that in the later development the elements of speech were used as an accompaniment to the different kinds of work carried on by primitive man. This work was performed by associated efforts, to the sound of rhythmically repeated utterances, the effect of which was to transfer a sexual interest to the work. Primitive man thus made his work agreeable, so to speak, by treating it as the equivalent of and substitute for sexual activities. The word uttered during the communal work had therefore two meanings, the one referring to the sexual act, the other to the labour which had come to be equivalent to it. In time the word was dissociated from its sexual significance and its application confined to the work. Generations later the same thing happened to a new word with a sexual signification, which was then applied to a new form of work. In this way a number of root-words arose which were all of sexual origin but had all lost their sexual meaning. If the statement here outlined be correct, a possibility at least of understanding dream-symbolism opens out before us. We should comprehend why it is that in dreams, which retain something of these primitive conditions, there is such an extraordinarily large number of sexual symbols; and why weapons and tools in general stand for the male, and materials and things worked on for the female. The symbolic relations would then be the survival of the old identity in words; things which once had the same name as the genitalia could now appear in dreams as symbolizing them.

Further, our parallels to dream-symbolism may assist you to appreciate what it is in psychoanalysis which makes it a subject of general interest, in a way that was not possible to either psychology or psychiatry; psychoanalytic work is so closely intertwined with so many other branches of science, the investigation of which gives promise of the most valuable conclusions: with mythology, philology, folk-lore, folk psychology and the study of religion. You will not be surprised to hear that a publication has sprung from psychoanalytic soil, of which the exclusive object is to foster these relations. I refer to *Imago*, first published in 1912 and edited by Hanns Sachs and Otto Rank. In its relation to all these other subjects, psychoanalysis has in the first instance given rather than received. True, analysis reaps the advantage of receiving confirmation of its own results, seemingly so strange, again in other fields; but on the whole it is psychoanalysis which supplies the technical methods and the points of view, the application of which is to prove fruitful in these other provinces. The mental life of the human individual yields, under psychoanalytic investigation, explanations which solve many a riddle in the life of the masses of mankind or at any rate can show these problems in their true light.

I have still given you no idea of the circumstances in which we may arrive at the deepest insight into that hypothetical "primordial language," or of the province in which it is for the most part retained. As long as you do not know this you cannot appreciate the true significance of the whole subject. I refer to the province of neurosis; the material is found in the symptoms and other modes of expression of nervous patients, for the explanation and treatment of which psychoanalysis was indeed devised.

My fourth point of view takes us back to the place from which we started and leads into the track we have already marked out. We said that even if there were no dream-censorship we should still find it difficult to interpret dreams, for we should then be confronted with the task of translating the symbolic language of dreams into the language of waking life. SYMBOLISM, then, is a second and independent factor in dream-distortion, existing side by side with the censorship. But the conclusion is obvious that it suits the censorship to make use of symbolism, in that both serve the same purpose: that of making the dream strange and incomprehensible.

Whether a further study of the dream will not introduce us to yet another contributing factor in the distortion, we shall soon see. But I must not leave the subject of dream-symbolism without once more touching on the puzzling fact that it has succeeded in rousing such strenuous opposition amongst educated persons, although the prevalence of symbolism in myth, religion, art and language is beyond all doubt. Is it not probable that, here again, the reason is to be found in its relation to sexuality?

ELEVENTH LECTURE

THE DREAM-WORK

WHEN YOU HAVE SUCCESSFULLY GRASPED THE DREAM-CENSOR-ship and symbolic representation, you will not, it is true, have mastered dream-distortion in its entirety, but you will never-theless be in a position to understand most dreams. To do so, you will make use of the two complementary methods: you will call up the dreamer's associations till you have penetrated from the substitute to the thought proper for which it stands, and you will supply the meaning of the symbols from your own knowledge of the subject. We will speak later of certain doubtful points which may arise in the process.

We can now return to a task which we attempted earlier with inadequate equipment, when we were studying the relations between dream-elements and the thoughts proper underlying them. We then determined the existence of four such main relations: substitution of the part for the whole, hints or allusions, symbolic connection, and plastic word-representation (images). We will now try to deal with this subject on a larger scale, by a comparison of the *manifest* dream-content as a whole with the *latent* dream as laid bare by our interpretation.

I hope you will never again confuse these two things. If you succeed in distinguishing between them, you will have ad-vanced further towards an understanding of dreams than in

all probability most of the readers of my *Interpretation of
Dreams* have done. Let me again remind you that *the process
by which the latent dream is transformed into the manifest
dream is called* THE DREAM-WORK; while the reverse process,
which seeks to progress from the manifest to the latent
thoughts, is our work of interpretation; the work of interpretation therefore aims at demolishing the dream-work. In dreams
of the infantile type in which the obvious wish-fulfilments
are easily recognized, the process of dream-work has nevertheless been operative to some extent, for the wish has been
transformed into a reality and, usually, the thoughts also
into visual images. Here no interpretation is necessary; we
only have to retrace both these transformations. The further
operations of the dream-work, as seen in the other types of
dreams, we call *dream-distortion,* and here the original ideas
have to be restored by our interpretative work.

Having had the opportunity of comparing many dream-
interpretations, I am in a position to give you a comprehensive
account of the manner in which the dream-work deals with
the material of the latent dream-thoughts. But please do not
expect to understand too much: it is a piece of description
which should be listened to quietly and attentively.

The first achievement of the dream-work is CONDENSATION;
by this term we mean to convey the fact that the content of
the manifest dream is less rich than that of the latent
thoughts, is, as it were, a kind of abbreviated translation of
the latter. Now and again condensation may be lacking, but
it is present as a rule and is often carried to a very high degree. It never works in the opposite manner, i.e. it never
happens that the manifest dream is wider in range or richer
in content than is the latent dream. Condensation is accomplished in the following ways: (1) certain latent elements
are altogether omitted; (2) of many complexes in the latent
dream only a fragment passes over into the manifest content;
(3) latent elements sharing some common characteristic are
in the manifest dream put together, blended into a single
whole.

If you prefer to do so, you can reserve the term "condensation" for this last process, the effects of which are particularly easy to demonstrate. Taking your own dreams, you will be able without any trouble to recall instances of the condensation of different persons into a single figure. Such a composite figure resembles A. in appearance, but is dressed like B., pursues some occupation which recalls C., and yet all the time you know that it is really D. The composite picture serves, of course, to lay special emphasis upon some characteristic common to the four people. And it is possible also for a composite picture to be formed with objects or places, as with persons, provided only that the single objects or places have some common attribute upon which the latent dream lays stress. It is as though a new and fugitive concept were formed, of which the common attribute is the kernel. From the superimposing of the separate parts which undergo condensation there usually results a blurred and indistinct picture, as if several photographs had been taken on the same plate.

The formation of such composite figures must be of great importance in the dream-work, for we can prove that the common properties necessary to their formation are purposely manufactured where at first sight they would seem to be lacking, as, for example, by the choice of some particular verbal expression for a thought. We have already met with instances of condensation and composite-formation of this sort; they played an important part in originating many slips of the tongue. You will remember the case of the young man who wished to "insort" a lady (*beleidigen* = insult, *begleiten* = escort, composite word *begleitdigen*). Besides, there are jokes in which the technique is traceable to condensation of this sort. Apart from this, however, we may venture to assert that this process is something quite unusual and strange. It is true that in many a creation of phantasy we meet with counterparts to the formation of the composite persons of our dreams, component parts which do not belong to one another in reality being readily united into a single whole by phantasy, as, for instance, in the centaurs and fabulous animals of ancient mythology or of Boecklin's pictures. "Creative" phantasy can, in fact, invent nothing new, but can only regroup elements from different sources. But the peculiar thing about the way in which the dream-work proceeds is this: its material consists of thoughts, some of which may be objectionable and disagreeable, but which nevertheless are correctly formed and expressed. The dream-work transmutes these thoughts into another form, and it is curious and incomprehensible that in this process of translation—of rendering them, as it were, into another script or language—the means of blending and combining are employed. The translator's endeavour in other cases must surely be to respect the distinctions observed in the text, and especially to differentiate between things which are similar but not the same; the dream-work, on the contrary, strives to condense two different thoughts by selecting, after the manner of wit, an ambiguous word which can suggest both thoughts. We must not expect to understand this characteristic straightaway, but it may assume great significance for our conception of the dream-work.

Although condensation renders the dream obscure, yet it does not give the impression of being an effect of the dream-censorship. Rather we should be inclined to trace it to mechanical or economic factors; nevertheless the censorship's interests are served by it.

What condensation can achieve is sometimes quite extraordinary: by this device it is at times possible for two completely different latent trains of thought to be united in a single manifest dream, so that we arrive at an apparently adequate interpretation of a dream and yet overlook a second possible meaning.

Moreover, one of the effects of condensation upon the relationship between the manifest and the latent dream is that the connection between the elements of the one and of the other nowhere remains a simple one; for by a kind of interlacing a manifest element represents simultaneously several latent ones and, conversely, a latent thought may enter into several manifest elements. Again, when we come to interpret dreams, we see that the associations to a single manifest element do not commonly make their appearance in orderly succession; we often have to wait until we have the interpretation of the whole dream.

The dream-work, then, follows a very unusual mode of transcription for the dream-thoughts; not a translation, word for word, or sign for sign; nor yet a process of selection according to some definite rule, for instance, as though the consonants only of the words were reproduced and the vowels omitted; nor again what one might call a process of representation, one element being always picked out to represent several others. It works by a different and much more complicated method.

The second achievement of the dream-work is DISPLACEMENT. Fortunately here we are not breaking perfectly fresh ground; indeed, we know that it is entirely the work of the dream-censorship. Displacement takes two forms: first, a latent element may be *replaced*, not by a part of itself, but by something more remote, something of the nature of an allusion; and, secondly, the *accent* may be transferred from an important element to another which is unimportant, so that the centre of the dream is shifted as it were, giving the dream a foreign appearance.

Substitution by allusion is familiar to us in our waking thoughts also, but with a difference; for it is essential in the latter that the allusion should be easily comprehensible, and that the content of the substitute should be associated to that of the thought proper. Allusion is also frequently employed in wit, where the condition of association in content is dispensed with and replaced by unfamiliar external associations, such as similarity of sound, ambiguity of meaning, etc. The condition of comprehensibility, however, is observed: the joke would lose all its point if we could not recognize without any effort what is the actual thing to which the allusion is made. But in dreams allusion by displacement is unrestricted by either limitation. It is connected most superficially and most remotely with the element for which it stands, and for that reason is not readily comprehensible; and, when the connection is traced, the interpretation gives the impression of an unsuccessful joke or of a "forced," far-fetched and "dragged in"

explanation. The object of the dream-censorship is only obtained when it has succeeded in making it impossible to trace
the thought proper back from the allusion.

Displacement of accent is not a legitimate device if our
object be the expression of thought; though we do sometimes
admit it in waking life in order to produce a comic effect. I
can to some extent convey to you the impression of confusion
which then results, by reminding you of an anecdote, according to which there was in a certain village a smith who had
committed a capital offence. The court decided that the smith
was guilty; but, since he was the only one of his trade in the
village and therefore indispensable, whereas there were three
tailors living there, one of these three was hanged in his place!

The third achievement of the dream-work is the most interesting from the psychological point of view. It consists in
the transformation of thoughts into *visual images*. Let us be
quite clear that not everything in the dream-thoughts is thus
transformed; much keeps its original form and appears also
in the manifest dream as thought or knowledge, on the part
of the dreamer; again, translation of them into visual images
is not the only possible transformation of thoughts. But it is
nevertheless the essential feature in the formation of dreams,
and, as we know, this part of the dream-work is, if we except
one other case, the least subject to variation; for single dream-
elements, moreover, *plastic word-representation* is a process
already familiar to us.

Obviously this achievement is by no means an easy one. In
order to get some idea of its difficulty, imagine that you had
undertaken to replace a political leading article in a newspaper by a series of illustrations; you would have to abandon
alphabetic characters in favour of hieroglyphics. The people
and concrete objects mentioned in the article could be easily
represented, perhaps even more satisfactorily, in pictorial
form; but you would expect to meet with difficulties when
you came to the portrayal of all the abstract words and all
those parts of speech which indicate relations between the
various thoughts, e.g. particles, conjunctions, and so forth.
With the abstract words you would employ all manner of de-

vices: for instance, you would try to render the text of the article into other words, more unfamiliar perhaps, but made up of parts more concrete and therefore more capable of such representation. This will remind you of the fact that most abstract words were originally concrete, their original significance having faded; and therefore you will fall back on the original concrete meaning of these words wherever possible. So you will be glad that you can represent the "possessing" of an object as a literal, physical "sitting upon" it (possess = *potis* + *sedeo*). This is just how the dream-work proceeds. In such circumstances you can hardly demand great accuracy of representation, neither will you quarrel with the dream-work for replacing an element which is difficult to reduce to pictorial form, such as the idea of breaking marriage vows, by some other kind of breaking, e.g. that of an arm or leg.[1] In this way you will to some extent succeed in overcoming the awkwardness of rendering alphabetic characters into hieroglyphs.

DIVINE RETRIBUTION

A BROKEN ARM FOR A BROKEN MARRIAGE-VOW

Frau Anna M., the wife of a soldier in the reserve, accused Frau Clementine K. of unfaithfulness to her husband. In her accusation she stated that Frau K. had had an illicit relationship with Karl M. during her husband's absence at the front, while he was sending her as much as 70 crowns a month. Besides this, she had already received a large sum of money from her (Frau M.'s) husband, while his wife and children had to live in hunger and misery. Some of her husband's comrades had informed her that he and Frau K. had visited public-houses together and remained there drinking late into the night. The accused woman had once actually asked the husband of the accuser, in the presence of several soldiers, whether he would not soon leave his "old woman" and come to her, and the caretaker of the house where Frau K. lived had repeatedly seen the plaintiff's husband in Frau K.'s room, in a state of complete undress.

[1] Whilst correcting these pages, my eye happened to fall upon a newspaper paragraph which I reproduce here as affording unexpected confirmation of the above words.

Yesterday, before a magistrate in the Leopoldstadt, Frau K. denied knowing M. at all: any intimate relations between them were out of the question, she said.

Albertine M., a witness, however, gave evidence of having surprised Frau K. in the act of kissing the accuser's husband.

M., who had been called as a witness in some earlier proceedings, had then denied any intimate relations with the accused. Yesterday, a letter was handed to the magistrate, in which the witness retracted his former denial and confessed that up to the previous June he had carried on illicit relations with Frau K. In the earlier proceedings he had denied his relations with the accused only because she had come to him before the action came into court and begged him on her knees to save her and say nothing. "To-day," wrote the witness, "I feel compelled to lay a full confession before the court, for I have broken my left arm and regard this as God's punishment for my offence."

The judge decided that the penal offence had been committed too long ago for the action to stand, whereupon the accuser withdrew her accusation and the accused was discharged.

When you come to represent those parts of speech which indicate thought-relations, e.g. "because," "therefore," "but," and so on, you have no such means as those described to assist you; so that these parts of the text must be lost, so far as your translation into pictorial form is concerned. Similarly, the content of the dream-thoughts is resolved by the dream-work into its "raw material," consisting of objects and activities. You may be satisfied if there is any possibility of indicating somehow, by a more minute elaboration of the images, certain relations which cannot be represented in themselves. In a precisely similar manner the dream-work succeeds in expressing much of the content of the latent thoughts by means of peculiarities in the *form* of the manifest dream, by its distinctness or obscurity, its division into various parts, etc. The number of parts into which a dream is divided corresponds as a rule with the number of its main themes, the successive trains of thought in the latent dream; a short preliminary dream often stands in an introductory or casual relation to the subsequent detailed main dream; whilst a subordinate dream-thought is represented by the interpolation into the

manifest dream of a change of scene, and so on. The form of
dreams, then, is by no means unimportant in itself, and itself
demands interpretation. Several dreams in the same night
often have the same meaning, and indicate an endeavour to
control more and more completely a stimulus of increasing
urgency. In a single dream, a specially difficult element may
be represented by "doubling" it, i.e. by more than one symbol.

If we continue the comparison of dream-thoughts with
the manifest dreams representing them, we discover in all
directions things we should never have expected, e.g. that
even nonsense and absurdity in dreams have their meaning;
in fact, at this point the contrast between the medical and
the psycho-analytic view of dreams becomes more marked
than ever before. According to the medical view, the dream
is absurd because while dreaming our mental activity has
renounced its functions; according to our view, on the other
hand, the dream becomes absurd when it has to represent a
criticism implicit in the latent thoughts—the opinion: "It is
absurd." The dream I told you, about the visit to the theatre
("three tickets for one florin and a half") is a good example
of this: the opinion thus expressed was as follows: "It was
absurd to marry so early."

Similarly, we find out when we interpret dreams what is the
real meaning of the doubts and uncertainties, so frequently
mentioned by dreamers, whether a certain element did actually appear in the dream, whether it was really this and not
rather something else. As a rule, there is nothing in the latent
thoughts corresponding with these doubts and uncertainties;
they originate wholly through the operation of the censorship
and are comparable to a not entirely successful attempt at
erasure.

One of our most surprising discoveries is the manner in
which *opposites* in the latent dream are dealt with by the
dream-work. We know already that points of agreement in
the latent material are replaced by condensation in the manifest dream. Now contraries are treated in just the same way
as similarities, with a marked preference for expression by
means of the *same* manifest element. An element in the mani-

fest dream which admits of an opposite may stand simply for itself, or for its opposite, or for both together; only the sense can decide which translation is to be chosen. It accords with this that there is no representation of a "No" in dreams, or at least none which is not ambiguous.

A welcome analogy to this strange behaviour of the dream-work is furnished in the development of language. Many philologists have maintained that in the oldest languages opposites such as: strong—weak, light—dark, large—small, were expressed by the same root word (*antithetical sense of primal words*). Thus, in old Egyptian *"ken"* stood originally for both "strong" and "weak." In speaking, misunderstanding was guarded against in the use of such ambivalent words by the intonation and accompanying gestures; in writing, by the addition of a so-called "determinative," that is to say, of a picture which was not meant to be expressed orally. Thus, *"ken"* = "strong" was written in such a way that after the letters there was a picture of a little man standing upright; when *"ken"* meant "weak," there was added the picture of a man in a slack, crouching attitude. Only at a later period did the two opposite meanings of the same primal word come to be designated in two different ways by slight modifications of the original. Thus, from *"ken"* meaning "strong—weak" were derived two words: *"ken"* = "strong" and *"kan"* = "weak." Nor is it only the oldest languages, in the last stages of their development, which have retained many survivals of these early words capable of meaning either of two opposites, but the same is true of much younger languages, even those which are to-day still living. I will quote some illustrations of this taken from the work of C. Abel (1884):

In Latin, such ambivalent words are:

> *altus* = high or deep. *sacer* = sacred or accursed.

As examples of modifications of the original root, I quote:

> *clamare* = to shout. *clam* = quietly, silently, secretly.
> *siccus* = dry. *succus* = juice.

and, in German, *Stimme* = voice. *stumm* = dumb.

A comparison of kindred languages yields a large number of examples:

English: lock = to shut. German: *Loch* = hole. *Lücke* = gap.
English: cleave.[1] German: *kleben* = to stick, adhere.

The English word "without," originally carrying with it both a positive and a negative connotation, is to-day used in the negative sense only, but it is clear that "with" has the signification, not merely of "adding to," but of "depriving of," from the compounds "withdraw," "withhold" (cf. the German *wieder*).

Yet another peculiarity of the dream-work has its counterpart in the development of language. In ancient Egyptian, as well as in other later languages, the sequence of sounds was transposed so as to result in different words for the same fundamental idea. Examples of this kind of parallels between English and German words may be quoted:

Topf (pot)—pot. Boat—tub. Hurry—*Ruhe* (rest).
Balken (beam)—*Kloben* (club). wait—*täuwen* (to wait).

Parallels between Latin and German:—

capere—*packen* (to seize). ren—*Niere* (kidney).

Such transpositions as have taken place here in the case of single words are made by the dream-work in a variety of ways. The inversion of the meaning, i.e. substitution by the opposite, is a device with which we are already familiar; but, besides this, we find in dreams inversion of situations or of the relations existing between two persons, as though the scene were laid in a "topsy-turvy" world. In dreams often enough the hare chases the hunter. Again, inversion is met with in the sequence of events, so that in dreams cause follows effect, which reminds us of what sometimes happens in a third-rate theatrical performance, when first the hero falls and then the

[1][Both senses of cleave are still alive in English: to cleave (= separate) and to cleave to (= adhere).—TR.]

shot which kills him is fired from the wings. Or there are dreams in which the whole arrangement of the elements is inverted, so that in interpreting them the last must be taken first, and the first last, in order to make sense at all. You remember that we also found this in our study of dream-symbolism, in which the act of plunging or falling into water has the same meaning as that of emerging from water, namely, giving birth or being born and going up steps or a ladder means the same as coming down them. We cannot fail to recognize the advantage reaped for dream-distortion by this freedom from restrictions in representing the dream-thoughts.

These features of the dream-work may be termed *archaic*. They cling to the primitive modes of expression of languages or scripts, and yield the same difficulties, which we shall touch upon later in the course of some critical observations on this topic.

Now let us consider some other aspects of the subject. Clearly what has to be accomplished by the dream-work is the transformation of the latent thoughts, as expressed in words, into perceptual forms, most commonly into visual images. Now our thoughts originated in such perceptual forms; their earliest material and the first stages in their development consisted of sense-impressions, or, more accurately, of memory-pictures of these. It was later that words were attached to these pictures and then connected so as to form thoughts. So that the dream-work subjects our thoughts to a *regressive* process and retraces the steps in their development; in the course of this REGRESSION all new acquisitions won during this development of memory-pictures into thoughts must necessarily fall away.

This then is what we mean by the dream-work. Beside what we have learnt of its processes our interest in the manifest dream is bound to recede far into the background; I will, however, devote still a few more remarks to the manifest dream, for, after all, that is the only part of the dream with which we have any direct acquaintance.

It is natural that the manifest dream should lose some of its importance in our eyes. It must strike us as a matter of indifference whether it is carefully composed or split up into a succession of disconnected pictures. Even when the outward form of the dream is apparently full of meaning, we know that this appearance has been arrived at by the process of dream-distortion, and can have as little organic connection with the inner content of the dream as exists between the *façade* of an Italian church and its general structure and ground-plan. At times, however, this *façade* of the dream has a meaning too, reproducing an important part of the latent thoughts with little or no distortion. But we cannot know this until we have interpreted the dream and thus arrived at an opinion with regard to the degree of distortion present. A similar doubt obtains where two elements seem to be closely connected; such connection may contain a valuable hint that the corresponding elements in the latent dream are similarly related, but at other times we can convince ourselves that what is connected in thought has become widely separated in the dream.

In general we must refrain from attempting to explain one part of the manifest dream by another part, as though the dream were a coherent conception and a pragmatic representation. It is in most cases comparable rather to a piece of Breccia stone, composed of fragments of different kinds of stone cemented together in such a way that the markings upon it are not those of the original pieces contained in it. There is, as a matter of fact, one mechanism in the dream-work, known as SECONDARY ELABORATION, the object of which is to combine the immediate results of the work into a single and fairly coherent whole; during this process the material is often so arranged as to give rise to total misunderstanding, and for this purpose any necessary interpolations are made.

On the other hand, we should not overrate the dream-work or attribute to it more than is its due. Its activity is limited to the achievements here enumerated; condensation, displacement, plastic representation and secondary elaboration of the whole dream; these are all that it can effect. Such manifestations of judgement, criticism, surprise, or deductive reasoning, as are met with in dreams are not brought about by the dream-work and are only very rarely the expression of subsequent reflection about the dream; but are for the most part fragments of the latent thoughts introduced into the manifest dream with more or less modification and in a form suited to the context. Again, the dream-work cannot create conversation in dreams; save in a few exceptional cases, it is imitated from, and made up of, things heard or even said by the dreamer himself on the previous day, which have entered into the latent thoughts as the material or incitement of his dream. Neither do mathematical calculations come into the province of the dream-work; anything of the sort appearing in the manifest dream is generally a mere combination of numbers, a pseudo-calculation, quite absurd as such, and again only a copy of some calculation comprised in the latent thoughts. In these circumstances it is not surprising that the interest which was felt in the dream-work soon becomes directed instead towards the latent thoughts which disclose themselves in a more or less distorted form through the manifest dream. We are not justified, however, in a theoretical consideration of the subject, in letting our interest stray so far that we altogether substitute the latent thoughts for the dream as a whole, and make some pronouncement on the latter which is only true of the former. It is strange that the findings of psychoanalysis could be so misused as to result in confusion between the two. The term "dream" can only be applied to the *results of the dream-work*, i.e. to the *form* into which the latent thoughts have been rendered by the dream-work.

This work is a process of a quite peculiar type; nothing like it has hitherto been known in mental life. This kind of condensation, displacement, and regressive translation of thoughts into images, is a novelty, the recognition of which in itself richly rewards our efforts in the field of psychoanalysis. You will again perceive, from the parallels to dream-work, the connections revealed between psychoanalytic and other research, especially in the fields of the development of speech and thought. You will only realize the further significance of the insight so acquired when you learn that the mechanism of the dream-work is a kind of model for the formation of neurotic symptoms.

I know too that it is not possible for us yet to grasp the full extent of the fresh gain accruing to psychology from these labours. We will only hint at the new proofs thereby afforded of the existence of unconscious mental activities—for this indeed is the nature of the latent dream-thoughts—and at the promise dream-interpretation gives of an approach, wider than we ever guessed at, to the knowledge of the unconscious life of the mind.

Now, however, I think the time has come to give you individual examples of various short dreams, which will illustrate the points for which I have already prepared you.

TWELFTH LECTURE

EXAMPLES OF DREAMS AND ANALYSIS OF THEM

YOU MUST NOT BE DISAPPOINTED IF I PRESENT YOU ONCE MORE
with fragments of dream-interpretations, instead of inviting
you to participate in the interpretation of one fine long dream.
You will say that after so much preparation you surely have a
right to expect that; and you will express your conviction that,
after successful interpretations of so many thousands of
dreams, it should long ago have been possible to collect a
number of striking examples by which the truth of all our assertions about the dream-work and dream-thoughts could be
demonstrated. Yes, but there are too many difficulties in the
way of fulfilling this wish of yours.

In the first place, I must confess that there is nobody who
makes the interpretation of dreams his main business. In what
circumstances, then, do we come to interpret them? At times
we may occupy ourselves, for no particular purpose, with the
dreams of a friend, or we may work out our own dreams over
a period of time in order to train ourselves for psychoanalytic
work; but chiefly we have to do with the dreams of nervous
patients who are undergoing psychoanalytic treatment. These
last dreams provide splendid material and are in no respect
inferior to those of healthy persons, but the technique of the
treatment obliges us to subordinate dream-interpretation to
therapeutic purposes and to desist from the attempt to inter-

pret a large number of the dreams as soon as we have extracted from them something of use for the treatment. Again, many dreams which occur during the treatment elude full interpretation altogether; since they have their origin in the whole mass of material in the mind which is as yet unknown to us, it is not possible to understand them until the completion of the cure. To relate such dreams would necessarily involve revealing all the secrets of a neurosis; this will not do for us, since we have taken up the problem of dreams in preparation for the study of the neuroses.

Now I expect you would willingly dispense with this material and would prefer to listen to the explanation of dreams of healthy persons or perhaps of your own. But the content of these dreams makes that impossible. One cannot expose oneself, nor anyone whose confidence has been placed in one, so ruthlessly as a thorough interpretation of a dream would necessitate; for, as you already know, they touch upon all that is most intimate in the personality. Apart from the difficulty arising out of the nature of the material, there is another difficulty as regards relating the dreams. You are aware that the dream seems foreign and strange to the dreamer himself; how much more so to an outsider to whom his personality is unknown. The literature of psychoanalysis shows no lack of good and detailed dream-analyses; I myself have published some which formed part of the history of certain pathological cases. Perhaps the best example of a dream-interpretation is that published by O. Rank, consisting of the analysis of two mutually related dreams of a young girl. These cover about two pages of print, while the analysis of them runs into 76 pages. It would need almost a whole term's lectures in order to take you through a work of this magnitude. If we selected some fairly long and considerably distorted dream we should have to enter into so many explanations, to adduce so much material in the shape of associations and recollections, and to go down so many sidetracks, that a single lecture would be quite inadequate and would give no clear idea of it as a whole So I must ask you to be content if I pursue a less difficult course, and relate some fragments from dreams of neurotic patients, in which this or that isolated feature may be recognized. Symbols are the easiest features to demonstrate and, after them, certain peculiarities of the regressive character of dream-representation. I will tell you why I regard each of the following dreams as worth relating.

1. A dream consisting only of two short pictures: *The dreamer's uncle was smoking a cigarette, although it was Saturday.—A woman was fondling and caressing the dreamer as though he were her child.*

With reference to the first picture, the dreamer (a Jew) remarked that his uncle was a very pious man who never had done, and never would do, anything so sinful as smoking on the Sabbath. The only association to the woman in the second picture was that of the dreamer's mother. These two pictures or thoughts must obviously be related to one another; but in what way? Since he expressly denied that his uncle would in reality perform the action of the dream, the insertion of the conditional "if" will at once suggest itself. "If my uncle, that deeply religious man, were to smoke a cigarette on the Sabbath, then I myself might be allowed to let my mother fondle me." Clearly, that is as much as to say that being fondled by the mother was something as strictly forbidden as smoking on the Sabbath is to the pious Jew. You will remember my telling you that in the dream-work all relations among the dream-thoughts disappear; the thoughts are broken up into their raw material, and our task in interpreting is to reinsert these connections which have been omitted.

2. My writings on the subject of dreams have placed me to some extent in the position of public consultant on the question, and for many years now I have received letters from the most diverse quarters communicating dreams to me or asking for my opinion. Naturally I am grateful to all those who have given me sufficient material with their dreams to make an interpretation possible, or have themselves volunteered one. The following dream of a medical student in Munich dating from 1910 belongs to this category; and I quote it because it may prove to you how hard it is, generally speaking, to understand a dream until the dreamer has given us what information he

can about it. For I have a suspicion that in the bottom of your hearts you think that the translating of the symbols is the ideal method of interpretation and that you would like to discard that of free association; I want, therefore, to clear your minds of so pernicious an error.

July 13th, 1910. Towards morning I had the following dream: *I was bicycling down a street in Tübingen, when a brown dachshund came rushing after me and caught hold of one of my heels. I rode a little further and then dismounted, sat down on a step and began to beat the creature off, for it had set its teeth fast in my heel.* (The dog's biting me and the whole scene roused no unpleasant sensations.) *Two elderly ladies were sitting opposite, watching me with grinning faces. Then I woke up and, as has frequently happened before, with the transition to waking consciousness the whole dream was clear to me.*

In this instance symbolism cannot help us much, but the dreamer goes on to tell us: "I recently fell in love with a girl, just from seeing her in the street; but I had no means of introduction to her. I should have liked best to make her acquaintance through her dachshund, for I am a great animal-lover myself and was attracted by seeing she was one too." He adds that several times he had separated fighting dogs very skilfully, often to the amazement of the onlookers. Now we learn that the girl who had taken his fancy was always seen walking with this particular dog. She, however, has been eliminated from the manifest dream; only the dog associated with her has remained. Possibly the elderly ladies who grinned at him represented her, but the rest of what he tells us does not clear up this point. The fact that he was riding a bicycle in the dream was a direct repetition of the situation as he remembered it, for he had not met the girl with the dog except when he was bicycling.

3. When a man has lost someone dear to him, for a considerable period afterwards he produces a special type of dream, in which the most remarkable compromises are effected between his knowledge that that person is dead and his desire to call him back to life. Sometimes the deceased is

dreamt of as being dead, and yet still alive because he does not know that he is dead, as if he would only really die if he did know it; at other times he is half dead and half alive, and each of these conditions has its distinguishing marks. We must not call these dreams merely nonsensical, for to come to life again is no more inadmissible in dreams than in fairy-tales, in which it is quite a common fate. As far as I have been able to analyse such dreams, it appeared that they were capable of a reasonable explanation, but that the pious wish to recall the departed is apt to manifest itself in the strangest ways. I will submit a dream of this sort to you, which certainly sounds strange and absurd enough, and the analysis of which will demonstrate many points already indicated in our theoretical discussions. The dreamer was a man who had lost his father some years previously:—

My father was dead but had been exhumed and looked ill. He went on living, and I did all I could to prevent his noticing it. Then the dream goes on to other matters, apparently very remote.

That the father was dead we know to be a fact; but the exhumation had not taken place in reality; indeed, the question of real fact has nothing to do with anything that follows. But the dreamer went on to say that after he returned from his father's funeral one of his teeth began to ache. He wanted to treat it according to the Jewish precept: "If thy tooth offend thee, pluck it out," and accordingly went to the dentist. The latter, however, said that that was not the way to treat a tooth; one must have patience with it. "I will put something in it," he said, "to kill the nerve, and you must come back in three days' time, when I will take it out again." "This 'taking out,' " said the dreamer suddenly, "is the exhuming."

Now was he right? True, the parallel is not exact, for it was not the tooth which was taken out, but only a dead part of it As a result of experience, however, we can well credit the dream-work with inaccuracies of this sort. We must suppose that the dreamer had, by a process of condensation, combined the dead father with the tooth, which was dead and which he yet retained. No wonder then that an absurdity was the result in the manifest dream, for obviously not all that was said about the tooth could apply to the father. What then are we to regard as the *tertium comparationis* between the father and the tooth,—what common factor makes the comparison possible?

Such a factor must have existed, for the dreamer went on to observe that he knew the saying that if one dreams of losing a tooth it means that one is about to lose a member of his family.

We know that this popular interpretation is incorrect or at least correct only in a very distorted sense. We shall therefore be the more surprised actually to discover the subject thus touched upon behind the other elements of the dream-content.

Without being pressed further, the dreamer then began to talk of his father's illness and death, and of the relations which had existed between father and son. The illness had been a long one, and the care and treatment of the invalid had cost the son a large sum of money. Yet it never seemed too much to him, nor did his patience ever fail or the wish occur to him that the end should come. He prided himself on his true Jewish filial piety and on his strict observance of the Jewish law. Does not a certain contradiction strike us here in the thoughts relating to the dream? He had identified the tooth with the father. He wanted to treat the former according to the Jewish law which commanded that a tooth which causes pain and annoyance should be plucked out. His father he also wanted to treat according to the precepts of the law, but here the command was that he must pay no heed to expense and annoyance, must take the whole burden upon himself, and not allow any hostile intention to arise against the cause of the trouble. Would not the agreement between the two situations be much more convincing if he had really gradually come to have the same feelings towards his sick father as he had towards his diseased tooth, that is to say, if he had wished for death to put a speedy end to his father's superfluous, painful and costly existence?

I have no doubt that this was, in reality, his attitude towards his father during the protracted illness and that his ostentatious assertions of filial piety were designed to divert his mind from any recollections of the sort. Under conditions such as these it is no uncommon thing for the death-wish against the father to be roused, and to mask itself with some ostensibly compassionate reflection, such as: "It would be a blessed release for him." But I want you particularly to notice that here in the latent thoughts themselves a barrier has been broken down. The first part of the thoughts was, we may be sure, only temporarily unconscious, that is, during the actual process of the dream-work; the hostile feelings towards the father, on the other hand, had probably been permanently so, possibly dating from childhood and having at times, during the father's illness, crept as it were timidly and in a disguised form into consciousness. We can maintain this with even greater certainty of other latent thoughts which have unmistakably contributed to the content of the dream. There are, it is true, no indications in it of hostile feelings towards the father; but when we enquire into the origin of such hostility in the life of the child we remember that fear of the father arises from the fact that in the earliest years of life it is he who opposes the sexual activity of the boy, as he is usually compelled to do again, after puberty, from motives of social expediency. This was the relation in which our dreamer stood to his father; his affection for him had been tinged with a good deal of respect and dread, the source of which was early sexual intimidation.

We can now explain the further phrases in the dream from the onanism complex. *"He looked ill"* was an allusion to another remark of the dentist's—that it did not look well for a tooth to be missing just there—but it also refers at the same time to the "looking ill" by which the young man, during the period of puberty, betrays, or fears lest he might betray, his excessive sexual activity. It was with a lightening of his own heart that in the manifest dream the dreamer transferred the look of illness from himself to his father, an inversion with which you are familiar as a device of the dream-work. *"He went on living"* accords both with the wish to recall the father to life and the promise of the dentist to save the tooth. The phrase *"I did everything I could to prevent his noticing"* is extremely subtly designed to lead us to complete it with the words "that he was dead." The only completion of them that really makes sense, however, is again to be traced to the onanism complex, where it is a matter of course that the young man should do all he can to conceal his sexual life from his father. Finally, I would remind you that the so-called "tooth-ache dreams" always refer to onanism, and the punishment for it that is feared.

You see how this incomprehensible dream is built up by a piece of remarkable and misleading condensation, by omitting from it all the thoughts that belong to the core of the latent train of thought, and by the creation of ambiguous substitute-formations to represent those thoughts which were deepest and most remote in time.

4. We have already tried repeatedly to get to the bottom of those prosaic and banal dreams which have nothing absurd or strange in them, but which suggest the question: Why should we dream about such trivialities at all? I will therefore quote a fresh example of this sort in the shape of three dreams connected with one another and dreamt by a young lady in the course of a single night.

(a) *She was going through the hall in her house and struck her head on a low-hanging chandelier with such force as to draw blood*. This episode did not remind her of anything that had actually happened; her remarks led in quite another direction: "You know how terribly my hair is coming out. Well, yesterday my mother said to me: 'My dear child, if it goes on like this, your head will soon be as bald as your buttocks.'" We see here that the head stands for the other end of the body. No further assistance is required to understand the symbolism of the chandelier: all objects capable of elongation are symbols of the male organ. The real subject of the dream then is a bleeding at the lower end of the body, caused by contact with the penis. This might still have other meanings; the dreamer's further associations show that the dream has to do with the belief that menstruation results from sexual intercourse with a man, a notion about sexual matters which is by no means uncommon amongst immature girls.

(*b*) *The dreamer saw in a vineyard a deep hole which she knew had been caused by the uprooting of a tree.* Her remark on this point was that "the tree was *missing*," meaning that she did not see the tree in the dream; but the same phrase serves to express another thought, which leaves us in no doubt as to the symbolic interpretation. The dream refers to another infantile notion on the subject of sex, to the belief that girls originally had the same genital organ as boys and that the later conformation of this organ has been brought about by castration (uprooting the tree).

(*c*) *The dreamer was standing in front of her writing-table drawer which she knows so well that, if anyone touched it, she would immediately be aware of it.* The writing-table drawer, like all drawers, chests and boxes, is a symbol of the female genital. She knew that when sexual intercourse (or, as she thought, any contact at all) has taken place the genital shows certain indications of the fact, and she had long had a fear of being convicted of this. I think that in all three dreams the main emphasis lies on the idea of *knowing*. She had in mind the time of childish investigations into sexual matters, of the results of which she had been very proud at the time.

5. Here is another example of symbolism. But this time I must preface it with a short account of the mental situation in which the dream occurred. A man and a woman who were in love had spent a night together; he described her nature as maternal, she was one of those women whose desire to have a child comes out irresistibly during caresses. The conditions of their meeting, however, made it necessary to take precautions to prevent the semen from entering the womb. On waking the next morning, the woman related the following dream:—

An officer with a red cap was pursuing her in the street. She fled from him and ran up the staircase, with him after her. Breathless, she reached her rooms and slammed and locked the door behind her. The man remained outside and, peeping through the keyhole in the door, she saw him sitting on a bench outside, weeping.

In the pursuit by the officer with the red cap and the breathless climbing of the stairs you will recognize the representation of the sexual act. That the dreamer shuts her pursuer out may serve as an example of the device of inversion so frequently employed in dreams, for in reality it was the man who withdrew before the completion of the sexual act. In the same way, she has projected her own feeling of grief on to her partner, for it is he who weeps in the dream, his tears at the same time alluding to the seminal fluid.

You will certainly have heard it said at some time or other that psycho-analysis maintains that all dreams have a sexual meaning. You are now in a position yourselves to form an opinion as to the falseness of this reproach. You have learnt of wish-fulfilment dreams, dealing with the gratification of the most obvious needs—hunger, thirst, and the longing for liberty —comfort-dreams, and impatient-dreams, as well as those which are frankly avaricious and egoistical. You may, however, certainly bear it in mind that, according to the results of psycho-analysis, dreams in which a marked degree of distortion is present *mainly* (but here again not exclusively) give expression to sexual desires.

6. I have a special motive in giving many instances of the use of symbols in dreams. In our first lecture I complained of the difficulty of demonstrating my statements in such a way as to carry conviction with regard to the findings of psychoanalysis, and since then you have doubtless agreed with me. Now the separate propositions of psychoanalysis are nevertheless so intimately related that conviction on a single point easily leads to acceptance of the greater part of the whole theory. It might be said of psychoanalysis that if you give it your little finger it will soon have your whole hand. If you accept the explanation of errors as satisfactory, you cannot logically stop short of belief in all the rest. Now dream-symbolism provides another, equally good, approach to such acceptance. I will recount to you a dream, which has already been published, of a woman of the poorer classes, whose husband was a watchman and of whom we may be sure that she had never heard of dream-symbolism and psychoanalysis.

You can then judge for yourselves whether the interpretation arrived at with the help of sexual symbols can justly be called arbitrary or forced.

"... Then someone broke into the house and in terror she cried for a watchman. But the watchman, accompanied by two tramps, had gone into a church, which had several steps leading up to it. Behind the church there was a mountain and, up above, a thick wood. The watchman wore a helmet, gorget and cloak, and had a full brown beard. The two tramps, who had gone along peaceably with him, had aprons twisted round their hips like sacks. A path led from the church to the mountain and was overgrown on both sides with grass and bushes which grew denser and denser, and at the top of the mountain there was a regular wood."

You will recognize without any trouble the symbols here employed: the male organ is represented by the trinity of *three* persons appearing, whilst the female sexual organs are symbolized by a landscape with a chapel, a mountain and a wood, and once more you have the act of going up steps as symbolic of the sexual act. The part of the body called in the dream "a mountain" is similarly termed in anatomy the mons veneris.

7. I will tell you another dream which is to be explained in the light of symbolism, a dream, moreover, which is noteworthy and convincing from the fact that the dreamer himself translated all the symbols, though he brought no previous theoretical knowledge to the interpretation. This is a very unusual circumstance and we have no accurate idea of the conditions which give rise to it.

He was walking with his father in a place which must have been the Prater,[1] *for they saw the Rotunda with a little building in front of it, to which was made fast a captive balloon which looked rather slack. His father asked him what it was all for; the son wondered at his asking, but explained it nevertheless. Then they came to a court-yard, where a large sheet of metal lay spread out. His father wanted to break off a big piece, but looked round first in case anyone should notice him. He said*

[1] [The principal park of Vienna.—TR.]

*to his son that all the same he need only tell the overseer and
then he could take it straightaway. Some steps led down from
this court to a shaft, the sides of which were upholstered with
some soft stuff, something like a leather armchair. At the bottom of this shaft was a rather long platform and, beyond it,
another shaft.*

The following is the dreamer's own interpretation:—"The
Rotunda stands for my genitals and the captive balloon in
front of it for the penis, which I have had to complain of for
being limp." A more detailed translation would then run thus:
the rotunda stands for the buttocks (regularly included by
children amongst the genitals), the smaller structure in front
is the scrotum. In the dream, his father asks him what all this
is, i.e. what are the purpose and function of the genitals. To
invert this situation so that the son asks the questions is an obvious idea, and, since these questions were never asked in
reality, we must construe the dream-thoughts as a wish or
take them in a conditional sense: "If I had asked my father
to explain. . . ." The sequel to this thought we shall find
presently.

The court-yard where the sheet-metal lay is not in the first
place to be explained symbolically, but is a reference to the
father's place of business. From motives of discretion I have
substituted "sheet-metal" for the actual material dealt with by
him, but otherwise I have made no alteration in the words of
the dream. The dreamer had entered his father's business and
had been much scandalized by the extremely questionable
practices upon which the high profits largely depended.
Hence the sequel to the dream-thought mentioned above
would run: "(If I had asked him), he would have deceived
me as he deceives his customers." The dreamer himself gives
a second explanation for the pulling off the piece of metal
which serves to represent commercial dishonesty: it means, he
says, the practice of masturbation. Not only is this an explanation with which we have long been familiar, but it is well in
accordance with this interpretation that the secret practice of
masturbation should be expressed by the opposite idea (*"We
may do it openly"*). So the fact that this practice is imputed

to the father, as was the questioning in the first scene of the
dream, is exactly what we should expect. The dreamer immediately interpreted the shaft, on account of the soft upholster-
ing of the walls, as the vagina, and I, on my own account,
offer the remark that going-down as well as going-up stands
for sexual intercourse.

The details of the long platform at the bottom of the first
shaft, and beyond that the second shaft, were explained by
the dreamer himself from his own history. He had practised
intercourse for some time and then given it up on account of
inhibitions, but hoped to be able to resume it by the help of
the treatment.

8. I quote the two following dreams, dreamt by a foreigner
with marked polygamous tendencies, because they may serve
to illustrate the statement that the dreamer's own person
is present in every dream, even when it is disguised in the
manifest content. The trunks in the dreams are female
symbols.

(a) *The dreamer was going on a journey and his luggage
was being taken to the station on a carriage. There were a
number of trunks piled one on the top of the other, and
amongst them two large black boxes like those of a commercial traveller. He said consolingly to someone: "You see
those are only going as far as the station."*

He does, as a matter of fact, travel with a great deal of luggage, and he also brings many stories about women to the
treatment. The two black trunks stand for two dark women
who at the moment are playing the principal part in his life.
One of them wanted to follow him to Vienna, but on my advice he had telegraphed to put her off.

(b) A scene at a customs house:—*A fellow-traveller opened
his trunk and said nonchalantly, smoking a cigarette: "There
is nothing to declare in that." The customs official seemed to
believe him, but felt in the trunk again and found a strictly
prohibited article. The traveller then said in a resigned way:
"Well, it can't be helped."* The dreamer himself is the traveller
and I am the official. He is generally very straightforward
with me, but had made up his mind to conceal from me a

relation which he had recently formed with a lady, for he assumed quite correctly that I knew her. He displaces on to a stranger the embarrassing situation of being detected, so that he himself does not seem to come into the dream at all.

9. Here we have an example of a symbol which I have not yet mentioned:—

The dreamer met his sister with two friends who were themselves sisters. He shook hands with these two, but not with his sister.

There was no real episode connected with this in his mind. Instead, his thoughts went back to a time when his observations led him to wonder why a girl's breasts are so late in developing. The two sisters, therefore, stand for the breasts; he would have liked to grasp them with his hand, if only it had not been his sister.

10. Here is an example of death symbolism in dreams:— *The dreamer was crossing a very high, steep, iron bridge, with two people whose names he knew, but forgot on waking. Suddenly both of them had vanished and he saw a ghostly man in a cap and an overall. He asked him whether he were the telegraph messenger . . . "No." Or the coachman? . . . "No." He then went on,* and in the dream, had a feeling of great dread; on waking, he followed it up with the phantasy that the iron bridge suddenly broke and that he fell into the abyss.

When stress is laid upon the fact that people in a dream are unknown to the dreamer, or that he has forgotten their names, they are, as a rule, persons with whom he is intimately connected. The dreamer was one of a family of three children; if he had ever wished for the death of the other two, it would be only just that he should be visited with the fear of death. With reference to the telegraph messenger, he remarked that they always bring bad news. From his uniform, the man in the dream might have been a lamp-lighter, who also puts out the lights, as the spirit of death extinguishes the torch of life. With the coachman he associated Uhland's poem of the voyage of King Karl, and recalled a dangerous sail on a lake with two companions, when he played the part of the king in the poem.

The iron bridge suggested to him a recent accident, also the stupid saying: "Life is a suspension bridge."

11. The following may be regarded as another example of a death-dream:—

An unknown gentleman was leaving a black-edged visiting card on the dreamer.

12. I give another dream which will interest you from several points of view; it is to be traced partly, however, to a neurotic condition in the dreamer:—

He was in a train which stopped in the open country. He thought there was going to be an accident and that he must make his escape, so he went through all the compartments, killing everyone he met,—driver, guard, and so on.

This dream recalls a story told him by a friend. On a certain Italian line, an insane man was being conveyed in a small compartment, but by some mistake a passenger was allowed to get in with him. The madman murdered the other traveller. Thus the dreamer identified himself with this insane man, his reason being that he was at times tormented by an obsession that he must make away with "everyone who shared his knowledge." Then he himself found a better motivation for the dream. The day before, he had seen at the theatre a girl he had meant to marry but had given up because she gave him cause for jealousy. Knowing the intensity which jealousy could assume in him, he would really have been mad to want to marry her. That is to say, he thought her so unreliable that his jealousy would have led him to murder everyone who got in his way. The going through a number of rooms, or, as here, compartments, we have already learnt to know as a symbol of marriage (the expression of monogamy according to the rule of opposites).

With reference to the train's stopping in the open country and the fear of an accident, he told the following story:—

Once when such a sudden halt occurred on the line outside a station, a young lady who was in the carriage said that perhaps there was going to be a collision, and that the best thing to do was to raise the legs high. This phrase "raise the legs" had associations with many walks and excursions into the country, which he had shared with the girl mentioned above in the happy early days of their love. Here was a new argument for the contention that he would be mad to marry her now; nevertheless, my knowledge of the situation led me to regard it as certain that there existed in him all the same the desire to fall a victim to this form of madness.

Thirteenth Lecture

Archaic and Infantile Features in Dreams

Let us start afresh from our conclusion that, under the influence of the censorship, the dream-work translates the latent dream-thoughts into another form. These thoughts are of the same nature as the familiar, conscious thoughts of waking life; the new form in which they are expressed is, owing to many peculiar characteristics, incomprehensible to us. We have said that it goes back to phases in our intellectual development which we have long outgrown—to hieroglyphic writing, to symbolic-connections, possibly to conditions which existed before the language of thought was evolved. On this account we called the form of expression employed by the dream-work *archaic* or *regressive*.

From this you may draw the inference that a more profound study of the dream-work must lead to valuable conclusions about the initial stages of our intellectual development, of which at present little is known. I hope it will be so, but so far this task has not been attempted. The era to which the dream-work takes us back is "primitive" in a twofold sense: in the first place, it means the early days of the *individual*—his childhood—and, secondly, in so far as each individual repeats in some abbreviated fashion during childhood the whole course of the development of the human race, the reference is *phylogenetic*. I believe it not impossible that we may be able to discriminate between that part of the latent mental processes which belongs to the early days of the individual and that which has its roots in the infancy of the race. It seems to me, for instance, that symbolism, a mode of expression which has never been individually acquired, may claim to be regarded as a racial heritage.

This, however, is not the only archaic feature in dreams. You are all familiar from actual experience with the peculiar *amnesia of childhood* to which we are subject. I mean that the first years of life, up to the age of five, six, or eight, have not left the same traces in memory as our later experiences. True, we come across individuals who can boast of continuous recollection from early infancy to the present time, but it is incomparably more common for the opposite, a blank in memory, to be found. In my opinion, this has not aroused sufficient surprise. At two years old the child can speak well and soon shows his capacity for adapting himself to complicated mental situations, and, moreover, says things which he himself has forgotten when they are repeated to him years later. And yet memory is more efficient in early years, being less overburdened than it is later. Again, there is no reason to regard the function of memory as an especially high or difficult form of mental activity; on the contrary, excellent memory may be found in people who are yet on a very low plane intellectually.

But I must draw your attention to a second peculiarity, based upon the first—namely, that from the oblivion in which the first years of childhood are shrouded certain clearly retained recollections emerge, mostly in the form of plastic images, for the retention of which there seems no adequate ground. Memory deals with the mass of impressions received in later life by a process of selection, retaining what is important and omitting what is not; but with the recollections retained from childhood this is not so. They do not necessarily reflect important experiences in childhood, not even such as must have seemed important from the child's standpoint, but are often so banal and meaningless in themselves that we can only ask ourselves in amazement why just this particular detail has escaped oblivion. I have tried, with the help of analysis, to attack the problem of childhood amnesia and of the fragments of recollection which break through it, and have come to the conclusion that, whatever may appear to the contrary, the child no less than the adult only retains in memory what is important; but that what is important is represented (by the processes of condensation and, more especially, of displacement, already familiar to you) in the memory by something apparently trivial. For this reason I have called these childhood recollections *screen-memories;* a thorough analysis can evolve from them all that has been forgotten.

It is a regular task in psycho-analytic treatment to fill in the blank in infantile memories, and, in so far as the treatment is successful to any extent at all (very frequently, therefore) we are enabled to bring to light the content of those early years long buried in oblivion. These impressions have never really been forgotten, but were only inaccessible and latent, having become part of the unconscious. But sometimes it happens that they emerge spontaneously from the unconscious, and it is in connection with dreams that this happens. It is clear that the dream-life knows the way back to these latent, infantile experiences. Many good illustrations of this are to be found in psychoanalytical literature, and I myself have been able to furnish a contribution of the sort. I once dreamt in a particular connection of someone who had evidently done me a service and whom I saw plainly. He was a one-eyed man, short, fat and high-shouldered; from the context I gathered that he was a doctor. Fortunately I was able to ask my mother, who was still living, what was the personal appearance of the doctor who attended us at the place where I was born and which I left at the age of three; she told me that he had only one eye and was short, fat and high-shouldered; I learnt also of the accident which was the occasion of this doctor's being called in and which I had forgotten. This command of the forgotten material of the earliest years of childhood is thus a further 'archaic' feature of dreams.

This knowledge has a bearing on another of the problems which up to the present have proved insoluble. You will re-

member the astonishment caused by our discovery that dreams
have their origin in actively evil or in excessive sexual desires,
which have made both the dream-censorship and dream-distortion necessary. Supposing now that we have interpreted a
dream of this sort, and the circumstances are specially favourable in that the dreamer does not quarrel with the interpretation itself, he does nevertheless invariably ask how any such
wish could come into his mind, since it seems quite foreign
to him and he is conscious of desiring the exact opposite. We
need have no hesitation in pointing out to him the origin of
the wish he repudiates: these evil impulses may be traced to
the past, often indeed to a past which is not so very far away.
It may be demonstrated that he once knew and was conscious
of them, even if this is no longer so. A woman who had a
dream meaning that she wished to see her only daughter (then
seventeen years old) lying dead found, with our help, that at
one time she actually had cherished this death-wish. The child
was the offspring of an unhappy marriage, which ended in
the speedy separation of husband and wife. Once when the
child was as yet unborn the mother, in an access of rage after
a violent scene with her husband, beat her body with her
clenched fists in order to kill the baby in her womb. How
many mothers who to-day love their children tenderly, perhaps with excessive tenderness, yet conceived them unwillingly and wished that the life within them might not develop
further; and have indeed turned this wish into various actions,
fortunately of a harmless kind. The later death-wish against
beloved persons, which appears so puzzling, thus dates from
the early days of the relationship to them.

A father, whose dream when interpreted shows that he
wished for the death of his eldest and favourite child, is in
the same way obliged to recall that there was a time when
this wish was not unknown to him. The man, whose marriage
had proved a disappointment, often thought when the child
was still an infant that if the little creature who meant nothing
to him were to die he would again be free and would make
better use of his freedom. A large number of similar impulses
of hate are to be traced to a similar source; they are recollec-

tions of something belonging to the past, something which was once in consciousness and played its part in mental life. From this you will be inclined to draw the conclusion that such dreams and such wishes would not occur in cases where there have been no changes of this sort in the relations between two persons, that is to say, where the relation has been of the same character from the beginning. I am prepared to grant you this conclusion, only I must warn you that you have to consider, not the literal meaning of the dream, but what it signifies on interpretation. It may be that the manifest dream of the death of some beloved person was only using this as a terrible mask, whilst really meaning something totally different, or it is possible that the beloved person is an illusory substitute for someone else.

This situation will, however, raise in you another and much more serious question. You will say: "Even though this death-wish did at one time actually exist and this is confirmed by recollection, that is still no true explanation; for the desire has long since been overcome and surely at the present time can exist in the unconscious merely as a recollection, of no affective value, and not as a powerful exciting agent. For this later assumption we have no evidence. Why is the wish recollected at all in dreams?" This is a question which you are really justified in asking; the attempt to answer it would take us far afield and would oblige us to define our position with regard to one of the most important points in the theory of dreams. But I must keep within the limits of our discussion and must forbear to follow up this question; so you must be reconciled to leaving it for the present. Let us content ourselves with the actual evidence that this wish, long since subdued, can be proved to have given rise to the dream, and let us continue our enquiry whether other evil wishes also can be traced in the same way to the past.

Let us keep to the death-wishes, which we shall certainly find mostly derived from the unbounded egoism of the dreamer. Wishes of this sort are very often found to be the underlying agents of dreams. Whenever anyone gets in our way in life—and how often must this happen when our relations to one another are so complicated!—a dream is immediately prepared to make away with that person, even if it be father, mother, brother or sister, husband or wife. It appeared to us amazing that such wickedness should be innate in humanity, and certainly we were not inclined to admit without further evidence that this result of our interpretation of dreams was correct. But, when once we had seen that the origin of wishes of this sort must be looked for in the past, we had little difficulty in finding the period in the past of the individual in which there is nothing strange in such egoism and such wishes, even when directed against the nearest and dearest. A child in his earliest years (which later are veiled in oblivion) is just the person who frequently displays such egoism in boldest relief; invariably, unmistakable tendencies of this kind, or, more accurately, surviving traces of them, are plainly visible in him. For a child loves himself first and only later learns to love others and to sacrifice something of his own ego to them. Even the people whom he seems to love from the outset are loved in the first instance because he needs them and cannot do without them—again therefore, from motives of egoism. Only later does the impulse of love detach itself from egoism: it is a literal fact that the child learns how to love through his own egoism.

In this connection it will be instructive to compare a child's attitude towards his brothers and sisters with his attitude towards his parents. The little child does not necessarily love his brothers and sisters, and often he is quite frank about it. It is unquestionable that in them he sees and hates his rivals, and it is well known how commonly this attitude persists without interruption for many years, till the child reaches maturity and even later. Of course it often gives place to a more tender feeling, or perhaps we should say it is overlaid by this, but the hostile attitude seems very generally to be the earlier. We can most easily observe it in children of two and a half to four years old when a new baby arrives, which generally meets with a very unfriendly reception; remarks such as "I don't like it. The stork is to take it away again" are very common. Subsequently every opportunity is seized to disparage the new-comer; attempts are even made to injure it and actual attacks upon it are by no means unheard-of. If the difference in age is less, by the time the child's mental activity is more fully developed the rival is already in existence and he adapts himself to the situation; if on the other hand there is a greater difference between their ages, the new baby may rouse certain kindly feelings from the first, as an object of interest, a sort of living doll; and when there is as much as eight years or more between them, especially if the elder child is a girl, protective, motherly impulses may at once come into play. But, speaking honestly, when we find a wish for the death of a brother or a sister latent in a dream we need seldom be puzzled, for we find its origin in early childhood without much trouble, or indeed, quite often in the later years when they still lived together.

There is probably no nursery without violent conflicts between the inhabitants, actuated by rivalry for the love of the parents, competition for possessions shared by them all, even for the actual space in the room they occupy. Such hostility is directed against older as well as younger brothers and sisters. I think it was Bernard Shaw who said: "If there is anyone whom a young English lady hates more than her mother it is her elder sister." Now there is something in this dictum which jars upon us; it is hard enough to bring ourselves to understand hatred and rivalry between brothers and sisters, but how can feelings of hate force themselves into the relation between mother and daughter, parents and children?

This relationship is no doubt a more favourable one, also from the children's point of view; and this too is what our expectations require: we find it far more offensive for love to be lacking between parents and children than between brothers and sisters. We have, so to speak, sanctified the former love while allowing the latter to remain profane. Yet everyday observation may show us how frequently the sentiments entertained towards each other by parents and grown-up children fall short of the ideal set up by society, and how much hostility lies smouldering, ready to burst into flame if it were not stifled by considerations of filial or parental duty and by other, tender impulses. The motives for this hostility are well known, and we recognize a tendency for those of the same sex to become alienated, daughter from mother and father from son. The daughter sees in her mother the authority which imposes limits to her will, whose task it is to bring her to that renunciation of sexual freedom which society demands; in certain cases, too, the mother is still a rival, who objects to being set aside. The same thing is repeated still more blatantly between father and son. To the son the father is the embodiment of the social compulsion to which he so unwillingly submits, the person who stands in the way of his following his own will, of his early sexual pleasures and, when there is family property, of his enjoyment of it. When a throne is involved this impatience for the death of the father may approach tragic intensity. The relation between father and daughter or mother and son would seem less liable to disaster; the latter relation furnishes the purest examples of unchanging tenderness, undisturbed by any egoistic consideration.

Why, you ask, do I speak of things so banal and so well-known to everybody? Because there exists an unmistakable tendency in people's minds to deny the significance of these things in real life and to pretend that the social ideal is much more frequently realized than it actually is. But it is better that psychology should tell the truth than that it should be left to cynics to do so. This general denial is only applied to real life, it is true; for fiction and drama are free to make use of the motives laid bare when these ideals are rudely disturbed.

There is nothing to wonder at therefore if the dreams of a great number of people bring to light the wish for the removal of their parents, especially of the parent whose sex is the same as the dreamer's. We may assume that the wish exists in waking life as well, sometimes even in consciousness if it can disguise itself behind another motive, as the dreamer in our third example disguised his real thought by pity for his father's useless suffering. It is but rarely that hostility reigns alone,—far more often it yields to more tender feelings which finally suppress it, when it has to wait in abeyance till a dream shows it, as it were, in isolation. That which the dream shows in a form magnified by this very isolation resumes its true proportions when our interpretation has assigned to it its proper place in relation to the rest of the dreamer's life. (H. Sachs.) But we also find this death-wish where there is no basis for it in real life and where the adult would never have to confess to entertaining it in his waking life. The reason for this is that the deepest and most common motive for estrangement, especially between parent and child of the same sex, came into play in the earliest years of childhood.

I refer to that rivalry of affections in which sexual elements are plainly emphasized. The son, when quite a little child, already begins to develop a peculiar tenderness towards his mother, whom he looks upon as his own property, regarding his father in the light of a rival who disputes this sole possession of his; similarly the little daughter sees in her mother someone who disturbs her tender relation to her father and occupies a place which she feels she herself could very well fill. Observation shows us how far back these sentiments date, sentiments which we describe by the term *Oedipus complex*, because in the Oedipus myth the two extreme forms of the wishes arising from the situation of the son—the wish to kill the father and to marry the mother—are realized in an only slightly modified form. I do not assert that the Oedipus complex exhausts all the possible relations which may exist between parents and children; these relations may well be a great deal more complicated. Again, this complex may be more or less strongly developed, or it may even become inverted, but it is a regular and very important factor in the mental life of the child; we are more in danger of underestimating than of overestimating its influence and that of the developments which may follow from it. Moreover, the parents themselves frequently stimulate the children to react with an Oedipus complex, for parents are often guided in their preferences by the difference in sex of their children, so that the father favours the daughter and the mother the son; or else, where conjugal love has grown cold, the child may be taken as a substitute for the love-object which has ceased to attract.

It cannot be said that the world has shown great gratitude to psychoanalytic research for the discovery of the Oedipus complex; on the contrary, the idea has excited the most violent opposition in grown-up people; and those who omitted to join in denying the existence of sentiments so universally reprehended and tabooed have later made up for this by proffering interpretations so wide of the mark as to rob the complex of its value. My own unchanged conviction is that there is nothing in it to deny or to gloss over. We ought to reconcile ourselves to facts in which the Greek myth itself saw the hand of inexorable destiny. Again, it is interesting to find that the Oedipus complex, repudiated in actual life and relegated to fiction, has there come to its own. O. Rank in a careful study of this theme has shown how this very complex has supplied dramatic poetry with an abundance of motives in countless variations, modifications and disguises, in short, subject to just the distortion familiar to us in the work of the dream-censorship. So we may look for the Oedipus complex even in those dreamers who have been fortunate enough to escape conflicts with their parents in later life; and closely connected with this we shall find what is termed the *castration complex*, the reaction to that intimidation in the field of sex or to that restraint of early infantile sexual activity which is ascribed to the father.

What we have already ascertained has guided us to the study of the child's mental life, and we may now hope to find in a similar way an explanation of the source of the other kind of prohibited wishes in dreams, i.e. the excessive sexual desires. We are impelled therefore to study the development of the sexual life of the child, and here from various sources we learn the following facts. In the first place, it is an untenable fallacy to suppose that the child has no sexual life and to assume that sexuality first makes its appearance at puberty, when the genital organs come to maturity. On the contrary he has from the very beginning a sexual life rich in content,

thought it differs in many points from that which later is regarded as normal. What in adult life are termed "perversions"
depart from the normal in the following respects: (1) in a
disregard for the barriers of species (the gulf between man
and beast), (2) in the insensibility to barriers imposed by disgust, (3) in the transgression of the incest-barrier (the prohibition against seeking sexual gratification with close blood-
relations), (4) in homosexuality and, (5) in the transferring
of the part played by the genital organs to other organs and
different areas of the body. All these barriers are not in existence from the outset, but are only gradually built up in the
course of development and education. The little child is free
from them: he does not perceive any immense gulf between
man and beast, the arrogance with which man separates himself from the other animals only dawns in him at a later period.
He shows at the beginning of life no disgust for excrement,
but only learns this feeling slowly under the influence of education; he attaches no particular importance to the difference
between the sexes, in fact he thinks that both have the same
formation of the genital organs; he directs his earliest sexual
desires and his curiosity to those nearest to him or to those
who for other reasons are specially beloved—his parents,
brothers and sisters or nurses; and finally we see in him a
characteristic which manifests itself again later at the height
of some love-relationship—namely, he does not look for gratification in the sexual organs only, but discovers that many other
parts of the body possess the same sort of sensibility and can
yield analogous pleasurable sensations, playing thereby the
part of genital organs. The child may be said then to be
polymorphously perverse, and even if mere traces of all these
impulses are found in him, this is due on the one hand to their
lesser intensity as compared with that which they assume in
later life and, on the other hand, to the fact that education
immediately and energetically suppresses all sexual manifestations in the child. This suppression may be said to be embodied in a theory; for grown-up people endeavour to overlook some of these manifestations, and, by misinterpretation,
to rob others of their sexual nature, until in the end the whole

thing can be altogether denied. It is often the same people who first inveigh against the sexual "naughtiness" of children in the nursery and then sit down to their writing-tables to defend the sexual purity of the same children. When they are left to themselves or when they are seduced children often display perverse sexual activity to a really remarkable extent. Of course grown-up people are right in not taking this too seriously and in regarding it, as they say, as "childish tricks" and "play," for the child cannot be judged either by a moral or legal code as if he were mature and fully responsible; nevertheless these things do exist, and they have their significance both as evidence of innate constitutional tendencies and inasmuch as they cause and foster later developments: they give us an insight into the child's sexual life and so into that of humanity as a whole. If then we find all these perverse wishes behind the distortions of our dreams, it only means that dreams in *this respect also* have regressed completely to the infantile condition.

Amongst these forbidden wishes special prominence must still be given to the incestuous desires, i.e. those directed towards sexual intercourse with parents or brothers and sisters. You know in what abhorrence human society holds, or at least professes to hold, such intercourse, and what emphasis is laid upon the prohibitions of it. The most preposterous attempts have been made to account for this horror of incest: some people have assumed that it is a provision of nature for the preservation of the species, manifesting itself in the mind by these prohibitions because in-breeding would result in racial degeneration; others have asserted that propinquity from early childhood has deflected sexual desire from the persons concerned. In both these cases, however, the avoidance of incest would have been automatically secured and we should be at a loss to understand the necessity for stern prohibitions, which would seem rather to point to a strong desire. Psychoanalytic investigations have shown beyond the possibility of doubt that *an incestuous love-choice* is in fact the first and the regular one, and that it is only later that any opposition is manifested towards it, the causes of which are not to be sought in the psychology of the individual.

Let us sum up the results which our excursions into child-psychology have brought to the understanding of dreams. We have learnt not only that the material of the forgotten childish experiences is accessible to the dream, but also that the child's mental life, with all its peculiarities, its egoism, its incestuous object-choice, persists in it and therefore in the unconscious, and that our dreams take us back every night to this infantile stage. This corroborates the belief that *the Unconscious is the infantile mental life,* and, with this, the objectionable impression that so much evil lurks in human nature grows somewhat less. For this terrible evil is simply what is original, primitive and infantile in mental life, what we find in operation in the child, but in part overlook in him because it is on so small a scale, and in part do not take greatly to heart because we do not demand a high ethical standard in a child. By regressing to this infantile stage our dreams appear to have brought the evil in us to light, but the appearance is deceptive, though we have let ourselves be dismayed by it; we are not so evil as the interpretation of our dreams would lead us to suppose.

If the evil impulses of our dreams are merely infantile, a re-version to the beginnings of our ethical development, the dream simply making us children again in thought and feel-ing, it is surely not reasonable to be ashamed of these evil dreams. But the reasoning faculty is only part of our mental life; there is much in it besides which is not reasonable, and so it happens that, although it is unreasonable, we neverthe-less are ashamed of such dreams. We subject them to the dream-censorship and are ashamed and indignant when one of these wishes by way of exception penetrates our conscious-ness in a form so undisguised that we cannot fail to recognize it; yes, we even at times feel just as much ashamed of a dis-torted dream as if we really understood it. Just think of the outraged comment of the respectable elderly lady upon her dream about "love service," although it was not interpreted to her. So the problem is not yet solved, and it is still possible that if we pursue this question of the evil in dreams we may arrive at another conclusion and another estimate of human nature.

Our whole enquiry has led to two results which, however, merely indicate the beginning of new problems and new doubts. In the first place: the regression in dreams is one not only of form but of substance. Not only does it translate our thoughts into a primitive form of expression, but it also re-awakens the peculiarities of our primitive mental life—the old supremacy of the ego, the initial impulses of our sexual life, even restores to us our old intellectual possession if we may conceive of symbolism in this way. And secondly: all these old infantile characteristics, which were once dominant and solely dominant, must to-day be accounted to the unconscious and must alter and extend our views about it. "Unconscious" is no longer a term for what is temporarily latent: the unconscious is a special realm, with its own desires and modes of expression and peculiar mental mechanisms not elsewhere operative. Yet the latent dream-thoughts disclosed by our interpretation do not belong to this realm; rather they correspond to the kind of thoughts we have in waking life also. And yet they are unconscious: how is the paradox to be resolved? We begin to realize that here we must discriminate. Something which has its origin in our conscious life and shares its characteristics—we call it the "residue" from the previous day—meets together with something from the realm of the unconscious in the formation of a dream, and it is between these two regions that the dream-work is accomplished. The influence of the unconscious impinging upon this residue probably constitutes the condition for regression. This is the deepest insight into the nature of dreams possible to us until we have explored further fields in the mind; but soon it will be time to give another name to the unconscious character of the latent dream-thoughts, in order to distinguish it from that unconscious material which has its origin in the province of the infantile.

We can of course also ask: What is it that forces our mental activity during sleep to such regression? Why cannot the mental stimuli that disturb sleep be dealt with without it? And if on account of the dream-censorship the mental activity has to disguise itself in the old, and now incomprehensible, form of expression, what is the object of re-animating the old impulses, desires and characteristics, now surmounted; what, in short, is the use of *regression in substance* as well as in *form?* The only satisfactory answer would be that this is the one possible way in which dreams can be formed, that, dynamically considered, the relief from the stimulus giving rise to the dream cannot otherwise be accomplished. But this is an answer for which, at present, we have no justification.

FOURTEENTH LECTURE

WISH-FULFILMENT

SHALL I REMIND YOU ONCE MORE OF THE STEPS BY WHICH WE have arrived at our present position? When in applying our technique we came upon the distortion in dreams, we made up our minds to avoid it for the moment and turned to the study of infantile dreams for some definite information about the nature of dreams in general. Next, equipped with the results of this investigation, we attacked the question of dream-distortion directly, and I hope that bit by bit we have also mastered that. Now, however, we are bound to admit that our findings in these two directions do not exactly tally, and it behoves us to combine and correlate our results.

Both enquiries have made it plain that the essential feature in the dream-work is the transformation of thoughts into hallucinatory experience. It is puzzling enough to see how this process is accomplished, but this is a problem for general psychology, and we have not to deal with it here. We have learnt from children's dreams that the object of the dream-work is to remove, by means of the fulfilment of some wish, a mental stimulus which is disturbing sleep. We could make no similar pronouncement with regard to distorted dreams until we understood how to interpret them, but from the outset we expected to be able to bring our ideas about them into line with our views on infantile dreams. This expectation was for the first time fulfilled when we recognized that all dreams are really children's dreams; that they make use of infantile material and are characterized by impulses and mechanisms which belong to the childish mind. When we feel we have mastered the distortion in dreams we must go on to find out whether the notion that dreams are WISH-FULFILMENTS holds good of distorted dreams also.

We have just subjected a series of dreams to interpretation, but without taking the question of wish-fulfilment into consideration at all. I feel certain that while we were talking about them the question repeatedly forced itself upon you: "What has become of the wish-fulfilment which is supposed to be the object of the dream-work?" Now this question is important, for it is the one which our lay critics are constantly asking. As you know, mankind has an instinctive antipathy to intellectual novelties; one of the ways in which this shows itself is that any such novelty is immediately reduced to its very smallest compass, and if possible embodied in some catch-word. "Wish-fulfilment" has become the catch-word for the new theory of dreams. Directly they hear that dreams are said to be wish-fulfilments, the laity asks: "Where does the wish-fulfilment come in?" and their asking the question amounts to a repudiation of the idea. They can immediately think of countless dreams of their own which were accompanied by feeling so unpleasant as sometimes to reach the point of agonizing dread; and so this statement of the psycho-analytical theory of dreams appears to them highly improbable. It is easy to reply that in distorted dreams the wish-fulfilment is not openly expressed, but has to be looked for, so that it cannot be shown until the dreams have been interpreted. We know too that the wishes underlying these distorted dreams are those which are prohibited and rejected by the censorship, and that it is just their existence which is the cause of distortion and the motive for the intervention of the censorship. But it is difficult to make the lay critic understand that we must not ask about the wish-fulfilment in a dream before it has been interpreted; he always forgets this. His reluctance to accept the theory of wish-fulfilment is really nothing but the effect of the dream-censorship, causing him to replace the real thought by a substitute, and following from his repudiation of these censored dream-wishes.

Of course we ourselves must feel the need to explain why so many dreams are painful in content; and in particular we shall want to know how we come to have 'anxiety-dreams.' Here for the first time we are confronted with the problem of the affects in dreams; a problem which deserves special study, but one which we cannot concern ourselves with just now, unfortunately. If the dream is a wish-fulfilment, it should be impossible for any painful emotions to come into it: on this point the lay critics seem to be right. But the matter is complicated by three considerations which they have overlooked.

First, it may happen that the dream-work is not wholly successful in creating a wish-fulfilment, so that part of the painful feeling in the latent thoughts is carried over into the manifest dream. Analysis would then have to show that these thoughts were a great deal more painful than the dream which is formed from them; this much can be proved in every instance. We admit then that the dream-work has failed in its purpose, just as a dream of drinking excited by the stimulus of thirst fails to quench that thirst. One is still thirsty after it and has to wake up and drink. Nevertheless, it is a proper dream: it has renounced nothing of its essential nature. We must say: "Ut desint vires, tamen est laudanda voluntas." The clearly recognizable intention remains a praiseworthy one, at any rate. Such instances of failure in the work are by no means rare, and one reason is that it is so much more difficult for the dream-work to produce the required change in the nature of the affect than to modify the content; affects are often very intractable. So it happens that in the process of the dream-work the painful *content* of the dream-thoughts is transformed into a wish-fulfilment while the painful *affect* persists unchanged. When this occurs the affect is quite out of harmony with the content, which gives our critics the opportunity of remarking that the dream is so far from being a wish-fulfilment that even a harmless content may be accompanied in it by painful feelings. Our answer to this rather unintelligent comment will be that it is just in dreams of this sort that the wish-fulfilling tendency of the dream-work is most apparent, because it is there seen in isolation. The mistake in this criticism arises because people who are not familiar with the neuroses imagine a more intimate connection between content and affect than actually exists, and so cannot understand that there may be an alteration in the content while the accompanying affect remains unchanged.

A second consideration, much more important and far-reaching but equally overlooked by the laity, is the following. A wish-fulfilment must certainly bring some pleasure; but we go on to ask: "To whom?" Of course to the person who has the wish. But we know that the attitude of the dreamer towards his wishes is a peculiar one: he rejects them, censors them, in short, he will have none of them. Their fulfilment then can afford him no pleasure, rather the opposite, and here experience shows that this "opposite," which has still to be explained, takes the form of *anxiety*. The dreamer, where his wishes are concerned, is like two separate people closely linked together by some important thing in common. Instead of enlarging upon this I will remind you of a well-known fairy-tale in which you will see these relationships repeated. A good fairy promised a poor man and his wife to fulfil their first three wishes. They were delighted and made up their minds to choose the wishes carefully. But the woman was tempted by the smell of some sausages being cooked in the next cottage and wished for two like them. Lo! and behold, there they were—and the first wish was fulfilled. With that, the man lost his temper and in his resentment wished that the sausages might hang on the tip of his wife's nose. This also came to pass, and the sausages could not be removed from their position; so the second wish was fulfilled, but it was the man's wish and its fulfilment was most unpleasant for the woman. You know the rest of the story: as they were after all man and wife, the third wish had to be that the sausages should come off the end of the woman's nose. We might make use of this fairy-tale many times over in other contexts, but here it need only serve to illustrate the fact that it is possible for the fulfilment of one person's wish to be very disagreeable to someone else, unless the two people are entirely at one.

It will not be difficult now to arrive at a still better understanding of anxiety-dreams. There is just one more observation to be made use of and then we may adopt an hypothesis which is supported by several considerations. The observation is that anxiety-dreams often have a content in which there is no distortion; it has, so to speak, escaped the censorship. This type of dream is frequently an undisguised wish-fulfilment, the wish being of course not one which the dreamer would accept but one which he has rejected; anxiety has developed in place of the working of the censorship. Whereas the infantile dream is an open fulfilment of a wish admitted by the dreamer, and the ordinary distorted dream is the disguised fulfilment of a repressed wish, the formula for the anxiety-dream is that it is the open fulfilment of a repressed wish. Anxiety is an indication that the repressed wish has proved too strong for the censorship and has accomplished or was about to accomplish its fulfilment in spite of it. We can understand that fulfilment of a repressed wish can only be, for us who are on the side of the censorship, an occasion for painful emotions and for setting up a defence. The anxiety then manifested in our dreams is, if you like to put it so, anxiety experienced because of the strength of wishes which at other times we manage to stifle. The study of dreams alone does not reveal to us why this defence takes the form of anxiety; obviously we must consider the latter in other connections.

The hypothesis which holds good for anxiety-dreams without any distortion may be adopted also for those which have undergone some degree of distortion, and for other kinds of unpleasant dreams in which the accompanying unpleasant feelings probably approximate to anxiety. Anxiety-dreams generally wake us; we usually break off our sleep before the repressed wish behind the dream overcomes the censorship and reaches complete fulfilment. In such a case the dream has failed to achieve its purpose, but its essential character is not thereby altered. We have compared the dream with a night-watchman, a guardian of sleep, whose purpose it is to protect sleep from interruption. Now night-watchmen also, just like dreams, have to rouse sleepers when they are not strong enough to ward off the cause of disturbance or danger alone. Nevertheless we do sometimes succeed in continuing to sleep even when our dreams begin to give us some uneasiness and to turn to anxiety. We say to ourselves in sleep: "It is only a dream after all," and go on sleeping.

You may ask *when* it happens that the dream-wish is able to overcome the censorship. This may depend either on the wish or on the censorship: it may be that for unknown reasons the strength of the wish at times becomes excessive; but our impression is that it is more often the attitude of the censorship which is responsible for this shifting in the balance of power. We have already heard that the censorship works with varying intensity in each individual instance, treating the different elements with different degrees of strictness; now we may add that it is very variable in its general behaviour and does not show itself always equally severe towards the same element. If then it chances that the censorship feels itself for once powerless against some dream-wish which threatens to overthrow it, it then, instead of making use of distortion, employs the last weapon left to it and destroys sleep by bringing about an access of anxiety.

At this point it strikes us that we still have no idea why these evil, rejected wishes rise up just at night-time, so as to disturb us when we sleep. The answer can hardly be found except in another hypothesis which goes back to the nature of sleep itself. During the day the heavy pressure of a censorship is exercised upon these wishes and, as a rule, it is impossible for them to make themselves felt at all. But in the night it is probable that this censorship, like all the other interests of mental life, is suspended, or at least very much weakened, in favour of the single desire for sleep. So it is due to this partial abrogation of the censorship at night that the forbidden wishes can again become active. There are nervous people suffering from insomnia who confess that their sleeplessness was voluntary in the first instance; for they did not dare to go to sleep because they were afraid of their dreams—that is to say, they feared the consequences of the diminished vigilance of the censorship. You will have no difficulty in understanding that this curtailment of the censorship does not argue any flagrant carelessness: sleep impairs our motor functions; even if our evil intentions do begin to stir within us the utmost they can do is to produce a dream, which is for all practical purposes harmless; and it is this comforting circumstance which gives rise to the sleeper's remark, made, it is true, in the night but yet not part of his dream-life: "It is only a dream." So we let it have its way and continue to sleep.

Thirdly, if you call to mind our idea that the dreamer striving against his own wishes is like a combination of two persons, separate and yet somehow intimately united, you will be able to understand another possible way in which something that is highly unpleasant may be brought about through wish-fulfilment: I am speaking of punishment. Here again the fairy-tale of the three wishes may help to make things clear. The sausages on the plate were the direct fulfilment of the first person's (the woman's) wish; the sausages on the tip of her nose were the fulfilment of the second person's (the husband's) wish, but at the same time they were the punishment for the foolish wish of the wife. In the neuroses we shall meet with wishes corresponding in motivation to the third wish of the fairy-tale, the only one left. There are many such punishment tendencies in the mental life of man; they are very strong and we may well regard them as responsible for some of our painful dreams. Now you will probably think that with all this there is very little of the famous wish-fulfilment left; but on closer consideration you will admit that you are wrong. In comparison with the manifold possibilities (to be discussed later) of what dreams might be—according to some writers, what they actually are—the solution: wish-fulfilment, anxiety-fulfilment, punishment-fulfilment, is surely quite a narrow one. Add to this, that anxiety is the direct opposite of a wish and that opposites lie very near one another in association and, as we have learned, actually coincide in the unconscious. Moreover, punishment itself is the fulfilment of a wish, namely, the wish of the other, censoring person.

On the whole then, I have made no concession to your objections to the wish-fulfilment theory; we are bound, however, to demonstrate its presence in any and every distorted dream, and we have certainly no desire to shirk this task. Let us go back to the dream we have already interpreted, about the three bad theatre tickets for one florin and a half, from which we have already learnt a good deal. I hope you still remember it: A lady, whose husband told her one day about the engagement of her friend Elise who was only three months younger than herself, dreamt on the following night that she and her husband were at the theatre and that one side of the stalls was almost empty. Her husband told her that Elise and her fiancé had wanted to go to the theatre too; but could not, because they could only get such bad seats, three tickets for a florin and a half. His wife said that they had not lost much by it. We discovered that the dream-thoughts had to do with her vexation at having been in such a hurry to marry and her dissatifaction with her husband. We may well be curious how these gloomy thoughts can have been transformed into a wish-fulfilment, and what trace of it can be found in the manifest content. Now we know already that the element "too soon, too great a hurry," was eliminated by the censorship; the empty stalls are an allusion to this element. The puzzling phrase *three for one florin and a half* is now more comprehensible to us than at first, through the knowledge of symbolism that we have acquired since then.[1] The number *three* really stands for a man and we can easily translate the manifest element to mean: "to buy a man (husband) with the dowry." ("I could have bought one ten times better for my dowry.") *Going to the theatre* obviously stands for marriage. *Getting the tickets too soon* is in fact a direct substitute for "marrying too soon." Now this substitution is the work of the wish-fulfilment. The dreamer had not always felt so dissatisfied with her premature marriage as she was on the day when she heard of her friend's

[1] Another interpretation of the number *three*, occurring in the dream of this childless woman, lies very close; but I will not mention it here, because this analysis did not furnish any material illustrating it.

engagement. She had been proud of her marriage at the time and considered herself more highly favoured than her friend. One hears that naïve girls, on becoming engaged, frequently express their delight at the idea that they will now soon be able to go to all plays and see everything hitherto forbidden them.

The indication of curiosity and a desire to "look on" evinced here comes, without doubt, originally from the sexual 'gazing impulse,' especially regarding the parents, and this became a strong motive impelling the girl to marry early; in this manner going to the theatre became an obvious allusive substitute for getting married. In her vexation at the present time on account of her premature marriage she therefore reverted to the time when this same marriage fulfilled a wish, by gratifying her skoptophilia; and so, guided by this old wish-impulse, she replaced the idea of marriage by that of going to the theatre.

We may say that the example we have chosen to demonstrate a hidden wish-fulfilment is not the most convenient one, but in all other distorted dreams we should have to proceed in a manner analogous to that employed above. It is not possible for me to do this here and now, so I will merely express my conviction that such procedure will invariably meet with success. But I wish to dwell longer upon this point in our theory: experience has taught me that it is one of the most perilous of the whole theory of dreams, exposed to many contradictions and misunderstandings. Besides, you are perhaps still under the impression that I have already retracted part of my statement by saying that the dream may be either a wish-fulfilment, or its opposite, an anxiety or a punishment, brought to actuality; and you may think this a good opportunity to force me to make further reservations. Also I have been reproached with presenting facts that seem obvious to myself in a manner too condensed to carry conviction.

When anyone has gone as far as this in dream-interpretation and has accepted all our conclusions up to this point, it often happens that he comes to a standstill at this question of wish-fulfilment and asks: "Admitting that every dream means something and that this meaning may be discovered by employing the technique of psychoanalysis, why must it always, in face of all the evidence to the contrary, be forced into the formula of wish-fulfilment? Why must our thoughts at night be any less many-sided than our thoughts by day; so that at one time a dream might be a fulfilment of some wish, at another time, as you say yourself, the opposite, the actualization of a dread; or, again, the expression of a resolution, a warning, a weighing of some problem with its pros and cons, or a reproof, some prick of conscience, or an attempt to prepare oneself for something which has to be done—and so forth? Why this perpetual insistence upon a wish or, at the most, its opposite?"

It might be supposed that a difference of opinion on this point is a matter of no great moment, if there is agreement on all others. Cannot we be satisfied with having discovered the meaning of dreams and the ways by which we can find out the meaning? We surely go back on the advance we have made if we try to limit this meaning too strictly. But this is not so. A misunderstanding on this head touches what is essential to our knowledge of dreams and imperils its value for the understanding of neuroses. Moreover, that readiness to "oblige the other party" which has its value in business life is not only out of place but actually harmful in scientific matters.

My first answer to the question why dreams should not be many-sided in their meaning is the usual one in such a case: I do not know why they should not be so, and should have no objection if they were. As far as I am concerned, they can be so! But there is just one trifling obstacle in the way of this wider and more convenient conception of dreams—that as a matter of fact they are not so. My second answer would emphasize the point that to assume that dreams represent manifold modes of thought and intellectual operations is by no means a novel idea to myself: once, in the history of a pathological case, I recorded a dream which occurred three nights running and never again; and gave it as my explanation that this dream corresponded to a resolution, the repetition of which became unnecessary as soon as that resolution was carried out. Later on, I published a dream which represented a confession. How is it possible for me then to contradict myself and assert that dreams are always and only wish-fulfilments?

I do it rather than permit a stupid misunderstanding which might cost us the fruit of all our labours on the subject of dreams; a misunderstanding that *confounds the dream with the latent dream-thoughts,* and makes statements with regard to the former which are applicable to the *latter and to the latter only.* For it is perfectly true that dreams can represent, and be themselves replaced by, all the modes of thought just enumerated: resolutions, warnings, reflections, preparations or attempts to solve some problem in regard to conduct, and so on. But when you look closely, you will recognize that all this is true only of the latent thoughts which have been transformed into the dream. You learn from interpretations of dreams that the unconscious thought-processes of mankind are occupied with such resolutions, preparations and reflections, out of which dreams are formed by means of the dream-work. If your interest at any given moment is not so much in the dream-work, but centres on the unconscious thought-processes in people, you will then eliminate the dream-formation and say of dreams themselves, what is for all practical purposes correct, that they represent a warning, a resolve, and so on. This is what is often done in psychoanalytic work: generally we endeavour simply to demolish the manifest form of dreams and to substitute for it the corresponding latent thoughts in which the dream originated.

Thus it is that we learn quite incidentally from our attempt to assess the latent dream-thoughts that all the highly complicated mental acts we have enumerated can be performed unconsciously—a conclusion surely as tremendous as it is bewildering.

But to go back a little: you are quite right in speaking of dreams as representing these various modes of thought, provided that you are quite clear in your own minds that you are using an abbreviated form of expression and do not imagine that the manifold variety of which you speak is in itself part of the essential nature of *dreams.* When you speak of "a dream" you must mean either the manifest dream, i.e. the product of the dream-work, or at most that work itself, i.e. the mental process which forms the latent dream-thoughts into the manifest dream. To use the word in any other sense is a confusion of ideas which is bound to be mischievous. If what you say is meant to apply to the latent thoughts behind the dream, then say so plainly, and do not add to the obscurity of the problem by your loose way of expressing yourselves. The latent dream-thoughts are the material which is transformed by the dream-work into the manifest dream. What makes you constantly confound the material with the process which deals with it? If you do that, in what way are you superior to those who know of the final product only, without being able to explain where it comes from or how it is constructed?

The only thing essential to the dream itself is the dreamwork which has operated upon the thought-material; and when we come to theory we have no right to disregard this, even if in certain practical situations it may be neglected. Further, analytic observation shows that the dream-work never consists merely in translating the latent thoughts into the archaic or regressive forms of expression described. On the contrary, something is invariably added which does not belong to the latent thoughts of the day-time, but which is the actual motive force in dream-formation; this indispensable component being the equally unconscious *wish*, to fulfil which the content of the dream is transformed. In so far, then, as you are considering only the thoughts represented in it, the dream may be any conceivable thing—a warning, a resolve, a preparation, and so on; but besides this, it itself is always the fulfilment of an unconscious wish, and, when you regard it as the result of the dream-work, it is this alone. A dream then is never simply the expression of a resolve or warning, and nothing more: in it the resolve, or whatever it may be, is translated into the archaic form with the assistance of an unconscious wish, and metamorphosed in such a way as to be a fulfilment of that wish. This single characteristic, that of fulfilling a wish, is the constant one: the other component varies it may indeed itself be a wish; in which event the dream represents the fulfilment of a latent wish from our waking hours brought about by the aid of an unconscious wish.

Now all this is quite clear to myself, but I do not know whether I have succeeded in making it equally clear to you; and it is difficult to prove it to you; for, on the one hand, proof requires the evidence afforded by a careful analysis of many dreams and, on the other hand, this, the crucial and most important point in our conception of dreams, cannot be presented convincingly without reference to considerations upon which we have not yet touched. Seeing how closely linked up all phenomena are, you can hardly imagine that we can penetrate very far into the nature of any one of them without troubling ourselves about others of a similar nature. Since as yet we know nothing about those phenomena which are so nearly akin to dreams—neurotic symptoms—we must once more content ourselves with what we actually have achieved. I will merely give you the explanation of one more example and adduce a new consideration.

Let us take once more that dream to which we have already reverted several times, the one about the three theatre tickets for one florin and a half. I can assure you that I had no ulterior motive in selecting it in the first instance for an illustration. You know what the latent thoughts were: the vexation, after hearing that her friend had only just become engaged, that she herself should have married so hastily; depreciation of her husband and the idea that she could have found a better one if only she had waited. We also know already that the wish which made a dream out of these thoughts was the desire to "look on," to be able to go to the theatre—very probably an offshoot of an old curiosity to find out at last what really does happen after marriage. It is well known that in children this curiosity is regularly directed towards the sexual life of the parents; that is to say, it is an infantile impulse and, wherever it persists later in life, it has its roots in the infantile period. But the news received on the day previous to the dream gave no occasion for the awakening of this skoptophilia; it only roused vexation and regret. This wish-impulse (of skoptophilia) was not at first connected with the latent thoughts, and the results of the dream-interpretation could have been used by the analysis without taking it into consideration at all. But again, the vexation was not in itself capable of producing a dream: no dream could be formed out of the thought: "It was folly to be in such a hurry to marry" until that thought had stirred up the early wish to see at last what happened after marriage. Then this wish formed the dream-content, substituting for marriage the going to the theatre; and the form was that of the fulfilment of the earlier wish: "Now I may go to the theatre and look at all that we have never been allowed to see; and you may not. I am married and you have got to wait." In this way the actual situation was transformed into its opposite and an old triumph substituted for the recent discomfiture; and incidentally, satisfaction both of a 'gazing' impulse and of one of egoistic rivalry was brought about. It is this latter satisfaction which determines the manifest content of the dream; for in it she is actually sitting in the theatre, while her friend cannot get in. Those portions of the dream-content behind which the latent thoughts still conceal themselves are to be found in the form of inappropriate and incomprehensible modifications of the gratifying situation. The business of *interpretation* is to put aside those features in the whole which merely represent a wish-fulfilment and to reconstruct the painful latent dream-thoughts from these indications.

The consideration which I said I wished to call to your notice is intended to direct your attention to these latent dream-thoughts now brought into prominence. I must beg you not to forget that, first, the dreamer is unconscious of them; secondly, that they are quite reasonable and coherent, so that we can understand them as comprehensible reactions to whatever stimulus has given rise to the dream; and, thirdly, that they may have the value of any mental impulse or intellectual operation. I will designate these thoughts more strictly now than hitherto as *the residue from the previous day;* the dreamer may acknowledge them or not. I then distinguish between this 'residue' and 'latent dream-thoughts,' so that, as we have been accustomed to do all along, I will call everything which we learn from the interpretation of the dream 'the latent dream-thoughts,' while 'the residue from the previous day' is only a part of the latent dream-thoughts. Then our conception of what happens is this: something has been added to the residue from the previous day, something which also belongs to the unconscious, a strong but repressed wish-impulse, and it is this alone which makes the formation of a dream possible. The wish-impulse, acting upon the 'residue,' creates the other part of the latent dream-thoughts, that part which no longer need appear rational or comprehensible from the point of view of our waking life.

To illustrate the relation between the residue and the unconscious wish I have elsewhere made use of a comparison which I cannot do better than repeat here. Every business undertaking requires a capitalist to defray the expenses and an entrepreneur who has the idea and understands how to carry it out. Now the part of the capitalist in dream-formation is always and only played by the unconscious wish; it supplies the necessary fund of mental energy for it: the entrepreneur is the residue from the previous day, determining the manner of the expenditure. It is, of course, quite possible for the capitalist himself to have the idea and the special knowledge needed, or for the entrepreneur himself to have capital. This simplifies the practical situation but makes the theory of it more difficult. In economics we discriminate between the man in his function of capitalist and the same man in his capacity as entrepreneur; and this distinction restores the fundamental situation upon which our comparison is based. The same variations are to be found in the formation of dreams: I leave you to follow them out for yourselves.

We cannot go any further at this point; for I think it likely that a disturbing thought has long since occurred to you and it deserves a hearing. You may ask: "Is the so-called 'residue' really unconscious in the sense in which the wish necessary for the formation of the dream is unconscious?" Your suspicion is justified: this is the salient point in the whole matter. They are not both unconscious in the same sense. The dream-wish belongs to a different type of UNCONSCIOUS, which, as we have seen, has its roots in the infantile period and is furnished with special mechanisms. It is very expedient to distinguish the two types of "unconscious" from one another by speaking of them in different terms. But, all the same, we will rather wait until we have familiarized ourselves with the phenomena of the neuroses. If our conception of the existence of any kind of unconscious be already regarded as fantastic, what will people say if we admit that to reach our solution we have had to assume two kinds?

Let us break off at this point. Once more you have heard only an incomplete statement; but is it not a hopeful thought that this knowledge will be carried further, either by ourselves or by those who come after us? And have not we ourselves learnt enough that is new and startling?

FIFTEENTH LECTURE

DOUBTFUL POINTS AND CRITICAL OBSERVATIONS

WE WILL NOT LEAVE THE SUBJECT OF DREAMS WITHOUT DEAL-ing with the most common doubts and uncertainties arising in connection with the novel ideas and conceptions we have been discussing: those of you who have followed these lectures attentively will have collected some material of the kind.

1. You may have received an impression that even with strict adherence to technique our work of dream-interpreta-tion leaves so much room for uncertainty that reliable trans-lation of manifest dreams into their latent dream-thoughts will be thereby frustrated. You will urge first that one never knows whether any particular element in a dream is to be understood literally or symbolically, since things employed as symbols do not thereby cease to be themselves. Where there is no objective evidence to decide the question the interpretation on that particular point will be left to be arbitrarily deter-mined by the interpreter. Further, since in the dream-work opposites coincide, it is in every instance uncertain whether a specific dream-element is to be understood in a positive or a negative sense, as itself or as its opposite—another opportu-nity for the interpreter to exercise a choice. Thirdly, on ac-count of the frequency with which inversion of every kind is employed in dreams, it is open to him to assume whenever he chooses that such an inversion has taken place. Finally

you will point to having heard that one is seldom certain that the interpretation arrived at is the only possible one, and that there is danger of overlooking another perfectly admissible interpretation of the same dream. In these circumstances, you will conclude, the discretion of the interpreter has a latitude that seems incompatible with any objective certainty in the result. Or you may also assume that the fault does not lie in dreams themselves, but that something erroneous in our conceptions and premises produces the unsatisfactory character of our interpretations.

All that you say is undeniable and yet I do not think it justifies either of your conclusions: that dream-interpretation as practised by us is at the mercy of the interpreter's arbitrary decisions or that the inadequacy of the results calls in question the correctness of our procedure. If for the "arbitrary decision" of the interpreter you will substitute his skill, his experience and his understanding, then I am with you. This kind of personal factor is of course indispensable, especially when interpretation is difficult; it is just the same in other scientific work, however; it can't be helped that one man will use any given technique less well, or apply it better, than another. The impression of arbitrariness made, for example, by the interpretation of symbols is corrected by the reflection that as a rule the connection of the dream-thoughts with one another, and of the dream with the life of the dreamer and the whole mental situation at the time of the dream, points directly to one of all the possible interpretations and renders all the rest useless. The conclusion that the imperfect character of the interpretations proceeds from fallacious hypotheses loses its force when consideration shows that, on the contrary, the ambiguity or indefiniteness of dreams is a quality which we should necessarily expect in them.

Let us call to mind our statement that the dream-work undertakes a translation of the dream-thoughts into a primitive mode of expression, analogous to hieroglyphics. Now all such primitive systems of expression are necessarily accompanied by ambiguity and indefiniteness; but we should not on that account be justified in doubting their practicability. You know that the coincidence of opposites in the dream-work is analogous to what is called the antithetical sense of primal words in the oldest languages. The philologist, R. Abel, to whom we owe this information, writing in 1884, begs us not on any account to imagine that there was any ambiguity in what one person said to another by means of ambivalent words of this sort. On the contrary, intonation, gestures and the whole context can have left no doubt whatever which of the two opposites the speaker had in mind to convey. In writing where gestures are absent the addition of little pictorial signs, not meant to receive separate oral expression, replaced them: e.g. a drawing of a little man, either crouching or standing upright, according as the ambiguous *ken* of the hieroglyphic meant "weak" or "strong." So that misunderstanding was avoided in spite of the ambiguity of sounds and signs.

In ancient systems of expression, for instance, in the scripts of the oldest languages, indefiniteness of various kinds is found with a frequency which we should not tolerate in our writings to-day. Thus in many Semitic writings only the consonants of the words appear: the omitted vowels have to be supplied by the reader from his knowledge and from the context. Hieroglyphic writing follows a similar principle, although not exactly the same; and this is the reason why nothing is known of the pronunciation of ancient Egyptian. There are besides other kinds of indefiniteness in the sacred writings of the Egyptians: for example, it is left to the writer's choice to inscribe the pictures from right to left or from left to right. To be able to read them, we have to remember that we must be guided by the direction of the faces of the figures, birds, and so forth. But it was also open to the writer to set the pictures in vertical columns and, in the case of inscriptions on smaller objects, he was led by considerations of what was pleasing to the eye, and of the space at his disposal, to introduce still further alterations in the arrangement of the signs. The most confusing feature in hieroglyphic script is that there is no spacing between the words. The pictures are all placed at equal intervals on the page, and it is generally impossible to know whether any given sign goes with the preceding one or forms the beginning of a new word. In Persian cuneiform writing, on the other hand, a slanting sign is used to separate the words.

The Chinese language, both spoken and written, is exceedingly ancient but is still used to-day by four hundred million people. Don't suppose that I understand it at all; I only obtained some information about it because I hoped to find in it analogies to the kinds of indefiniteness occurring in dreams; nor was I disappointed in my expectation, for Chinese is so full of uncertainties as positively to terrify one. As is well known, it consists of a number of syllabic sounds which are pronounced singly or doubled in combination. One of the chief dialects has about four hundred of these sounds, and since the vocabulary of this dialect is estimated at somewhere about four thousand words it is evident that every sound has an average of ten different meanings—some fewer, but some all the more. For this reason there are a whole series of devices to escape ambiguity, for the context alone will not show which of the ten possible meanings of the syllable the speaker wishes to convey to the hearer. Amongst these devices is the combining of two sounds into a single word and the use of four different "tones" in which these syllables may be spoken. For purposes of our comparison a still more interesting fact is that this language is practically without grammar: it is impossible to say of any of the one-syllabled words whether it is a noun, a verb or an adjective; and, further, there are no inflections to show gender, number, case, tense or mood. The language consists, as we may say, of the raw material only; just as our thought-language is resolved into its raw material by the dream-work omitting to express the relations in it. Wherever there is any uncertainty in Chinese the decision is left to the intelligence of the listener, who is guided by the context. I made a note of a Chinese saying, which literally translated runs thus: "Little what see, much what wonderful." This is simple enough to understand. It may mean: "The less a man has seen, the more he finds to wonder at," or "There is much to wonder at for the man who has seen little." Naturally there is no occasion to choose between these two translations which differ only in grammatical construction. We are assured that in spite of these uncertainties the Chinese language is a quite exceptionally good medium of expression; so it is clear that indefiniteness does not necessarily lead to ambiguity.

Now we must certainly admit that the position of affairs is far less favourable in regard to the mode of expression in dreams than it is with these ancient tongues and scripts; for these latter were originally designed as a means of communication; that is, they were intended to be understood, no matter what ways or means they had to employ. But just this character is lacking to dreams: their object is not to tell anyone anything; they are not a means of communication; on the contrary, it is important to them not to be understood. So we ought not to be surprised or misled if the result is that a number of the ambiguities and uncertainties in dreams cannot be determined. The only certain piece of knowledge gained from our comparison is that this indefiniteness (which people would like to make use of as an argument against the accuracy of our dream-interpretations) is rather to be recognized as a regular characteristic of all primitive systems of expression.

Practice and experience alone can determine the extent to which dreams can in actual fact be understood. My own opinion is that this is possible to a very great extent; and a comparison of the results obtained by properly trained analysts confirms my view. It is well known that the lay public, even in scientific circles, delights to make a parade of superior scepticism in the face of the difficulties and uncertainties which beset a scientific achievement; I think they are wrong in so doing. You may possibly not all know that the same thing happened at the time when the Babylonian and Assyrian inscriptions were being deciphered. There was a point at which public opinion was active in declaring that the men deciphering the cuneiform writing were victims of a chimera and that the whole business of investigation was a fraud. But in the year 1857 the Royal Asiatic Society made a conclusive test. They challenged four of the most distinguished men engaged in this branch of research—Rawlinson, Hincks, Fox Talbot and Oppert—to send to the Society in sealed envelopes independent translations of a newly discovered inscription, and, after comparing the four versions, they were able to announce that there was sufficient agreement between the four to justify belief in what had been achieved and confidence in further progress. The mockery of the learned laity then gradually came to an end, and certainty in the reading of cuneiform documents has advanced enormously since then.

2. A second series of objections is closely connected with an impression which you also have probably not escaped; namely, that a number of the solutions achieved by our method of dream-interpretation seem strained, specious, "dragged in,"—in other words, forced, or even comical or joking. These criticisms are so frequent that I will take at random the last that has come to my ears. Now listen: a head-master in Switzerland —that free country—was recently asked to resign his post on account of his interest in psychoanalysis. He protested and a Berne paper published the decision of the school authorities on his case. I shall quote a few sentences from the article which refer to psychoanalysis: "Further, we are amazed at the far-fetched and factitious character of many of the examples given in the said book by Dr. Pfister of Zurich. . . . It is indeed a matter for surprise that the head-master of a Training College should accept so credulously all these assertions and such specious evidence." These sentences purport to be the final opinion of "One who judges calmly." I am much more inclined to think this "calm" factitious. Let us examine these remarks more closely in the expectation that a certain amount of reflection and knowledge of the subject will do no harm, even to a "calm judgement."

It is really quite refreshing to see how swiftly and unerringly anyone relying merely on his first impressions can arrive at an opinion on some critical question of psychology in its more abstruse aspects. The interpretations seem to him far-fetched and strained, and do not commend themselves to him; consequently, they are wrong and the whole business is rubbish. Such critics never give even a passing thought to the possibility that there may be good reasons why the interpretations are bound to convey this very impression—a thought which would lead to the further question what these good reasons are.

The circumstance which calls forth this criticism is essentially related to the effect of displacement, which you have learnt to know as the most powerful instrument in the service of the dream-censorship. With its aid the substitute-formations which we call allusions are created; but these allusions are of a kind not easy to recognize as such; nor is it easy to discover the thought proper by working back from them, for they are connected with it by the most extraordinary and unusual extrinsic associations. But the whole matter throughout concerns things which are meant to be hidden, intended to be concealed: that is exactly the object of the dream-censorship. We must not expect, though, to find something that has been hidden by looking in the very place where it ordinarily belongs. The frontier surveillance authorities nowadays are a good deal more cunning in this respect than the Swiss school authorities; for they are not content with examining portfolios and letter-cases when hunting for documents and plans; but consider the possibility that spies and smugglers may conceal anything compromising about their persons, in places where it is most difficult to detect and where such things certainly do not belong, for example, between the double soles of their boots. If the concealed articles are found there, it is certainly true that they have been "dragged" to light, but they are none the less a very good "find."

In admitting the possibility that the connection between a latent dream-element and its manifest substitute may appear most remote and extraordinary, sometimes even comical or joking, we are guided by our wide experience of instances in which we did not as a rule find the meaning ourselves. It is often impossible to arrive at such interpretations by our own efforts: no sane person could guess the bridge connecting the two. The dreamer either solves the riddle straightaway by a direct association (*he* can do it because it is in his mind that the substitute-formation originated); or else he provides so much material that there is no longer any need for special penetration in order to solve it—the solution thrusts itself upon us as inevitable. If the dreamer does not help us in either of these two ways the manifest element in question will remain for ever incomprehensible. Let me give you one more instance of this kind which happened recently. A patient of mine lost her father during the course of the treatment, after which she seized every opportunity to bring him back to life in her dreams. In one of these her father appeared in a certain connection otherwise not applicable and said: *"It is quarter past eleven, it is half past eleven, it is quarter to twelve."* For the interpretation of this curious detail she could only provide the association that her father was pleased when his older children were punctual at the midday meal. This certainly fitted in with the dream-element, but it threw no light on its origin. The situation which had just been reached in the treatment gave good grounds for the suspicion that a carefully suppressed critical antagonism to her much loved and honoured father had played a part in this dream. Following out her further associations, apparently quite remote from the dream, she told how she had heard a long discussion of psychological questions on the day before and a relative had said: "Primitive man (*Urmensch*) survives in all of us." Now a light dawns on us. Here was again a splendid opportunity for her to imagine that her dead father survived, and so in the dream she made him a "clock-man" (*Uhrmensch*), telling the quarters up to the time of the midday meal.

The likeness to a pun in this cannot be ignored, and as a matter of fact it has often happened that a dreamer's pun has been ascribed to the interpreter; there are yet other examples in which it is not at all easy to decide whether we are dealing with a joke or a dream. But you will remember that the same sort of doubt arose with some slips of the tongue. A man related as a dream that he and his uncle were sitting in the latter's *auto* (automobile) and his uncle kissed him. The dreamer himself instantly volunteered the interpretation: it meant *"auto-erotism"* (a term used in our theory of the libido, signifying gratification obtained without any external love-object). Now was this man allowing himself a joke at our expense and pretending that a pun which occurred to him was part of a dream? I do not think so: he really did dream it. But where does this bewildering resemblance between dreams and jokes come from? At one time this question took me somewhat out of my way, for it necessitated my making a thorough investigation into the question of wit itself. This led to the conclusion that wit originates as follows: a preconscious train of thought is for a moment left to a process of unconscious elaboration, from which it emerges in the form of a witticism. While under the influence of the unconscious it is subject to the mechanisms there operative—to condensation and displacement; that is to say, to the same processes as we found at work in the dream-work; and the similarity sometimes found between dreams and wit is to be ascribed to this character common to both. But the unintentional "dream joke" does not amuse us as does an ordinary witticism; a deeper study of wit may show you why this is so. The "dream joke" strikes us as a poor form of wit; it does not make us laugh, it leaves us cold.

Now in this we are following the path of the ancient method of dream-interpretation, which has given us, besides much that is useless, many a valuable example of interpretation upon which we ourselves could not improve. I will tell you a dream of historic importance which is related in slightly different versions by Plutarch and Artemidorus of Daldis, the dreamer being Alexander the Great. When he was laying siege to the city of Tyre, which was putting up an obstinate resistance (B.C. 322), he dreamt one night that he saw a dancing satyr. The dream-interpreter Aristandros, who accompanied the army on its campaigns, interpreted this dream by dividing the word "satyros" into σὰ Τύρος ("Tyre is thine"), and prophesied from this the king's victory over the city. This interpretation decided Alexander to continue the siege and eventually the city fell. The interpretation, factitious as it seems, was undoubtedly the right one.

3. I can well imagine that you will be especially impressed on being told that even people who have long studied the interpretation of dreams in the course of their work as psycho-

analysts have raised objections to our conception of dreams. It would indeed have been exceptional if so excellent an opportunity for new mistakes had been let slip; and so assertions have been made, due to confusion of ideas and based on unjustifiable generalizations, which are hardly less incorrect than the medical conception of dreams. One of these statements you know already: that dreams deal with attempts at adaptation to the situation at the moment and with the solution of future problems; in other words, that they pursue a "prospective tendency" or aim (A. Maeder). We have already demonstrated that this statement rests upon a confusion between dreams and the latent dream-thoughts and ignores the process of dream-work. If those who speak of this "prospective tendency" mean thereby to characterize the unconscious mental activity to which the latent thoughts belong, then, on the one hand, they tell us nothing new and, on the other hand, the description is not exhaustive; for unconscious mental activity occupies itself with many other things besides preparation for the future. There seems to be a much worse confusion behind the assurance that the "death clause" may be found underlying every dream; I am not quite clear what this formula is intended to mean, but I suspect that behind it the dream is confounded with the whole personality of the dreamer.

An unjustifiable generalization, based on a few striking examples, is contained in the statement that every dream admits of two kinds of interpretation: one of the kind we have described, the so-called "psychoanalytic" interpretation, and the other the so-called "anagogic," which disregards the instinctual tendencies and aims at a representation of the higher mental functions (H. Silberer); there are dreams of this kind, but you will seek in vain to extend this conception to include even a majority of dreams. After all you have heard, the statement that all dreams are to be interpreted bisexually, as a combination of two tendencies which may be called male and female (A. Adler), will seem to you quite incomprehensible. Here again, single dreams of this sort do of course occur and later on you may learn that their structure is similar to that of certain hysterical symptoms. I mention all these discoveries of new general characteristics of dreams in order to warn you against them, or at least to leave you in no doubt about my own opinion of them.

4. At one time the objective value of research into dreams seemed to be discredited by the fact that patients treated analytically appeared to suit the content of their dreams to the favourite theories of their doctors, one class dreaming mainly of sexual impulses, and another of impulses for mastery, others again even of rebirth (W. Stekel). The force of this observation is weakened by the reflection that people dreamed dreams before there was any such thing as psychoanalytic treatment to influence their dreams and that the patients undergoing treatment nowadays also used to dream before they began it. The actual fact in this supposedly new observation is soon shown to be self-evident and of no consequence for the theory of dreams. The residue from the previous day which gives rise to dreams is a residue from the great interests of waking life. If the physician's words and the stimuli which he gives have become of importance to the patient they then enter into whatever constitutes the residue and can act as mental stimuli for dream-formation, just like other interests of affective value roused on the preceding day which have not subsided; they operate in the same way as bodily stimuli which affect the sleeper during sleep. Like these other factors inciting dreams, the trains of thought roused by the physician can appear in the manifest dream-content or be revealed in the latent thoughts. We know indeed that dreams can be experimentally produced, or, to speak more accurately, a part of the dream-material can be thus introduced into the dream. In influencing his patients thus the analyst plays a part no different from that of an experimenter, like Mourly Vold, who placed in certain positions the limbs of the person upon whom he experimented.

We can often influence what a man shall dream *about*, but never *what* he will dream; for the mechanism of the dream-work and the unconscious dream-wish are inaccessible to

external influence of any sort. We realized, when we were
considering dreams arising out of bodily stimuli, that in the reaction to the bodily or mental stimuli brought to bear upon
the dreamer the peculiarity and independence of dream-life
is clearly seen. The criticism I have just discussed which tends
to cast a doubt upon the objectivity of dream investigation is
again an assertion based upon confounding, this time confounding dreams with—their material.

I wanted to tell you as much as this about the problems
of dreams. You will guess that I have passed over a great deal
and will have discovered for yourselves that my treatment of
nearly every point has necessarily been incomplete; but this
is due to the phenomena of dreams being so closely connected with those of the neuroses. Our plan was to study
dreams as an introduction to the study of the neuroses and it
was certainly a better one than beginning the other way about;
but since dreams prepare us for comprehension of the neuroses, so also can a correctly formed estimate of dreams be acquired only after some knowledge of neurotic manifestations
has been gained.

I do not know how you may think about it, but I can assure
you that I do not regret having taken up so much of your interest and of the time at our disposal in the consideration of
problems connected with dreams. I know no other way by
which one can so speedily arrive at conviction of the correctness of those statements by which psychoanalysis stands or
falls. It requires strenuous work for many months, and even
years, to demonstrate that the symptoms in a case of neurotic
illness have a meaning, serve a purpose, and arise from the
patient's experiences in life. On the other hand, a few hours'
effort may be enough to show these things in some dream
which at first seemed utterly confused and incomprehensible,
and in this way to confirm all the premises upon which
psychoanalysis rests—the existence of unconscious mental
processes, the special mechanisms which they obey, and the
instinctive propelling forces which are expressed by them.
And when we remember how far-reaching is the analogy in

the structure of dreams to that of neurotic symptoms and, with that, reflect how rapid is the transformation of a dreamer into a wide-awake, reasonable human being, we acquire an assurance that the neuroses too depend only upon an alteration in the balance of the forces at work in mental life.

PART III

GENERAL THEORY OF THE NEUROSES

IT PLEASES ME GREATLY TO SEE YOU HERE AGAIN TO CONTINUE our discussions after a year has passed. Last year the subject of my lectures was the application of psychoanalysis to errors and to dreams; I hope this year to lead you to some comprehension of neurotic phenomena which, as you will soon discover, have much in common with both our former subjects. I must tell you before I begin, however, that I cannot concede you the same attitude towards me now as I did last year. Then I endeavoured to make no step without being in agreement with your judgement; I debated a great deal with you, submitted to your objections, in fact, recognized you and your "healthy common-sense" as the deciding factor. That is no longer possible and for a very simple reason. Errors and dreams are phenomena which were familiar to you; one might say you had as much experience of them as I, or could easily have obtained it. The manifestations of neurosis, however, are an unknown region to you; those of you who are not yourselves medical men have no access there except through the accounts I give you; and of what use is the most excellent judgement where there is no knowledge of the subject under debate?

However, do not receive this announcement as though I were going to give these lectures *ex cathedra* or to demand unconditional acceptance from you. Any such misconception would do me a gross injustice. I do not aim at producing conviction—my aim is to stimulate enquiry and to destroy prejudices. If owing to ignorance of the subject you are not in a position to adjudicate, then you should neither believe nor reject. You should only listen and allow what I tell you to make its own effect upon you. Convictions are not so easily acquired, or, when they are achieved without much trouble, they soon prove worthless and unstable. No one has a right to conviction on these matters who has not worked at this subject for many years, as I have, and has not himself experienced the same new and astonishing discoveries. Then why these sudden convictions in intellectual matters, lightning conversions, and instantaneous repudiations? Do you not see that the *coup de foudre*, "love at first sight," proceeds from a very different mental sphere, from the affective one? We do not require even our patients to bring with them any conviction in favour of psychoanalysis or any devotion to it. It would make us suspicious of them. Benevolent scepticism is the attitude in them which we like best. Therefore will you also try to let psychoanalytical conceptions develop quietly in your minds alongside the popular or the psychiatric view, until opportunities arise for them to influence each other and be united into a decisive opinion.

On the other hand, you are not for a moment to suppose that the psychoanalytic point of view which I shall lay before you is a speculative system of ideas. On the contrary, it is the result of experience, being founded either on direct observations or on conclusions drawn from observation. Whether these have been drawn in an adequate or a justifiable manner future advances in science will show; after nearly two and a half decades and now that I am fairly well advanced in years I may say, without boasting, that it was particularly difficult, intense, and all-absorbing work that yielded these observations. I have often had the impression that our opponents were unwilling to consider this source of our statements, as if they looked upon them as ideas derived subjectively which anyone could dispute at his own sweet will. This attitude on the part of my opponents is not quite comprehensible to me. Perhaps it comes from the circumstance that physicians pay so little attention to neurotics and listen so carelessly to what they say that it has become impossible for them to perceive anything in the patients' communications or to make detailed observations from them. I will take this opportunity of assuring you that in these lectures I shall make few controversial references, least of all to individuals. I have never been able to convince myself of the truth of the saying that "strife is the father of all things." I think the source of it was the philosophy of the Greek sophists and that it errs, as does the latter, through the overestimation of dialectics. It seems to me, on the contrary, that scientific controversy, so-called, is on the whole quite unfruitful, apart from the fact that it is almost always conducted in a highly personal manner. Until a few years ago I could boast that I had only once been engaged in a regular scientific dispute, and that with one single investigator, Löwenfeld of Munich. The end of it was that we became friends and have remained so to this day. But I did not repeat the experiment for a very long time because I was not certain that the outcome would be the same.

Now you will surely judge that a refusal of this kind to discuss matters publicly points to a high degree of inaccessibility to criticism, to obstinacy, or, in the polite colloquialism of the scientific world, to "pig-headedness."[1] My reply to you would be that, should you have arrived at a conviction by means of such hard work, you would also thereby derive a certain right to maintain it with some tenacity. Further, on my own behalf, I can say that in the course of my work I have modified my views on important points, changed them or replaced them by others, and have of course in each case published the fact. What has been the result of this frankness? Some people have ignored my corrections of myself altogether and still to-day criticize me in respect of views which no longer mean the same to me. Others positively reproach me for these changes and declare me to be unreliable on that account. No one who changes his views once or twice deserves

[1] *Verranntheit.*

to be believed, for it is only too likely that he will be mistaken again in his latest assertions; but anyone who sticks to anything he has once said, or refuses to give way upon it easily enough, is obstinate or pig-headed; is it not so? What is to be done in the face of these self-contradictory criticisms except to remain as one is and behave as seems best to one? This is what I decided to do; and I am not deterred from remodelling and improving my theories in accordance with later experience. I have so far found nothing to alter in my fundamental standpoint and I hope this will never be necessary.

So now I have to lay before you the psychoanalytic theory of neurotic manifestations. For this purpose it will be simplest, on account of both the analogy and the contrast, to take an example which links up with the phenomena we have already considered. I will take a 'symptomatic act' which I see many people commit in my own consulting-room. The analyst has little to offer to the people who come to a physician's consulting-room for half-an-hour to recount the lifelong misery of their fate. His deeper comprehension makes it difficult for him to give, as another might, the opinion that there is nothing wrong with them and that they had better take a light course of hydro-therapy. One of our colleagues once replied, with a shrug, when asked how he dealt with consultation patients, that he "fined them so many crowns for 'wasting the time of the court.'" You will therefore not be surprised to hear that even the busiest psychoanalysts are not much sought after for consultations. I have had the ordinary door between the waiting-room and my consulting-room supplemented by another door and covered with felt. The reason for this is obvious. Now it constantly happens when I admit people from the waiting-room that they omit to close these doors, leaving even both doors open behind them. When I see this happen, I at once, with some stiffness, request him or her to go back and make good the omission, no matter how fine a gentleman he may be or how many hours she has spent on her toilet. My action gives the impression of being uncalled-for and pedantic; occasionally too I have found myself in the wrong, when the person turned out to be one of those who cannot themselves grasp a door-handle and are glad when those with them avoid it. But in the majority of cases I was right, for anyone who behaves in this way and leaves the door of a physician's consulting-room open into the waiting-room belongs to the rabble and deserves to be received with coldness. Now don't allow yourselves to be biassed before you have heard the rest. This omission on the part of a patient occurs only when he has been waiting alone in the outer room and thus leaves an empty room behind him, never when others, strangers to him, have also been waiting there. In the latter case he knows very well that it is to his own interest not to be overheard while he talks to the physician and he never neglects to close both doors carefully.

Occurring in this way, the patient's omission is neither accidental nor meaningless, and not even unimportant, for it betrays the visitor's attitude to the physician. He belongs to that large class who seek those in high places, and wish to be dazzled and intimidated. Perhaps he had made enquiries by telephone at what time he would be most likely to gain admittance and had been expecting to find a crowd of applicants in a queue, as if at the grocer's in war-time. Then he is shown into an empty room which, moreover, is most modestly furnished, and he is dumbfounded. He must somehow make the physician atone for the superfluous respect he had been prepared to show him; and so he omits to close the doors between the waiting- and the consulting-rooms. He intends this to mean: "Pooh! there is no one here and I daresay there won't be, however long I stay!" He would behave during the interview in an uncivil and supercilious manner, too, if his presumption were not curbed at the outset by a sharp reminder.

In the analysis of this little symptomatic act you find nothing that is not already known to you; namely, the conclusion that it is no accident but has in it motive, meaning, and intention; that it belongs to a mental context which can be specified; and that it provides a small indication of a more important mental process. But above all it implies that the process thus indicated is not known to the consciousness of the person who carries it out; for not one of the patients who left the two doors open would have admitted that he wished to show any depreciation of me by his neglect. Many of them could probably recall a sense of disappointment on entering the empty waiting-room, but the connection between this impression and the succeeding symptomatic act certainly remained outside their consciousness.

Now let us place this little analysis of a symptomatic act by the side of an observation made on a patient. I will choose one which is fresh in my memory, and also because it can be described in comparatively few words. A certain amount of detail is indispensable for any such account.

A young officer, home on short leave of absence, asked me to treat his mother-in-law, who was living in the happiest surroundings and yet was embittering her own and her family's lives by a nonsensical idea. I found her a well-preserved lady, fifty-three years of age, of a friendly, simple disposition, who gave without hesitation the following account of herself. She is most happily married, and lives in the country with her husband who manages a large factory. She cannot say enough of her husband's kindness and consideration; theirs had been a love-marriage thirty years ago, since when they had never had a cloud, a quarrel, or a moment's jealousy. Her two children have both married well, but her husband's sense of duty keeps him still at work. A year before, an incredible and, to her, incomprehensible thing happened. She received an anonymous letter telling her that her excellent husband was carrying on an intrigue with a young girl, and believed it on the spot—since then her happiness has been destroyed. The details were more or less as follows: she had a housemaid with whom she discussed confidential matters, perhaps rather too freely. This young woman cherished a positively venomous hatred for another girl who had succeeded better in life than herself, although of no better origin. Instead of going into service, the other young woman had had a commercial training, been taken into the factory and, owing to vacancies caused by the absence of staff on service in the field, had been promoted to a good position. She lived in the factory, knew all the gentlemen, and was even addressed as "Miss." The other one who had been left behind in life was only too ready to accuse her former schoolmate of all possible evil. One day our patient and her housemaid were discussing an elderly gentleman who had visited the house and of whom it was said that he did not live with his wife but kept a mistress. Why, she did not know, but she suddenly said: "I cannot imagine anything more awful than to hear that my husband had a mistress." The next day she received by post an anonymous letter in disguised handwriting which informed her of the very thing she had just imagined. She concluded—probably correctly—that the letter was the handiwork of her malicious housemaid, for the woman who was named as the mistress of her husband was the very girl who was the object of this housemaid's hatred. Although she at once saw through the plot and had seen enough of such cowardly accusations in her own surroundings to place little credence in them, our patient was nevertheless prostrated by this letter. She became terribly excited and at once sent for her husband to overwhelm him with reproaches. The husband laughingly denied the accusation and did the best thing he could. He sent for the family physician (who also attended the factory), and he did his best to calm the unhappy lady. The next thing they did was also most reasonable. The housemaid was dismissed, but not the supposed mistress. From that time on the patient claims to have repeatedly brought herself to a calm view of the matter, so that she no longer believes the contents of the letter; but it has never gone very deep nor lasted very long. It was enough to hear the young woman's name mentioned, or to meet her in the street, for a new attack of suspicion, agony, and reproaches to break out.

This is the clinical picture of this excellent woman's case. It did not require much experience of psychiatry to perceive that, in contrast to other neurotics, she described her symptoms too mildly—as we say, dissimulated them—and that she had never really overcome her belief in the anonymous letter.

Now what attitude does a psychiatrist take up to such a case? We know already what he would say to the symptomatic act of a patient who does not close the waiting-room doors. He explains it as an accident, without interest psychologically, and no concern of his. But he cannot continue to take up this attitude in regard to the case of the jealous lady. The symptomatic action appears to be unimportant; the symptom calls for notice as a grave matter. Subjectively it involves intense suffering, and objectively it threatens to break up a family; its claim to psychiatric interest is therefore indisputable. First the psychiatrist tries to characterize the symptom by some essential attribute. The idea with which this lady torments herself cannot be called nonsensical in itself; it does happen that elderly husbands contract relationships with young women. But there is something else about it that is nonsensical and incomprehensible. The patient has absolutely no grounds, except the anonymous letter, for supposing that her loving and faithful husband belongs to this category of men, otherwise not so uncommon. She knows that this communication carries no proof, she can explain its origin satisfactorily; she ought therefore to be able to say to herself that she has no grounds for her jealousy and she does even say so, but she suffers just as much as if she regarded her jealousy as well-founded. Ideas of this kind that are inaccessible to logic and the arguments of reality are unanimously described as *delusions*. The good lady suffers therefore, from a *delusion of jealousy*. That is evidently the essential characteristic of the case.

Having established this first point, our psychiatric interest increases. When a delusion cannot be dissipated by the facts of reality, it probably does not spring from reality. Where else then does it spring from? Delusions can have the most various contents; why is the content of it in this case jealousy? What kind of people have delusions, and particularly delusions of jealousy? Now we should like to listen to the psychiatrist, but he leaves us in the lurch here. He considers only one of our questions. He will examine the family history of this woman and will *perhaps* bring us the answer that the kind of people who suffer from delusions are those in whose families similar or different disorders have occurred repeatedly. In other words, this lady has developed a delusion because she had an hereditary predisposition to do so. That is certainly something; but is it all that we want to know? Is it the sole cause of her disease? Does it satisfy us to assume that it is unimportant, arbitrary, or inexplicable that one kind of delusion should have been developed instead of another? And are we to understand the proposition—that the hereditary predisposition is decisive—also in a negative sense; that is, that no matter what experiences and emotions life had brought her she was destined some time or other to produce a delusion? You will want to know why scientific psychiatry gives no further explanation. And I reply: "Only a rogue gives more than he has." The psychiatrist knows of no path leading to any further explanation in such a case. He has to content himself with a diagnosis and, in spite of wide experience, with a very uncertain prognosis of its future course.

Now can psychoanalysis do better than this? Yes, certainly I hope to show you that even in such an obscure case as this it is possible to discover something which makes closer comprehension possible. First, I shall ask you to notice this incomprehensible detail; that the anonymous letter on which her delusion is founded was positively provoked by the patient herself, by her saying to the scheming housemaid the day before that nothing could be more awful than to hear that her husband had an intrigue with a young woman. She first put the idea of sending the letter into the servant's mind by this. So the delusion acquires a certain independence of the letter; it existed beforehand as a fear—or, as a wish?—in her mind. Besides this, the further small indications revealed in the bare two hours of analysis are noteworthy. The patient responded very coldly, it is true, to the request to tell me her further thoughts, ideas, and recollections, after she had finished her story. She declared that nothing came to her mind, she had told me everything; and after two hours the attempt had to be given up, because she announced that she felt quite well already and was certain that the morbid idea would not return. Her saying this was naturally due to resistance and to the fear of further analysis. In these two hours she had let fall some remarks, nevertheless, which made a certain interpretation not only possible but inevitable, and this interpretation threw a sharp light on the origin of the delusion of jealousy. There actually existed in her an infatuation for a young man, for the very son-in-law who had urged her to seek my assistance. Of this infatuation she herself knew nothing or only perhaps very little; in the circumstances of their relationship it was easily possible for it to disguise itself as harmless tenderness on her part. After what we have already learnt it is not difficult to see into the mind of this good woman and excellent mother. Such an infatuation, such a monstrous, impossible thing, could not come into her conscious mind; it persisted, nevertheless, and unconsciously exerted a heavy pressure. Something had to happen, some sort of relief had to be found; and the simplest alleviation lay in that mechanism of displacement which so regularly plays its part in the formation of delusional jealousy. If not merely she, old woman that she was, were in love with a young man, but if only her old husband too were in love with a young mistress, then her torturing conscience would be absolved from the infidelity. The phantasy of her husband's infidelity was thus a cooling balm on her burning wound. Of her own love she never became conscious; but its reflection in the delusion, which brought such advantages, thus became compulsive, delusional and conscious. All arguments against it could naturally avail nothing; for they were directed only against the reflection, and not against the original to which its strength was due and which lay buried out of reach in the unconscious.

Let us now piece together the results of this short, obstructed psychoanalytic attempt to understand this case. It is assumed of course that the information acquired was correct, a point which I cannot submit to your judgement here. First of all, the delusion is no longer senseless and incomprehensible; it is sensible, logically motivated, and has its place in connection with an affective experience of the patient's. Secondly, it has arisen as a necessary reaction to another mental process which has itself been revealed by other indications; and it owes its delusional character, its quality of resisting real and logical objections, to this relation with this other mental process. It is something desired in itself, a kind of consolation. Thirdly, the fact that the delusion is one of jealousy and no other is unmistakably determined by the experience under-lying the disease. You will also recognize the two important analogies with the symptomatic act we analysed; namely, the discovery of the sense or intention behind the symptom and the relation of it to something in the given situation which is unconscious.

This does not, of course, answer all the questions arising out of this case. On the contrary, it bristles with further problems, some of which have not yet proved soluble at all, while others cannot be solved owing to the unfavourable circumstances met with in this case. For instance, why does this happily married lady fall in love with her son-in-law, and why does relief come to her in the form of this kind of reflection, this projection of her own state of mind on to her husband, when other forms of relief were also possible? Do not think that it is idle and un-called-for to propound these questions. We have already a good deal of material at hand to provide possible answers. The patient had come to that critical time of life which brings a sudden and unwelcome increase of sexual desire to a woman; that may have been sufficient in itself. Or there may have been an additional reason, in that the sexual capacity of her excellent and faithful husband may have been for some years insufficient for the still vigorous woman's needs. Observation has taught us that it is just such men, whose fidelity is thus a matter of course, who treat their wives with particular tender-ness and are unusually considerate of their nervous ailments. Neither is it unimportant, moreover, that the object of this ab-normal infatuation should be her daughter's young husband. A strong erotic attachment to the daughter, with its roots in the individual sexual constitution of the mother, often manages to maintain itself in such a transformation. I may perhaps re-mind you in this connection that the relation between mother-in-law and son-in-law has from time immemorial been re-garded by mankind as a particularly sensitive one, which among primitive races has given rise to very powerful taboos and precautions.[1] On the positive as well as on the negative side it frequently exceeds the limits regarded as desirable in

[1] Cf. *Totem und Tabu,* 1913.

civilized society. Of these three possible factors, whether one of them has been at work in the case before us, or two of them, or whether all three together have taken part, I cannot tell you; though only because the analysis of the case could not be continued beyond the second hour.

I perceive now that I have been speaking entirely of things which you were not yet prepared to understand. I did so in order to carry out the comparison between psychiatry and psychoanalysis. But I may ask you one thing at this point: Have you observed anything in the nature of a contradiction between the two? Psychiatry does not employ the technical methods of psychoanalysis, neglects any consideration of the content of the delusion, and in pointing to heredity gives us but a general and remote ætiology instead of first disclosing the more scientific and immediate one. But is any contradiction or opposition contained in this? Is not the one rather a supplement to the other? Is the hereditary factor inconsistent with the importance of experience and would they not both work together most effectively? You will admit that there is nothing essential in the work of psychiatry which could oppose psychoanalytic researches. It is therefore the psychiatrists who oppose it, and not psychiatry itself. Psychoanalysis stands to psychiatry more or less as histology does to anatomy; in one, the outer forms of organs are studied, in the other, the construction of these out of the tissues and constituent elements. It is not easy to conceive of any contradiction between these two fields of study, in which the work of the one is continued in the other. You know that nowadays anatomy is the basis of the scientific study of medicine; but time was when dissecting human corpses in order to discover the internal structure of the body was as much a matter for severe prohibition as practising psychoanalysis in order to discover the internal workings of the human mind seems to-day to be a matter for condemnation. And, presumably at a not too distant date, we shall have perceived that there can be no psychiatry which is scientifically radical without a thorough knowledge of the deep-seated unconscious processes in mental life.

There may be some of you who perhaps are friendly enough

towards psychoanalysis, often attacked as it is, to wish that it would justify itself in another direction also, that is, therapeutically. You know that psychiatric therapy has hitherto been unable to influence delusions. Can psychoanalysis do so perhaps, by reason of its insight into the mechanism of these symptoms? No, I have to tell you that it cannot; for the present, at any rate, it is just as powerless as any other therapy to heal these sufferers. It is true that we can understand what has happened to the patient; but we have no means by which we can make him understand it himself. You have heard that I could not continue the analysis of this delusion beyond the first preliminaries. Would you then maintain that analysis of such cases is undesirable because it remains fruitless? I do not think so. It is our right, yes, and our duty, to pursue our researches without respect to the immediate gain effected. The day will come, where and when we know not, when every little piece of knowledge will be converted into power, and into therapeutic power. Even if psychoanalysis showed itself as unsuccessful with all other forms of nervous and mental diseases as with delusions, it would still remain justified as an irreplaceable instrument of scientific research. It is true that we should not be in a position to practise it; the human material on which we learn lives, and has its own will, and must have its own motives in order to participate in the work; and it would then refuse to do so. I will therefore close my lecture for to-day by telling you that there are large groups of nervous disturbances for which this conversion of our own advance in knowledge into therapeutic power has actually been carried out; and that with these diseases, otherwise so refractory, our measures yield, under certain conditions, results which give place to none in the domain of medical therapy.

In the last lecture i explained to you that clinical psychiatry troubles itself little about the actual form of the individual symptom or the content of it; but that psychoanalysis has made this its starting-point, and has ascertained that the symptom itself has a meaning and is connected with experiences in the life of the patient. The meaning of neurotic symptoms was first discovered by J. Breuer in the study and successful cure of a case of hysteria (1880–82), which has since then become famous. It is true that P. Janet independently reached the same result; in fact, priority in publication must be granted to the French investigator, for Breuer did not publish his observations until more than a decade later (1893–95), during the period of our work together. Incidentally, it is of no great importance to us who made the discovery, for you know that every discovery is made more than once, and none is made all at once, nor is success meted out according to deserts. America is not called after Columbus. Before Breuer and Janet, the great psychiatrist Leuret expressed the opinion that even the delusions of the insane would prove to have some meaning, if only we knew how to translate them. I confess that for a long time I was willing to accord Janet very high recognition for his explanation of neurotic symptoms, because he regarded them as expressions of *"idées inconscientes"* possessing the patient's mind. Since then, however, Janet has taken up an attitude of undue reserve, as if he meant to imply that the Unconscious had been nothing more to him than a manner of speaking, a makeshift, *une façon de parler*, and that he had nothing "real" in mind. Since then I have not understood Janet's views, but I believe that he has gratuitously deprived himself of great credit.

Neurotic symptoms then, just like errors and dreams, have their meaning and, like these, are related to the life of the person in whom they appear. This is an important matter which I should like to demonstrate to you by some examples. I can merely assert, I cannot prove, that it is so in every case; anyone observing for himself will be convinced of it. For certain reasons though, I shall not take these examples from cases of hysteria, but from another very remarkable form of neurosis, closely allied in origin to the latter, about which I must say a few preliminary words. This, which we call *the obsessional neurosis*, is not so popular as the widely known *hysteria;* it is, if I may so express myself, not so noisily ostentatious, behaves more as if it were a private affair of the patients, dispenses almost entirely with bodily manifestations and creates all its symptoms in the mental sphere. The obsessional neurosis and hysteria are the two forms of neurotic disease upon the study of which psychoanalysis was first built up, and in the treatment of which also our therapy celebrates its triumphs. In the obsessional neurosis, however, that mysterious leap from the mental to the physical is absent, and it has really become more intimately comprehensible and transparent to us through psychoanalytic research than hysteria; we have come to understand that it displays far more markedly certain extreme features of the neurotic constitution.

The obsessional neurosis[1] takes this form: the patient's mind is occupied with thoughts that do not really interest him, he feels impulses which seem alien to him, and he is impelled to perform actions which not only afford him no pleasure but from which he is powerless to desist. The thoughts (obses-

[1][*Zwangsneurose*, sometimes called in English compulsion-neurosis.—TR.]

sions) may be meaningless in themselves or only of no interest to the patient; they are often absolutely silly; in every case they are the starting-point of a strained concentration of thought which exhausts the patient and to which he yields most unwillingly. Against his will he has to worry and speculate as if it were a matter of life or death to him. The impulses which he perceives within him may seem to be of an equally childish and meaningless character; mostly, however, they consist of something terrifying, such as temptations to commit serious crimes, so that the patient not only repudiates them as alien, but flees from them in horror, and guards himself by prohibitions, precautions, and restrictions against the possibility of carrying them out. As a matter of fact he never, literally not even once, carries these impulses into effect; flight and precautions invariably win. What he does really commit are very harmless, certainly trivial acts—what are termed the obsessive actions—which are mostly repetitions and ceremonial elaborations of ordinary every-day performances, making these common necessary actions—going to bed, washing, dressing, going for walks, etc.—into highly laborious tasks of almost insuperable difficulty. The morbid ideas, impulses, and actions are not by any means combined in the same proportions in individual types and cases of the obsessional neurosis; on the contrary, the rule is that one or another of these manifestations dominates the picture and gives the disease its name; but what is common to all forms of it is unmistakable enough.

This is a mad disease, surely. I don't think the wildest psychiatric phantasy could have invented anything like it, and if we did not see it every day with our own eyes we could hardly bring ourselves to believe in it. Now do not imagine that you can do anything for such a patient by advising him to distract himself, to pay no attention to these silly ideas, and to do something sensible instead of his nonsensical practices. This is what he would like himself; for he is perfectly aware of his condition, he shares your opinion about his obessional symptoms, he even volunteers it quite readily. Only he simply cannot help himself; the actions performed in an obsessional condition are supported by a kind of energy which probably has no counterpart in normal mental life. Only one thing is open to him—he can displace and he can exchange; instead of one silly idea he can adopt another of a slightly milder character, from one precaution or prohibition he can proceed to another, instead of one ceremonial rite he can perform another. He can displace his sense of compulsion, but he cannot dispel it. This capacity for displacing all the symptoms, involving radical alteration of their original forms, is a main characteristic of the disease; it is, moreover, striking that in this condition the 'opposite-values' (polarities) pervading mental life appear to be exceptionally sharply differentiated. In addition to compulsions of both positive and negative character, doubt appears in the intellectual sphere, gradually spreading until it gnaws even at what is usually held to be certain. All these things combine to bring about an ever-increasing indecisiveness, loss of energy, and curtailment of freedom; and that although the obsessional neurotic is originally always a person of a very energetic disposition, often highly opinionated, and as a rule intellectually gifted above the average. He has usually attained to an agreeably high standard of ethical development, is over-conscientious, and more than usually correct. You may imagine that it is a sufficiently arduous task to find one's bearings in this maze of contradictory character-traits and morbid manifestations. At the moment our aim is merely to interpret some symptoms of this disease.

Perhaps in view of our previous discussions you would like to know what present-day psychiatry has to offer concerning the obsessional neurosis; it is but a miserable contribution, however. Psychiatry has given names to the various compulsions; and has nothing more to say about them. It asserts instead that persons exhibiting these symptoms are "degenerate." That is not much satisfaction to us; it is no more than an estimate of their value, a condemnation instead of an explanation. We are intended, I suppose, to conclude that deterioration from type would naturally produce all kinds of oddities in people. Now, we do believe that people who develop such symptoms must be somewhat different in type from other human beings; but we should like to know whether they are more "degenerate" than other nervous patients, than hysterical or insane people. The characterization is clearly again much too general. One may even doubt whether it is justified at all when one learns that such symptoms occur in men and women of exceptional ability who have left their mark on their generation. Thanks to their own discretion and the untruthfulness of biographers we usually learn very little of an intimate nature about our exemplary great men; but it does happen occasionally that one of them is a fanatic about truth like Émile Zola,[1] and then we hear of the many extraordinary obsessive habits from which he suffered throughout life.

Psychiatry has got out of this difficulty by dubbing these people *"dégénerés superieurs."* Very well; but psychoanalysis has shown that these extraordinary obsessional symptoms can be removed permanently, like the symptoms of other diseases, and as in other people who are not degenerate. I myself have frequently succeeded in doing so.

I shall only give you two examples of analysis of obsessional symptoms; one is an old one, but I have never found a better; and one is a recent one. I shall limit myself to these two because an account of this kind must be very explicit and go into great detail.

A lady of nearly thirty years of age suffered from very severe obsessional symptoms. I might perhaps have been able to help her if my work had not been destroyed by the caprice of fate—perhaps I shall tell you about it later. In the course of a day she would perform the following peculiar obsessive act, among others, several times over. She would run out of her room into the adjoining one, there take up a certain position at the table in the centre of the room, ring for her maid, give her a trivial order or send her away without, and then run back again. There was certainly nothing very dreadful about this, but it might well arouse curiosity. The explanation presented itself in the simplest and most unexceptionable manner, without any assistance on the part of the analyst. I cannot

[1] E. Toulouse, *Émile Zola. Enquête medico-psychologique.* Paris, 1896.

imagine how I could even have suspected the meaning of this obsession or could possibly have suggested an interpretation for it. Every time I had asked the patient, "Why do you do this? What is the meaning of it?" she had answered, "I don't know." But one day, after I had succeeded in overcoming a great hesitation on her part, involving a matter of principle, she suddenly did know, for she related the history of the obsessive act. More than ten years previously she had married a man very much older than herself, who had proved impotent on the wedding-night. Innumerable times on that night he had run out of his room into hers in order to make the attempt, but had failed every time. In the morning he had said angrily: "It's enough to disgrace one in the eyes of the maid who does the beds," and seizing a bottle of red ink which happened to be at hand he poured in on the sheet, but not exactly in the place where such a mark might have been. At first I did not understand what this recollection could have to do with the obsessive act in question; for I could see no similarity between the two situations, except in the running from one room into the other, and perhaps also in the appearance of the servant on the scene. The patient then led me to the table in the adjoining room, where I found a great mark on the table-cover. She explained further that she stood by the table in such a way that when the maid came in she could not miss seeing this mark. After this, there could no longer be any doubt about the connection between the current obsessive act and the scene of the wedding-night, though there was still a great deal to learn about it.

It was clear, first of all, that the patient identified herself with her husband; in imitating his running from one room into another she acted his part. To keep up the similarity we must assume that she has substituted the table and table-cover for the bed and sheet. This might seem too arbitrary; but then we have not studied dream-symbolism in vain. In dreams a table is very often found to represent a bed. "Bed and board" together mean marriage, so that the one easily stands for the other.

All this would be proof enough that the obsessive act is full of meaning; it *seems* to be a representation, a repetition of that all-important scene. But we are not bound to stop at this semblance; if we investigate more closely the relation between the two situations we shall probably find out something more, the purpose of the obsessive act. The kernel of it evidently lies in the calling of the maid, to whom she displays the mark, in contrast to her husband's words: "It's enough to disgrace one before the servant." In this way he, whose part she is playing, is *not* ashamed before the servant, the stain is where it ought to be. We see therefore that she has not simply repeated the scene, she has continued it and corrected it, transformed it into what it ought to have been. This implies something else, too, a correction of the circumstance which made that night so distressing, and which made the red ink necessary: namely, the husband's impotence. The obsessive act thus says: "No, it is not true, he was not disgraced before the servant, he was not impotent." As in a dream she represents this wish as fulfilled, in a current obsessive act, which serves the purpose of restoring her husband's credit after that unfortunate incident.

Everything else which I could tell you about this lady fits in with this, or, more correctly stated, everything else that we know about her points to this interpretation of the obsessive act, in itself so incomprehensible. She had been separated from her husband for years and was trying to make up her mind to divorce him legally. But there would have been no prospect of being free from him in her mind; she forced herself to be true to him. She withdrew from the world and from everyone so that she might not be tempted, and in her phantasies she excused and idealized him. The deepest secret of her illness was that it enabled her to shield him from malicious gossip, to justify her separation from him, and to make a comfortable existence apart from her possible for him. The analysis of a harmless obsessive act thus leads straight to the inmost core of the patient's disease, and at the same time betrays a great deal of the secret of the obsessional neurosis in general. I am quite willing that you should spend some time over this example, for it unites conditions which cannot reasonably be expected in all cases. The interpretation of the symptom was discovered by the patient herself in a flash, without guidance or interference from the analyst, and it had arisen in connection with an event which did not belong, as it commonly does, to a forgotten period in childhood, but which had occurred in the patient's adult life and was clear in her memory. All those objections which critics habitually raise against our interpretations of symptoms are quite out of place here. To be sure, we cannot always be so fortunate.

And one thing more! Has it not struck you that this innocent obsessive act leads directly to this lady's most private affairs? A woman can hardly have anything more intimate to relate than the story of her wedding-night; and is it by chance and without special significance that we are led straight to the innermost secrets of her sexual life? It might certainly be due to the choice I made of this example. Let us not decide this point too quickly; but let us turn to the second example, which is of a totally different nature, and belongs to a very common type, that of rituals preparatory to sleep.

A well-grown clever girl of 19, the only child of her parents, superior to them in education and intellectual activity, was a wild, high-spirited child, but of late years had become very nervous without any apparent cause. She was very irritable, particularly with her mother, was discontented and depressed, inclined to indecision and doubt, finally confessing that she could no longer walk alone through squares and wide streets. We will not go very closely into her complicated condition, which requires at least two diagnoses: agoraphobia and obsessional neurosis; but will turn our attention to the ritual elaborated by this young girl preparatory to going to bed, as a result of which she caused her parents great distress. In a certain sense, every normal person may be said to carry out a ritual before going to sleep, or at least, he requires certain conditions without which he is hindered in going to sleep; the transition from waking life to sleep has been made into a regular formula which is repeated every night in the same manner. But everything that a healthy person requires as a condition of sleep can be rationally explained, and if the external circumstances make any alteration necessary he adapts himself easily to it without waste of time. The morbid ritual on the other hand is inexorable, it will be maintained at the greatest sacrifices; it is disguised, too, under rational motives and appears superficially to differ from the normal only in a certain exaggerated carefulness of execution. On a closer examination, however, it is clear that the disguise is insufficient, that the ritual includes observances which go far beyond what reason can justify and even some which directly contravene this. As the motive of her nightly precautions, our patient declares that she must have silence at night and must exclude all possibility of noise. She does two things for this purpose; she stops the large clock in her room and removes all other clocks out of the room, including even the tiny wrist-watch on her bed-table. Flower-pots and vases are placed carefully together on the writing-table, so that they cannot fall down in the night and break, and so disturb her sleep. She knows that these precautions have only an illusory justification in the demand for quiet; the ticking of the little watch could not be heard, even if it lay on the table by the bed; and we all know that the regular ticking of a pendulum-clock never disturbs sleep, but is more likely to induce it. She also admits that her fear that the flower-pots and vases, if left in their places at night, might fall down of themselves and break is utterly improbable. For some other practices in her ritual this insistence upon silence as a motive is dropped; indeed, by ordaining that the door between her bedroom and that of her parents shall remain half-open (a condition which she ensures by placing various objects in the doorway) she seems, on the contrary, to open the way to sources of noise. The most important observances are concerned with the bed itself, however. The bolster at the head of the bed must not touch the back of the wooden bedstead. The pillow must lie across the bolster exactly in a diagonal position and in no other; she then places her head exactly in the middle of this diamond, lengthways. The eiderdown must be shaken before she puts it over her, so that all the feathers sink to the foot-end; she never fails, however, to press this out and redistribute them all over it again.

I will pass over other trivial details of her ritual; they would teach us nothing new and lead us too far from our purpose. Do not suppose, though, that all this is carried out with perfect smoothness. Everything is accompanied by the anxiety that it has not all been done properly; it must be tested and repeated; her doubts fix first upon one, then another, of the precautions; and the result is that one or two hours elapse before the girl herself can sleep, or lets the intimidated parents sleep.

The analysis of these torments did not proceed so simply as that of the former patient's obsessive act. I had to offer hints and suggestions of its interpretation which were invariably received by her with a positive denial or with scornful doubt. After this first reaction of rejection, however, there followed a period in which she herself took up the possibilities suggested to her, noted the associations they aroused, produced memories, and established connections until she herself had accepted all the interpretations in working them out for herself. In proportion as she did this she began to relax the performance of her obsessive precautions and before the end of the treatment she had given up the whole ritual. I must also tell you that analytic work, as we conduct it nowadays, definitely excludes any uninterrupted concentration on a single symptom until its meaning becomes fully clear. It is necessary, on the contrary, to abandon a given theme again and again, in the assurance that one will come upon it anew in another context. The interpretation of the symptom, which I am now going to tell you, is therefore a synthesis of the results which, amid the interruptions of work on other points, took weeks and months to procure.

The patient gradually learnt to understand that she banished clocks and watches from her room at night because they were symbols of the female genitals. Clocks, which we know may have other symbolic meanings besides this, acquire this significance of a genital organ by their relation to periodical processes and regular intervals. A woman may be heard to boast that menstruation occurs in her as regularly as clockwork. Now this patient's special fear was that the ticking of the clocks would disturb her during sleep. The ticking of a clock is comparable to the throbbing of the clitoris in sexual excitation. This sensation, which was distressing to her, had actually on several occasions wakened her from sleep; and now her fear of an erection of the clitoris expressed itself by the imposition of a rule to remove all going clocks and watches far away from her during the night. Flower-pots and vases are, like all receptacles, also symbols of the female genitals. Precautions to prevent them from falling and breaking during the night are therefore not lacking in meaning. We know the very widespread custom of breaking a vessel or a plate on the occasion of a betrothal; everyone present possesses himself of a fragment in symbolic acceptance of the fact that he may no longer put forward any claims to the bride, presumably a custom which arose with monogamy. The patient also contributed a recollection and several associations to this part of her ritual. Once as a child she had fallen while carrying a glass or porcelain vessel, and had cut her finger which had bled badly. As she grew up and learnt the facts about sexual intercourse, she developed the apprehension that on her wedding-night she would not bleed and so would prove not to be a virgin. Her precautions against the vases breaking signified a rejection of the whole complex concerned with virginity and with the question of bleeding during the first act of intercourse; a rejection of the anxiety both that she would bleed and that she would not bleed. These precautions were in fact only remotely connected with the prevention of noise.

One day she divined the central idea of her ritual when she suddenly understood her rule not to let the bolster touch the back of the bed. The bolster had always seemed a woman to her, she said, and the upright back of the bedstead a man. She wished therefore, by a magic ceremony, as it were, to keep man and woman apart; that is to say, to separate the parents and prevent intercourse from occurring. Years before the institution of her ritual, she had attempted to achieve this end by a more direct method. She had simulated fear, or had exploited a tendency to fear, so that the door between her bedroom and that of her parents should not be closed. This regulation was still actually included in her present ritual; in this way she managed to make it possible to overhear her parents; a proceeding which at one time had caused her months of sleeplessness. Not content with disturbing her parents in this way, she at that time even succeeded occasionally in sleeping between the father and mother in their bed. "Bolster" and "bedstead" were then really prevented from coming together. As she finally grew too big to be comfortable in the same bed with the parents, she achieved the same thing by consciously simulating fear and getting her mother to change places with her and to give up to her her place by the father. This incident was undoubtedly the starting-point of phantasies, the effect of which was evident in the ritual.

If the bolster was a woman, then the shaking of the eiderdown till all the feathers were at the bottom, making a protuberance there, also had a meaning. It meant impregnating a woman; she did not neglect, though, to obliterate the pregnancy again, for she had for years been terrified that intercourse between her parents might result in another child and present her with a rival. On the other hand, if the large bolster meant the mother then the small pillow could only represent the daughter. Why had this pillow to be placed diamond-wise upon the bolster and her head be laid exactly in its middle lengthways? She was easily reminded that a diamond is repeatedly used in drawings on walls to signify the open female genitals. The part of the man (the father) she thus played herself and replaced the male organ by her own head. (Cf. Symbolism of beheading for castration.)

Horrible thoughts, you will say, to run in the mind of a virgin girl. I admit that; but do not forget that I have not invented these ideas, only exposed them. A ritual of this kind before sleep is also peculiar enough, and you cannot deny the correspondence, revealed by the interpretation, between the ceremonies and the phantasies. It is more important to me, however, that you should notice that the ritual was the outcome, not of one single phantasy, but of several together which of course must have had a nodal point somewhere. Note, too, that the details of the ritual reflect the sexual wishes both positively and negatively, and serve in part as expressions of them, in part as defences against them.

It would be possible to obtain much more out of the analysis of this ritual by bringing it into its place in connection with the patient's other symptoms. But that is not our purpose at the moment. You must be content with a reference to an erotic attachment to the father, originating very early in childhood, which had enslaved this girl. It was perhaps for this reason that she was so unfriendly towards her mother. Also we cannot overlook the fact that the analysis of this symptom has again led to the patient's sexual life. The more insight we gain into the meaning and purpose of neurotic symptoms, the less surprising will this seem.

From two selected examples I have now shown you that neurotic symptoms have meaning, like errors and like dreams, and that they are closely connected with the events of the patient's life. Can I expect you to believe this exceptionally significant statement on the strength of two examples? No. But can you expect me to go on quoting examples to you until you declare yourselves convinced? Again, no; for in view of the exhaustive treatment given to each individual case I should have to devote five hours a week for a whole term to the consideration of this one point in the theory of the neuroses. I will content myself therefore with the samples given, as evidence of my statement; and will refer you for more to the literature on the subject, to the classical interpretation of symptoms in Breuer's first case (hysteria), to the striking elucidations of very obscure symptoms in dementia præcox, so-called, made by C. G. Jung at a time when this investigator was a mere psychoanalyst and did not yet aspire to be a prophet, and to all the subsequent contributions with which our periodicals have been filled since then. Precisely this type of investigation is plentiful. Analysis, interpretation, and translation of neurotic symptoms has proved so attractive to psycho-analysts that in comparison they have temporarily neglected the other problems of the neuroses.

Any one of you who makes the necessary effort to look up this question will certainly be strongly impressed by the wealth of evidential material. But he will also meet with a difficulty. The meaning of a symptom lies, as we have seen, in its connection with the life of the patient. The more individually the symptom has been formed, the more clearly may we expect to establish this connection. Then the task resolves itself specifically into a discovery, for every nonsensical idea and every useless action, of the past situation in which the idea was justified and the action served a useful purpose. The obsessive act of the patient who ran to the table and rang for the maid is a perfect model of this kind of symptom. But symptoms of quite a different type are very frequently seen. They are what we call *typical* symptoms of a disease, in each case they are practically identical, the individual differences in them vanish or at least fade away, so that it is difficult to connect them with the patient's life or to relate them to special situations in his past. Let us consider the obsessional neurosis again. The second patient's ceremonies preparatory to sleep are in many ways quite typical, although showing enough individual features as well to make an "historical" interpretation, so to speak, possible. But all obsessional patients are given to repetitions, to isolating certain of their actions and to rhythmic performances. Most of them wash too much. Those patients who suffer from agoraphobia (topophobia, fear of space), no longer reckoned as an obsessional neurosis but now classified as anxiety-hysteria, reproduce the same features of the pathological picture often with fatiguing monotony. They fear enclosed spaces, wide, open squares, long stretches of road, and avenues; they feel protected if accompanied, or if a vehicle drives behind them, and so on. Nevertheless, on this groundwork of similarity the various patients construct individual conditions of their own, moods, one might call them, which directly contrast with other cases. One fears narrow streets only, another wide streets only, one can walk only when few people are about, others only when surrounded with people. Similarly in hysteria, beside the wealth of individual features there are always plenty of common typical symptoms which appear to resist an easy interpretation on historical lines. Do not let us forget that it is these typical symptoms which enable us to take our bearings in forming a diagnosis. Supposing we do trace back a typical symptom in a case of hysteria to an experience or to a chain of similar experiences (for instance, an hysterical vomiting to a series of impressions of a disgusting nature), it will be confusing to discover in another case of vomiting an entirely dissimilar series of apparently causative experiences. It almost looks as though hysterical patients must vomit, for some unknown reason, and as though the historical factors revealed by analysis were but pretexts, seized upon by an inner necessity, when opportunity offered, to serve its purpose.

This brings us to the discouraging conclusion that although individual forms of neurotic symptoms can certainly be satisfactorily explained by their relation to the patient's experiences, yet our science fails us for the far more frequent typical symptoms in the same cases. In addition to this, I have not nearly explained to you all the difficulties that arise during a resolute pursuit of the historical meaning of a symptom. Nor shall I do so; for although my intention is to conceal nothing from you and to gloss over nothing, I do not need to confuse you and stupefy you at the outset of our studies together. It is true that our understanding of symptom-interpretation has only just begun, but we will hold fast to the knowledge gained and proceed to overcome step by step the difficulties of the unknown. I will try to cheer you with the thought that it is hardly possible to presume a fundamental difference between the one kind of symptom and the other. If the individual form of symptom is so unmistakably connected with the patient's experiences, it is possible that the typical symptom relates to an experience which is itself typical and common to all humanity. Other regularly recurring features of a neurosis, such as the repetition and doubt of the obsessional neurosis, may be universal reactions which the patient is compelled to exaggerate by the nature of the morbid change. In short, there is no reason to give up hastily in despair; let us see what more we can find out.

There is a very similar difficulty met with in the theory of dreams, one which I could not deal with in the course of our previous discussions of dreams. The manifest content of dreams is multifarious and highly differentiated individually, and we have shown exhaustively what can be obtained by analysis from this content. But there are also dreams which may in the same way be called *typical* and occur in everybody, dreams with an identical content, which present the same difficulties to analysis. These are the dreams of falling, flying, floating, swimming, of being hindered, of being naked, and certain other anxiety-dreams; which yield first this, then that, interpretation, according to the person concerned, without any explanation of their monotonous and typical recurrence. But we notice that in these dreams also the common groundwork is embroidered with additions of an individually varying character. Most probably they too will prove to fit in with other knowledge about the dream-life, gained from a study of other kinds of dreams—not by any forcible twist, but by a gradual widening of our comprehension of these things.

Eighteenth Lecture

Fixation upon Traumas: The Unconscious

I said last time that we would take, as a starting-point for further work, the knowledge we have gained already, and not the doubts which it has roused in us. We have not yet even begun to discuss two of the most interesting conclusions arising from the analysis of the two examples.

First: both the patients give the impression that they are *"fixed"* to a particular point in their past, that they do not know how to release themselves from it, and are consequently alienated from both present and future. They are marooned in their illness, as it were; just as in former times people used to withdraw to the cloister to live out their unhappy fate there. In the case of the first patient, it was the marriage to the husband, which in reality had long ago come to an end, that had settled this doom upon her. Her symptoms enabled her to continue her relationship with him; we could perceive in them the voices which pleaded for him, excused him, exalted him, lamented his loss. Although she is young and could attract other men, she has seized upon every possible real and imaginary (magical) precaution that will preserve her fidelity to him. She will not meet strangers, she neglects her appearance, moreover, she cannot readily rise from any chair which she sits upon, and she refuses to sign her name and can give no presents, because no one must have anything which is hers.

With the second patient, the young girl, it is the erotic attachment to the father established in the years before puberty that plays this part in her life. She also has herself perceived that she cannot marry as long as she is so ill. We may suspect that she became so ill in order to be unable to marry and so to remain with her father.

We cannot avoid asking the question how, by what means, and impelled by what motives, anyone can take up such an extraordinary and unprofitable attitude towards life. Provided, that is, that this attitude is a universal character of neurosis and is not a special peculiarity of these two patients. As a matter of fact, this is so; it is a universal trait common to every neurosis, and one of great practical significance. Breuer's first hysterical patient was *fixated*, in the same way, to the time when her father was seriously ill and she nursed him. In spite of her recovery, she has remained to some extent cut off from life since that time; for although she has remained healthy and active, she did not take up the normal career of a woman. In every one of our patients we learn through analysis that the symptoms and their effects have set the sufferer back into some past period of his life. In the majority of cases it is actually a very early phase of the life-history which has been thus selected, a period in childhood, even, absurd as it may sound, the period of existence as a suckling infant.

The closest analogy to this behaviour in our nervous patients is provided by the forms of illness recently made so common by the war—the so-called *traumatic neuroses*. Of course similar cases have occurred before the war, after railway accidents and other terrifying experiences involving danger to life. The traumatic neuroses are not fundamentally the same as those which occur spontaneously, which we investigate analytically and are accustomed to treat; neither have we been successful so far in correlating them with our views on other subjects; later on I hope to show you where this limitation lies. Yet there is a complete agreement between them on one point

which may be emphasized. The traumatic neuroses demonstrate very clearly that a fixation to the moment of the traumatic occurrence lies at their root. These patients regularly
produce the traumatic situation in their dreams; in cases
showing attacks of an hysterical type in which analysis is
possible, it appears that the attack constitutes a complete
reproduction of this situation. It is as though these persons
had not yet been able to deal adequately with the situation,
as if this task were still actually before them unaccom-
plished. We take this attitude of theirs in all seriousness; it
points the way to what we may call an *economic* conception
of the mental processes. The term '*traumatic*' has actually no
other meaning but this *economic* one. An experience which
we call traumatic is one which within a very short space of
time subjects the mind to such a very high increase of stimulation that assimilation or elaboration of it can no longer be
effected by normal means, so that lasting disturbances must
result in the distribution of the available energy in the mind.

This analogy tempts us also to classify as traumatic those
experiences to which our nervous patients seem to be fixated. In this way we should be provided with a simple condition for a neurotic illness; it would be comparable to a
traumatic illness and would result from an incapacity to
deal with an overpowering affective experience. Indeed,
the first formula in which Breuer and I, in 1893–95, reduced our new observations to a theory was expressed very
similarly. A case like that of the first patient described, the
young woman separated from her husband, fits very well
into this description; she had not been able to "get over"
the impracticability of her marriage and was still attached
to her trauma. But the second case of the young girl who
was tied to her father shows us at once that the formula
is not comprehensive enough. On the one hand, an infantile adoration of her father by a little girl is such a common experience and so frequently grown out of that the
term 'traumatic' would lose all its meaning if applied to it;
on the other hand, the history of the case shows that this
first erotic fixation was gone through by the patient quite
harmlessly at the time, to all appearances, and only several

years later came to expression in the obsessional neurosis. So we see that there are complications ahead, a considerable variety and number of determining factors in neurosis; but we divine that the traumatic view will not necessarily be abandoned as false, and that it will fit in and have to be co-ordinated properly elsewhere.

Here again we must leave the path we have been follow-ing. At the moment it will take us no further, and we have much more to learn before we can find a satisfactory continu-ation of it. But before leaving the subject of fixation to traumas it should be noted that it is a phenomenon mani-fested extensively outside the neuroses; every neurosis con-tains such a fixation, but not every fixation leads to a neurosis, or is necessarily combined with a neurosis, or arises in the course of a neurosis. Grief is a prototype and perfect example of an affective fixation upon something that is past, and, like the neuroses, it also involves a state of complete alienation from the present and the future. But even the lay public dis-tinguishes clearly between grief and neurosis. On the other hand, there are neuroses which may be described as morbid forms of grief.

It does also happen that persons may be brought to a com-plete standstill in life by a traumatic experience which has shaken the whole structure of their lives to the foundations, so that they give up all interest in the present and the future, and live permanently absorbed in their retrospections; but these unhappy persons do not necessarily become neurotic. Therefore this single feature must not be overestimated as a characteristic of neurosis, however invariable and significant it may be otherwise.

Now let us turn to the second conclusion to be drawn from our analyses; it is one upon which we shall not need to im-pose any subsequent limitation. With the first patient we have heard of the senseless obsessive act she performed and of the intimate memories she recalled in connection with it; we also considered the relation between the two, and deduced the purpose of the obsessive act from its connection with the memory. But there is one factor which we have entirely

neglected, and yet it is one which deserves our fullest attention. As long as the patient continued this performance she
did not know that it was in any way connected with the previous experience; the connection between the two things was
hidden; she could quite truly answer that she did not know
what impulse led her to do it. Then it happened suddenly
that, under the influence of the treatment, she found this connection and was able to tell it. But even then she knew nothing of the purpose she had in performing the action, the purpose that was to correct a painful event of the past and to
raise the husband she loved in her own estimation. It took a
long time and much effort for her to grasp, and admit to me,
that such a motive as this alone could have been the driving
force behind the obsessive act.

The connection with the scene on the morning after the
unhappy bridal-night, and the patient's own tender feeling
for her husband, together, make up what we have called the
"meaning" of the obsessive act. But both sides of this meaning were hidden from her, she understood neither the *whence*
nor the *whither* of her act, as long as she carried it on. Mental
processes had been at work in her, therefore, of which the
obsessive act was the effect; she was aware in a normal manner
of their effect; but nothing of the mental antecedents of this
effect had come to the knowledge of her consciousness. She
was behaving exactly like a subject under hypnotism whom
Bernheim had ordered to open an umbrella in the ward five
minutes after he awoke, but who had no idea why he was
doing it. This is the kind of occurrence we have in mind
when we speak of the existence of *unconscious mental processes;* we may challenge anyone in the world to give a more
correctly scientific explanation of this matter, and will then
gladly withdraw our inference that unconscious mental processes exist. Until they do, however, we will adhere to this inference and, when anyone objects that in a scientific sense
the unconscious has no reality, that it is a mere makeshift,
une façon de parler, we must resign ourselves with a shrug
to rejecting his statement as incomprehensible. Something

unreal, which can nevertheless produce something so real and palpable as an obsessive action!

In the second patient fundamentally the same thing is found. She has instituted a rule that the bolster must not touch the back of the bedstead, and she had to carry out this rule, but she does not know whence it comes, what it means, or to what it owes its strength. Whether she regards it indifferently, or struggles against it, or rages against it, or determines to overcome it, matters not; it will be followed. It must be followed; in vain she asks herself why. It is undeniable that these symptoms of the obsessional neurosis, these ideas and these impulses which arise no man knows where and which oppose such a powerful resistance against all the influences to which an otherwise normal mental life is susceptible, give the impression, even to the patients themselves, of being all-powerful visitants from another world, immortal beings mingling in the whirlpool of mortal things. In these symptoms lies the clearest indication of a special sphere of mental activity cut off from all the rest. They show the way unmistakably to conviction on the question of the unconscious in the mind; and for that very reason clinical psychiatry, which only recognizes a psychology of consciousness, can do nothing with these symptoms except to stigmatize them as signs of a special kind of degeneration. Naturally, the obsessive ideas and impulses are not themselves unconscious, any more than is the performance of the obsessive acts. They would not have become symptoms if they had not penetrated into consciousness. But the mental antecedents of them disclosed by analysis, the connections into which they fit after interpretation, are unconscious, at least until the time when we make the patient conscious of them by the work of the analysis.

Consider now, in addition, that the facts established in these two cases are confirmed in every symptom of every neurotic disease; that always and everywhere the meaning of the symptoms is unknown to the sufferer; that analysis invariably shows that these symptoms are derived from unconscious mental processes which can, however, under various favourable conditions, become conscious. You will then understand that we cannot dispense with the unconscious part of the mind in psycho-analysis, and that we are accustomed to deal with it as with something actual and tangible. Perhaps you will also be able to realize how unfitted all those who only know the unconscious as a phrase, who have never analysed, never interpreted dreams, or translated neurotic symptoms into their meaning and intention, are to form an opinion on this matter. I will repeat the substance of it again in order to impress it upon you: The fact that it is possible to find meaning in neurotic symptoms by means of analytic interpretation is an irrefutable proof of the existence—or, if you prefer it, of the necessity for assuming the existence—of unconscious mental processes.

But that is not all. Thanks to a second discovery of Breuer's, for which he alone deserves credit and which seems to me even more far-reaching in its significance than the first, more still has been learnt about the relation between the unconscious and the symptoms of neurotics. Not merely is the meaning of the symptom invariably unconscious; there exists also a connection of a substitutive nature between the two; the existence of the symptom is only possible by reason of this unconscious activity. You will soon understand what I mean. With Breuer, I maintain the following: Every time we meet with a symptom we may conclude that definite unconscious activities which contain the meaning of the symptom are present in the patient's mind. Conversely, this meaning must be unconscious before a symptom can arise from it. Symptoms are not produced by conscious processes; as soon as the unconscious processes involved are made conscious the symptom must vanish. You will perceive at once that here is an opening for therapy, a way by which symptoms can be made to disappear. It was by this means that Breuer actually achieved the recovery of his patient, that is, freed her from her symptoms; he found a method of bringing into her consciousness the unconscious processes which contained the meaning of her symptoms and the symptoms vanished.

This discovery of Breuer's was not the result of any specu-

lation but of a fortunate observation made possible by the
co-operation of the patient. Now you must not rack your
brains to try and understand this by seeking to compare it
with something similar that is already familiar to you; but
you must recognize in it a fundamentally new fact, by means
of which much else becomes explicable. Allow me therefore
to express it again to you in other words.

The symptom is formed as a substitute for something else
which remains submerged. Certain mental processes would,
under normal conditions, develop until the person became
aware of them consciously. This has not happened; and, instead, the symptom has arisen out of these processes which
have been interrupted and interfered with in some way and
have had to remain unconscious. Thus something in the nature of an exchange has occurred; if we can succeed in re-
versing this process by our therapy we shall have performed
our task of dispersing the symptom.

Breuer's discovery still remains the foundation of psychoanalytic therapy. The proposition that symptoms vanish when
their unconscious antecedents have been made conscious has
been borne out by all subsequent research; although the most
extraordinary and unexpected complications are met with in
attempting to carry this proposition out in practice. Our
therapy does its work by transforming something unconscious
into something conscious, and only succeeds in its work in so
far as it is able to effect this transformation.

Now for a rapid digression, lest you should run the risk of
imagining that this therapeutic effect is achieved too easily.
According to the conclusions we have reached so far, neurosis
would be the result of a kind of ignorance, a not-knowing of
mental processes which should be known. This would approach very closely to the well-known Socratic doctrine according to which even vice is the result of ignorance. Now
it happens in analysis that an experienced practitioner can
usually surmise very easily what those feelings are which have
remained unconscious in each individual patient. It should
not therefore be a matter of great difficulty to cure the patient
by imparting his knowledge to him and so relieving his igno-

rance. At least, one side of the unconscious meaning of the symptom would be easily dealt with in this way, although it is true that the other side of it, the connection between the symptom and the previous experiences in the patient's life, can hardly be divined thus; for the analyst does not know what the experiences have been, he has to wait till the patient remembers them and tells him. But one might find a substitute even for this in many cases. One might ask for information about his past life from the friends and relations; they are often in a position to know what events have been of a traumatic nature, perhaps they can even relate some of which the patient is ignorant because they took place at some very early period of childhood. By a combination of these two means it would seem that the pathogenic ignorance of the patients might be overcome in a short time without much trouble.

If only it were so! But we have made discoveries that we were quite unprepared for at first. There is knowing and knowing; they are not always the same thing. There are various kinds of knowing, which psychologically are not by any means of equal value. *Il y a fagots et fagots*, as Molière says. Knowing on the part of the physician is not the same thing as knowing on the part of the patient and does not have the same effect. When the physician conveys his knowledge to the patient by telling him what he knows, it has effect. No, it would be incorrect to say that. It does not have the effect of dispersing the symptoms; but it has a different one, it sets the analysis in motion, and the first result of this is often an energetic denial. The patient has learned something that he did not know before—the meaning of his symptom—and yet he knows it as little as ever. Thus we discover that there is more than one kind of ignorance. It requires a considerable degree of insight and understanding of psychological matters in order to see in what the difference consists. But the proposition that symptoms vanish with the acquisition of knowledge of their meaning remains true, nevertheless. The necessary condition is that the knowledge must be founded upon an inner change in the patient which can only come about by a mental operation directed to that end. We are here confronted by problems which to us will soon develop into the *dynamics* of symptom-formation.

Now I must really stop and ask you whether all that I have been saying is not too obscure and complicated? Am I confusing you by so often qualifying and restricting, spinning out trains of thought and then letting them drop? I should be sorry if it were so. But I have a strong dislike of simplification at the expense of truth, I am not averse from giving you a full impression of the many-sidedness and intricacy of the subject, and also I believe that it does no harm to tell you more about each point than you can assimilate at the moment. I know that every listener and every reader arranges what is offered him as suits him in his own mind, shortens it, simplifies it, and extracts from it what he will retain. Within certain limits it is true that the more we begin with the more we shall have at the end. So let me hope that, in spite of the elaboration, you will have grasped the essential substance of my remarks concerning the meaning of symptoms, the unconscious, and the connection between the two. You have probably understood also that our further efforts will proceed in two directions; first, towards discovering how people become ill, how they come to take up the characteristic neurotic attitude towards life, which is a clinical problem; and secondly, how they develop the morbid symptoms out of the conditions of a neurosis, which remains a problem of mental dynamics. The two problems must somewhere have a point of contact.

I shall not go further into this to-day; but as our time is not yet up I propose to draw your attention to another characteristic of our two analyses; namely, *the memory gaps or amnesias*, again a point which only later will appear in its full significance. You have heard that the task of the psychoanalytic treatment can be summed up in this formula: everything pathogenic in the unconscious must be transferred into consciousness. Now you will be perhaps astonished to hear that another formula may be substituted for that one: all gaps in the patient's memory must be filled in, his amnesias removed. It amounts to the same thing; which means that an

important connection is to be recognized between the development of the symptoms and the amnesias. If you consider
the case of the first patient analysed you will, however, not
find this view of amnesia justified; the patient had not forgotten the scene from which the obsessive act is derived; on
the contrary, it was vivid in her memory, nor is there any
other forgotten factor involved in the formation of her symptom. The situation is quite analogous, although less clear, in
the second case, the girl with the obsessional ceremonies. She,
too, had not really forgotten her behaviour in former years,
the fact that she had insisted upon the open door between
her parents' bedroom and her own, and that she had turned
her mother out of her place in the parents' bed; she remembered it quite clearly, although with hesitation and unwillingness. What is remarkable about it is that the first patient, although she had carried out her obsessive act such a countless
number of times, had not *once* been reminded of its similarity
to the scene after the wedding-night, nor did this recollection
ever occur to her when she was directly asked to search for
the origin of her obsessive act. The same thing is true in the
case of the girl, where not merely the ritual, but the situation
which gave rise to it, was repeated identically every evening.
In neither case was there really an amnesia, a lapse of
memory; but a connection, which should have existed intact
and have led to the reproduction, the recollection, of the
memory, had been broken. This kind of disturbance of
memory suffices for the obsessional neurosis; in hysteria it is
different. This latter neurosis is usually characterized by
amnesias on a grand scale. As a rule the analysis of each
single hysterical symptom leads to a whole chain of former
impressions, which upon their return may be literally described as having been hitherto forgotten. This chain reaches,
on the one hand, back to the earliest years of childhood, so
that the hysterical amnesia is seen to be a direct continuation
of the infantile amnesia which hides the earliest impressions
of our mental life from all of us. On the other hand, we are
astonished to find that the most recent experiences of the
patient are liable to be forgotten also, and that in particular

the provocations which induced the outbreak of the disease or aggravated it are at least partially obliterated, if not entirely wiped out, by amnesia. From the complete picture of any such recent recollection important details have invariably disappeared or been replaced by falsifications. It happens again and again, almost invariably, that not until shortly before the completion of an analysis do certain recollections of recent experiences come to the surface, which had managed to be withheld throughout it and had left noticeable gaps in the context.

These derangements in the capacity to recall memories are, as I have said, characteristic of hysteria, in which disease it also happens even that states occur as symptoms (the hysterical attacks) without necessarily leaving a trace of recollection behind them. Since it is otherwise in the obsessional neurosis, you may infer that these amnesias are part of the psychological character of the hysterical change and are not a universal trait of neurosis in general. The importance of this difference will be diminished by the following consideration. Two things are combined to constitute the meaning of a symptom; its *whence* and its *whither* or *why*; that is, the impressions and experiences from which it sprang, and the purpose which it serves. The *whence* of a symptom is resolved into impressions which have been received from without, which were necessarily at one time conscious, and which may have become unconscious by being forgotten since that time. The *why* of the symptom, its tendency, is however always an endopsychic process, which may possibly have been conscious at first, but just as possibly may never have been conscious and may have remained in the unconscious from its inception. Therefore it is not very important whether the amnesia has also infringed upon the *whence*, the impressions upon which the symptom is supported, as happens in hysteria; the *whither*, the tendency of the symptom, which may have been unconscious from the beginning, is what maintains the symptom's dependence upon the unconscious, in the obsessional neurosis no less strictly than in hysteria.

By thus emphasizing the unconscious in mental life we have

called forth all the malevolence in humanity in opposition to psycho-analysis. Do not be astonished at this and do not suppose that this opposition relates to the obvious difficulty of conceiving the unconscious or to the relative inaccessibility of the evidence which supports its existence. I believe it has a deeper source. Humanity has in the course of time had to endure from the hands of science two great outrages upon its naïve self-love. The first was when it realized that our earth was not the centre of the universe, but only a tiny speck in a world-system of a magnitude hardly conceivable; this is associated in our minds with the name of Copernicus, although Alexandrian doctrines taught something very similar. The second was when biological research robbed man of his peculiar privilege of having been specially created, and relegated him to a descent from the animal world, implying an ineradicable animal nature in him: this transvaluation has been accomplished in our own time upon the instigation of Charles Darwin, Wallace, and their predecessors, and not without the most violent opposition from their contemporaries. But man's craving for grandiosity is now suffering the third and most bitter blow from present-day psychological research which is endeavouring to prove to the "ego" of each one of us that he is not even master in his own house, but that he must remain content with the veriest scraps of information about what is going on unconsciously in his own mind. We psychoanalysts were neither the first nor the only ones to propose to mankind that they should look inward; but it appears to be our lot to advocate it most insistently and to support it by empirical evidence which touches every man closely. This is the kernel of the universal revolt against our science, of the total disregard of academic courtesy in dispute, and the liberation of opposition from all the constraints of impartial logic. And besides this, we have been compelled to disturb the peace of the world in yet another way, as you will soon hear.

NINETEENTH LECTURE

RESISTANCE AND REPRESSION

WE NOW NEED MORE DATA BEFORE WE CAN ADVANCE FURTHER in our understanding of the neuroses; two observations lie to hand for us. Both are very remarkable and at first were very surprising. You are of course prepared for both of them by the work we did last year.

First: when we undertake to cure a patient of his symptoms he opposes against us a vigorous and tenacious *resistance* throughout the entire course of the treatment. This is such an extraordinary thing that we cannot expect much belief in it. It is best to say nothing about it to the patient's relations, for they invariably regard it as a pretext set up by us to excuse the length or the failure of the treatment. The patient, too, exhibits all the manifestations of this resistance without recognizing it as such, and it is a great step forward when we have brought him to realize this fact and to reckon with it. To think that the patient, whose symptoms cause him and those about him such suffering, who is willing to make such sacrifices in time, money, effort, and self-conquest in order to be freed from them,—that he should, in the interests of his illness, resist the help offered him. How improbable this statement must sound! And yet it is so, and if the improbability is made a reproach against us we need only reply that it is not without its analogies; for a man who has rushed off to a dentist

298 A General Introduction to Psychoanalysis

with a frightful toothache may very well fend him off when he takes his forceps to the decayed tooth.

The resistance shown by patients is highly varied and exceedingly subtle, often hard to recognize and protean in the manifold forms it takes; the analyst needs to be continually suspicious and on his guard against it. In psychoanalytic therapy we employ the technique which is already familiar to you through dream-interpretation: we require the patient to put himself into a condition of calm self-observation, without trying to think of anything, and then to communicate everything which he becomes inwardly aware of, feelings, thoughts, remembrances, in the order in which they arise in his mind. We expressly warn him against giving way to any kind of motive which would cause him to select from or to exclude any of the ideas (associations), whether because they are too "disagreeable," or too "indiscreet" to be mentioned, or too "unimportant" or "irrelevant" or "nonsensical" to be worth saying. We impress upon him that he has only to attend to what is on the surface consciously in his mind, and to abandon all objections to whatever he finds, no matter what form they take; and we inform him that the success of the treatment, and, above all, its duration, will depend upon his conscientious adherence to this fundamental technical rule. We know from the technique of dream-interpretation that it is precisely those associations against which innumerable doubts and objections are raised that invariably contain the material leading to the discovery of the unconscious.

The first thing that happens as a result of instituting this technical rule is that it becomes the first point of attack for the resistance. The patient attempts to escape from it by every possible means. First he says nothing comes into his head, then that so much comes into his head that he can't grasp any of it. Then we observe with displeasure and astonishment that he is giving in to his critical objections, first to this, then to that; he betrays it by the long pauses which occur in his talk. At last he admits that he really cannot say something, he is ashamed to, and he lets this feeling get the better of his promise. Or else, he has thought of something but it concerns

NINETEENTH LECTURE   299

someone else and not himself, and is therefore to be made an exception to the rule. Or else, what he has just thought of is really too unimportant, too stupid and too absurd, I could never have meant that he should take account of such thoughts. So it goes on, with untold variations, to which one continually replies that telling everything really means telling everything.

One hardly ever meets with a patient who does not attempt to make a reservation in some department of his thoughts, in order to guard them against intrusion by the analysis. One patient, who in the ordinary way was remarkably intelligent, concealed a most intimate love-affair from me for weeks in this way; when accused of this violation of the sacred rule he defended himself with the argument that he considered this particular story his private affair. Naturally analytic treatment cannot countenance a right of sanctuary like this; one might as well try to allow an exception to be made in certain parts of a town like Vienna, and forbid that any arrests should be made in the market-place or in the square by St. Stephen's church, and then attempt to take up a "wanted" man. Of course he would never be found anywhere but in those safe places. Once I decided to permit a man to make an exception of such a point; for a great deal depended on his recovering his capacity for work and he was bound by his oath as a civil servant not to communicate certain matters to any other person. He was content with the result, it is true, but I was not: I made up my mind never again to repeat the attempt under such conditions.

Obsessional patients are exceedingly clever at making the technical rule almost useless by bringing their over-conscientiousness and doubt to bear upon it. Patients with anxiety-hysteria sometimes succeed in reducing it to absurdity by only producing associations which are so far removed from what is wanted that they yield nothing for analysis. However, I do not intend to introduce you to these technical difficulties of the treatment. It is enough to know that finally, with resolution and perseverance, we do succeed in extracting from the patient a certain amount of obedience for the rule of the technique; and then the resistance takes another line altogether. It appears as intellectual opposition, employs arguments as weapons, and turns to its own use all the difficulties and improbabilities which normal but uninstructed reasoning finds in analytical doctrines. We then have to hear from the mouth of the individual patient all the criticisms and objections which thunder about us in chorus in scientific literature. What the critics outside shout at us is nothing new, therefore. It is indeed a storm in a teacup. Still, the patient can be argued with; he is very glad to get us to instruct him, teach him, defeat him, point out the literature to him so that he can learn more; he is perfectly ready to become a supporter of psychoanalysis on the condition that analysis shall spare him personally. We recognize resistance in this desire for knowledge, however; it is a digression from the particular task in hand and we refuse to allow it. In the obsessional neurosis the resistance makes use of special tactics which we are prepared for. It permits the analysis to proceed uninterruptedly along its course, so that more and more light is thrown upon the problems of the case, until we begin to wonder at last why these explanations have no practical effect and entail no corresponding improvement in the symptoms. Then we discover that the resistance has fallen back upon the doubt characteristic of the obsessional neurosis and is holding us successfully at bay from this vantage-point. The patient has said to himself something of this kind: "This is all very pretty and very interesting. I should like to go on with it. I am sure it would do me a lot of good if it were true. But I don't believe it in the least, and as long as I don't believe it, it doesn't affect my illness." So it goes on for a long time, until at last this reservation itself is reached and then the decisive battle begins.

The intellectual resistances are not the worst; one can always get the better of them. But the patient knows how to set up resistances within the boundaries of analysis proper, and the defeat of these is one of the most difficult tasks of the technique. Instead of remembering certain of the feelings and states of mind of his previous life, he reproduces them, lives through again such of them as, by means of what is called the 'transference,' may be made effective in opposition against the physician and the treatment. If the patient is a man, he usually takes this material from his relationship with his father, in whose place he has now put the physician; and in so doing he erects resistances out of his struggles to attain to personal independence and independence of judgement, out of his ambition, the earliest aim of which was to equal or to excel the father, out of his disinclination to take the burden of gratitude upon himself for the second time in his life. There are periods in which one feels that the patient's desire to put the analyst in the wrong, to make him feel his impotence, to triumph over him, has completely ousted the worthier desire to bring the illness to an end. Women have a genius for exploiting in the interests of resistance a tender erotically tinged transference to the analyst; when this attraction reaches a certain intensity all interest in the actual situation of treatment fades away, together with every obligation incurred upon undertaking it. The inevitable jealousy and the embitterment consequent upon the unavoidable rejection, however considerately it is handled, is bound to injure the personal relationship with the physician, and so to put out of action one of the most powerful propelling forces in the analysis.

Resistances of this kind must not be narrowly condemned. They contain so much of the most important material from the patient's past life and bring it back in so convincing a fashion that they come to be of the greatest assistance to the analysis, if a skilful technique is employed correctly to turn them to the best use. What is noteworthy is that this material always serves at first as a resistance and comes forward in a guise which is inimical to the treatment. Again it may be said that they are character-traits, individual attitudes of the ego, which are thus mobilized to oppose the attempted alterations. One learns then how these character-traits have been developed in connection with the conditions of the neurosis and in reaction against its demands, and observes features in this character which would not otherwise have appeared, at least, not so clearly: that is, which may be designated latent. Also you must not carry away the impression that we look upon the appearance of these resistances as an unforeseen danger threatening our analytic influence. No, we know that these resistances are bound to appear; we are dissatisfied only if we cannot rouse them definitely enough and make the patient perceive them as such. Indeed, we understand at last that the overcoming of these resistances is the essential work of the analysis, that part of the work which alone assures us that we have achieved something for the patient.

Besides this, you must take into account that all accidental occurrences arising during the treatment are made use of by the patient to interfere with it, anything which could distract him or deter him from it, every hostile expression of opinion from anyone in his circle whom he can regard as an authority, any chance organic illness or one complicating the neurosis; indeed, he even converts every improvement in his condition into a motive for slackening his efforts. Then you will have obtained an approximate, though still incomplete, picture of the forms and the measures taken by the resistances which must be met and overcome in the course of every analysis. I have given such a detailed consideration to this point because I am about to inform you that our dynamic conception of the neuroses is founded upon this experience of ours of the resistances that neurotic patients set up against the cure of their symptoms. Breuer and I both originally practised psychotherapy by the hypnotic method. Breuer's first patient was treated throughout in a state of hypnotic suggestibility; at first I followed his example. I admit that at that time my work went forward more easily and agreeably and also took much less time: but the results were capricious and not permanent; therefore I finally gave up hypnotism. And then I understood that no comprehension of the dynamics of these affections was possible as long as hypnosis was employed. In this condition the very existence of resistances is concealed from the physician's observation. Hypnosis drives back the resistances and frees a certain field for the work of the analysis, but dams them up at the boundaries of this field so that they are insurmountable; it is similar in effect to the doubt of the obsessional neurosis. Therefore I may say that true psychoanalysis only began when the help of hypnosis was discarded.

If it is a matter of such importance to establish these resistances then surely it would be wise to allow caution and doubt full play, in case we have been too ready with our assumption that they exist. Perhaps cases of neurosis may be found in which the associations really fail for other reasons, perhaps the arguments against our theories really deserve serious attention, and we may be wrong in so conveniently disposing of the patient's intellectual objections by stigmatizing them as resistance. Well, I can only assure you that our judgement in this matter has not been formed hastily; we have had opportunity to observe these critical patients both before the resistance comes to the surface and after it disappears. In the course of the treatment the resistance varies in intensity continually; it always increases as a new topic is approached, it is at its height during the work upon it, and dies down again when this theme has been dealt with. Unless certain technical errors have been committed we never have to meet the full measure of resistance, of which any patient is capable, at once. Thus we could definitely ascertain that the same man would take up and then abandon his critical objections over and over again in the course of the analysis. Whenever we are on the point of bringing to his consciousness some piece of unconscious material which is particularly painful to him, then he is critical in the extreme; even though he may have previously understood and accepted a great deal, yet now all these gains seem to be obliterated; in his struggles to oppose at all costs he can behave just as though he were mentally deficient, a form of 'emotional stupidity.' If he can be successfully helped to overcome this new resistance he regains his insight and comprehension. His critical faculty is not functioning independently, and therefore is not to be respected as if it were; it is merely a maid-of-all-work for his affective attitudes and is directed by his resistance. When he dislikes anything he can defend himself against it most ingeniously; but when anything suits his book he can be credulous enough. We are perhaps all much the same; a person being analysed shows this dependence of the intellect upon the affective life so clearly because in the analysis he is so hard-pressed.

In what way can we now account for this fact observed, that the patient struggles so energetically against the relief of his symptoms and the restoration of his mental processes to normal functioning? We say that we have come upon the traces of powerful forces at work here opposing any change in the condition; they must be the same forces that originally induced the condition. In the formation of symptoms some process must have been gone through, which our experience in dispersing them make us able to reconstruct. As we already know from Breuer's observations, it follows from the existence of a symptom that some mental process has not been carried through to an end in a normal manner so that it could become conscious; the symptom is a substitute for that which has not come through. Now we know where to place the forces which we suspect to be at work. A vehement effort must have been exercised to prevent the mental process in question from penetrating into consciousness and as a result it has remained unconscious; being unconscious it had the power to construct a symptom. The same vehement effort is again at work during analytic treatment, opposing the attempt to bring the unconscious into consciousness. This we perceive in the form of resistances. The pathogenic process which is demonstrated by the resistances we call REPRESSION.

It will now be necessary to make our conception of this process of *repression* more precise. It is the essential preliminary condition for the development of symptoms, but it is also something else, a thing to which we have no parallel. Let us take as a model an impulse, a mental process seeking to convert itself into action: we know that it can suffer rejection, by virtue of what we call "repudiation" or "condemnation"; whereupon the energy at its disposal is withdrawn, it becomes powerless, but it can continue to exist as a memory. The whole process of decision on the point takes place with the full cognizance of the ego. It is very different when we imagine the same impulse subject to *repression:* it would then retain its energy and no memory of it would be left behind; the process of repression, too, would be accomplished without the cognizance of the ego. This comparison therefore brings us no nearer to the nature of repression.

I will expound to you those theoretical conceptions which alone have proved useful in giving greater definiteness to the term *repression*. For this purpose it is first necessary that we should proceed from the purely descriptive meaning of the word "unconscious" to its systematic meaning; that is, we resolve to think of the consciousness or unconsciousness of a mental process as merely one of its qualities and not necessarily definitive. Suppose that a process of this kind has remained unconscious, its being withheld from consciousness may be merely a sign of the fate it has undergone, not necessarily the fate itself. Let us suppose, in order to gain a more concrete notion of this fate, that every mental process—there is one exception, which I will go into later—first exists in an unconscious state or phase, and only develops out of this into a conscious phase, much as a photograph is first a negative and then becomes a picture through the printing of the positive. But not every negative is made into a positive, and it is just as little necessary that every unconscious mental process should convert itself into a conscious one. It may be best expressed as follows: Each single process belongs in the first place to the unconscious psychical system; from this system it can under certain conditions proceed further into the conscious system.

The crudest conception of these systems is the one we shall find most convenient, a spatial one. The unconscious system may therefore be compared to a large ante-room, in which the various mental excitations are crowding upon one another, like individual beings. Adjoining this is a second, smaller apartment, a sort of reception-room, in which consciousness resides. But on the threshold between the two there stands a personage with the office of door-keeper, who examines the various mental excitations, censors them, and denies them admittance to the reception-room when he disapproves of them. You will see at once that it does not make much difference whether the door-keeper turns any one impulse back at the threshold, or drives it out again once it has entered the reception-room; that is merely a matter of the degree of his vigilance and promptness in recognition. Now this metaphor may be employed to widen our terminology. The excitations in the unconscious, in the ante-chamber, are not visible to consciousness, which is of course in the other room, so to begin with they remain unconscious. When they have pressed forward to the threshold and been turned back by the door-keeper, they are '*incapable of becoming conscious*'; we call them then *repressed*. But even those excitations which are allowed over the threshold do not necessarily become conscious; they can only become so if they succeed in attracting the eye of consciousness. This second chamber therefore may be suitably called *the preconscious system*. In this way the process of becoming conscious retains its purely descriptive sense. Being repressed, when applied to any single impulse, means being unable to pass out of the unconscious system because of the door-keeper's refusal of admittance into the preconscious. The door-keeper is what we have learnt to know as resistance in our attempts in analytic treatment to loosen the repressions.

Now I know very well that you will say that these conceptions are as crude as they are fantastic and not at all permissible in a scientific presentation. I know they are crude; further indeed, we even know that they are incorrct, and unless I am mistaken, we have something better ready as a substitute for them; whether you will then continue to think them so fantastic, I do not know. At the moment they are useful aids to understanding, like *Ampère's* manikin swimming in the electric current, and, in so far as they do assist comprehension, are not to be despised. Still, I should like to assure you that these crude hypotheses, the two chambers, the door-keeper on the threshold between the two, and consciousness as a spectator at the end of the second room, must indicate an extensive approximation to the actual reality. I should also like to hear you admit that our designations, unconscious, preconscious, and conscious, are less prejudicial and more easily defensible than some others which have been suggested or have come into use, e.g. sub-conscious, inter-conscious, co-conscious, etc.

If so, I should think it more significant if you then went on to point out that any such constitution of the mental apparatus as I have assumed in order to account for neurotic symptoms can only be of universal validity and must throw light on normal functioning. In this, of course, you are perfectly right. We cannot follow up this conclusion at the moment; but our interest in the psychology of symptom-development would certainly be enormously increased if we could see any prospect of obtaining, by the study of pathological conditions, an insight into normal mental functioning, hitherto such a mystery.

Do you not recognize, moreover, what it is that supports these conceptions of the two systems and the relationship between them and consciousness? The door-keeper between the unconscious and the preconscious is nothing else than the *censorship* to which we found the form of the manifest dream subjected. The residue of the day's experiences which we found to be the stimuli exciting the dream, was preconscious material which at night during sleep had been influenced by unconscious and repressed wishes and excitations; and had thus by association with them been able to form the latent dream, by means of their energy. Under the dominion of the unconscious system this material had been elaborated (worked over)—by condensation and displacement—in a way which in normal mental life, i.e. in the preconscious system, is unknown or admissible very rarely. This difference in their manner of functioning is what distinguishes the two systems for us; the relationship to consciousness, which is a permanent feature of the preconscious, indicates to which of the two systems any given process belongs. Neither is dreaming a pathological phenomenon; every healthy person may dream while asleep. Every inference concerning the constitution of the mental apparatus which comprises an understanding of both dreams and neurotic symptoms has an irrefutable claim to be regarded as applying also to normal mental life.

This is as much as we will say about repression for the present. Moreover, it is but a necessary preliminary condition, a prerequisite, of symptom-formation. We know that the symptom is a substitute for some other process which was held back by repression; but even given repression we have still a long way to go before we can obtain comprehension of this substitute-formation. There are other sides to the problem of repression itself which present questions to be answered: What kind of mental excitations suffer repression? What forces effect it? and from what motives? On one point only, so far, have we gained any knowledge relevant to these questions. While investigating the problem of resistance we learned that the forces behind it proceed from the ego, from character-traits, recognizable or latent: it is these forces therefore which have also effected the repression, or at least they have taken a part in it. We know nothing more than this at present.

The second observation for which I prepared you will help us now. By means of analysis we can always discover the purpose behind the neurotic symptom. This is of course nothing new to you: I have already pointed it out in two cases of neurosis. But, to be sure, what do two cases signify? You have a right to demand two hundred cases, innumerable cases, in demonstration of it. But then, I cannot comply with that. So you must fall back on personal experience, or upon belief, which in this matter can rely upon the unanimous testimony of all psychoanalysts.

You will remember that in the two cases in which we submitted the symptoms to detailed investigation analysis led to the innermost secrets of the patient's sexual life. In the first case, moreover, the purpose or tendency of the symptom under examination was particularly evident; in the second case, it was perhaps to some extent veiled by another factor to be mentioned later. Well now, what we found in these two examples we should find in every case we submitted to analysis. Every time we should be led by analysis to the sexual experiences and desires of the patient, and every time we should have to affirm that the symptom served the same purpose. This purpose shows itself to be the gratification of sexual wishes; the symptoms serve the purpose of sexual gratification for the patient; they are a substitute for satisfactions which he does not obtain in reality.

Think of the obsessive act of our first patient. This woman

has to do without the husband she loved so intensely; on account of his deficiencies and short-comings she could not share his life. She had to be faithful to him; she could not put anyone else in his place. Her obsessional symptom gives her what she so much desires; it exalts her husband, denies and corrects his deficiencies, above all, his impotence. This symptom is fundamentally a wish-fulfilment, in that respect exactly like a dream; it is, moreover, what a dream is not always, an erotic wish-fulfilment. In the case of the second patient you could see that her ritual aims at preventing intercourse between the parents or at hindering the procreation of another child; you have probably also divined that fundamentally it seeks to set her in her mother's place. It again therefore constitutes a removal of hindrances to sexual satisfaction and the fulfilment of the subject's own sexual wishes. Of the complications referred to in the second case I shall speak shortly.

I wish to avoid making reservations later on about the universal applicability of these statements, and therefore I will ask you to notice that all I have just been saying about repression, symptom-formation and symptom-interpretation has been obtained from the study of three types of neurosis, and for the present is only applicable to these three types—namely, *anxiety-hysteria, conversion-hysteria,* and *the obsessional neurosis.* These three disorders, which we are accustomed to combine together in a group as the TRANSFERENCE NEUROSES, constitute the field open to psycho-analytic therapy. The other neuroses have been far less closely studied psychoanalytically; in one group of them the impossibility of therapeutic influence has no doubt been one reason for this neglect. You must not forget that psychoanalysis is still a very young science, that much time and trouble are required for the study of it, and that not so very long ago there was only one man practising it: yet we are approaching from all directions to a nearer comprehension of these other conditions which are not transference neuroses. I hope I shall still be able to tell you of the developments that our hypotheses and conclusions have undergone in the course of adaptation to this new material, and to show you that these further studies have not yielded contradictions but have led to a higher degree of unification in our knowledge. Everything that has been said, then, applies only to the three transference neuroses and I will now add another piece of information which throws further light upon the significance of the symptoms. A comparative examination of the situations out of which the disease arose yields the following result, which may be reduced to a formula—namely, that these persons have fallen ill from the PRIVATION (FRUSTRATION) which they suffer when reality withholds from them gratification of their sexual wishes. You will perceive how beautifully these two conclusions supplement one another. The symptoms are now explicable as substitute-gratifications for desires which are unsatisfied in life.

It is certainly possible to make all kinds of objections to the proposition that neurotic symptoms are substitutes for sexual gratifications. I will discuss two of them to-day. If any one of you has himself undertaken the analysis of a large number of neurotics, he will perhaps shake his head and say: "In certain cases this is not at all applicable, in them the symptoms seem rather to contain the opposite purpose, of excluding or of discontinuing sexual gratification." I shall not dispute your interpretation. In psychoanalysis things are often a good deal more complicated than we could wish: if they had been simpler psychoanalysis would perhaps not have been required to bring them to light. Certain features of the ritual of our second patient are distinctly recognizable as being of this ascetic character, inimical to sexual satisfaction; e.g., her removing the clocks for the magic purpose of preventing erections at night, or her trying to prevent the falling and breaking of vessels, which amounts to a protection of her virginity. In other cases of ceremonials on going to bed which I have analysed this negative character was far more marked; the whole ritual could consist of defensive regulations against sexual recollections and temptations. But we have long ago learnt from psychoanalysis that opposites do not constitute a contradiction. We might extend our proposition and say that the purpose of the symptom is either a sexual gratification or a defence against it; in hysteria the positive, wish-fulfilling character predominates on the whole, and in the obsessional neurosis the negative ascetic character. The symptoms can serve the purpose both of sexual gratification and of its opposite so well because this double-sidedness, or *polarity,* has a most suitable foundation in one element of their mechanism which we have not yet had an opportunity to mention. They are in fact, as we shall see, the effects of *compromises* between two opposed tendencies, acting on one another; they represent both that which is repressed, and also that which has effected the repression and has co-operated in bringing them about. The representation of either one or another of these two factors may predominate in the symptom, but it happens very rarely that one of them is absent altogether. In hysteria a collaboration of the two tendencies in one symptom is usually achieved. In the obsessional neurosis the two parts are often distinct: the symptom is then a double one and consists of two successive actions which cancel each other.

It will not be so easy to dispose of a second difficulty. When you consider a whole series of symptom-interpretations your first opinion would probably be that the conception of a sexual substitute-gratification has to be stretched to its widest limits in order to include them. You will not neglect to point out that these symptoms offer nothing real in the way of gratification, that often enough they are confined to re-animating a sensation, or to enacting a phantasy arising from some sexual complex. Further, that the ostensible sexual gratification is very often of an infantile and unworthy character, perhaps approximating to a masturbatory act, or is reminiscent of dirty habits which long ago in childhood had been forbidden and abandoned. And further still, you will express your astonishment that anyone should reckon among sexual gratifications those which can only be described as gratifications of cruel or horrible appetites, or which may be termed unnatural. Indeed, we shall come to no agreement on these latter points until we have submitted human sexuality to a thorough investigation and have thus established what we are justified in calling sexual.

Twentieth Lecture

The Sexual Life of Man

One would certainly think that there could be no doubt about what is to be understood by the term "sexual." First and foremost, of course, it means the "improper," that which must not be mentioned. I have been told a story about some pupils of a famous psychiatrist, who once endeavoured to convince their master that the symptoms of an hysteric are frequently representations of sexual things. With this object, they took him to the bedside of an hysterical woman whose attacks were unmistakable imitations of childbirth. He objected, however: "Well, there is nothing sexual about childbirth." To be sure, childbirth is not necessarily always improper.

I perceive that you don't approve of my joking about such serious matters. It is not altogether a joke, however. Seriously, it is not so easy to define what the term sexual includes. Everything connected with the difference between the two sexes is perhaps the only way of hitting the mark; but you will find that too general and indefinite. If you take the sexual act itself as the central point, you will perhaps declare sexual to mean everything which is concerned with obtaining pleasurable gratification from the body (and particularly the sexual organs) of the opposite sex; in the narrowest sense, everything which is directed to the union of the genital organs and the performance of the sexual act. In doing so, however, you come very near to reckoning the sexual and the improper as identical, and childbirth would really have nothing to do with sex. If then you make the function of reproduction the kernel of sexuality you run the risk of excluding from it a whole host of things like masturbation, or even kissing, which are not directed towards reproduction, but which are nevertheless undoubtedly sexual. However, we have already found that attempts at definition always lead to difficulties; let us give up trying to do any better in this particular case. We may suspect that in the development of the concept "sexual" something has happened which has resulted in what H. Silberer has aptly called a 'covering error.' On the whole, indeed, we know pretty well what is meant by sexual.

In the popular view, which is sufficient for all practical purposes in ordinary life, sexual is something which combines references to the difference between the sexes, to pleasurable excitement and gratification, to the reproductive function, and to the idea of impropriety and the necessity for concealment. But this is no longer sufficient for science. For painstaking researches (only possible, of course, in a spirit of self-command maintained by self-sacrifice) have revealed that classes of human beings exist whose sexual life deviates from the usual one in the most striking manner. One group among these "perverts" has, as it were, expunged the difference between the sexes from its scheme of life. In these people, only the same sex as their own can rouse sexual desire; the other sex (especially the genital organ of the other sex) has absolutely no sexual attraction for them, can even in extreme cases be an object of abhorrence to them. They have thus of course foregone all participation in the process of reproduction. Such persons are called homosexuals or inverts. Often, though not always, they are men and women who otherwise have reached an irreproachably high standard of mental growth and development, intellectually and ethically, and are only afflicted with this one fateful peculiarity. Through the mouths of their scientific spokesmen they lay claim to be a special variety of the human race, a "third sex," as they call it, standing with equal rights alongside the other two. We may perhaps have an opportunity of critically examining these claims. They are not, of course, as they would gladly maintain, the "elect" of mankind; they contain in their ranks at least as many inferior and worthless individuals as are to be found among those differently constituted sexually.

These perverts do at least seek to achieve very much the same ends with the objects of their desires as normal people do with theirs. But after them comes a long series of abnormal types, in whom the sexual activities become increasingly further removed from anything which appears attractive to a reasonable being. In their manifold variety and their strangeness these types may be compared to the grotesque monstrosities painted by P. Breughel to represent the temptation of St. Anthony, or to the long procession of effete gods and worshippers which G. Flaubert shows us passing before his pious penitent, and to nothing else. The chaotic assembly calls out for classification if it is not to bewilder us completely. We divide them into those in whom the *sexual object* has been altered, as with the homosexuals, and those in whom, first and foremost, the *sexual aim* has been altered. In the first group belong those who have dispensed with the mutual union of the genital organs and who have substituted for the genitals, in one of the partners in the act, another organ or part of the body (mouth or anus, in place of the vagina) making light of both the anatomical difficulties and the suppression of disgust involved. There follow others who, it is true, still retain the genital organs as object; not, however, by virtue of their sexual function, but on account of other functions in which they take part anatomically or by reason of their proximity. These people demonstrate that the excretory functions, which in the course of the child's upbringing are relegated to a limbo as indecent, remain capable of attracting the entire sexual interest. There are others who have given up altogether the genital organs as object; and, instead, have exalted some other part of the body to serve as the object of desire, a woman's breast, foot, or plait of hair. There are others yet to whom even a part of the body is meaningless, while a particle of clothing, a shoe or a piece of underclothing, will gratify all their desires; these are the fetichists. Farther on in the scale come those who indeed demand the object as a whole: but whose requirements in regard to it take specific forms, of an extraordinary or horrible nature —even to the point of seeking it as a defenceless corpse and, urged on by their criminal obsessions, of making it one in order so to enjoy it. But enough of these horrors!

Foremost in the second group are those perverts whose sexual desires aim at the performance of an act which normally is but an introductory or preparatory one. They are those who seek gratification in looking and touching, or in watching the other person's most intimate doings; or those who expose parts of their own bodies which should be concealed, in the vague expectation of being rewarded by a similar action on the part of the other. Then come the incomprehensible sadists, in whom all affectionate feeling strains towards the one goal of causing their object pain and torture, ranging in degree from mere indications of a tendency to humiliate the other up to the infliction of severe bodily injuries. Then, as though complementary to these, come the masochists whose only longing is to suffer, in real or in symbolic form, humiliations and tortures at the hands of the loved object. There are others yet, in whom several abnormal characteristics of this kind are combined and interwoven with one another. Finally, we learn that the persons belonging to each of these groups may be divided again: into those who seek their particular form of sexual satisfaction in reality and those who are satisfied merely to imagine it in their own minds, needing no real object at all but being able to substitute for it a creation of phantasy.

There is not the slightest possible doubt that these mad, extraordinary and horrible things do actually constitute the sexual activities of these people. Not merely do they themselves so regard them, recognizing their substitutive character; but we also have to acknowledge that they play the same part in their lives as normal sexual satisfaction plays in ours, exacting the same, often excessive, sacrifices. It is possible to trace out, both broadly and in great detail, where these abnormalities merge into the normal and where they diverge from it. Nor will it escape you that that quality of impropriety which adheres inevitably to a sexual activity is not absent from these forms of it: in most of them it is intensified to the point of odium.

Well, now, what attitude are we to take up to these unusual forms of sexual satisfaction? Indignation and expressions of our personal disgust, together with assurances that we do not share these appetites, will obviously not carry us very far. That is not the point at issue. After all, this is a field of phenomena like any other; attempts to turn away and flee from it, on the pretext that these are but rarities and curiosities, could easily be rebutted. On the contrary, the phenomena are common enough and widely distributed. But if it is objected that our views on the sexual life of mankind require no revision on this account, since these things are one and all aberrations and divagations of the sexual instinct, a serious reply will be necessary. If we do not understand these morbid forms of sexuality and cannot relate them to what is normal in sexual life, then neither can we understand normal sexuality. It remains, in short, our undeniable duty to account satisfactorily in theory for the existence of all the perversions described and to explain their relation to normal sexuality, so-called.

In this task we can be helped by a point of view, and by two new evidential observations. The first we owe to Ivan Bloch; according to him, the view that all the perversions are "signs of degeneration" is incorrect; because of the evidence existing that such aberrations from the sexual aim, such erratic relationships to the sexual object, have been manifested since the beginning of time through every age of which we have knowledge, in every race from the most primitive to the most highly civilized, and at times have succeeded in attaining to toleration and general prevalence. The two evidential observations have been made in the course of psychoanalytic investigations of neurotic patients; they must undoubtedly influence our conception of sexual perversions in a decisive manner.

We have said that neurotic symptoms are substitutes for sexual satisfactions and I have already indicated that many difficulties will be met with in proving this statement from the analysis of symptoms. It is, indeed, only accurate if the "perverse" sexual needs, so-called, are included under the sexual satisfactions; for an interpretation of the symptoms on this basis is forced upon us with astonishing frequency. The claim made by homosexuals or inverts, that they constitute a select class of mankind, falls at once to the ground when we discover that in every single neurotic evidence of homosexual tendencies is forthcoming and that a large proportion of the symptoms are expressions of this latent inversion. Those who openly call themselves homosexuals are merely those in whom the inversion is conscious and manifest; their number is negligible compared with those in whom it is latent. We are bound, in fact, to regard the choice of an object of the same sex as a regular type of offshoot of the capacity to love, and are learning every day more and more to recognize it as especially important. The differences between manifest homosexuality and the normal attitude are certainly not thereby abrogated; they have their practical importance, which remains, but theoretically their value is very considerably diminished. In fact, we have even come to the conclusion that one particular mental disorder, paranoia, no longer to be reckoned among the transference neuroses, invariably arises from an attempt to subdue unduly powerful homosexual tendencies. Perhaps you will remember that one of our patients,[1] in her obsessive act, played the part of a man—of her own husband, that is, whom she had left; such symptoms, representing the impersonation of a man, are very commonly produced by neurotic women. If this is not actually attributable to homosexuality, it is certainly very closely connected with its origins.

As you probably know, the neurosis of hysteria can create its symptoms in all systems of the body (circulatory, respiratory, etc.) and may thus disturb all the functions. Analysis shows that all those impulses, described as perverse, which

[1] See p. 273.

aim at replacing the genital organ by another come to expression in these symptoms. These organs thus behave as substitutes for the genital organs: it is precisely from the study of hysterical symptoms that we have arrived at the view that, besides their functional rôle, a sexual—*erotogenic*—significance must be ascribed to the bodily organs; and that the needs of the former will be interfered with if the demands of the latter upon them are too great. Countless sensations and innervations, which we meet as hysterical symptoms, in organs apparently not concerned with sexuality, are thus discovered to be essentially fulfilments of perverse sexual desires, by the other organs having usurped the function of the genitalia. In this way also the very great extent to which the organs of nutrition and of excretion, in particular, may serve in yielding sexual excitement is brought home to us. It is indeed the same thing as is manifested in the perversions; except that in the latter it is unmistakable and recognizable without any difficulty, whereas in hysteria we have to make the *détour* of interpreting the symptom, and then do not impute the perverse sexual impulse in question to the person's consciousness, but account it to the unconscious part of his personality.

Of the many types of symptom characteristic of the obsessional neurosis the most important are found to be brought about by the undue strength of one group of sexual tendencies with a perverted aim, i.e. the sadistic group. These symptoms, in accordance with the structure of the obsessional neurosis, serve mainly as a defence against these wishes or else they express the conflict between satisfaction and rejection. Satisfaction does not find short shrift, however; it knows how to get its own way by a roundabout route in the patient's behaviour, by preference turning against him in self-inflicted torment. Other forms of this neurosis are seen in excessive "worry" and brooding; these are the expressions of an exaggerated sexualization of acts which are normally only preparatory to sexual satisfaction: the desire to see, to touch and to investigate. In this lies the explanation of the very great importance dread of contact and obsessive washing attains to in this disease. An unsuspectedly large proportion of obsessive actions are found to be disguised repetitions and modifications of masturbation, admittedly the only uniform act which accompanies all the varied flights of sexual phantasy.

It would not be difficult to show you the connections between perversion and neurosis in a much more detailed manner, but I believe that I have said enough for our purposes. We must beware, however, of overestimating the frequency and intensity of the perverse tendencies in mankind, after these revelations of their importance in the interpretation of symptoms. You have heard that frustration of normal sexual satisfactions may lead to the development of neurosis. In consequence of this frustration in reality the need is forced into the abnormal paths of sexual excitation. Later you will be able to understand how this happens. You will at any rate understand that a "collateral" damming-up of this kind must swell the force of the perverse impulses, so that they become more powerful than they would have been had no hindrance to normal sexual satisfaction been present in reality. Incidentally, a similar factor may be recognized also in the manifest perversions. In many cases they are provoked or activated by the unduly great difficulties in the way of normal satisfaction of the sexual instinct which are produced either by temporary conditions or by permanent social institutions. In other cases, certainly, perverse tendencies are quite independent of such conditions; they are, as it were, the natural kind of sexual life for the individual concerned.

Perhaps you are momentarily under the impression that all this tends to confuse rather than to explain the relations between normal and perverted sexuality. But keep in mind this consideration. If it is correct that real obstacles to sexual satisfaction or frustration in regard to it bring to the surface perverse tendencies in people who would otherwise have shown none, we must conclude that something in these people is ready to embrace the perversions; or, if you prefer it, the tendencies must have been present in them in a latent form. Thus we come to the second of the new evidential observations of which I spoke. Psychoanalytic investigation has found it necessary also to concern itself with the sexual life of children, for the reason that in the analysis of symptoms the forthcoming reminiscences and associations invariably lead back to the earliest years of childhood. That which we discovered in this way has since been corroborated point by point by the direct observation of children. In this way it has been found that all the perverse tendencies have their roots in childhood, that children are disposed towards them all and practise them all to a degree conforming with their immaturity; in short, *perverted sexuality* is nothing else but infantile sexuality, magnified and separated into its component parts.

Now you will see the perversions in an altogether different light and no longer ignore their connection with the sexual life of mankind; but what distressing emotions these astonishing and grotesque revelations will provoke in you! At first you will certainly be tempted to deny everything—the fact that there is anything in children which can be termed sexual life, the accuracy of our observations, and the justification of our claim to see in the behaviour of children any connection with that which in later years is condemned as perverted. Permit me first to explain to you the motives of your antagonism and then to put before you a summary of our observations. That children should have no sexual life—sexual excitement, needs, and gratification of a sort—but that they suddenly acquire these things in the years between twelve and fourteen would be, apart from any observations at all, biologically just as improbable, indeed, nonsensical, as to suppose that they are born without genital organs which first begin to sprout at the age of puberty. What does actually awake in them at this period is the reproductive function, which then makes use for its own purposes of material lying to hand in body and mind. You are making the mistake of confounding sexuality and reproduction with each other and thus you obstruct your own way to the comprehension of sexuality, the perversions, and the neuroses. This mistake, moreover, has a meaning in it. Strange to say, its origin lies in the fact that you yourselves have all been children and as children were subject to the influences of education. For it is indeed one of the most important social tasks of education to restrain, confine, and subject to an individual control (itself identical with the demands of society) the sexual instinct when it breaks forth in the form of the reproductive function. In its own interests, accordingly, society would postpone the child's full development until it has attained a certain stage of intellectual maturity, since educability practically ceases with the full onset of the sexual instinct. Without this the instinct would break all bounds and the laboriously erected structure of civilization would be swept away. Nor is the task of restraining it ever an easy one; success in this direction is often poor and, sometimes, only too great. At bottom society's motive is economic; since it has not means enough to support life for its members without work on their part, it must see to it that the number of these members is restricted and their energies directed away from sexual activities on to their work—the eternal primordial struggle for existence, therefore, persisting to the present day.

Experience must have taught educators that the task of moulding the sexual will of the next generation can only be carried out by beginning to impose their influence very early, and intervening in the sexual life of children before puberty, instead of waiting till the storm bursts. Consequently almost all infantile sexual activities are forbidden or made disagreeable to the child; the ideal has been to make the child's life asexual, and in course of time it has come to this that it is really believed to be asexual, and is given out as such, even at the hands of science. In order then to avoid any contradiction with established beliefs and aims, the sexual activity of children is overlooked—no small achievement, by the way—while science contents itself with otherwise explaining it away. The little child is supposed to be pure and innocent; he who says otherwise shall be condemned as a hardened blasphemer against humanity's tenderest and most sacred feelings.

The children alone take no part in this convention; they assert their animal nature naïvely enough and demonstrate persistently that they have yet to learn their "purity." Strange to say, those who deny sexuality in children are the last to relax educative measures against it; they follow up with the greatest severity every manifestation of the "childish tricks" the existence of which they deny. Moreover, it is theoretically of great interest that the time of life which most flagrantly contradicts the prejudice about asexual childhood, the years of infancy up to five or six, is precisely the period which is veiled by oblivion in most people's memories; an oblivion which can only be dispelled completely by analysis but which even before this was sufficiently penetrable to allow some of the dreams of childhood to be retained.

I will now tell you the most clearly recognizable of the child's sexual activities. It will be expedient if I first introduce you to the term LIBIDO. In every way analogous to *hunger*, libido is the force by means of which the instinct, in this case the sexual instinct, as, with hunger, the nutritional instinct, achieves expression. Other terms, such as sexual excitation and satisfaction, require no definition. Interpretation finds most to do in regard to the sexual activities of the infant, as you will easily perceive; and no doubt you will find a reason for objections. This interpretation is formed on the basis of analytic investigation, working backwards from a given symptom. The infant's first sexual excitations appear in connection with the other functions important for life. Its chief interest, as you know, is concerned with taking nourishment; as it sinks asleep at the breast, utterly satisfied, it bears a look of perfect content which will come back again later in life after the experience of the sexual orgasm. This would not be enough to found a conclusion upon. However, we perceive that infants wish to repeat, without really getting any nourishment, the action necessary to taking nourishment; they are therefore not impelled to this by hunger. We call this action "pleasure-sucking" (German: *lutschen*, signifying the enjoyment of sucking for its own sake—as with a rubber "comforter"); and as when it does this the infant again falls asleep with a blissful expression we see that the action of sucking is sufficient in itself to give it satisfaction. Admittedly, it very soon contrives not to go to sleep without having sucked in this way. An old physician for children in Budapest, Dr. Lindner, was the first to maintain the sexual nature of this procedure. Nurses and people who look after children appear to take the same view of this pleasure-sucking, though without taking up any theoretic attitude about it. They have no doubt that its only purpose is in the pleasure derived; they account it one of the child's "naughty tricks"; and take severe measures to force it to give it up, if it will not do so of its own accord. And so we learn that an infant performs actions with no other object but that of obtaining pleasure. We believe that this pleasure is first of all experienced while nourishment is being taken, but that the infant learns rapidly to enjoy it apart from this condition. The gratification obtained can only relate to the region of the mouth and lips; we therefore call these areas of the body *erotogenic zones* and describe the pleasure derived from this sucking as a *sexual one*. To be sure, we have yet to discuss the justification for the use of this term.

If the infant could express itself it would undoubtedly acknowledge that the act of sucking at its mother's breast is far and away the most important thing in life. It would not be wrong in this, for by this act it gratifies at the same moment the two greatest needs in life. Then we learn from psycho-analysis, not without astonishment, how much of the mental significance of this act is retained throughout life. Sucking for nourishment becomes the point of departure from which the whole sexual life develops, the unattainable prototype of every later sexual satisfaction, to which in times of need phantasy often enough reverts. The desire to suck includes within it the desire for the mother's breast, which is therefore the first *object* of sexual desire; I cannot convey to you any adequate idea of the importance of this first object in determining every later object adopted, of the profound influence it exerts, through transformation and substitution, upon the most distant fields of mental life. First of all, however, as the infant takes to sucking for pleasure this object is given up and is replaced by a part of its own body, it sucks its thumb or its own tongue. For purposes of obtaining pleasure it thus makes itself independent of the concurrence of the outer world and, in addition, it extends the region of excitation to a second area of the body, thus intensifying it. The erotogenic zones are not all equally capable of yielding enjoyment; it is therefore an important experience when, as Dr. Lindner says, the infant in feeling about on its own body discovers the particularly excitable region of its genitalia, and so finds the way from pleasure-sucking to onanism.

This assessment of the nature of pleasure-sucking has now brought to our notice two of the decisive characteristics of infantile sexuality. It appears in connection with the satisfaction of the great organic needs, and it behaves *auto-erotically*, that is to say, it seeks and finds its objects in its own person. What is most clearly discernible in regard to the taking of nourishment is to some extent repeated with the process of excretion. We conclude that infants experience pleasure in the evacuation of urine and the contents of the bowels, and that they very soon endeavour to contrive these actions so that the accompanying excitation of the membranes in these erotogenic zones may secure them the maximum possible gratification. As Lou Andreas has pointed out, with fine intuition, the outer world first steps in as a hindrance at this point, a hostile force opposed to the child's desire for pleasure —the first hint he receives of external and internal conflicts to be experienced later on. He is not to pass his excretions whenever he likes but at times appointed by other people. To induce him to give up these sources of pleasure he is told that everything connected with these functions is "improper," and must be kept concealed. In this way he is first required to exchange pleasure for value in the eyes of others. His own attitude to the excretions is at the outset very different. His own fæces produce no disgust in him; he values them as part of his own body and is unwilling to part with them, he uses them as the first "present" by which he can mark out those people whom he values especially. Even after education has succeeded in alienating him from these tendencies, he continues to feel the same high regard for his "presents" and his "money"; while his achievements in the way of urination appear to be the subject of particular pride.

I know that for some time you have been longing to interrupt me with cries of: "Enough of these monstrosities! The motions of the bowels a source of pleasurable sexual satisfaction exploited even by infants! Fæces a substance of great values and the anus a kind of genital organ! We do not believe it; but we understand why children's physicians and educationists have emphatically rejected psychoanalysis and its conclusions!" Not at all; you have merely forgotten for the moment that I have been endeavouring to show you the connection between the actual facts of infantile sexual life and the actual facts of the sexual perversions. Why should you not know that in many adults, both homosexual and heterosexual, the anus actually takes over the part played by the vagina in sexual intercourse? And that there are many persons who retain the pleasurable sensations accompanying evacuations of the bowels throughout life and describe them as far from insignificant? You may hear from children themselves, when they are a little older and able to talk about these things, what an interest they take in the act of defæcation and what pleasure they find in watching others in the act. Of course if you have previously systematically intimidated these children they will understand very well that they are not to speak of such things. And for all else that you refuse to believe I refer you to the evidence brought out in analysis and to the direct observation of children and I tell you that it will require the exercise of considerable ingenuity to avoid seeing all this or to see it in a different light. Nor am I at all averse from your thinking the relationship between childish sexual activities and the sexual perversions positively striking. It is a matter of course that there should be this relationship; for if a child has a sexual life at all it must be of a perverted order, since apart from a few obscure indications he is lacking in all that transforms sexuality into the reproductive function. Moreover, it is a characteristic common to all the perversions that in them reproduction as an aim is put aside. This is actually the criterion by which we judge whether a sexual activity is perverse—if it departs from reproduction in its aims and pursues the attainment of gratification independently. You will understand therefore that the gulf and turning-point in the development of the sexual life lies at the point of its subordination to the purposes of reproduction. Everything that occurs before this conversion takes place, and everything which refuses to conform to it and serves the pursuit of gratification alone, is called by the unhonoured title of "perversion" and as such is despised.

So let me continue my brief account of infantile sexuality. I could supplement what I have told you concerning two of the bodily systems by extending the same scrutiny to the others. The sexual life of the child consists entirely in the activities of a series of component-instincts which seek for gratification independently of one another, some in his own body and others already in an external object. Among the organs of these bodily systems the genitalia rapidly take the first place; there are people in whom pleasurable gratification in their own genital organ, without the aid of any other genital organ or object, is continued without interruption from the onanism habitual in the suckling period of infancy to the onanism of necessity occurring in the years of puberty, and then maintained indefinitely beyond that. Incidentally, the subject of onanism is not so easily exhausted; it contains material for consideration from various angles.

In spite of my wish to limit the extent of this discussion I must still say something about sexual curiosity in children. It is too characteristic of childish sexuality and too important for the symptom-formation of the neuroses to be omitted. Infantile sexual curiosity begins very early, sometimes before the third year. It is not connected with the difference between the sexes, which is nothing to children, since they—boys, at least—ascribe the same male genital organ to both sexes. If then a boy discovers the vagina in a little sister or playmate he at once tries to deny the evidence of his senses; for he cannot conceive of a human being like himself without his most important attribute. Later, he is horrified at the possibilities it reveals to him; the influence of previous threats occasioned by too great a preoccupation with his own little member now begins to be felt. He comes under the dominion of the castration complex, which will play such a large part in the formation of his character if he remains healthy, and of his neurosis if he falls ill, and of his resistances if he comes under analytic treatment. Of little girls we know that they feel themselves heavily handicapped by the absence of a large visible penis and envy the boy's possession of it; from this source primarily springs the wish to be a man which is resumed again later in the neurosis, owing to some mal-adjustment to a female development. The clitoris in the girl, moreover, is in every way equivalent during childhood to the penis; it is a region of especial excitability in which auto-erotic satisfaction is achieved. In the transition to womanhood very much depends upon the early and complete relegation of this sensitivity from the clitoris over to the vaginal orifice. In those women who are sexually anæsthetic, as it is called, the clitoris has stubbornly retained this sensitivity.

The sexual interest of children is primarily directed to the problem of birth—the same problem that lies behind the riddle of the Theban Sphinx. This curiosity is for the most part aroused by egoistic dread of the arrival of another child. The answer which the nursery has ready for the child, that the stork brings the babies, meets with incredulity even in little children much more often than we imagine. The feeling of having been deceived by grown-up people, and put off with lies, contributes greatly to a sense of isolation and to the development of independence. But the child is not able to solve this problem on his own account. His undeveloped sexual constitution sets definite limits to his capacity to understand it. He first supposes that children are made by mixing some special thing with the food taken; nor does he know that only women can have children. Later, he learns of this limitation and gives up the idea of children being made by food, though it is retained in fairy-tales. A little later he soon sees that the father must have something to do with making babies, but he cannot discover what it is. If by chance he is witness of the sexual act he conceives it as an attempt to overpower the woman, as a combat, the sadistic misconception of coitus; at first, however, he does not connect this act with the creation

of children; if he discovers blood on the mother's bed or underlinen he takes it as evidence of injury inflicted by the father.
In still later years of childhood he probably guesses that the
male organ of the man plays an essential part in the procreation of children, but cannot ascribe to this part of the body
any function but that of urination.

Children are all united from the outset in the belief that the
birth of a child takes place by the bowel; that is to say, that
the baby is produced like a piece of fæces. Not until all interest has been weaned from the anal region is this theory
abandoned and replaced by the supposition that the navel
opens, or that the area between the two nipples is the birth-
place of the child. In some such manner as this the enquiring
child approaches some knowledge of the facts of sex, unless,
misled by his ignorance, he overlooks them until he receives
an imperfect and discrediting account of them, usually in the
period before puberty, which not infrequently affects him
traumatically.

Now you will probably have heard that the term "sexual"
has suffered an unwarrantable expansion of meaning at the
hands of psychoanalysis, in order that its assertions regarding the sexual origin of the neuroses and the sexual significance of the symptoms may be maintained. You can now
judge for yourselves whether this amplification is justified or
not. We have extended the meaning of the concept "sexuality"
only so far as to include the sexual life of perverted persons
and also of children; that is to say, we have restored to it
its true breadth of meaning. What is called sexuality outside
psychoanalysis applies only to the restricted sexual life that
is subordinated to the reproductive function and is called
normal.

Twenty-First Lecture

Development of the Libido and Sexual Organizations

It is my impression that I have not succeeded in bringing home to you with complete conviction the importance of the perversions for our conception of sexuality I wish therefore, as far as I am able, to review and improve upon what I have already said on this subject.

Now I do not wish you to think that it was the perversions alone that required us to make the alteration in the meaning of the term sexuality which has aroused such vehement opposition. The study of infantile sexuality has contributed even more to it, and the unanimity between the two was decisive. But, however unmistakably they may be in the later years of childhood, the manifestations of infantile sexuality in its earliest forms do seem to fade away indefinably. Those who do not wish to pay attention to evolution and to the connections brought out by analysis will dispute the sexual nature of them, and will ascribe in consequence some other, undifferentiated character to them. You must not forget that as yet we have no generally acknowledged criterion for the sexual nature of a phenomenon, unless it is some connection with the reproductive function—a definition which we have had to reject as too narrow. The biological criteria, such as the periodicities of twenty-three and twenty-eight days, suggested by W. Fliess, are exceedingly debatable; the peculiar chemical features which we may perhaps assume for sexual processes are yet to be discovered. The sexual perversions in adults, on the other hand, are something definite and unambiguous. As their generally accepted description implies, they are unquestionably of a sexual nature; whether you call them marks of degeneration or anything else, no one has yet been so bold as to rank them anywhere but among the phenomena of sexual life. In view of them alone we are justified in maintaining that sexuality and the reproductive function are not identical, for they one and all abjure the aim of reproduction.

I notice a not uninteresting parallel here. Whereas, for most people, the word 'mental' means 'conscious,' we found ourselves obliged to widen the application of the term 'mental' to include a part of the mind that is not conscious. In a precisely similar way, most people declare 'sexual' identical with 'pertaining to reproduction'—or, if you like it expressed more concisely, with 'genital'; whereas we cannot avoid admitting things as 'sexual' that are not 'genital' and have nothing to do with reproduction. It is only a formal analogy, but it is not without deeper significance.

However, if the existence of sexual perversions is such a forcible argument on this point, why has it not long ago done its work and settled the question? I really am unable to say. It seems to me that the sexual perversions have come under a very special ban, which insinuates itself into the theory, and interferes even with scientific judgement on the subject. It seems as if no one could forget, not merely that they are detestable, but that they are also something monstrous and terrifying; as if they exerted a seductive influence; as if at bottom a secret envy of those who enjoy them had to be strangled—the same sort of feeling that is confessed by the count who sits in judgement in the famous parody of *Tannhäuser:*

> So in the Mount of Venus conscience, duty, are forgot!
> —Remarkable that such a thing has never been my lot!

In reality, perverts are more likely to be poor devils who have to pay most bitterly for the satisfactions they manage to procure with such difficulty.

That which makes perverse activities so unmistakably sexual, in spite of all that seems unnatural in their objects or their aims, is the fact that in perverse satisfaction the act still terminates usually in a complete orgasm with evacuation of the genital product. This is of course only the consequence of adult development in the persons concerned; in children, orgasm and genital excretion are not very well possible; as substitutes they have approximations to them which are again not recognized definitely as sexual.

I must still add something more in order to complete our assessment of the sexual perversions. Abominated as they are, sharply distinguished from normal sexual activity as they may be, simple observation will show that very rarely is one feature or another of them absent from the sexual life of a normal person. The kiss to begin with has some claim to be called a perverse act, for it consists of the union of the two erotogenic mouth zones instead of the two genital organs. But no one condemns it as perverse; on the contrary, in the theatre it is permitted as a refined indication of the sexual act. Nevertheless, kissing is a thing that can easily become an absolute perversion—namely, when it occurs in such intensity that orgasm and emission directly accompany it, which happens not at all uncommonly. Further, it will be found that gazing at and handling the object are in one person an indispensable condition of sexual enjoyment, while another at the height of sexual excitement pinches or bites; that in another lover not always the genital region, but some other bodily region in the object, provokes the greatest excitement, and so on in endless variety. It would be absurd to exclude people with single idiosyncrasies of this kind from the ranks of the normal and place them among perverts; rather, it becomes more and more clear that what is essential to the perversions lies, not in the overstepping of the sexual aim, not in the replacement of the genitalia, not always even in the variations in the object, but solely in the *exclusiveness* with which these deviations are maintained, so that the sexual act which serves the reproductive process is rejected altogether. In so far as perverse performances are included in order to intensify or to lead up to the performance of the normal sexual act, they are no longer actually perverse. Facts of the kind just described naturally tend to diminish the gulf between normal and perverse sexuality very considerably. The obvious inference is that normal sexuality has arisen, out of something existing prior to it, by a process of discarding some components of this material as useless, and by combining the others so as to subordinate them to a new aim, that of reproduction.

The point of view thus gained in regard to the perversions can now be employed by us in penetrating more deeply, with a clear perspective, into the problem of infantile sexuality; but before doing this I must draw your attention to an important difference between the two. Perverse sexuality is as a rule exceedingly concentrated, its whole activity is directed to one—and mostly to only one—aim; one particular component-impulse is supreme; it is either the only one discernible or it has subjected the others to its own purposes. In this respect there is no difference between perverse and normal sexuality, except that the dominating component-impulse, and therefore the sexual aim, is a different one. Both of them constitute a well-organized tyranny; only that in one case one ruling family has usurped all the power, and in the other, another. This concentration and organization, on the other hand, is in the main absent from infantile sexuality; its component-impulses are equally valid, each of them strives independently after its own pleasure. Both the lack of this concentration (in childhood) and the presence of it (in the adult) correspond well with the fact that both normal and perverse sexuality are derived from the same source, namely, infantile sexuality. There are indeed also cases of perversion which correspond even more closely to infantile sexuality in that numerous component-instincts, independently of one another, with their aims, are developed or, better, perpetuated in them. With these cases it is more correct to speak of infantilism than of perversion of the sexual life.

Thus prepared we may now go on to consider a suggestion which we shall certainly not be spared. It will be said: "Why are you so set upon declaring as already belonging to sexuality

those indefinite manifestations of childhood out of which what
is sexual later develops, and which you yourself admit to be
indefinite? Why are you not content rather to describe them
physiologically and simply to say that activities, such as sucking for its own sake and the retaining of excreta, may be observed already in young infants, showing that they seek
pleasure in their organs? In that way you would have avoided
the conception of a sexual life even in babies which is so
repugnant to all our feelings." Well, I can only answer that
I have nothing against pleasure derived from the organs of
the body; I know indeed that the supreme pleasure of the
sexual union is also only a bodily pleasure, derived from the
activity of the genital organ. But can you tell me when this
originally indifferent bodily pleasure acquires the sexual character that it undoubtedly possesses in later phases of development? Do we know any more about this 'organ-pleasure' than
we know about sexuality? You will answer that the sexual
character is added to it when the genitalia begin to play their
part; sexuality simply means genital. You will even evade the
obstacle of the perversions by pointing out that after all with
most of them a genital orgasm occurs, although brought about
by other means than the union of the genitalia. If you were
to eliminate the relation to reproduction from the essential
characteristics of sexuality since this view is untenable in
consequence of the existence of the perversions, and were to
emphasize instead activity of the genital organs, you would
actually take up a much better position. But then we should
no longer differ very widely; it would be a case of the genital
organs *versus* the other organs. What do you now make of
the abundant evidence that the genital organs may be replaced by other organs for the purpose of gratification, as in
the normal kiss, or the perverse practices of loose living, or
in the symptomatology of hysteria? In this neurosis it is quite
usual for stimulation phenomena, sensations, innervations, and
even the processes of erection, which properly belong to the
genitalia to be displaced on to other distant areas of the body
(e.g. the displacement from below upwards to the head and
face). Thus you will find that nothing is left of all that you

cling to as essentially characteristic of sexuality; and you will have to make up your minds to follow my example and extend the designation 'sexual' to include those activities of early infancy which aim at 'organ-pleasure.'

And now will you permit me to bring forward two further considerations in support of my view. As you know, we call the doubtful and indefinable activities of earliest infancy towards pleasure 'sexual,' because in the course of analysing symptoms we reach them by way of material that is undeniably sexual. They would not thereby necessarily be sexual themselves, let us grant; but let us take an analogous case. Suppose that there were no way to observe the development from seed of two dicotyledonous plants—the apple-tree and the bean; but imagine that in both it was possible to follow back its development from the fully developed plant to the first seedling with two cotyledons. The two cotyledons are indistinguishable in each; they look exactly alike in both plants. Shall I conclude from this that they actually are exactly alike and that the specific differences between apple-tree and bean-plant arise *later* in the plant's development? Or is it not more correct biologically to believe that this difference exists *already* in the seedlings, although I cannot see any in the cotyledons? This is what we do when we call infantile pleasurable activities sexual. Whether each and every organ-pleasure may be called sexual or whether there exists, besides the sexual, another kind of pleasure that does not deserve this name is a matter I cannot discuss here. I know too little about organ-pleasure and its conditions; and I am not at all surprised that in consequence of the retrogressive character of analysis I arrive finally at factors which at the present time do not permit of definite classification.

One thing more. You have on the whole gained very little for what you are so eager to maintain, the sexual purity of children, even if you can convince me that the infant's activities had better not be regarded as sexual. For from the third year onwards there is no longer any doubt about sexual life in the child; at this period the genital organs begin already to show signs of excitation; there is a perhaps regular period of infantile masturbation, that is, of gratification in the genital organs. The mental and social sides of sexual life need no longer be overlooked: choice of object, distinguishing of particular persons with affection, even decision in favour of one sex or the other, and jealousy, were conclusively established independently by impartial observation before the time of psycho-analysis; they may be confirmed by any observer who will use his eyes. You will object that you never doubted the early awakening of affection but only that this affection was of a 'sexual' quality. Children between the ages of three and eight have certainly learnt to conceal this element in it; but nevertheless if you look attentively you will collect enough evidence of the 'sensual' nature of this affection, and whatever still escapes your notice will be amply and readily supplied by analytic investigation. The sexual aims in this period of life are in closest connection with the sexual curiosity arising at the same time, of which I have given you some description. The perverse character of some of these aims is a natural result of the immature constitution of the child who has not yet discovered the aim of the act of intercourse.

From about the sixth or eighth year onwards a standstill or retrogression is observed in the sexual development, which in those cases reaching a high cultural standard deserves to be called a *latency period*. This latency period, however, may be absent; nor does it necessarily entail an interruption of sexual activities and sexual interests over the whole field. Most of the mental experiences and excitations occurring before the latency period then succumb to the infantile amnesia, already discussed, which veils our earliest childhood from us and estranges us from it. It is the task of every psychoanalysis to bring this forgotten period of life back into recollection; one cannot resist the supposition that the beginnings of sexual life belonging to this period are the motive for this forgetting, that is, that this oblivion is an effect of repression.

From the third year onwards the sexual life of children shows much in common with that of adults; it is differentiated from the latter, as we already know, by the absence of a stable organization under the primacy of the genital organs, by inevitable traits of a perverse order, and of course also by far less intensity in the whole impulse. But those phases of the sexual development, or as we will call it, of the *libido-development*, which are of greatest interest theoretically lie before this period. This development is gone through so rapidly that direct observation alone would perhaps never have succeeded in determining its fleeting forms. Only by the help of psychoanalytic investigation of the neuroses has it become possible to penetrate so far back and to discover these still earlier phases of libido-development. These phases are certainly only theoretic constructions, but in the practice of psychoanalysis you will find them necessary and valuable constructions. You will soon understand how it happens that a pathological condition enables us to discover phenomena which we should certainly overlook in normal conditions.

Thus we can now define the forms taken by the sexual life of the child before the primacy of the genital zone is reached; this primacy is prepared for in the early infantile period, before the latent period, and is permanently organized from puberty onwards. In this early period a loose sort of organization exists which we shall call *pre-genital;* for during this phase it is not the genital component-instincts, but the *sadistic* and *anal*, which are most prominent. The contrast between *masculine* and *feminine* plays no part as yet; instead of it there is the contrast between *active* and *passive*, which may be described as the forerunner of the sexual polarity with which it also links up later. That which in this period seems masculine to us, regarded from the stand-point of the genital phase, proves to be the expression of an impulse to mastery, which easily passes over into cruelty. Impulses with a passive aim are connected with the erotogenic zone of the rectal orifice, at this period very important; the impulses of skoptophilia (gazing) and curiosity are powerfully active; the function of excreting urine is the only part actually taken by the genital organ in the sexual life. Objects are not wanting to the component-instincts in this period, but these objects are not necessarily all comprised in one object. The sadistic-anal organization is the stage immediately preceding the phase of primacy of the genital zone. Closer study reveals how much of it is retained intact in the later final structure, and what are the paths by which these component-instincts are forced into the service of the new *genital organization*. Behind the sadistic-anal phase of the libido-development we obtain a glimpse of an even more primitive stage of development, in which the erotogenic mouth zone plays the chief part. You can guess that the sexual activity of sucking (for its own sake) belongs to this stage; and you may admire the understanding of the ancient Egyptians in whose art a child, even the divine Horus, was represented with a finger in the mouth. Abraham has quite recently published work showing that traces of this primitive *oral* phase of development survive in the sexual life of later years.

I can indeed imagine that you will have found this last information about the sexual organizations less of an enlightenment than an infliction. Perhaps I have again gone too much into detail; but have patience! what you have just heard will be of more use when we employ it later. Keep in view at the moment the idea that the sexual life—the *libido-function*, as we call it—does not first spring up in its final form, does not even expand along the lines of its earliest forms, but goes through a series of successive phases unlike one another; in short, that many changes occur in it, like those in the development of the caterpillar into the butterfly. The turning-point of this development is the *subordination of all the sexual component-instincts under the primacy of the genital zone* and, together with this, the enrolment of sexuality in the service of the reproductive function. Before this happens the sexual life is, so to say, disparate—independent activities of single component-impulses each seeking *organ-pleasure* (pleasure in a bodily organ). This anarchy is modified by attempts at *pregenital* 'organizations,' of which the chief is the sadistic-anal phase, behind which is the oral, perhaps the most primitive. In addition there are the various processes, about which little is known as yet, which effect the transition from one stage of organization to the next above it. Of what significance this long journey over so many stages in the development of the libido is for comprehension of the neuroses we shall learn later on.

To-day we will follow up another aspect of this development—namely, the relation of the sexual component-impulses to an *object;* or, rather, we will take a fleeting glimpse over this development so that we may spend more time upon a comparatively late result of it. Certain of the component-impulses of the sexual instinct have an object from the very beginning and hold fast to it: such are the impulses to mastery (sadism), to gazing (skoptophilia) and curiosity. Others, more plainly connected with particular erotogenic areas in the body, only have an object in the beginning, so long as they are still dependent upon the non-sexual functions, and give it up when they become detached from these later. Thus the first object of the oral component of the sexual instinct is the mother's breast which satisfies the infant's need for nutrition. In the act of sucking for its own sake the erotic component, also gratified in sucking for nutrition, makes itself independent, gives up the object in an external person, and replaces it by a part of the child's own person. The oral impulse becomes *auto-erotic,* as the anal and other erotogenic impulses are from the beginning. Further development has, to put it as concisely as possible, two aims: first, to renounce auto-erotism, to give up again the object found in the child's own body in exchange again for an external one; and secondly, to combine the various objects of the separate impulses and replace them by one single one. This naturally can only be done if the single object is again itself complete, with a body like that of the subject; nor can it be accomplished without some part of the auto-erotic impulse-excitations being abandoned as useless.

The processes by which an object is found are rather involved, and have not so far received comprehensive exposition. For our purposes it may be emphasized that, when the process has reached a certain point in the years of childhood before the latency period, the object adopted proves almost identical with the first object of the oral pleasure impulse, adopted by reason of the child's dependent relationship to it; it is, namely, the mother, although not the mother's breast.

We call the mother the first *love*-object. We speak of 'love'
when we lay the accent upon the mental side of the sexual
impulses and disregard, or wish to forget for a moment, the
demands of the fundamental physical or 'sensual' side of the
impulses. At about the time when the mother becomes the
love-object, the mental operation of repression has already begun in the child and has withdrawn from him the knowledge
of some part of his sexual aims. Now with this choice of the
mother as love-object is connected all that which, under the
name of 'the Oedipus complex,' has become of such great importance in the psychoanalytic explanation of the neuroses,
and which has had a perhaps equally important share in causing the opposition against psycho-analysis.

Here is a little incident which occurred during the present
war. One of the staunch adherents of psychoanalysis was
stationed in his medical capacity on the German front in
Poland; he attracted the attention of his colleagues by the fact
that he occasionally effected an unexpected influence upon a
patient. On being questioned, he admitted that he worked
with psychoanalytic methods and with readiness agreed to
impart his knowledge to his colleagues. So every evening the
medical men of the corps, his colleagues and superiors, met to
be initiated into the mysteries of psychoanalysis. For a time
all went well; but when he had introduced his audience to the
Oedipus complex a superior officer rose and announced that
he did not believe this, it was the behaviour of a cad for the
lecturer to relate such things to brave men, fathers of families,
who were fighting for their country, and he forbade the continuation of the lectures. This was the end; the analyst got himself transferred to another part of the front. In my opinion,
however, it is a bad outlook if a victory for German arms depends upon an 'organization' of science such as this, and German science will not prosper under any such organization.

Now you will be impatiently waiting to hear what this terrible Oedipus complex comprises. The name tells you: you all
know the Greek myth of King Oedipus, whose destiny it was
to slay his father and to wed his mother, who did all in his
power to avoid the fate prophesied by the oracle, and who in

self-punishment blinded himself when he discovered that in ignorance he had committed both these crimes. I trust that many of you have yourselves experienced the profound effect of the tragic drama fashioned by Sophocles from this story. The Attic poet's work portrays the gradual discovery of the deed of Oedipus, long since accomplished, and brings it slowly to light by skilfully prolonged enquiry, constantly fed by new evidence; it has thus a certain resemblance to the course of a psychoanalysis. In the dialogue the deluded mother-wife, Jocasta, resists the continuation of the enquiry; she points out that many people in their dreams have mated with their mothers, but that dreams are of no account. To us dreams are of much account, especially typical dreams which occur in many people; we have no doubt that the dream Jocasta speaks of is intimately related to the shocking and terrible story of the myth.

It is surprising that Sophocles' tragedy does not call forth indignant remonstrance in its audience; this reaction would be much better justified in them than it was in the blunt army doctor. For at bottom it is an immoral play; it sets aside the individual's responsibility to social law, and displays divine forces ordaining the crime and rendering powerless the moral instincts of the human being which would guard him against the crime. It would be easy to believe that an accusation against destiny and the gods was intended in the story of the myth; in the hands of the critical Euripides, at variance with the gods, it would probably have become such an accusation. But with the reverent Sophocles there is no question of such an intention; the pious subtlety which declares it the highest morality to bow to the will of the gods, even when they ordain a crime, helps him out of the difficulty. I do not believe that this moral is one of the virtues of the drama, but neither does it detract from its effect; it leaves the hearer indifferent; he does not react to this, but to the secret meaning and content of the myth itself. He reacts as though by self-analysis he had detected the Oedipus complex in himself, and had recognized the will of the gods and the oracle as glorified disguises of his own unconscious; as though he remembered in himself the wish to do away with his father and in his place to wed his mother, and must abhor the thought. The poet's words seem to him to mean: "In vain do you deny that you are accountable, in vain do you proclaim how you have striven against these evil designs. You are guilty, nevertheless; for you could not stifle them; they still survive unconsciously in you." And psychological truth is contained in this; even though man has repressed his evil desires into his Unconscious and would then glady say to himself that he is no longer answerable for them, he is yet compélled to feel his responsibility in the form of a sense of guilt for which he can discern no foundation.

There is no possible doubt that one of the most important sources of the sense of guilt which so often torments neurotic people is to be found in the Oedipus complex. More than this: in 1913, under the title of *Totem und Tabu*, I published a study of the earliest forms of religion and morality in which I expressed a suspicion that perhaps the sense of guilt of mankind as a whole, which is the ultimate source of religion and morality, was acquired in the beginnings of history through the Oedipus complex. I should much like to tell you more of this, but I had better not; it is difficult to leave this subject when once one begins upon it, and we must return to individual psychology.

Now what does direct observation of children, at the period of object-choice before the latency period, show us in regard to the Oedipus complex? Well, it is easy to see that the little man wants his mother all to himself, finds his father in the way, becomes restive when the latter takes upon himself to caress her, and shows his satisfaction when the father goes away or is absent. He often expresses his feelings directly in words and promises his mother to marry her; this may not seem much in comparison with the deeds of Oedipus, but it is enough in fact; the kernel of each is the same. Observation is often rendered puzzling by the circumstance that the same child on other occasions at this period will display great affection for the father; but such contrasting—or, better, *ambivalent*—states of feeling, which in adults would lead to conflicts, can be tolerated alongside one another in the child for a long time, just as later on they dwell together permanently in the unconscious. One might try to object that the little boy's behaviour is due to egoistic motives and does not justify the conception of an erotic complex; the mother looks after all the child's needs and consequently it is to the child's interest that she should trouble herself about no one else. This too is quite correct; but it is soon clear that in this, as in similar dependent situations, egoistic interests only provide the occasion on which the erotic impulses seize. When the little boy shows the most open sexual curiosity about his mother, wants to sleep with her at night, insists on being in the room while she is dressing, or even attempts physical acts of seduction, as the mother so often observes and laughingly relates, the erotic nature of this attachment to her is established without a doubt. Moreover, it should not be forgotten that a mother looks after a little daughter's needs in the same way without producing this effect; and that often enough a father eagerly vies with her in trouble for the boy without succeeding in winning the same importance in his eyes as the mother. In short, the factor of sex preference is not to be eliminated from the situation by any criticisms. From the point of view of the boy's egoistic interests it would merely be foolish if he did not tolerate two people in his service rather than only one of them.

As you see, I have only described the relationship of a boy to his father and mother; things proceed in just the same way, with the necessary reversal, in little girls. The loving devotion to the father, the need to do away with the superfluous mother and to take her place, the early display of coquetry and the arts of later womanhood, make up a particularly charming picture in a little girl, and may cause us to forget its seriousness and the grave consequences which may later result from this situation. Let us not fail to add that frequently the parents themselves exert a decisive influence upon the awakening of the Oedipus complex in a child, by themselves following the sex attraction where there is more than one child; the father in an unmistakable manner prefers his little daughter with marks of tenderness, and the mother, the son; but even this factor does not seriously impugn the spontaneous nature of the infantile Oedipus complex. When other children appear, the Oedipus complex expands and becomes a family complex. Reinforced anew by the injury resulting to the egoistic interests, it actuates a feeling of aversion towards these new arrivals and an unhesitating wish to get rid of them again. These feelings of hatred are as a rule much more often openly expressed than those connected with the parental complex. If such a wish is fulfilled and after a short time death removes the unwanted addition to the family, later analysis can show what a significant event this death is for the child, although it does not necessarily remain in memory. Forced into the second place by the birth of another child and for the first time almost entirely parted from the mother, the child finds it very hard to forgive her for this exclusion of him; feelings which in adults we should describe as profound embitterment are roused in him, and aften become the ground-work of a lasting estrangement. That sexual curiosity and all its consequences is usually connected with these experiences has already been mentioned. As these new brothers and sisters grow up the child's attitude to them undergoes the most important transformations. A boy may take his sister as love-object in place of his faithless mother; where there are several brothers to win the favour of a little sister hostile rivalry, of great importance in after life, shows itself already in the nursery. A little girl takes an older brother as a substitute for the father who no longer treats her with the same tenderness as in her earliest years; or she takes a little sister as a substitute for the child that she vainly wished for from her father.

So much and a great deal more of a similar kind is shown by direct observation of children, and by consideration of clear memories of childhood, uninfluenced by any analysis. Among other things you will infer from this that a child's position in the sequence of brothers and sisters is of very great significance for the course of his later life, a factor to be considered in every biography. What is even more important, however, is that in the face of these enlightening considerations, so easily to be obtained, you will hardly recall without smiling the scientific theories accounting for the prohibition of incest. What has not been invented for this purpose! We are told that sexual attraction is diverted from the members of the opposite sex in one family owing to their living together from early childhood; or that a biological tendency against in-breeding has a mental equivalent in the horror of incest! Whereby it is entirely overlooked that no such rigorous prohi-bitions in law and custom would be required if any trust-worthy natural barriers against the temptation to incest ex-isted. The opposite is the truth. The first choice of object in mankind is regularly an incestuous one, directed to the mother and sister of men, and the most stringent prohibitions are re-quired to prevent this sustained infantile tendency from being carried into effect. In the savage and primitive peoples sur-viving to-day the incest prohibitions are a great deal stricter than with us; Theodor Reik has recently shown in a brilliant work that the meaning of the savage rites of puberty which represent re-birth is the loosening of the boy's incestuous at-tachment to the mother and his reconciliation with the father.

Mythology will show you that incest, ostensibly so much ab-horred by men, is permitted to their gods without a thought; and from ancient history you may learn that incestuous mar-riage with a sister was prescribed as a sacred duty for kings (the Pharaohs of Egypt and the Incas of Peru); it was there-fore in the nature of a privilege denied to the common herd.

Incest with the mother is one of the crimes of Oedipus and parricide the other. Incidentally, these are the two great of-fences condemned by totemism, the first social-religious insti-tution of mankind. Now let us turn from the direct observation of children to the analytic investigation of adults who have become neurotic; what does analysis yield in further knowl-edge of the Oedipus complex? Well, this is soon told. The complex is revealed just as the myth relates it; it will be seen that every one of these neurotics was himself an Oedipus or, what amounts to the same thing, has become a Hamlet in his reaction to the complex. To be sure, the analytic picture of the Oedipus complex is an enlarged and accentuated edition of the infantile sketch; the hatred of the father and the death-wishes against him are no longer vague hints, the affection for the mother declares itself with the aim of possessing her as a woman. Are we really to accredit such grossness and intensity of the feelings to the tender age of childhood; or does the analysis deceive us by introducing another factor? It is not difficult to find one. Every time anyone describes anything past, even if he be a historian, we have to take into account all that he unintentionally imports into that past period from present and intermediate times, thereby falsifying it. With the neurotic it is even doubtful whether this retroversion is altogether unintentional; we shall hear later on that there are motives for it and we must explore the whole subject of the 'retrogressive phantasy-making' which goes back to the remote past. We soon discover, too, that the hatred against the father has been strengthened by a number of motives arising in later periods and other relationships in life, and that the sexual desires towards the mother have been moulded into forms which would have been as yet foreign to the child. But it would be a vain attempt if we endeavoured to explain the whole of the Oedipus complex by 'retrogressive phantasy-making,' and by motives originating in later periods of life. The infantile nucleus, with more or less of the accretions to it, remains intact, as is confirmed by direct observation of children.

The clinical fact which confronts us behind the form of the Oedipus complex as established by analysis now becomes of the greatest practical importance. We learn that at the time of puberty, when the sexual instinct first asserts its demands in full strength, the old familiar incestuous objects are taken up again and again invested by the libido. The infantile object-choice was but a feeble venture in play, as it were, but it laid down the direction for the object-choice of puberty. At this time a very intense flow of feeling towards the Oedipus complex or in reaction to it comes into force; since their mental antecedents have become intolerable, however, these feelings must remain for the most part outside consciousness. From the time of puberty onward the human individual must devote himself to the great task of *freeing himself from the parents;* and only after this detachment is accomplished can he cease to be a child and so become a member of the social community. For a son, the task consists in releasing his libidinal desires from his mother, in order to employ them in the quest of an external love-object in reality; and in reconciling himself with his father if he has remained antagonistic to him, or in freeing himself from his domination if, in the reaction to the infantile revolt, he has lapsed into subservience to him. These tasks are laid down for every man; it is noteworthy how seldom they are carried through ideally, that is, how seldom they are solved in a manner psychologically as well as socially satisfactory. In neurotics, however, this detachment from the parents is not accomplished at all; the son remains all his life in subjection to his father, and incapable of transferring his libido to a new sexual object. In the reversed relationship the daughter's fate may be the same. In this sense the Oedipus complex is justifiably regarded as the kernel of the neuroses.

You will imagine how incompletely I am sketching a large number of the connections bound up with the Oedipus complex which practically and theoretically are of great importance. I shall not go into the variations and possible inversions of it at all. Of its less immediate effects I should like to allude to one only, which proves it to have influenced literary production in a far-reaching manner. Otto Rank has shown in a very valuable work that dramatists throughout the ages have drawn their material principally from the Oedipus and incest complex and its variations and masked forms. It should also be remarked that long before the time of psychoanalysis the two criminal offences of Oedipus were recognized as the true expressions of unbridled instinct. Among the works of the Encyclopædist Diderot you will find the famous dialogue, *Le neveu de Rameau*, which was translated into German by no less a person than Goethe. There you may read these remarkable words: *Si le petit sauvage était abandonné à lui-même, qu'il conserva toute son inbecillité et qu'il réunit au peu de raison de l'enfant au berceau la violence des passions de l'homme de trente ans, il tordrait le cou à son père et coucherait avec sa mère.*

There is yet one thing more which I cannot pass over. The

mother-wife of Oedipus must not remind us of dreams in vain. Do you still remember the results of our dream-analyses, how so often the dream-forming wishes proved perverse and incestuous in their nature, or betrayed an unsuspected enmity to near and beloved relatives? We then left the source of these evil strivings of feeling unexplained. Now you can answer this question yourselves. They are dispositions of the libido, and investments of objects by libido, belonging to early infancy and long since given up in conscious life, but which at night prove to be still present and in a certain sense capable of activity. But, since all men and not only neurotic persons have perverse, incestuous, and murderous dreams of this kind, we may infer that those who are normal to-day have also made the passage through the perversions and the object-investments of the Oedipus complex; and that this is the path of normal development; only that neurotics show in a magnified and exaggerated form what we also find revealed in the dream-analyses of normal people. And this is one of the reasons why we chose the study of dreams to lead up to that of neurotic symptoms.

Twenty-Second Lecture

Aspects of Development and Regression. Ætiology

As we have heard, the libido-function goes through an extensive development before it can enter the service of reproduction in the way that is called normal. Now I wish to show you the significance of this fact for the causation of the neuroses.

I think that it will be in agreement with the doctrines of general pathology to assume that such a development involves two dangers; first, that of *inhibition*, and secondly, that of *regression*. That is to say, owing to the general tendency to variation in biological processes it must necessarily happen that not all these preparatory phases will be passed through and completely outgrown with the same degree of success; some parts of the function will be permanently arrested at these early stages, with the result that with the general development there goes a certain amount of inhibited development.

Let us seek analogies to these processes in other fields. When a whole people leaves its dwellings in order to seek a new country, as often happened in earlier periods of human history, their entire number certainly did not reach the new destination. Apart from losses due to other causes, it must invariably have happened that small groups or bands of the migrating people halted on the way, and settled down in these stopping-places, while the main body went further. Or, to take a nearer comparison, you know that in the higher mammals the seminal glands, which are originally located deep in the abdominal cavity, begin a movement at a certain period of intra-uterine development which brings them almost under the skin of the pelvic extremity. In a number of males it is found that one of this pair of organs has remained in the pelvic cavity, or else that it has taken up a permanent position in the inguinal canal which both of them had to pass through on the journey, or at least that this canal has not closed as it normally should after the passage of the seminal glands through it. When as a young student I was doing my first piece of scientific research under v. Brücke, I was working on the origin of the dorsal nerve-roots in the spinal cord of a small fish, still very archaic in form. I found that the nerve-fibres of these roots grew out of large cells in the posterior horn of the grey matter, a condition which is no longer found in other vertebrates. But soon after I discovered that similar nerve-cells were to be found outside the grey matter along the whole length to the so-called spinal ganglion of the posterior roots, from which I concluded that the cells of this ganglion had moved out of the spinal cord along the nerve-roots. Evolutionary development shows this too; in this little fish, however, the whole route of this passage was marked by cells arrested on the way. Closer consideration will soon show you the weak points of these comparisons. Therefore let me simply say that we consider it possible that single portions of every separate sexual impulse may remain in an early stage of development, although at the same time other portions of it may have reached their final goal. You will see from this that we conceive each such impulse as a current continuously flowing from the beginning of life, and that we have divided its flow to some extent artificially into separate successive forward movements. Your impression that these conceptions require further elucidation is correct, but the attempt would lead us too far afield. We will, however, decide at this point to call this *arrest* in a component impulse at an early stage a FIXATION (of the impulse).

The second danger in a development by stages such as this we call REGRESSION; it also happens that those portions which have proceeded further may easily revert in a backward direction to these earlier stages. The impulse will find occasion to *regress* in this way when the exercise of its function in a later and more developed form meets with powerful external obstacles, which thus prevent it from attaining the goal of satisfaction. It is a short step to assume that fixation and regression are not independent of each other; the stronger the fixations in the path of development the more easily will the function yield before the external obstacles, by regressing on to those fixations; that is, the less capable of resistance against the external difficulties in its path will the developed function be. If you think of a migrating people who have left large numbers at the stopping-places on their way, you will see that the foremost will naturally fall back upon these positions when they are defeated or when they meet with an enemy too strong for them. And again, the more of their number they leave behind in their progress, the sooner will they be in danger of defeat.

It is important for comprehension of the neuroses that you should keep in mind this relation between fixation and regression. You will thus acquire a secure foothold from which to investigate the causation of the neuroses—their ætiology—which we shall soon consider.

For the present we will keep to the question of regression. After what you have heard about the development of the libido you may anticipate two kinds of regression; a return to the first objects invested with libido, which we know to be incestuous in character, and a return of the whole sexual organization to earlier stages. Both kinds occur in the transference neuroses, and play a great part in their mechanism. In particular, the return to the first incestuous objects of the libido is a feature found with quite fatiguing regularity in neurotics. There is much more to be said about the regressions of libido if another group of neuroses, called the narcissistic, is taken into account; but this is not our intention at the moment. These affections yield conclusions about other developmental processes of the libido-function, not yet mentioned, and also show us new types of regression corresponding with them. I think, however, that I had better warn you now above all not to confound *Regression* with *Repression* and that I must assist you to clear your minds about the relation between the two processes. *Repression,* as you will remember, is the process by which a mental act capable of becoming conscious (that is, one which belongs to the preconscious system) is made unconscious and forced back into the unconscious system. And we also call it *repression* when the unconscious mental act is not permitted to enter the adjacent preconscious system at all, but is turned back upon the threshold by the censorship. There is therefore no connection with sexuality in the concept 'repression'; please mark this very carefully. It denotes a purely psychological process; and would be even better described as *topographical,* by which we mean that it has to do with the spatial relationships we assume within the mind, or, if we again abandon these crude aids to the formulation of theory, with the structure of the mental apparatus out of separate psychical systems.

The comparisons just now instituted showed us that hitherto we have not been using the word 'regression' in its general sense but in a quite specific one. If you give it its general sense, that of a reversion from a higher to a lower stage of development in general, then repression also ranges itself under regression; for repression can also be described as reversion to an earlier and lower stage in the development of a mental act. Only, in repression this retrogressive direction is not a point of any moment to us; for we also call it repression in a dynamic sense when a mental process is arrested before it leaves the lower stage of the unconscious. Repression is thus a topographic-dynamic conception, while regression is a purely descriptive one. But what we have hitherto called 'regression' and considered in its relation to fixation signified exclusively the return of *the libido* to its former halting-places in development, that is, something which is essentially quite different from repression and quite independent of it Nor can we call regression of the libido a purely psychical process; neither

A General Introduction to Psychoanalysis

do we know where to localize it in the mental apparatus; for though it may exert the most powerful influence upon mental life, the organic factor in it is nevertheless the most prominent.

Discussions of this sort tend to be rather dry; therefore let us turn to clinical illustrations of them in order to get a more vivid impression of them. You know that the group of the transference neuroses consists principally of hysteria and the obsessional neurosis. Now in hysteria, a regression of the libido to the primary incestuous sexual objects is without doubt quite regular, but there is little or no regression to an earlier stage of sexual organization. Consequently the principal part in the mechanism of hysteria is played by repression. If I may be allowed to supplement by a construction the certain knowledge of this neurosis acquired up to the present I might describe the situation as follows: The fusion of the component-impulses under the primacy of the genital zone has been accomplished; but the results of this union meet with resistance from the direction of the preconscious system with which consciousness is connected. The genital organization therefore holds good for the unconscious, but not also for the preconscious, and this rejection on the part of the preconscious results in a picture which has a certain likeness to the state prior to the primacy of the genital zone. It is nevertheless actually quite different. Of the two kinds of regression of the libido, that on to an earlier phase of sexual organization is much the more striking. Since it is absent in hysteria and our whole conception of the neuroses is still far too much dominated by the study of hysteria which came first in point of time, the significance of libido-regression was recognized much later than that of repression. We may be sure that our points of view will undergo still further extensions and alterations when we include consideration of still other neuroses (the narcissistic) in addition to hysteria and the obsessional neurosis.

In the obsessional neurosis, on the other hand, regression of the libido to the antecedent stage of the sadistic-anal organization is the most conspicuous factor and determines the form taken by the symptoms. The impulse to love must then mask itself under the sadistic impulse. The obsessive thought, "I should like to murder you," means (when it has been detached from certain superimposed elements that are not, however, accidental but indispensable to it) nothing else but "I should like to enjoy love of you." When you consider in addition that regression to the primary objects has also set in at the same time, so that this impulse concerns only the nearest and most beloved persons, you can gain some idea of the horror roused in the patient by these obsessive ideas and at the same time how unaccountable they appear to his conscious perception. But repression also has its share, a great one, in the mechanism of this neurosis, and one which is not easy to expound in a rapid survey such as this. Regression of libido without repression would never give rise to a neurosis, but would result in a perversion. You will see from this that repression is the process which distinguishes the neuroses particularly and by which they are best characterized. Perhaps, however, I may have an opportunity at some time of expounding to you what we know of the mechanism of the perversions, and you will then see that there again nothing proceeds so simply as we should like to imagine in our constructions.

I think that you will be soonest reconciled to this exposition of fixation and regression of the libido if you will regard it as preparatory to a study of the *ætiology* of the neuroses. So far I have only given you one piece of information on this subject, namely, that people fall ill of a neurosis when the possibility of satisfaction for the libido is removed from them—they fall ill in consequence of a 'frustration,' as I called it, therefore— and that their symptoms are actually substitutes for the missing satisfaction. This of course does not mean that every frustration in regard to libidinal satisfaction makes everyone who meets with it neurotic, but merely that in all cases of neurosis investigated the factor of frustration was demonstrable. The statement therefore cannot be reversed. You will no doubt have understood that this statement was not intended to reveal the whole secret of the ætiology of the neuroses, but that it merely emphasized an important and indispensable condition.

Now in order to consider this proposition further we do not know whether to begin upon the nature of the frustration or the particular character of the person affected by it. The frustration is very rarely a comprehensive and absolute one; in order to have a pathogenic effect it would probably have to strike at the only form of satisfaction which that person desires, the only form of which he is capable. In general, there are very many ways by which it is possible to endure lack of libidinal satisfaction without falling ill. Above all we know of people who are able to take such abstinence upon themselves without injury; they are then not happy, they suffer from unsatisfied longing, but they do not become ill. We therefore have to conclude that the sexual impulse-excitations are exceptionally 'plastic,' if I may use the word. One of them can step in in place of another; if satisfaction of one is denied in reality, satisfaction of another can offer full recompense. They are related to one another like a network of communicating canals filled with fluid, and this in spite of their subordination to the genital primacy, a condition which is not at all easily reduced to an image. Further, the component-instincts of sexuality, as well as the united sexual impulse which comprises them, show a great capacity to change their object, to exchange it for another—i.e. for one more easily attainable; this capacity for displacement and readiness to accept surrogates must produce a powerful counter-effect to the effect of a frustration. One amongst these processes serving as protection against illness arising from want has reached a particular significance in the development of culture. It consists in the abandonment, on the part of the sexual impulse, of an aim previously found either in the gratification of a component-impulse or in the gratification incidental to reproduction, and the adoption of a new aim—which new aim, though genetically related to the first, can no longer be regarded as sexual, but must be called social in character. We call this process SUBLI-MATION, by which we subscribe to the general standard which estimates social aims above sexual (ultimately selfish) aims. Incidentally, sublimation is merely a special case of the connections existing between sexual impulses and other, asexual ones. We shall have occasion to discuss this again in another context.

Your impression now will be that we have reduced want of satisfaction to a factor of negligible proportions by the recognition of so many means of enduring it. But no; this is not so: it retains its pathogenic power. The means of dealing with it are not always sufficient. The measure of unsatisfied libido that the average human being can take upon himself is limited. The plasticity and free mobility of the libido is not by any means retained to the full in all of us; and sublimation can never discharge more than a certain proportion of libido, apart from the fact that many people possess the capacity for sublimation only in a slight degree. The most important of these limitations is clearly that referring to the mobility of the libido, since it confines the individual to the attaining of aims and objects which are very few in number. Just remember that incomplete development of the libido leaves behind it very extensive (and sometimes also numerous) libido-fixations upon earlier phases of organization and types of object-choice, mostly incapable of satisfaction in reality; you will then recognize fixation of libido as the second powerful factor working together with frustration in the causation of illness. We may condense this schematically and say that libido-fixation represents the internal, predisposing factor, while frustration represents the external, accidental factor, in the ætiology of the neuroses.

I will take this opportunity to warn you against taking sides in a quite superfluous dispute. It is a popular habit in scientific matters to seize upon one side of the truth and set it up as the whole truth, and then in favour of that element of truth to dispute all the rest which is equally true. More than one faction has already split off in this way from the psychoanalytic movement; one of them recognizes only the egoistic impulses and denies the sexual; another perceives only the influence of real tasks in life but overlooks that of the individual's past life, and so on. Now here is occasion for another of these antitheses and moot-points: Are the neuroses exogenous or endogenous diseases—the inevitable result of

a certain type of constitution or the product of certain injurious (traumatic) events in the person's life? In particular,
are they brought about by the fixation of libido and the rest
of the sexual constitution, or by the pressure of frustration?
This dilemma seems to me about as sensible as another I
could point to: Is the child created by the father's act of
generation or by the conception in the mother? You will
properly reply: Both conditions are alike indispensable. The
conditions underlying the neuroses are very similar, if not
exactly the same. From the point of view of causation, cases
of neurotic illness fall into a *series*, within which the two factors—sexual constitution and events experienced, or, if you
wish, fixation of libido and frustration—are represented in
such a way that where one of them predominates the other
is proportionately less pronounced. At one end of the series
stand those extreme cases of whom one can say: These people
would have fallen ill whatever happened, whatever they
experienced, however merciful life has been to them, because
of their anomalous libido development. At the other end stand
cases which call forth the opposite verdict—they would undoubtedly have escaped illness if life had not put such and
such burdens upon them. In the intermediate cases in the
series, more or less of the disposing factor (the sexual constitution) is combined with less or more of the injurious im-
positions of life. Their sexual constitution would not have
brought about their neurosis if they had not gone through
such and such experiences, and life's vicissitudes would not
have worked traumatically upon them if the libido had been
otherwise constituted. In this series I can perhaps admit a
certain preponderance in the effect of the predisposing factor,
but this admission again depends upon where you draw the
line in marking the boundaries of nervousness.

I shall now suggest to you that we should call series such as
these *complemental series,* and will inform you beforehand
that we shall find occasion to establish others of this kind.

The tenacity with which the libido holds to particular
channels and particular objects, the 'adhesiveness' of the
libido, so to say, seems to be an independent factor, varying

in individuals, the determining conditions of which are completely unknown to us, but the importance of which in the
ætiology of the neuroses we shall certainly no longer underestimate. At the same time we should not overestimate the
close relation between the two things. A similar 'adhesiveness'
of the libido occurs—from unknown causes—in normal people
under numerous conditions, and is found as a decisive factor
in those persons who in a certain sense are the extreme opposite of neurotics—namely, perverted persons. It was known
before the time of psychoanalysis that in the anamnesis of
such persons a very early impression, relating to an abnormal
instinct-tendency or object-choice, is frequently discovered,
to which the libido of that person henceforth remains attached for life (Binet). It is often hard to say what has
enabled this impression to exert such an intense power of attraction upon the libido. I will describe a case of this kind
observed by myself. A man to whom the genitals and all the
other attractions in a woman now mean nothing can be
aroused to irresistible sexual excitation only by a shoe-clad
foot of a certain shape; he can remember an event in his
sixth year which determined this fixation of libido. He was
sitting upon a stool by the side of his governess who was to
give him an English lesson. She was a plain, elderly, shrivelled
old maid, with watery blue eyes and a snub nose, and on this
day she had hurt her foot and had it therefore stretched out
on a cushion in a velvet slipper, with the leg itself most
decorously concealed. Later on, after a timid attempt at
normal sexual activity during puberty, a thin sinewy foot like
that of the governess became his only sexual object; and if
still other features in the person reminded him of the type of
woman represented by the English governess, the man was
helplessly attracted. This fixation of the libido, however, rendered him not neurotic but perverse; he became, as we say,
a foot-fetichist. So you see that although an excessive and,
in addition, premature fixation of libido is an indispensable
condition in the causation of neurosis, the extent of its influence far exceeds the boundaries of the neuroses. This con-

dition by itself is also as little decisive as the frustration mentioned previously.

So the problem of the causation of the neuroses seems to become more complicated. In fact, psychoanalytic investigation acquaints us with yet a new factor, not considered in our ætiological series, and best observed in someone whose previous good health is suddenly disturbed by falling ill of a neurosis. In these people signs of contradictory and opposed wishes, or, as we say, of *mental conflict*, are regularly found. One side of the personality stands for certain wishes, while another part struggles against them and fends them off. There is no neurosis without such a CONFLICT. There might seem to be nothing very special in this; you know that mental life in all of us is perpetually engaged with conflicts that have to be decided. Therefore it would seem that special conditions must be fulfilled before such a conflict can become pathogenic; we may ask what these conditions are, what forces in the mind take part in these pathogenic conflicts, and what relation conflict bears to the other causative factors.

I hope to be able to give you answers to these questions which will be satisfactory although perhaps schematically condensed. Conflict is produced by frustration, in that the libido which lacks satisfaction is urged to seek other paths and other objects. A condition of it then is that these other paths and objects arouse disfavour in one side of the personality, so that a veto ensues, which at first makes the new way of satisfaction impossible. This is the point of departure for the formation of symptoms, which we shall follow up later. The rejected libidinal longings manage to pursue their course by circuitous paths, though not indeed without paying toll to the prohibition in the form of certain disguises and modifications. The circuitous paths are the ways of symptom-formation; the symptoms are the new and substitutive satisfactions necessitated by the fact of the frustration.

The significance of the mental conflict can be defined in another way, thus: in order to become pathogenic *external* frustration must be supplemented by *internal* frustration. When this is so, the external and the internal frustration relate of course to different paths and different objects; external frustration removes one possibility of satisfaction, internal frustration tries to exclude another possibility, and it is this second possibility which becomes the debatable ground of the conflict. I choose this form of presentation because it contains a certain implication; it implies that the internal impediment arose originally, in primitive phases of human development, out of real external obstacles.

But what are these forces out of which the prohibition against the libidinal longings proceeds, the other parties in the pathogenic conflict? Speaking very broadly, we may say that they are the non-sexual instincts. We include them all under the name 'ego-instincts'; analysis of the transference neuroses offers no adequate opportunity for further investigation of them; at most we learn something of them from the resistances opposed to the analysis. The pathogenic conflict is, therefore, one between the ego-instincts and the sexual instincts. In a whole series of cases it looks as though there might also be conflict between various purely sexual impulses; at bottom, however, this is the same thing, because of the two sexual impulses engaged in a conflict one will always be found 'consistent with the ego' (ego-syntonic) while the other calls forth a protest from the ego. It remains, therefore, a conflict between ego and sexuality.

Over and over again when psychoanalysis has regarded something happening in the mind as an expression of the sexual instincts indignant protests have been raised to the effect that other instincts and other interests exist in mental life besides the sexual, that one should not derive "everything" from sexuality, and so on. Well, it is a real pleasure for once to be in agreement with one's opponets. Psychoanalysis has never forgotten that non-sexual instincts also exist; it has been built upon a sharp distinction between sexual instincts and ego-instincts; and in the face of all opposition it has insisted, *not* that they arise from sexuality, but that the neuroses owe their origin to a *conflict* between ego and sexuality. It has no conceivable motive in denying the existence or the significance of the ego-instincts while it investigates the part played by

sexual instincts in disease and in life generally. Only, psychoanalysis has been destined to concern itself first and foremost with the sexual instincts, because in the transference
neuroses these are the most accessible to investigation, and
because it was obliged to study what others had neglected.

It is not any more accurate to say that psychoanalysis has
not occupied itself at all with the non-sexual side of the personality. The very distinction between the ego and sexuality
has shown us with particular clearness that the ego-instincts
also undergo an important development which is neither entirely independent of the development of the libido nor without influence upon the latter. We certainly understand the
development of the ego much less well than the development
of the libido, because it is only by the study of the narcissistic
neuroses that we have just reached some hope of insight into
the structure of the ego. Nevertheless, we have already a
notable attempt on the part of Ferenczi[1] to reconstruct theoretically the developmental stages of the ego; and there are at
least two points at which we have a secure foothold from
which to examine this development further. We are not at all
disposed to think that the libidinal interests of a human being
are from the outset in opposition to the interests of self-preservation; the ego is rather impelled at every stage to attempt
to remain in harmony with the corresponding stage of sexual
organization and to accommodate itself to that. The succession
of the separate phases in the development of the libido probably follows a prescribed course; it is undeniable, however,
that this course may be influenced from the direction of the
ego. A certain parallelism, a definite correspondence between
the phases in the two developments (of the ego and of the
libido) may also be assumed; indeed, a disturbance in this
correspondence may become a pathogenic factor. More important to us is the question how the ego behaves when the
libido has undergone a powerful fixation at an earlier point
in its development. The ego may countenance the fixation and
will then be perverse to that extent, or, what is the same

[1]Ferenczi, *Contributions to Psycho-Analysis*. English translation
by Ernest Jones, 1916. Chap. viii, p. 181.

thing, infantile; it may, however, hold itself averse from this attachment of libido, the result of which is that where the libido undergoes a *fixation* there the ego institutes an act of *repression*.

In this way we arrive at the conclusion that the third factor in the ætiology of the neuroses, the susceptibility to conflict, is as much connected with the development of the ego as with the development of the libido; our insight into the causation of the neuroses is thus enlarged. First, there is the most general condition of privation, then the fixation of libido (forcing it into particular channels), and thirdly, the *susceptibility to conflict* produced by the development of the ego having repudiated libidinal excitations of that particular kind. The thing is therefore not so very obscure and intricate—as you probably thought it during the course of my exposition. To be sure, though, after all, we have not done with it yet; there is still something new to add and something we already know to dissect further.

In order to demonstrate the effect of the development of the ego upon the tendency to conflict and therewith upon the causation of the neurosis, I will quote an example which, although entirely imaginary, is not at all improbable in any respect. I will give it the title of Nestroy's farce: *On the Ground-Floor and in the Mansion*. Suppose that a caretaker is living on the ground-floor of a house, while the owner, a rich and well-connected man, lives above. They both have children, and we will assume that the owner's little girl is permitted to play freely without supervision with the child of lower social standing. It may then very easily happen that their games become "naughty," that is, take on a sexual character: that they play "father and mother," watch each other in the performance of intimate acts, and stimulate each other's genital parts. The caretaker's daughter may have played the temptress in this, since in spite of her five or six years she has been able to learn a great deal about sexual matters. These occurrences, even though they are only kept up for a short period, will be enough to rouse certain sexual excitations in both children which will come to expression in the practice of masturbation for a few years, after the games have been discontinued. There is common ground so far, but the final result will be very different in the two children. The caretaker's daughter will continue masturbation, perhaps up to the onset of menstruation, and then give it up without difficulty; a few years later will find a lover, perhaps bear a child; choose this or that path in life, perhaps become a popular actress and end as an aristocrat. Probably her career will turn out less brilliantly, but in any case she will be unharmed by the premature sexual activity, free from neurosis, and able to live her life. Very different is the result in the other child. She will very soon, while yet a child, acquire a sense of having done wrong; after a fairly short time she will give up the masturbatory satisfaction, though perhaps only with a tremendous struggle, but will nevertheless retain an inner feeling of subdued depression. When later on as a young girl she comes to learn something of sexual intercourse, she will turn from it with inexplicable horror and wish to remain ignorant. Probably she will then again suffer a fresh irresistible impulse to masturbation about which she will not dare to unburden herself to anyone. When the time comes for a man to choose her as a wife the neurosis will break out and cheat her out of marriage and the joy of life. If analysis makes it possible to obtain an insight into this neurosis, it will be found that this well-brought-up, intelligent and idealistic girl has completely repressed her sexual desires; but that they are, unconsciously, attached to the few little experiences she had with the childish play-mate.

The differences which ensue in these two destinies in spite of the common experiences undergone, arise because in one girl the ego has sustained a development absent in the other. To the caretaker's daughter sexual activity seemed as natural and harmless in later years as in childhood. The gentleman's daughter had been "well-brought-up" and had adopted the standards of her education. Thus stimulated, her ego had formed ideals of womanly purity and absence of desire that were incompatible with sexual acts; her intellectual training had caused her to depreciate the feminine rôle for which she is intended. This higher moral and intellectual development in her ego has brought her into conflict with the claims of her sexuality.

I will explore one more aspect of the development of the libido to-day, both because it leads out upon certain wide prospects, and also because it is well-suited to justify the sharp, and not immediately obvious, line of demarcation we are wont to draw between ego-instincts and sexual instincts. In considering the two developments undergone by the ego and by the libido we must emphasize an aspect which hitherto has received little attention. Both of them are at bottom inheritances, abbreviated repetitions of the evolution undergone by the whole human race through long-drawn-out periods and from prehistoric ages. In the development of the libido this phylogenetic origin is readily apparent, I should suppose. Think how in one class of animals the genital apparatus is in closest relation with the mouth, in another it is indistinguishable from the excretory mechanism, in another it is part of the organs of motility; you will find a delightful description of these facts in W. Bölsche's valuable book. One sees in animals all the various perversions, ingrained, so to speak, in the form taken by their sexual organizations. Now the phylogenetic aspect is to some extent obscured in man by the circumstance that what is fundamentally inherited is nevertheless individually acquired anew, probably because the same conditions that originally induced its acquisition still prevail and exert their influence upon each individual. I would say, where they originally created a new response they now stimulate a predisposition. Apart from this, it is unquestionable that the course of the prescribed development in each individual can be disturbed and altered by current impressions from without. But the power which has enforced this development upon mankind, and still to-day maintains its pressure in the same course, is known to us; it is, again, the frustration exacted by reality; or, if we give it its great real name, it is *necessity*, the struggle for life, ἀνάγκη. Necessity has been a severe task-mistress, and she has taught us a great deal. Neurotics are those of her children upon whom this severity

has had evil effects, but that risk is inevitable in any education. Incidentally, this view of the struggle for existence as
the motive force in evolution need not detract from the
significance of "inner evolutionary tendencies," if such are
found to exist.

Now it is very noteworthy that sexual instincts and self-
preservative instincts do not behave alike when confronted
with the necessity of real life. The self-preservative instincts
and all that hangs together with them are more easily
moulded; they learn early to conform to necessity and to
adapt their development according to the mandates of reality.
This is comprehensible, for they cannot obtain the objects
they require by any other means, and without these objects
the individual must perish. The sexual instincts are less easily
moulded; for in the beginning they do not know any lack of
objects. Since they are connected parasitically, as it were,
with the other physical functions and at the same time can be
auto-erotically gratified on their own body, they are at first
isolated from the educative influence of real necessity; and
in most people they retain throughout life, in some respect
or other, this character of obstinacy and inaccessibility to influence which we call "unreasonableness." Moreover, the
educability of a young person as a rule comes to an end when
sexual desire breaks out in its final strength. Educators know
this and act accordingly; but perhaps they will yet allow
themselves to be influenced by the results of psychoanalysis
so that they will transfer the main emphasis in education to
the earliest years of childhood, from the suckling period onward. The little human being is frequently a finished product
in his fourth or fifth year, and only gradually reveals in later
years what lies buried in him.

To appreciate the full significance of this difference between
the two groups of instincts we must digress some distance,
and include one of those aspects which deserve to be called
economic; we enter here upon one of the most important, but
unfortunately one of the most obscure, territories of psychoanalysis. We may put the question whether a main purpose is
discernible in the operation of the mental apparatus; and our

first approach to an answer is that this purpose is directed to the attainment of pleasure. It seems that our entire psychical activity is bent upon *procuring pleasure* and *avoiding pain,* that it is automatically regulated by the PLEASURE-PRINCIPLE. Now of all things in the world we should like to know what are the conditions giving rise to pleasure and pain, but that is just where we fall short. We may only venture to say that pleasure is *in some way* connected with lessening, lowering, or extinguishing the amount of stimulation present in the mental apparatus; and that pain involves a heightening of the latter. Consideration of the most intense pleasure of which man is capable, the pleasure in the performance of the sexual act, leaves little doubt upon this point. Since pleasurable processes of this kind are bound up with the distribution of quantities of mental excitation and energy, we term considerations of this kind *economic* ones. It appears that we can describe the tasks and performances of the mental apparatus in another way and more generally than by emphasizing the attainment of pleasure. We can say that the mental apparatus serves the purpose of mastering and discharging the masses of supervening stimuli, the quantities of energy. It is quite plain that the sexual instincts pursue the aim of gratification from the beginning to the end of their development; throughout they keep up this primary function without alteration. At first the other group, the ego-instincts, do the same; but under the influence of necessity, their mistress, they soon learn to replace the pleasure-principle by a modification of it. The task of avoiding pain becomes for them almost equal in importance to that of gaining pleasure; the ego learns that it must inevitably go without immediate satisfaction, postpone gratification, learn to endure a degree of pain, and altogether renounce certain sources of pleasure. Thus trained, the ego becomes "reasonable," is no longer controlled by the pleasure-principle, but follows the REALITY-PRINCIPLE, which at bottom also seeks pleasure—although a delayed and diminished pleasure, one which is assured by its realization of fact, its relation to reality.

The transition from the pleasure-principle to the reality-principle is one of the most important advances in the develop-

ment of the ego. We already know that the sexual instincts
follow late and unwillingly through this stage; presently we
shall learn what the consequences are to man that his sexuality is satisfied with such a slight hold upon external reality.
And now in conclusion one more observation relevant in this
connection. If the ego in mankind has its evolution like the
libido, you will not be surprised to hear that there exist 'ego-
regressions' too, and will wish to know the part this reversion
of the ego to earlier stages in development can play in neurotic disease.

Twenty-Third Lecture

The Paths of Symptom-Formation

In the eyes of the general public the symptoms are the essence of a disease, and to them a cure means the removal of the symptoms. In medicine, however, we find it important to differentiate between symptoms and disease, and state that the disappearance of the symptoms is by no means the same as the cure of the disease. The only tangible element of the disease that remains after the removal of the symptoms, however, is the capacity to form new symptoms. Therefore for the moment let us adopt the lay point of view and regard a knowledge of the foundation of the symptoms as equivalent to understanding the disease.

The symptoms—of course we are here dealing with mental (or psychogenic) symptoms, and mental disease—are activities which are detrimental, or at least useless, to life as a whole; the person concerned frequently complains of them as obnoxious to him or they involve distress and suffering for him. The principal injury they inflict lies in the expense of mental energy they entail and, besides this, in the energy needed to combat them. Where the symptoms are extensively developed, these two kinds of effort may exact such a price that the person suffers a very serious impoverishment in available mental energy, which consequently disables him for all the important tasks of life. This result depends principally upon the amount

of energy taken up in this way, therefore you will see that
"illness" is essentially a practical conception. But if you look
at the matter from a theoretical point of view and ignore this
question of degree you can very well say that we are all ill,
i.e. neurotic; for the conditions required for symptom-formation are demonstrable also in normal persons.

Of neurotic symptoms we already know that they are the
result of a conflict arising when a new form of satisfaction of
libido is sought. The two powers which have entered into opposition meet together again in the symptom and become
reconciled by means of the *compromise* contained in symptom-
formation. That is why the symptom is capable of such re-
sistence; it is sustained from both sides. We also know that
one of the two partners to the conflict is the unsatisfied libido,
frustrated by reality and now forced to seek other paths to satisfaction. If reality remains inexorable, even when the libido
is prepared to take another object in place of that denied, the
libido will then finally be compelled to resort to regression,
and to seek satisfaction in one of the organizations it had already surmounted or in one of the objects it had relinquished
earlier. The libido is drawn into the path of regression by the
fixations it has left behind it at these places in its development.

Now the path of perversion branches off sharply from that
of neurosis. If these regressions do not call forth a prohibition
on the part of the ego, no neurosis results; the libido succeeds
in obtaining a real, although not a normal satisfaction. But if
the ego, which controls not merely consciousness but also the
approaches to motor innervation and hence the realization in
actuality of mental impulses, is not in agreement with these
regressions, conflict ensues. The libido is blocked, as it were,
and must seek an escape by which it can find an outlet for its
cathexis (charge of energy) in conformity with the demands
of the pleasure-principle: it must elude, eschew the ego. The
fixations upon the path of development now regressively trav-
ersed—fixations against which the ego had previously guarded
itself by repressions—offer just such an escape. In streaming
backward and re-'cathecting' these repressed positions, the

libido withdraws itself from the ego and its laws; but it also abandons all the training acquired under the influence of the ego. It was docile as long as satisfaction was in sight; under the double pressure of external and internal frustration it becomes intractable and harks back to former happier days. That is its essential unchangeable character. The ideas to which the libido now transfers its cathexis belong to the unconscious system and are subject to the special processes characteristic of that system—namely, condensation and displacement. Conditions are thus set up which correspond exactly with those of dream-formation. Just as the latent dream, first formed in the unconscious out of the thoughts proper, and constituting the fulfilment of an unconscious wish-phantasy, meets with some (pre)conscious activity which exerts a censorship upon it and permits, according to its verdict, the formation of a compromise in the manifest dream, so the ideas to which the libido is attached ('libido-representatives') in the unconscious have still to contend with the power of the preconscious ego. The opposition against it in the ego follows it as an anti-cathexis (counter-charge) and forces it to adopt a form of expression by which the opposing forces also can at the same time express themselves. In this way the symptom then comes into being, as a derivative, distorted in manifold ways, of the unconscious libidinal wish-fulfilment, as a cleverly chosen ambiguity with two completely contradictory significations. In this last point alone is there a difference between dream-formation and symptom-formation; for the preconscious purpose in dream-formation is merely to preserve sleep and to allow nothing that would disturb it to penetrate consciousness; it does not insist upon confronting the unconscious wish-impulse with a sharp prohibiting "No, on the contrary." It can be more tolerant because a sleeping person is in a less dangerous position; the condition of sleep is enough in itself to prevent the wish from being realized in actuality.

You see that this escape of the libido under the conditions of conflict is rendered possible by the existence of fixations. The regressive cathexis (with libido) of these fixations leads to a circumventing of the repressions and to a discharge—or a satisfaction—of the libido, in which the conditions of a compromise have nevertheless to be maintained. By this détour through the unconscious and the old fixations the libido finally succeeds in attaining to a real satisfaction, though the satisfaction is certainly of an exceedingly restricted kind and hardly recognizable as such. Let me add two remarks on this outcome. First, will you notice how closely connected the libido and the unconscious, on the one hand, and the ego, consciousness, and reality, on the other, show themselves to be, although there were no such connections between them originally; and secondly, let me tell you that all I have said and have still to say on this point concerns the neurosis of hysteria only.

Where does the libido find the fixations it needs in order to break through the repressions? In the activities and experiences of infantile sexuality, in the component-tendencies and the objects of childhood which have been relinquished and abandoned. It is to them, therefore, that the libido turns back. The significance of childhood is a double one; on the one hand the congenitally determined instinct-dispositions are first shown at that time, and secondly, other instincts are then first awakened and activated by external influences and accidental events experienced. In my opinion we are quite justified in laying down this dichotomy. That the innate predisposition comes to expression will certainly not be disputed; but analytic observation even requires us to assume that purely accidental experiences in childhood are capable of inducing fixations of libido. Nor do I see any theoretical difficulty in this. Constitutional predispositions are undoubtedly the after-effects of the experiences of an earlier ancestry; they also have been at one time acquired; without such acquired characters there would be no heredity. And is it conceivable that the acquisition of characters which will be transmitted further should suddenly cease in the generation which is being observed to-day? The importance of the infantile experiences should not, however, be entirely overlooked, as so often happens, in favour of ancestral experiences or of experiences in adult life; but on the contrary they should be particularly appreciated. They are all the more pregnant with consequences because they occur at a time of uncompleted development, and for this very reason are likely to have a traumatic effect. The work done by Roux and others on the mechanism of development has shown that a needle pricked into an embryonic cell-mass undergoing division results in serious disturbances of the development; the same injury to a larva or a full-grown animal would be innocuous.

The libido-fixation of an adult, which we have referred to as representing the constitutional factor in the ætiology of the neuroses, may therefore now be divided into two further elements: the inherited predisposition and the predisposition acquired in early childhood. Since a schematic mode of presentation is always acceptable to a student, let us formulate these relations as follows:

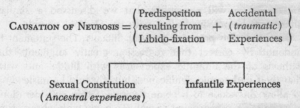

The hereditary sexual constitution provides a great variety of predispositions, according as this or that component-impulse, alone or in combination with others, is specially strongly accentuated. Together with the infantile experiences the sexual constitution forms another 'complemental series,' quite similar to that already described as being formed out of the predisposition and accidental experiences of an adult. In each series similar extreme cases are met with, and also similar degrees and relationships between the factors concerned. It would be appropriate at this point to consider whether the more striking of the two kinds of libido-regression (that which reverts to earlier stages of sexual organization) is not predominantly conditioned by the hereditary constitutional factor; but the answer to this question is best postponed until a wider range of forms of neurotic disease can be considered.

Now let us devote attention to the fact that analytic investigation shows the libido of neurotics to be attached to their infantile sexual experiences. In this light these experiences seem to be of enormous importance in the lives and illnesses of mankind. This importance remains undiminished in so far as the therapeutic work of analysis is concerned; but regarded from another point of view it is easy to see that there is a danger of a misunderstanding here, one which might delude us into regarding life too exclusively from the angle of the situation in neurotics. The importance of the infantile experiences is after all diminished by the reflection that the libido reverts regressively to them *after* it has been driven from its later positions. This would lead us towards the opposite conclusion, that the libido-experiences had no importance at the time of their occurrence, but only acquired it later by regression. You will remember that we discussed a similar alternative before, in dealing with the Oedipus complex.

To decide this point is again not difficult. The statement is undoubtedly correct that regression greatly augments the cathexis of the infantile experiences with libido—and with that their pathogenic significance; but it would be misleading to allow this alone to become decisive. Other considerations must be taken into account as well. To begin with, observation shows in a manner excluding all doubt that infantile experiences have their own importance which is demonstrated already during childhood. There are, indeed, neuroses in children too; in their neuroses the factor of displacement backwards in time is necessarily much diminished, or quite absent, the outbreak of illness following immediately upon a traumatic experience. The study of infantile neuroses guards us from many risks of misunderstanding the neuroses of adults, just as children's dreams gave us the key to comprehension of the dreams of adults. Neurosis in children is very common, far more common than is usually supposed. It is often overlooked, regarded as a manifestation of bad behaviour or naughtiness, and often subdued by the authorities in the nursery; but in retrospect it is always easily recognizable. It appears most often in the form of anxiety-hysteria; we shall learn what that means on another occasion. When a neurosis breaks out in later life analysis invariably reveals it to be a direct continuation of that infantile neurosis, which had perhaps been expressed in a veiled and incipient form only; as has been said, however, there are cases in which the childish nervousness is carried on into lifelong illness without a break. In a few instances we have been able to analyse a child actually in a condition of neurosis; far more often we have had to be satisfied with the retrospective insight into a childhood-neurosis that can be gained through someone who has fallen ill in mature years, a situation in which due corrections and precautions must not be neglected.

In the second place, it would certainly be inexplicable that the libido should regress so regularly to the time of childhood if there had been nothing there which could exert an attraction upon it. The fixation upon certain stages of development, which we assume, only has meaning if we regard it as attaching to itself a definite amount of libidinal energy. Finally, I may point out that a complemental relationship exists here between the intensity and pathogenic importance of the *infantile* and of the *later* experiences, again a similar relationship to that found in the other two series we have already studied. There are cases in which the whole accent of causation falls on the sexual experiences in childhood; cases in which these impressions undoubtedly had a traumatic effect, nothing more than the average sexual constitution and its immaturity being required to supplement them. Then there are others in which all the accent lies on the later conflicts, and the analytic emphasis upon the childhood-impressions seems to be the effect of regression alone. There exist, therefore, the two extremes—'inhibited development' and 'regression'—and between them every degree of combination of the two factors.

This state of things has a certain interest for those looking to pedagogy for the prevention of neuroses by early intervention in the matter of the child's sexual development. As long as attention is directed mainly to the infantile sexual experiences one would think everything in the way of prophylaxis of later neurosis could be done by ensuring that this development should be retarded and the child secured against this kind of experience. But we know that the conditions causing neurosis are more complicated than this and that they cannot be influenced in a general way by attending to one factor only. Strict supervision in childhood loses value because it is helpless against the constitutional factor; more than this, it is less easy to carry out than specialists in education imagine; and it entails two new risks, which are not to be lightly disregarded. It may accomplish too much; in that it favours an exaggerated degree of sexual repression which is harmful in its effects, and it sends the child into life without power to resist the urgent demands of his sexuality that must be expected at puberty. It therefore remains most doubtful how far prophylaxis in childhood can go with advantage, and whether a changed attitude to actuality would not constitute a better point of departure for attempts to forestall the neuroses.

Let us return to consideration of the symptoms. They yield a satisfaction in place of one lacking in reality; they achieve this by means of a regression of the libido to a previous time of life, with which regression is indissolubly connected, a reversion to earlier phases in the object-choice or in the organization. We learned some time ago that the neurotic is in some way *tied* to a period in his past life; we know now that this period in the past is one in which his libido could attain satisfaction, one in which he was happy. He looks back on his life-story, seeking some such period, and goes on seeking it, even if he must go back to the time when he was a suckling infant to find it according to his recollection or his imagination of it under later influences. In some way the symptom reproduces that early infantile way of satisfaction, disguised though it is by the censorship implicit in the conflict, converted as it usually is into a sensation of suffering, and mingled with elements drawn from the experiences leading up to the outbreak of the illness. The kind of satisfaction which the symptom brings has much about it which estranges us, quite apart from the fact that the person concerned is unaware of the satisfaction and perceives this that we call satis-

faction much more as suffering, and complains of it. This
transformation belongs to the mental conflict, by the pressure
of which the symptom had to be formed; what was at one
time a satisfaction must to-day arouse resistance or horror in
him. We are familiar with a simple but instructive instance
of such a change of feeling: the same child that sucked milk
with voracity from its mother's breast often shows, some years
later, a strong dislike of milk which can with difficulty be
overcome by training; this dislike is intensified to the point
of horror if the milk or any other kind of liquid containing it
has a skin formed upon it. It is possible that this skin calls
up reverberations of a memory of the mother's breast, once
so ardently desired; it is true that the traumatic experience
of weaning has intervened meanwhile.

There is still something else which makes the symptoms
seem remarkable and inexplicable as a means of libidinal
satisfaction. They so entirely fail to remind us of all that we
are accustomed normally to connect with satisfaction. They
are mostly quite independent of an object and thus have given
up a relation to external reality. We understand this as a
consequence of the rejection of the reality-principle and the
return to the pleasure-principle; it is also, however, a return
to a kind of amplified auto-erotism, the kind which offered
the sexual instinct its first gratifications. In the place of effecting a change in the outer world they set up a change in the
body itself; that is, an internal action instead of an external
one, an adaptation instead of an activity—from a phylogenetic
point of view again a very significant regression. We shall
understand this better when we consider it in connection with
a new factor yet to be learnt from among those which analytic
research has yielded in regard to symptom-formation. Further,
we remember that in symptom-formation the same unconscious processes are at work as in dream-formation, namely,
condensation and displacement. Like the dream, the symptom
represents something as fulfilled, a satisfaction infantile in
character; but by the utmost condensation this satisfaction
can be compressed into a single sensation or innervation, or
by farthest displacement can be whittled away to a tiny de-

tail out of the entire libidinal complex. It is no wonder that we often find it difficult to recognize in the symptom the libidinal satisfaction which we suspect and can always verify in it.

I have indicated that we have still to learn of a new element; it is really something most surprising and bewildering. You know that from analysis of symptoms we arrive at a knowledge of the infantile experiences to which the libido is fixated and out of which the symptoms are made up. Now the astonishing thing is that these scenes of infancy are not always true. Indeed, in the majority of cases they are untrue, and in some cases they are in direct opposition to historical truth. You will see that this discovery is more likely than any other to discredit either the analysis which leads to such results, or the patient, upon whose testimony the analysis and comprehension of the neuroses as a whole is built up. There is besides this still something utterly bewildering about it. If the infantile experiences brought to light by the analysis were in every case real we should have the feeling that we were on firm ground; if they were invariably falsified and found to be inventions and phantasies of the patient's we should have to forsake this insecure foothold and save ourselves some other way. But it is neither one thing nor the other; for what we find is that the childhood-experiences reconstructed or recollected in analysis are on some occasions undeniably false, while others are just as certainly quite true, and that in most cases truth and falsehood are mixed up. So the symptoms are thus at one minute reproductions of experiences which actually took place and which one can credit with an influence on the fixation of the libido; and at the next a reproduction of phantasies of the patient's to which, of course, it is difficult to ascribe any ætiological significance. It is hard to find one's way here. We may perhaps find our first clue in a discovery of a similar kind, namely, that the meagre childish recollections which people have always, long before analysis, consciously preserved can be falsified in the same way, or at least can contain a generous admixture of truth and falsehood; evidence of error in them is nearly always plainly visible, and so we have at least the reassurance that not the analysis, but the patient in some way, must bear the responsibility for this unexpected disappointment.

After a little reflection we can easily understand what it is that is so bewildering in this matter. It is the depreciation of reality, the neglect of the difference between reality and phantasy; we are tempted to be offended with the patient for taking up our time with invented stories. According to our way of thinking heaven and earth are not farther apart than fiction from reality, and we value the two quite differently. The patient himself, incidentally, takes the same attitude when he is thinking normally. When he brings forward the material that leads us to the wished-for situations (which underlie the symptoms and are formed upon the childhood experiences), we are certainly in doubt at first whether we have to deal with reality or with phantasies. Decision on this point becomes possible later by means of certain indications, and we are then confronted with the task of making this result known to the patient. This is never accomplished without difficulty. If we tell him at the outset that he is now about to bring to light the phantasies in which he has shrouded the history of his childhood, just as every race weaves myths about its forgotten early history, we observe to our dissatisfaction that his interest in pursuing the subject further suddenly declines—he also wishes to find out facts and despises what is called "imagination." But if we leave him to believe until this part of the work has been carried through that we are investigating the real events of his early years, we run the risk of being charged with the mistake later and of being laughed at for our apparent gullibility. It takes him a long time to understand the proposal that phantasy and reality are to be treated alike and that it is to begin with of no account whether the childhood-experiences under consideration belong to the one class or to the other. And yet this is obviously the only correct attitude towards these products of his mind. They have indeed also a kind of reality; it is a fact that the patient has created these phantasies, and for the neurosis this fact is hardly less important than the other—if he had really experienced what they contain. In contrast to *material* reality these phantasies possess *psychical* reality, and we gradually come to understand that *in the world of neurosis* PSYCHICAL REALITY *is the determining factor*.

Among the occurrences which continually recur in the story of a neurotic's childhood, and seem hardly ever absent, are some of particular significance which I therefore consider worthy of special attention. As models of this type I will enumerate: observation of parental intercourse, seduction by an adult, and the threat of castration. It would be a great mistake to suppose that they never occur in reality; on the contrary, they are often confirmed beyond doubt by the testimony of older relatives. Thus, for example, it is not at all uncommon for a little boy, who is beginning to play with his penis and has not yet learnt that he must conceal such activities, to be threatened by parents or nurses that his member or his offending hand will be cut off. Parents will often admit the fact on being questioned, since they imagine that such intimidation was the right course to take; many people have a clear conscious recollection of this threat, especially if it took place in later childhood. If the mother or some other woman makes the threat she usually shifts the execution of it to someone else, indicating that the father or the doctor will perform the deed. In the famous *Struwelpeter* by the Frankfort physician for children, Hoffmann, which owes its popularity precisely to his understanding of the sexual and other complexes of children, you will find the castration idea modified and replaced by cutting off the thumbs as a punishment for stubborn sucking of them. It is, however, highly improbable that the threat of castration has been delivered as often as would appear from the analysis of a neurotic. We are content to understand that the child concocts a threat of this kind out of its knowledge that auto-erotic satisfactions are forbidden, on the basis of hints and allusions, and influenced by the impression received on discovering the female genital organ. Similarly, it is not at all impossible that a small child, credited as he is with no understanding and no memory, may be witness of the sexual act on the part of his parents or other adults in other

families besides those of the proletariat; and there is reason
to think that the child can *subsequently* understand the impression received and react to it. But when this act of intercourse is described with minute details which can hardly have
been observed, or when it appears, as it most frequently does,
to have been performed from behind, *more ferarum,* there can
be little doubt that this phantasy has grown out of the observation of copulating animals (dogs) and that its motive force
lies in the unsatisfied skoptophilia (gazing-impulse) of the
child during puberty. The greatest feat achieved by this kind
of phantasy is that of observing parental intercourse while
still unborn in the mother's womb.

The phantasy of seduction has special interest, because
only too often it is no phantasy but a real remembrance;
fortunately, however, it is still not as often real as it seemed
at first from the results of analysis. Seduction by children of
the same age or older is more frequent than by adults; and
when girls who bring forward this event in the story of their
childhood fairly regularly introduce the father as the seducer,
neither the phantastic character of this accusation nor the
motive actuating it can be doubted. When no seduction has
occurred, the phantasy is usually employed to cover the childhood period of auto-erotic sexual activity; the child evades
feelings of shame about onanism by retrospectively attributing
in phantasy a desired object to the earliest period. Do not
suppose, however, that sexual misuse of children by the nearest
male relatives is entirely derived from the world of phantasy;
most analysts will have treated cases in which such occurrences actually took place and could be established beyond
doubt; only even then they belonged to later years of childhood and had been transposed to an earlier time.

All this seems to lead to but one impression, that childhood
experiences of this kind are in some way necessarily required
by the neurosis, that they belong to its unvarying inventory.
If they can be found in real events, well and good; but if
reality has not supplied them they will be evolved out of hints
and elaborated by phantasy. The effect is the same, and even
to-day we have not succeeded in tracing any variation in the

results according as phantasy or reality plays the greater part in these experiences. Here again is one of those complemental series so often referred to already; it is certainly the strangest of all those we have encountered. Whence comes the necessity for these phantasies, and the material for them? There can be no doubt about the instinctual sources; but how is it to be explained that the same phantasies are always formed with the same content? I have an answer to this which I know will seem to you very daring. I believe that these *primal phantasies* (as I should like to name these, and certainly some others also) are a phylogenetic possession. In them the individual, wherever his own experience has become insufficient, stretches out beyond it to the experience of past ages. It seems to me quite possible that all that to-day is narrated in analysis in the form of phantasy, seduction in childhood, stimulation of sexual excitement upon observation of parental coitus, the threat of castration—or rather, castration itself—was in prehistoric periods of the human family a reality; and that the child in its phantasy simply fills out the gaps in its true individual experiences with true prehistoric experiences. We have again and again been led to suspect that more knowledge of the primordial forms of human development is stored up for us in the psychology of the neuroses than in any other field we may explore.

Now these things that we have been discussing require us to consider more closely the origin and meaning of that mental activity called "phantasy-making." In general, as you know, it enjoys high esteem, although its place in mental life has not been clearly understood. I can tell you as much as this about it. You know that the ego in man is gradually trained by the influence of external necessity to appreciate reality and to pursue the reality-principle, and that in so doing it must renounce temporarily or permanently various of the objects and aims—not only sexual—of its desire for pleasure. But renunciation of pleasure has always been very hard to man; he cannot accomplish it without some kind of compensation. Accordingly he has evolved for himself a mental activity in which all these relinquished sources of pleasure and aban-

doned paths of gratification are permitted to continue their
existence, a form of existence in which they are free from the
demands of reality and from what we call the exercise of 'test-
ing reality.' Every longing is soon transformed into the idea of
its fulfilment; there is no doubt that dwelling upon a wish-
fulfilment in phantasy brings satisfaction, although the knowledge that it is not reality remains thereby unobscured. In
phantasy, therefore, man can continue to enjoy a freedom
from the grip of the external world, one which he has long
relinquished in actuality. He has contrived to be alternately
a pleasure-seeking animal and a reasonable being; for the
meagre satisfaction that he can extract from reality leaves
him starving. "There is no doing without accessory constructions," said Fontane. The creation of the mental domain of
phantasy has a complete counterpart in the establishment of
"reservations" and "nature-parks" in places where the inroads
of agriculture, traffic, or industry threaten to change the
original face of the earth rapidly into something unrecognizable. The "reservation" is to maintain the old condition of
things which has been regretfully sacrificed to necessity everywhere else; there everything may grow and spread as it
pleases, including what is useless and even what is harmful.
The mental realm of phantasy is also such a reservation re-
claimed from the encroaches of the reality-principle.

The best-known productions of phantasy have already been
met by us; they are called day-dreams, and are imaginary
gratifications of ambitious, grandiose, erotic wishes, dilating
the more extravagantly the more reality admonishes humility
and patience. In them is shown unmistakably the essence of
imaginary happiness, the return of gratification to a condition
in which it is independent of reality's sanction. We know that
these day-dreams are the kernels and models of night-dreams;
fundamentally the night-dream is nothing but a day-dream
distorted by the nocturnal form of mental activity and made
possible by the nocturnal freedom of instinctual excitations.
We are already familiar with the idea that a day-dream is not
necessarily conscious, that unconscious day-dreams also exist;

such unconscious day-dreams are therefore just as much the source of night-dreams as of neurotic symptoms.

The significance of phantasy for symptom-formation will become clear to you in what follows. We said that under frustration the libido regressively invests the positions it had left but to which nevertheless some portions of its energy had remained attached. We shall not retract or correct this statement, but we shall have to interpolate a connecting-link in it. How does the libido find its way back to these fixation-points? Now the objects and channels which have been forsaken by the libido have not been forsaken in every sense; they, or their derivatives, are still retained to some degree of intensity in the conceptions of phantasy. The libido has only to withdraw on to the phantasies in order to find the way open to it back to all the repressed fixations. These phantasies had enjoyed a certain sort of toleration; no conflict between them and the ego had developed, however sharp an opposition there was between them, as long as a certain condition was preserved— a condition of a *quantitative* nature, now disturbed by the return of the libido-stream on to the phantasies. By this accession, the cathexis of the phantasies with energy becomes so much augmented that they become assertive and begin to press towards realization; then, however, conflict between them and the ego becomes unavoidable. Although previously they were preconscious or conscious, now they are subject to repression from the side of the ego and are exposed to the attraction exerted from the side of the unconscious. The libido travels from the phantasies, now unconscious, to their sources in the unconscious—back to its own fixation-points again.

The return of the libido on to phantasy is an intermediate step on the way to symptom-formation which well deserves a special designation. C. G. Jung has coined for it the very appropriate name of INTROVERSION, but inappropriately he uses it also to describe other things. We will adhere to the position that *introversion* describes the deflection of the libido away from the possibilities of real satisfaction and its excessive accumulation upon phantasies previously tolerated as harmless. An introverted person is not yet neurotic, but he is in an unstable condition; the next disturbance of the shifting forces will cause symptoms to develop, unless he can yet find other outlets for his pent-up libido. The unreal character of neurotic satisfaction and the disregard of the difference between phantasy and reality are already determined by the arrest at this stage of introversion.

You will doubtless have noticed that in these last remarks I have introduced a new factor into the concatenation of the ætiological chain—namely, the *quantity*, the magnitude of the energies concerned; we must always take this factor into account as well. A purely qualitative analysis of the ætiological conditions does not suffice; or, to put it in another way, a purely *dynamic* conception of these processes is insufficient, the *economic* aspect is also required. We have to realize that the conflict between the two forces in opposition does not break out until a certain intensity in the degree of investment is reached, even though the substantive conditions have long been in existence. In the same way, the pathogenic significance of the constitutional factor is determined by the preponderance of one of the component-instincts in *excess* over another in the disposition; it is even possible to conceive disposition as qualitatively the same in all men and only differentiated by this quantitative factor. No less important is this quantitative factor for the capacity to withstand neurotic illness; it depends upon the *amount* of undischarged libido that a person can hold freely suspended, and upon *how large* a portion of it he can deflect from the sexual to a non-sexual goal in sublimation. The final aim of mental activity, which can be qualitatively described as a striving towards pleasure and avoidance of pain, is represented economically in the task of mastering the distribution of the quantities of excitation (stimulus-masses) present in the mental apparatus, and in preventing the accumulation of them which gives rise to pain.

I set out to tell you as much as this about symptom-formation in the neuroses. Yes, but I must not neglect to mention once more that everything said to-day relates only to symptom-formation in hysteria. Even the obsessional neurosis shows great differences, although the essentials are the same. The 'counter-charges' from the ego against the demands made by instincts for satisfaction, mentioned already in connection with hysteria, are more strongly marked in the obsessional neurosis and govern the clinical picture in the form of what we call 'reaction-formations.' Similar and more extensive deviations still are found in the other neuroses, in which field researches into the mechanisms of symptom-formation are not yet complete in any direction.

Before you leave to-day I should like to direct your attention for a moment to a side of phantasy-life of very general interest. There is, in fact, a path from phantasy back again to reality, and that is—art. The artist has also an introverted disposition and has not far to go to become neurotic. He is one who is urged on by instinctual needs which are too clamorous; he longs to attain to honour, power, riches, fame, and the love of women; but he lacks the means of achieving these gratifications. So, like any other with an unsatisfied longing, he turns away from reality and transfers all his interest, and all his libido too, on to the creation of his wishes in the life of phantasy, from which the way might readily lead to neurosis. There must be many factors in combination to prevent this becoming the whole outcome of his development; it is well known how often artists in particular suffer from partial inhibition of their capacities through neurosis. Probably their constitution is endowed with a powerful capacity for sublimation and with a certain flexibility in the repressions determining the conflict. But the way back to reality is found by the artist thus: He is not the only one who has a life of phantasy; the intermediate world of phantasy is sanctioned by general human consent, and every hungry soul looks to it for comfort and consolation. But to those who are not artists the gratification that can be drawn from the springs of phantasy is very limited; their inexorable repressions prevent the enjoyment of all but the meagre day-dreams which can become conscious. A true artist has more at his disposal. First of all he understands how to elaborate his day-dreams, so that they lose that personal note which grates upon strange ears and become enjoyable to others; he knows too how to modify them sufficiently so that their origin in prohibited sources is not easily detected. Further, he possesses the mysterious ability to mould his particular material until it expresses the ideas of his phantasy faithfully; and then he knows how to attach to this reflection of his phantasy-life so strong a stream of pleasure that, for a time at least, the repressions are out-balanced and dispelled by it. When he can do all this, he opens out to others the way back to the comfort and consolation of their own unconscious sources of pleasure, and so reaps their gratitude and admiration; then he has won—through his phantasy—what before he could only win in phantasy: honour, power, and the love of women.

TWENTY-FOURTH LECTURE

ORDINARY NERVOUSNESS

AFTER SUCH A DIFFICULT PIECE OF WORK AS WE GOT THROUGH
in our last lecture I shall leave the subject for a time and turn
to my audience.

For I know that you are dissatisfied. You imagined that *A
General Introduction to Psychoanalysis* would be something
quite different. You expected illustrations from life instead of
theories; you will tell me that the story of the two children,
on the ground-floor and in the mansion, revealed something
of the causation of neurosis to you, except that it ought to have
been an actual fact instead of an invention of my own. Or you
will say that, when at the beginning I described two symptoms to you (not also imaginary, let us hope), and unfolded
the solution of them and their connection with the lives of
the patients, it threw some light on the meaning of symptoms,
and you had hoped I would continue in the same way. Instead of doing so I gave you long-drawn-out and very obscure
theories which were never complete, and to which I was constantly adding something; I dealt with conceptions which I
had not yet introduced to you; I let go of descriptive explanation and took up the dynamic aspect and dropped this again
for a so-called economic one; made it difficult for you to understand how many of these technical terms mean the same
thing and are only exchanged for one another on account of

euphony; I let vast conceptions, such as those of the pleasure and reality principles, and the inherited residue of phylogenetic development, appear, and then instead of explaining anything to you I let them drift away before your eyes out of sight.

Why did I not begin the introduction to the study of the neuroses with what you all know of nervousness, a thing that has long roused your interest, or with the peculiar nature of nervous persons, their incomprehensible reactions to human intercourse and external influences, their excitability, their unreliability, and their inability to do well in anything? Why not lead you step by step from an explanation of the simple every-day forms of nervousness to the problems of the enigmatic extreme manifestations?

Indeed, I cannot deny any of this or say that you are wrong. I am not so much in love with my powers of presentation as to imagine that every blemish in it is a peculiar charm. I think myself that I might with advantage to you have proceeded differently, and, indeed, such was my intention. But one cannot always carry through a reasoned scheme; something in the material itself often intervenes and takes possession of one and turns one from one's first intentions. Even such an ordinary task as the arrangement of familiar material is not entirely subject to the author's will; it comes out in its own way and one can but wonder afterwards why it happened so and not otherwise.

One of the reasons probably is that my theme, an introduction to psychoanalysis, no longer covers this section dealing with the subject of the neuroses. The introduction to psychoanalysis lies in the study of errors and of dreams; the theory of neurosis is psychoanalysis itself. I do not think that in such a short time I could have given you any knowledge of the material contained in the theory of the neuroses except in this very concentrated form. It was a matter of presenting to you in their proper context the sense and meaning of symptoms, together with the external and internal conditions and mechanisms of symptom-formation. This I attempted to do; it is more or less the core of what psychoanalysis is able to offer to-day. In conjunction with it there was much to be said about the libido and its development, and something about that of the ego. You were already prepared by the preliminary lectures for the main principles of our method and for the broad aspects involved in the conceptions of the unconscious and of repression (resistance). In one of the following lectures you will learn at what point the work of psychoanalysis finds its organic continuation. So far I have not concealed from you that all our results proceed from the study of one single group only of nervous disorders—namely, the transference neuroses; and even so I have traced out the mechanism of symptom-formation only in the hysterical neurosis. Though you will probably have gained no very thorough knowledge and have not retained every detail, yet I hope that you have acquired a general idea of the means with which psychoanalysis works, the problems it has to deal with, and the results it has to offer.

I have ascribed to you a wish that I had begun the subject of the neuroses with a description of the neurotic's behaviour, and of the ways in which he suffers from his disorder, protects himself against it, and adapts himself to it. This is certainly a very interesting subject, well worth studying, and not difficult to treat: nevertheless there are reasons against beginning with this aspect. The danger is that the unconscious will be overlooked, the great importance of the libido ignored, and that everything will be judged as it appears to the patient's own ego. Now it is obvious that his ego is not a reliable and impartial authority. The ego is after all the force which denies the existence of the unconscious and has subjected it to repressions; how then can we trust its good faith where the unconscious is concerned? That which has been repressed consists first and foremost of the repudiated claims of the sexuality; it is perfectly self-evident that we shall never learn their extent and their significance from the ego's view of the matter. As soon as the nature of repression begins to dawn upon us we are advised not to allow one of the two contending parties, and certainly not the victorious one, to be judged in the dispute. We are forewarned against being misled by what the ego tells us. According to its evidence it would appear to have been the active force throughout, so that the symptoms arise by its will and agency; we know that to a large extent it has played a passive part, a fact which it then endeavours to conceal and to gloss over. It is true that it cannot always keep up this pretence—in the symptoms of the obsessional neurosis it has to confess to being confronted by something alien which it must strenuously resist.

It is certainly plain sailing enough for anyone who does not heed these warnings against taking the falsifications of the ego at their face-value; he will escape all the opposition which psychoanalysis has to encounter in accentuating the unconscious, sexuality, and the passivity of the ego. He can agree with Alfred Adler that the "nervous character" is the cause of the neurosis, instead of the result; but he will not be in a position to account for a single detail of symptom-formation or a single dream.

You will ask: May it not be possible to do justice to the part played by the ego in nervousness and in symptom-formation without absolutely glaring neglect of the other factors discovered by psychoanalysis? I reply: Certainly it must be possible, and some time or other it will be done; but the work which lies at hand for psycho-analysis is not suited for a beginning at this end. One can, no doubt, predict the point at which this task also will be included. There are neuroses, called by us the *narcissistic* neuroses, in which the ego is far more deeply involved than in those we have studied; analytic investigation of these disorders will enable us to estimate impartially and reliably the share taken by the ego in neurotic disease.

One of the relations the ego bears to its neurosis is, however, so conspicuous that it was quite appreciable from the beginning. It never seems to be absent; but it is most clearly discernible in a form of disorder which we are far from understanding, the traumatic neurosis. You must know that in the causation and mechanism of all the various different forms of neurosis the same factors are found at work over and over again, only that in one type this factor and in another type that factor is of greatest significance in symptom-formation.

It is just the same as with the personnel of a theatrical company, where every member plays a special type of part—hero, confidant, villain, etc.; each of them will choose a different piece for his own benefit-performance. Hence, the phantasies which are transformed into the symptoms are nowhere so manifest as in hysteria; the 'counter-charges' (anti-cathexes) or reaction-formations of the ego dominate the picture in the obsessional neurosis; the mechanism which in dreams we called 'secondary elaboration' is the prominent feature in the delusions of paranoia, and so on.

In the *traumatic neuroses,* especially in those arising from the terrors of war, we are particularly impressed by a self-seeking, egoistic motive, a straining towards protection and self-interest; this alone perhaps could not produce the disease, but it gives its support to the latter and maintains it once it has been formed. This tendency aims at protecting the ego from the dangers which led by their imminence to the outbreak of illness; nor does it permit of recovery until a repetition of the dangers appears to be no longer possible, or until some gain in compensation for the danger undergone has been received.

The ego takes a similar interest in the origin and maintenance of all the other forms of neurosis; we have said already that the symptom is supported by the ego because one side of it offers a satisfaction to the repressing ego-tendency. More than this, a solution of the conflict by a symptom-formation is the most convenient one, most in accordance with the pleasure-principle; for it undoubtedly spares the ego a severe and painful piece of internal labour. There are indeed cases in which the physician himself must admit that the solution of a conflict by a neurosis is the one most harmless and most tolerable socially. Do not be astonished to hear then that the physician himself occasionally takes sides with the illness which he is attacking. It is not for him to confine himself in all situations in life to the part of fanatic about health; he knows that there is *other* misery in the world besides neurotic misery—real unavoidable suffering—that necessity may even demand of a man that he sacrifice his health to it, and he learns that such suffering in one individual may often avert incalculable hardship for many others. Therefore, although it may be said of every neurotic that he has taken 'flight into illness,' it must be admitted that in many cases this flight is fully justified, and the physician who has perceived this state of things will silently and considerately retire.

But let us continue our discussion without regard to these exceptional cases. In the ordinary way it is apparent that by flight into neurosis the ego gains a certain internal 'advantage through illness,' as we call it; under certain conditions a tangible external advantage, more or less valuable in reality, may be combined with this. To take the commonest case of this kind: a woman who is brutally treated and mercilessly exploited by her husband fairly regularly takes refuge in a neurosis, if her disposition admits of it. This will happen if she is too cowardly or too conventional to console herself secretly with another man, if she is not strong enough to defy all external reasons against it and separate from her husband, if she has no prospect of being able to maintain herself or of finding a better husband, and last of all, if she is still strongly attached sexually to this brutal man. Her illness becomes her weapon in the struggle against him, one that she can use for her protection, or misuse for purposes of revenge. She can complain of her illness, though she probably dare not complain of her marriage; her doctor is her ally; the husband who is otherwise so ruthless is required to spare her, to spend money on her, to grant her absence from home and thus some freedom from marital oppression. Whenever this external or 'accidental' advantage through illness is at all pronounced, and no substitute for it can be found in reality, you need not look forward very hopefully to influencing the neurosis by your therapy.

You will now say that what I have just told you about the 'advantage through illness' is all in favour of the view I have rejected, namely, that the ego itself desires the neurosis and creates it. But just a moment! Perhaps it means merely this: that the ego is pleased to accept the neurosis which it is in any case unable to prevent, and that if there is anything at all to be made out of it it makes the best of it. This is only one side of the matter. In so far as there is advantage in it the ego is quite happy to be on good terms with a neurosis, but there are also disadvantages to be considered. As a rule it is soon apparent that by accepting a neurosis the ego has made a bad bargain. It has paid too heavily for the solution of the conflict; the sufferings entailed by the symptoms are perhaps as bad as those of the conflict they replace, and they may quite probably be very much worse. The ego wishes to be rid of the pain of the symptoms, but not to give up its advantage through illness; and that is just what it cannot succeed in doing. It appears therefore that the ego was not quite so actively concerned in the matter throughout as it had thought, and we will keep this well in mind.

If, as physicians, you have much to do with neurotics, you will soon cease to expect that those who complain most bitterly of their illness will be most ready to accept your help and make least difficulty—quite the contrary. You will at all events easily understand that everything which contributes to the advantage through illness reinforces the resistance arising from the repressions, and increases the therapeutic difficulties. And there is yet another kind of advantage through illness, one which supervenes later than that born with the symptom, so to speak. When such a mental organization as the disease has persisted for a considerable time it seems finally to acquire the character of an independent entity; it displays something like a self-preservative instinct; it forms a kind of pact, a *modus vivendi,* with the other forces in mental life, even with those fundamentally hostile to it, and opportunities can hardly fail to arise in which it once more manifests itself as useful and expedient, thus acquiring a *secondary function* which again strengthens its position. Instead of taking an example from pathology let us consider a striking illustration in everyday life. A capable working-man earning his living is crippled by an accident in the course of his employment; he can work no more, but he gets a small periodical dole in compensation and learns how to exploit his mutilation as a beggar. His new life, although so inferior, nevertheless is supported by the very thing which destroyed his old life; if you were to remove his disability you would deprive him for a time of his means of subsistence, for the question would arise whether he would still be capable of resuming his former work. When a secondary exploitation of the illness such as this is formed in a neurosis we can range it alongside the first and call it a 'secondary advantage through illness.'

I should like to advise you in a general way not to underestimate the practical importance of the advantage through illness, and yet not to be too much impressed by its theoretical significance. Apart from the exceptions previously recognized, this factor always reminds one of the illustrations of "Intelligence in Animals" by Oberländer in *Fliegende Blätter*. An Arab is riding a camel along a narrow path cut in the side of a steep mountain. At a turn in the path he suddenly finds himself confronted by a lion ready to spring at him. There is no escape; on one side the abyss, on the other the sheer wall; retreat and flight are impossible; he gives himself up for lost. Not so the camel. He takes one leap with his rider into the abyss—and the lion is left a spectator. The remedies provided by neurosis avail the patient no better as a rule; perhaps because the solution of the conflict by a symptom-formation is after all an automatic process which may show itself inadequate to meet the demands of life, and involves man in a renunciation of his best and highest powers. The more honourable choice, if there be a choice, is to go down in fair fight with destiny.

I still owe you a further explanation of my motive in not taking ordinary nervousness as my starting-point. Perhaps you think I avoided doing so because it would have been more difficult to bring in evidence of the sexual origin of the neuroses is that way; but in this you would be mistaken. In the transference neuroses the symptoms have to be submitted to interpretation before we arrive at this; but in the ordinary forms of what are called the ACTUAL NEUROSES the ætiological significance of the sexual life is a crudely obvious fact which courts notice. I became aware of it more than twenty years ago, as one day I began to wonder why, when we examine nervous patients, we so invariably exclude from consideration all matters concerning their sexual life. Investigations on this point led to the sacrifice of my popularity with my patients, but in a very short time my efforts had brought me to this conclusion: that no neurosis—actual neurosis, I meant—is present where sexual life is normal. It is true that this statement ignores the individual differences in people rather too much, and it also suffers from the indefinite connotation inseparable from the word "normal"; but as a broad outline it has retained its value to this day. At that time I got so far as to be able to establish particular connections between certain forms of nervousness and certain injurious sexual conditions; I do not doubt that I could repeat these observations to-day if I still had similar material for investigation. I noticed often enough that a man who contented himself with some kind of incomplete sexual satisfaction, e.g. with manual masturbation, would suffer from a definite type of actual neurosis, and that this neurosis would promptly give way to another form if he adopted some other equally unsatisfactory form of sexual life. I was then in a position to infer the change in his mode of sexual life from the alteration in the patient's condition; and I learnt to abide stubbornly by my conclusions until I had overcome the prevarications of my patients and had compelled them to give me confirmation. It is true that they then thought it advisable to seek other physicians who would not take so much interest in their sexual life.

It did not escape me at that time either that sexuality was not always indicated as the cause of a neurosis; one person certainly would fall ill because of some injurious sexual condition, but another because he had lost his fortune or recently sustained a severe organic illness. The explanation of these variations was revealed later, when insight was obtained into the interrelationships suspected between the ego and the libido; and the further this subject was explored the more satisfactory became our insight into it. A person only falls ill of a neurosis when the ego loses its capacity to deal in some way or other with the libido. The stronger the ego the more easily can it accomplish this task; every weakening of the ego, from what-

ever cause, must have the same effect as an increase in the demands of the libido; that is, make a neurosis possible. There
are yet other and more intimate relations between the ego
and the libido, which I shall not go into now as we have not
yet come to them in the course of our discussions. The most
essential and most instructive point for us is that the fund of
energy supporting the symptoms of a neurosis, in every case
and regardless of the circumstances inducing their outbreak,
is provided by the libido, which is thus put to an abnormal
use.

Now I must point out to you the decisive difference between the symptoms of the *actual neuroses* and those of the
psychoneuroses, with the first group of which (the transference neuroses) we have hitherto been so much occupied.
In both the actual neuroses and the psychoneuroses the symptoms proceed from the libido; that is, they are abnormal ways
of using it, substitutes for satisfaction of it. But the symptoms
of an actual neurosis—headache, sensation of pain, an irritable
condition of some organ, the weakening or inhibition of some
function—have no 'meaning,' no signification in the mind. Not
merely are they manifested principally in the body, as also
happens, for instance with hysterical symptoms, but they are
in themselves purely and simply physical processes; they arise
without any of the complicated mental mechanisms we have
been learning about. They really are, therefore, what psychoneurotic symptoms were for so long held to be. But then, how
can they be expressions of the libido which we have come to
know as a force at work in the mind? Now, really, the answer
to that is very simple. Let me resurrect one of the very first
objections ever made against psychoanalysis. It was said that
the theories were an attempt to account for neurotic symptoms by psychology alone and that the outlook was consequently hopeless, since no illness could ever be accounted for
by psychological theories. These critics were pleased to forget
that the sexual function is not a purely mental thing, any
more than it is merely a physical thing. It affects bodily life as
well as mental life. Having learnt that the symptoms of the
psychoneuroses express the mental consequences of some dis-

turbance in this function, we shall not be surprised to find that the actual neuroses represent the direct somatic consequences of sexual disturbances.

Clinical medicine gives us a useful hint (recognized by many different investigators) towards comprehension of the actual neuroses. In the details of their symptomatology, and also in the peculiarity by which all the bodily systems and functions are affected together, they exhibit an unmistakable similarity with pathological conditions resulting from the chronic effect or the sudden removal of foreign toxins—i.e. with states of intoxication or of abstinence. The two groups of affections are brought still closer together by comparison with conditions like Basedow's disease[1] that have also been found to result from poisoning, not, however, from poisons derived externally, but from such as arise in the internal metabolism. In my opinion these analogies necessitate our regarding the neuroses as the effects of disturbances in the sexual metabolism, due either to more of these sexual toxins being produced than the person can dispose of, or else to internal and even mental conditions which interfere with the proper disposal of these substances. Assumptions of this kind about the nature of sexual desire have found acceptance in the mind of the people since the beginning of time; love is called an "intoxication," it can be induced by "potions"—in these ideas the agency at work is to some extent projected on to the outer world. We find occasion at this point to remember the erotogenic zones, and to reflect upon the proposition that sexual excitation may arise in the most various organs. Beyond this the subject of 'sexual metabolism' or the 'chemistry of sexuality' is an empty chapter: we know nothing about it, and cannot even determine whether to assume two kinds of sexual substances, to be called 'male' and 'female,' or to content ourselves with *one* sexual toxin as the agent of all the stimuli effected by the libido. The edifice of psychoanalytic doctrine which we have erected is in reality but a superstructure, which will have to be set on its organic foundation at some time or other; but this foundation is still unknown to us.

[1] [I.e. Grave's disease, exophthalmic goitre.—TR.]

As a science psychoanalysis is characterized by the methods with which it works, not by the subject-matter with which it deals. These methods can be applied without violating their essential nature to the history of civilization, to the science of religion, and to mythology as well as to the study of the neuroses. Psychoanalysis aims at and achieves nothing more than the discovery of the unconscious in mental life. The problems of the actual neuroses, in which the symptoms probably arise through direct toxic injury, offer no point of attack for psycho-analysis; it can supply little towards elucidation of them and must leave this task to biological and medical research. Now perhaps you understand better why I chose this arrangement of my material. If I had intended an *Introduction to the Study of the Neuroses* it would undoubtedly have been correct to begin with the simple forms of (actual) neuroses and proceed from them to the more complicated psychical disorders resulting from disturbances of the libido. I should have had to collect from various quarters what we know or think we know about the former, and about the latter psychoanalysis would have been introduced as the most important technical means of obtaining insight into these conditions. An *Introduction to Psychoanalysis* was what I had undertaken and announced, however; I thought it more important to give you an idea of psychoanalysis than to teach you something about the neuroses; and therefore the actual neuroses which yield nothing towards the study of psychoanalysis could not suitably be put in the foreground. I think too that my choice was the wiser for you, since the radical axioms and far-reaching connections of psychoanalysis make it worthy of every educated person's interest; the theory of the neuroses, however, is a chapter of medicine like any other.

However, you are justified in expecting that we should take some interest in the actual neuroses; their close clinical connection with the psychoneuroses even necessitates this. I will tell you then that we distinguish three pure forms of actual neurosis: *neurasthenia, anxiety-neurosis* and *hypochondria*. Even this classification has been disputed; the terms are certainly all in use, but their connotation is vague and unsettled.

There are some medical men who are opposed to all discrimination in the confusing world of neurotic manifestations, who
object to any distinguishing of clinical entities or types of
diseases, and do not even recognize the difference between
actual neuroses and psychoneuroses; in my opinion they go
too far, and the direction they have chosen does not lead to
progress. The three kinds of neurosis named above are occasionally found in a pure form; more frequently, it is true,
they are combined with one another and with a psychoneurotic affection. This fact need not make us abandon the distinctions between them. Think of the difference between the
science of minerals and that of ores in mineralogy: the minerals are classified individually, in part no doubt because they
are frequently found as crystals, sharply differentiated from
their surroundings; the ores consist of mixtures of minerals
which have indeed coalesced, not accidentally, but according
to the conditions at their formation. In the theory of the neuroses we still understand too little of the process of their development to formulate anything similar to our knowledge of
ores; but we are certainly working in the right direction in
first isolating from the mass the recognizable clinical elements,
which are comparable to the individual minerals.

A noteworthy connection between the symptoms of the
actual neuroses and the psychoneuroses adds a valuable contribution to our knowledge of symptom-formation in the latter;
the symptom of the actual neurosis is frequently the nucleus
and incipient stage of the psychoneurotic symptom. A connection of this kind is most clearly observable between neurasthenia and the transference neurosis known as conversion-
hysteria, between the anxiety-neurosis and anxiety-hysteria,
but also between hypochondria and forms of a neurosis which
we shall deal with later on, namely, paraphrenia (dementia
præcox and paranoia). As an example, let us take an hysterical
headache or backache. Analysis shows that by means of condensation and displacement it has become a substitutive satisfaction for a whole series of libidinal phantasies or memories;
at one time, however, this pain was real, a direct symptom of
a sexual toxin, the bodily expression of a sexual excitation. We

do not by any means maintain that all hysterical symptoms have a nucleus of this kind, but it remains true that this very often is so, and that all effects (whether normal or pathological) of the libidinal excitation upon the body are especially adapted to serve the purposes of hysterical symptom-formation. They play the part of the grain of sand which the oyster envelops in mother-of-pearl. The temporary signs of sexual excitation accompanying the sexual act serve the psychoneurosis in the same way, as the most suitable and convenient material for symptom-formation.

There is a similar process of special diagnostic and therapeutic interest. In persons who are disposed to be neurotic without having yet developed a neurosis on a grand scale, some morbid organic condition—perhaps an inflammation, or an injury—very commonly sets the work of symptom-formation in motion; so that the latter process swiftly seizes upon the symptom supplied by reality, and uses it to represent those unconscious phantasies that have only been lying in wait for some means of expression. In such a case the physician will try first one therapy and then the other; will either endeavour to abolish the organic foundation on which the symptom rests, without troubling about the clamorous neurotic elaboration of it; or will attack the neurosis which this opportunity has brought to birth, while leaving on one side the organic stimulus which incited it. Sometimes one and sometimes the other procedure will be found justified by success; no general rules can be precribed for mixed cases of this kind.

Twenty-Fifth Lecture

Anxiety

You will certainly have judged the information that I gave you in the last lecture about ordinary nervousness as the most fragmentary and most inadequate of all my accounts. I know that it was; and I expect that nothing surprised you more than that I made no mention of the 'anxiety' which most nervous people complain of and themselves describe as their most terrible burden. Anxiety or dread can really develop tremendous intensity and in consequence be the cause of the maddest precautions. But in this matter at least I wished not to cut you short; on the contrary, I had determined to put the problem of nervous anxiety to you as clearly as possible and to discuss it at some length.

Anxiety (or *dread*)[1] itself needs no description; everyone has personally experienced this sensation, or to speak more correctly this affective condition, at some time or other. But in my opinion not enough serious consideration has been given to the question why nervous persons in particular suffer from anxiety so much more intensely, and so much more altogether, than others. Perhaps it has been taken for granted that they should; indeed, the words "nervous" and "anxious" are used

[1][*Angst*. The German word denotes a more intense feeling than the English 'anxiety'; the latter, however, derived from the same root, has become established as the technical English term.—Tr.]

interchangeably, as if they meant the same thing. This is not justifiable, however; there are anxious people who are otherwise not in any way nervous and there are, besides, neurotics with numerous symptoms who exhibit no tendency to dread.

However this may be, one thing is certain, that the problem of anxiety is a nodal point, linking up all kinds of most important questions; a riddle, of which the solution must cast a flood of light upon our whole mental life. I do not claim that I can give you a complete solution; but you will certainly expect psychoanalysis to have attacked this problem too in a different manner from that adopted by academic medicine. Interest there centres upon the anatomical processes by which the anxiety condition comes about. We learn that the medulla oblongata is stimulated, and the patient is told that he is suffering from a neurosis in the vagal nerve. The medulla oblongata is a wondrous and beauteous object; I well remember how much time and labour I devoted to the study of it years ago. But to-day I must say I know of nothing less important for the psychological comprehension of anxiety than a knowledge of the nerve-paths by which the excitations travel.

One may consider anxiety for a long time without giving a thought to nervousness. You will understand me at once when I describe this form of anxiety as OBJECTIVE ANXIETY, in contrast to neurotic anxiety. Now *real* anxiety or dread appears to us a very natural and rational thing; we should call it a reaction to the perception of an external danger, of an injury which is expected and foreseen; it is bound up with the reflex of flight, and may be regarded as an expression of the instinct of self-preservation. The occasions of it, i.e. the objects and situations about which anxiety is felt, will obviously depend to a great extent upon the state of the person's knowledge and feeling of power regarding the outer world. It seems to us quite natural that a savage should be afraid of a cannon or of an eclipse of the sun, while a white man who can handle the weapon and foretell the phenomenon remains unafraid in the same situation. At other times it is knowledge itself which inspires fear, because it reveals the danger sooner; thus a savage will recoil with terror at the sight of a track in the jungle which conveys nothing to an ignorant white man, but means that some wild beast is near at hand; and an experienced sailor will perceive with dread a little cloud on the horizon because it means an approaching hurricane, while to a passenger it looks quite insignificant.

The view that objective anxiety is rational and expedient, however, will on deeper consideration be admitted to need thorough revision. In face of imminent danger the only expedient behaviour, actually, would be first a cool appraisement of the forces at disposal as compared with the magnitude of the danger at hand, and then a decision whether flight or defence, or possibly attack, offered the best prospect of a successful outcome. Dread, however, has no place in this scheme; everything to be done will be accomplished as well and probably better if dread does not develop. You will see too that when dread is excessive it becomes in the highest degree inexpedient; it paralyses every action, even that of flight. The reaction to danger usually consists in a combination of the two things, the fear-affect and the defensive action; the frightened animal is afraid *and* flees, but the expedient element in this is the 'flight,' not the 'being afraid.'

One is tempted therefore to assert that the development of anxiety is never expedient; perhaps a closer dissection of the situation in dread will give us a better insight into it. The first thing about it is the 'readiness' for danger, which expresses itself in heightened sensorial perception and in motor tension. This expectant readiness is obviously advantageous; indeed, absence of it may be responsible for grave results. It is then followed on the one hand by a motor action, taking the form primarily of flight and, on a higher level, of defensive action; and on the other hand by the condition we call a sensation of 'anxiety' or dread. The more the development of dread is limited to a flash, to a mere signal, the less does it hinder the transition from the state of anxious readiness to that of action, and the more expediently does the whole course of events proceed. The *anxious readiness* therefore seems to me the expedient element, and the *development* of anxiety the inexpedient element, in what we call anxiety or dread.

I shall not enter upon a discussion whether the words anxiety, fear, fright, mean the same or different things in common usage. In my opinion, *anxiety* relates to the condition and ignores the object, whereas in the word *fear* attention is directed to the object; *fright* does actually seem to possess a special meaning—namely, it relates specifically to the condition induced when danger is unexpectedly encountered without previous anxious readiness. It might be said then that anxiety is a protection against fright.

It will not have escaped you that a certain ambiguity and indefiniteness exists in the use of the word 'anxiety.' It is generally understood to mean the subjective condition arising upon the perception of what we have called 'developed' anxiety; such a condition is called an affect. Now what is an affect, in a dynamic sense? It is certainly something very complex. An affect comprises first of all certain motor innervations or discharges; and, secondly, certain sensations, which moreover are of two kinds—namely, the perceptions of the motor actions which have been performed, and the directly pleasurable or painful sensations which give the affect what we call its dominant note. But I do not think that this description penetrates to the essence of an affect. With certain affects one seems to be able to see deeper, and to recognize that the core of it, binding the whole complex structure together, is of the nature of a *repetition* of some particular very significant previous experience. This experience could only have been an exceedingly early impression of a universal type, to be found in the previous history of the species rather than of the individual. In order to be better understood I might say that an affective state is constructed like an hysterical attack, i.e. is the precipitate of a reminiscence. An hysterical attack is therefore comparable to a newly formed individual affect, and the normal affect to a universal hysteria which has become a heritage.

Do not imagine that what I am telling you now about affects is the common property of normal psychology. On the contrary, these conceptions have grown on the soil of psychoanalysis and are only indigenous there. What psychology has to say about affects—the James-Lange theory, for instance—is utterly incomprehensible to us psychoanalysts and impossible for us to discuss. We do not however regard what we know of affects as at all final; it is a first attempt to take our bearings in this obscure region. To continue, then: we believe we know what this early impression is which is reproduced as a repetition in the anxiety affect. We think it is the experience of *birth* —an experience which involves just such a concatenation of painful feelings, of discharges of excitation, and of bodily sensations, as to have become a prototype for all occasions on which life is endangered, ever after to be reproduced again in us as the dread or 'anxiety' condition. The enormous increase in stimulation effected by the interruption of the renewal of blood (the internal respiration) was the cause of the anxiety experience at birth—the first anxiety was therefore toxically induced. The name *Angst* (anxiety)—*angustiœ, Enge,* a narrow place, a strait—accentuates the characteristic tightening in the breathing which was then the consequence of a real situation and is subsequently repeated almost invariably with an affect. It is very suggestive too that the first anxiety state arose on the occasion of the separation from the mother. We naturally believe that the disposition to reproduce this first anxiety condition has become so deeply ingrained in the organism, through countless generations, that no single individual can escape the anxiety affect; even though, like the legendary Macduff, he 'was from his mother's womb untimely ripped' and so did not himself experience the act of birth. What the prototype of the anxiety condition may be for other animals than mammals we cannot say; neither do we know what the complex of sensations in them is which is equivalent to fear in us.

It may perhaps interest you to know how it was possible to arrive at such an idea as this—that birth is the source and prototype of the anxiety affect. Speculation had least of all to do with it; on the contrary, I borrowed a thought from the naïve intuitive mind of the people. Many years ago a number of young house-physicians, including myself, were sitting round a dinner-table, and one of the assistants at the obstetrical clinic was telling us all the funny stories of the last midwives' examination. One of the candidates was asked what it meant when the meconium (child's excreta) was present in the waters at birth, and promptly replied: "That the child is frightened." She was ridiculed and failed. But I silently took her part and began to suspect that the poor unsophisticated woman's unerring perception had revealed a very important connection.

Now let us turn to neurotic anxiety; what are the special manifestations and conditions found in the anxiety of nervous persons? There is a great deal to be described here. First of all, we find a general apprehensiveness in them, a 'free-floating' anxiety, as we call it, ready to attach itself to any thought which is at all appropriate, affecting judgements, inducing expectations, lying in wait for any opportunity to find a justification for itself. We call this condition '*expectant dread*' or 'anxious expectation.' People who are tormented with this kind of anxiety always anticipate the worst of all possible outcomes, interpret every chance happening as an evil omen, and exploit every uncertainty to mean the worst. The tendency to this kind of expectation of evil is found as a character-trait in many people who cannot be described as ill in any other way, and we call them 'over-anxious' or pessimistic; but a marked degree of expectant dread is an invariable accompaniment of the nervous disorder which I have called anxiety-neurosis and include among the actual neuroses.

In contrast to this type of anxiety, a second form of it is found to be much more circumscribed in the mind, and attached to definite objects and situations. This is the anxiety of the extraordinarily various and often very peculiar phobias. Stanley Hall, the distinguished American psychologist, has recently taken the trouble to designate a whole series of these phobias by gorgeous Greek titles; they sound like the ten plagues of Egypt, except that there are far more than ten of them. Just listen to the things that can become the object or content of a phobia: darkness, open air, open spaces, cats, spiders, caterpillars, snakes, mice, thunder, sharp points, blood, enclosed places, crowds, loneliness, crossing bridges, travelling by land or sea, and so on. As a first attempt to take one's bearings in this chaos we may divide them into three

406 A GENERAL INTRODUCTION TO PSYCHOANALYSIS

groups. Many of the objects and situations feared are rather sinister, even to us normal people, they have some connection with danger; and these phobias are not entirely incomprehensible to us, although their intensity seems very much exaggerated. Most of us, for instance, have a feeling of repulsion upon encountering a snake. It may be said that the snake-phobia is universal in mankind. Charles Darwin has described most vividly how he could not control his dread of a snake that darted at him, although he knew that he was protected from it by a thick plate of glass. The second group consists of situations that still have some relation to danger, but to one that is usually belittled or not emphasized by us; most situation-phobias belong to this group. We know that there is more chance of meeting with a disaster in a railway train than at home—namely, a collision; we also know that a ship may sink, whereupon it is usual to be drowned; but we do not brood upon these dangers and we travel without anxiety by train and boat. Nor can it be denied that if a bridge were to break at the moment we were crossing it we should be hurled into the torrent, but that only happens so very occasionally that it is not a danger worth considering. Solitude too has its dangers, which in certain circumstances we avoid, but there is no question of never being able to endure it for a moment under any conditions. The same thing applies to crowds, enclosed spaces, thunderstorms, and so on. What is foreign to us in these phobias is not so much their content as their intensity. The anxiety accompanying a phobia is positively indescribable! And we sometimes get the impression that neurotics are not really at all fearful of those things which can, under certain conditions, arouse anxiety in us and which they call by the same names.

There remains a third group which is entirely unintelligible to us. When a strong full-grown man is afraid to cross a street or square in his own so familiar town, or when a healthy well-developed woman becomes almost senseless with fear because a cat has brushed against her dress or a mouse has scurried through the room, how can we see the connection with danger which is obviously present to these people? With this kind of animal-phobia it is no question of an increased intensity of common human antipathies; to prove the contrary, there are numbers of people who, for instance, cannot pass a cat without attracting and petting it. A mouse is a thing that so many women are afraid of, and yet it is at the same time a very favourite pet name;[1] many a girl who is delighted to be called so by her lover will scream with terror at the sight of the dainty little creature itself. The behaviour of the man who is afraid to cross streets and squares only suggests one thing to us—that he behaves like a little child. A child is directly taught that such situations are dangerous, and the man's anxiety too is allayed when he is led by someone across the open space.

The two forms of anxiety described, the 'free-floating' expectant dread and that attached to phobias, are independent of each other. The one is not the other at a further stage; they are only rarely combined, and then as if fortuitously. The most intense general apprehensiveness does not necessarily lead to a phobia; people who have been hampered all their lives by agoraphobia may be quite free from pessimistic expectant dread. Many phobias, e.g. fear of open spaces, of railway travelling, are demonstrably acquired first in later life; others, such as fear of darkness, thunder, animals, seem to have existed from the beginning. The former signify serious illness, the latter are more of the nature of idiosyncrasies, peculiarities; anyone exhibiting one of these latter may be suspected of harbouring others similar to it. I must add that we group all these phobias under *anxiety-hysteria,* that is, we regard them as closely allied to the well-known disorder called conversion-hysteria.

The third form taken by neurotic anxiety brings us to an enigma; there is no visible connection at all between the anxiety and the danger dreaded. This anxiety occurs in hysteria, for instance, accompanying the hysterical symptoms; or under various conditions of excitement in which, it is true, we should expect some affect to be displayed, but least of all an anxiety-

[1][In Germany it replaces the use of "duck" for this purpose in English.—Tr.]

affect; or without reference to any conditions, incomprehensible both to us and to the patient, an unrelated anxiety-attack. We may look far and wide without discovering a danger or an occasion which could even be exaggerated to account for it. These spontaneous attacks show therefore that the complex condition which we describe as anxiety can be split up into components. The whole attack can be represented (as a substitute) by a single intensively developed symptom—shuddering, faintness, palpitation of the heart, inability to breathe—and the general feeling which we recognize as anxiety may be absent or may have become unnoticeable. And yet these states which are termed 'anxiety equivalents' have the same clinical and ætiological validity as anxiety itself.

Two questions arise now: Is it possible to bring neurotic anxiety, in which such a small part or none at all is played by danger, into relation with 'objective anxiety,' which is essentially a reaction to danger? And, how is neurotic anxiety to be understood? We will at present hold fast to the expectation that where there is anxiety there must be something of which one is afraid.

Clinical observation yields various clues to the comprehension of neurotic anxiety, and I will now discuss their significance with you.

(a) It is not difficult to see that expectant dread or general apprehensiveness stands in intimate relation to certain processes in the sexual life—let us say, to certain modes of libido-utilization. The simplest and most instructive case of this kind arises in people who expose themselves to what is called frustrated excitation, i.e. when a powerful sexual excitation experiences insufficient discharge and is not carried on to a satisfying termination. This occurs, for instance, in men during the time of an engagement to marry, and in women whose husbands are not sufficiently potent, or who perform the sexual act too rapidly or incompletely with a view to preventing conception. Under these conditions the libidinal excitation disappears and anxiety appears in place of it, both in the form of expectant dread and in that of attacks and anxiety-equivalents. The precautionary measure of *coitus interruptus,* when practised as a customary sexual régime, is so regularly the cause of anxiety-neurosis in men, and even more so in women, that medical practitioners would be wise to enquire first of all into the possibility of such an ætiology in all such cases. Innumerable examples show that the anxiety-neurosis vanishes when the sexual malpractice is given up.

So far as I know, the fact that a connection exists between sexual restraint and anxiety conditions is no longer disputed, even by physicians who hold aloof from psychoanalysis. Nevertheless I can well imagine that they do not neglect to invert the connection, and to put forward the view that such persons are predisposed to apprehensiveness and consequently practice caution in sexual matters. Against this, however, decisive evidence is found in the reactions in women, in whom the sexual function is essentially passive, so that its course is determined by the treatment accorded by the man. The more 'temperament,' i.e. the more inclination for sexual intercourse and capacity for satisfaction, a woman has, the more certainly will she react with anxiety manifestations to the man's impotence or to *coitus interruptus;* whereas such abuse entails far less serious results with anæsthetic women or those in whom the sexual hunger is less strong.

Sexual abstinence, which is nowadays so warmly recommended by physicians, of course only has the same significance for anxiety conditions when the libido which is denied a satisfactory outlet is correspondingly insistent, and is not being utilized to a large extent in sublimation. Whether or not illness will ensue is indeed always a matter of the quantitative factor. Even apart from illness, it is easy to see in the sphere of character-formation that sexual restraint goes hand in hand with a certain anxiousness and cautiousness, whereas fearlessness and a boldly adventurous spirit bring with them a free tolerance of sexual needs. However these relations may be altered and complicated by the manifold influences of civilization, it remains incontestible that for the average human being anxiety is closely connected with sexual restriction.

I have by no means told you all the observations which point to this genetic connection between libido and anxiety.

There is, for instance, the effect upon anxiety states of certain periods of life, such as puberty and the menopause, in which the production of libido is considerably augmented. In many states of excitement too, the mingling of sexual excitation with anxiety may be directly observed, as well as the final replacement of the libidinal excitation by anxiety. The impression received from all this is a double one; first, that it is a matter of an accumulation of libido, debarred from its normal utilization; and secondly, that the question is one of somatic processes only. How anxiety develops out of sexual desire is at present obscure; we can only ascertain that desire is lacking and anxiety is found in its place.

(b) A second clue is obtained from analysis of the psychoneuroses, in particular, of hysteria. We have heard that anxiety frequently accompanies the symptoms in this disease, and that unattached anxiety may also be chronically present or come to expression in attacks. The patients cannot say what it is they fear; they link it up by unmistakable secondary elaboration to the most convenient phobias: of dying, of going mad, of having a stroke, etc. When we subject to analysis the situation in which the anxiety, or the symptom accompanied by anxiety, arose, we can as a rule discover what normal mental process has been checked in its course and replaced by a manifestation of anxiety. To express it differently: we construe the unconscious process as though it had not undergone repression and had gone through unhindered into consciousness. This process would have been accompanied by a particular affect and now we discover, to our astonishment, that this affect, which would normally accompany the mental process through into consciousness, is in every case replaced by anxiety, no matter what particular type it had previously been. So that when we have a hysterical anxiety condition before us, its unconscious correlative may be an excitation of a similar character, such as apprehension, shame, embarrassment; or quite as possibly a 'positive' libidinal excitation; or an antagonistic, aggressive one, such as rage or anger. Anxiety is thus general current coin for which all the affects are exchanged, or can be exchanged, when the corresponding ideational content is under repression.

(c) A third observation is provided by patients whose symptoms take the form of obsessive acts, and who seem to be remarkably immune from anxiety. When we restrain them from carrying out their obsessive performances, their washing, their ceremonies, etc., or when they themselves venture an attempt to abandon one of their compulsions, they are forced by an appalling dread to yield to the compulsion and to carry out the act. We perceive that the anxiety was concealed under the obsessive act and that this is only performed to escape the feeling of dread. In the obsessional neurosis, therefore, the anxiety which would otherwise ensue is replaced by the symptom-formation; and when we turn to hysteria we find a similar relation existing—as a consequence of the process of repression either a pure developed anxiety, or anxiety with symptom-formation, or symption-formation without anxiety. In an abstract sense, therefore, it seems correct to say that symptoms altogether are formed purely for the purpose of escaping the otherwise inevitable development of anxiety. Thus anxiety comes to the forefront of our interest in the problems of the neuroses.

We concluded from our observations on the anxiety-neurosis that the diversion of the libido away from its normal form of utilization, a diversion which releases anxiety, took place on the basis of somatic processes. The analyses of hysterical and obsessional neuroses furnish the additional conclusion that a similar diversion with a similar result can follow from opposition on the part of institutions in the mind. We know as much as this, therefore, about the origin of neurotic anxiety; it still sounds rather indefinite. But for the moment I know of no path which will take us further. The second task we undertook, that of establishing a connection between neurotic anxiety (abnormally utilized libido) and 'objective anxiety' (which corresponds with the reaction to danger), seems even more difficult to accomplish. One would think there could be no comparison between the two things, and yet there are no means by which the sensations of neurotic anxiety can be distinguished from those of real anxiety.

The desired connection may be found with the help of the antithesis, so often put forward, between the ego and the libido. As we know, the development of anxiety is the reaction of the ego to danger and the signal preparatory to flight; it is then not a great step to imagine that in neurotic anxiety also the ego is attempting a flight, from the demands of its libido, and is treating this internal danger as if it were an external one. Then our expectation, that where anxiety is present there must be something of which one is afraid, would be fulfilled. The analogy goes further than this, however. Just as the tension prompting the attempt to flee from external danger is resolved into holding one's ground and taking appropriate defensive measures, so the development of neurotic anxiety yields to a symptom-formation, which enables the anxiety to be 'bound.'

Our difficulty in comprehension now lies elsewhere. The anxiety which signifies the flight of the ego from its libido is nevertheless supposed to have had its source in that libido. This is obscure, and we are warned not to forget that the libido of a given person is fundamentally part of that person and cannot be contrasted with him as if it were something external. It is the question of the topographical dynamics of anxiety-development that is still obscure to us—what kind of mental energies are being expended and to what systems do they belong? I cannot promise you to answer this question also; but we will not neglect to follow up two other clues, and in so doing will again summon direct observation and analytic investigation to aid our speculation. We will turn to the sources of anxiety in children, and to the origin of the neurotic anxiety which is attached to phobias.

Apprehensiveness is very common among children, and it is difficult enough to decide whether it is objective or neurotic anxiety. Indeed the very value of this distinction is called in question by the attitude of children themselves. For on the one hand we are not surprised that children are afraid of strangers, of strange objects and situations, and we account for this reaction to ourselves very easily by reflecting on their weakness and ignorance. Thus we ascribe to the child a strong tendency to objective anxiety and should regard it as only practical if this apprehensiveness had been transmitted by inheritance. The child would only be repeating the behaviour of prehistoric man and of primitive man to-day who, in consequence of his ignorance and helplessness, experiences a dread of anything new and strange, and of much that is familiar to him, none of which any longer inspires fear in us. It would also correspond to our expectations if the phobias of children were at least in part such as might be attributed to those primeval periods of human development.

On the other hand, it cannot be overlooked that children are not all equally apprehensive, and that the very children who are more than usually timid in the face of all kinds of objects and situations are just those who later on become neurotic. The neurotic disposition is therefore betrayed, amongst other signs, by a marked tendency to objective anxiety; apprehensiveness rather than nervousness appears to be primary; and we arrive at the conclusion that the child, and later the adult, experiences a dread of the strength of his libido simply because he is afraid of everything. The derivation of anxiety from the libido itself would then be discarded; and investigation of the conditions of real anxiety would logically lead to the view that consciousness of personal weakness and helplessness—inferiority, as A. Adler calls it—when it is able to maintain itself into later life is the final cause of neurosis.

This sounds so simple and plausible that it has a claim on our attention. It is true that it would involve shifting the point of view from which we regard the problem of nervousness. That such feelings of inferiority do persist into later life—together with a disposition to anxiety and symptom-formation—seems so well established that much more explanation is required when, in an exceptional case, what we call 'health' is the outcome. But what can be learnt from the close observation of apprehensiveness in children? The small child is first of all afraid of strange people; situations become important only on account of the people concerned in them, and objects always much later. But the child is not afraid of these strange people because he attributes evil intentions to them, comparing their strength with his weakness, and thus recognizing in them a danger to his existence, his safety, and his freedom from pain. Such a conception of a child, so suspicious and terrified of an overpowering aggressivity in the world, is a very poor sort of theoretical construction. On the contrary, the child starts back in fright from a strange figure because he is used to—and therefore expects—a beloved and familiar figure, primarily his mother. It is his disappointment and longing which are transformed into dread—his libido, unable to be expended, and at that time not to be held suspended, is discharged through being converted into dread. It can hardly be a coincidence too that in this situation, which is the prototype of childish anxiety, the condition of the primary anxiety state during birth, a separation from the mother, is again reproduced.

The first phobias of situations in children concern darkness and loneliness; the former is often retained throughout life; common to both is the desire for the absent attendant, for the mother, therefore. I once heard a child who was afraid of the darkness call out: "Auntie, talk to me, I'm frightened." "But what good will that do? You can't see me;" to which the child replied: "If someone talks, it gets lighter." The longing felt *in* the darkness is thus transformed into fear *of* the darkness. Far from finding that neurotic anxiety is only secondary and a special case of objective anxiety, we see on the contrary that there is something in the small child which behaves like real anxiety and has an essential feature in common with neurotic anxiety—namely, origin in undischarged libido. Of genuine 'objective anxiety' the child seems to bring very little into the world. In all those situations which can become the conditions of phobias later, on heights, on narrow bridges over water, in trains and boats, the small child shows no fear—the less it knows the less it fears. It is much to be wished that it had inherited more of these life-preserving instincts; the task of looking after it and preventing it from exposing itself to one danger after another would have been very much lightened. Actually, you see, a child overestimates his powers, to begin with, and behaves without fear because he does not recognize dangers. He will run along the edge of the water, climb upon the window-sill, play with sharp things and with fire, in short, do anything that injures him and alarms his attendants. Since he cannot be allowed to learn it himself through bitter experience, it is entirely due to training that real anxiety does eventually awake in him.

Now if some children embrace this training in apprehensiveness very readily, and then find for themselves dangers which they have not been warned against, it is explicable on the ground that these children have inherently a greater amount of libidinal need in their constitution than others, or else that they have been spoiled early with libidinal gratifications. It is no wonder if those who later become nervous also belong to this type as children; we know that the most favourable circumstance for the development of a neurosis lies in the inability to tolerate a considerable degree of pent-up libido for any length of time. You will observe now that here the constitutional factor, which we have never denied, comes into its own. We protest only when others emphasize it to the exclusion of all other claims, and when they introduce the constitutional factor even where according to the unanimous findings both of observation and of analysis, it does not belong, or only plays a minor part.

Let us sum up the conclusions drawn from the observation of apprehensiveness in children: Infantile dread has very little to do with objective anxiety (dread of real danger), but is, on the other hand, closely allied to the neurotic anxiety of adults. It is derived like the latter from undischarged libido, and it substitutes some other external object or some situation for the love-object which it misses.

Now you will be glad to hear that the analysis of phobias has little more to teach us than we have learnt already. The same thing happens in them as in the anxiety of children; libido that cannot be discharged is continuously being converted into an apparently 'objective' anxiety, and so an insignificant external danger is taken as a representative of what the libido desires. The agreement between the two forms of anxiety is not surprising; for infantile phobias are not merely prototypes of those which appear later in anxiety-hysteria, but they are a direct preliminary condition and prelude of them. Every hysterical phobia can be traced back to a childish dread, of which it is a continuation, even if it has a different content and must be called by a different name. The difference between the two conditions lies in their mechanism. In order that the libido should be converted into anxiety in the adult it is no longer sufficient that the libido should be momentarily unable to be utilized. The adult has long since learned to maintain such libido suspended, or to apply it in different ways. But, when the libido is attached to a mental excitation which has undergone repression, conditions similar to those in the child, in whom there is not yet any distinction between conscious and unconscious, are re-established; and by a regression to the infantile phobia a bridge, so to speak, is provided by which the conversion of libido into anxiety can be conveniently effected. As you will remember, we have treated repression at some length, but in so doing we have been concerned exclusively with the fate of the *idea* to be repressed; naturally, because this was easier to recognize and to present. But we have so far ignored the question of what happened to the *affect* attached to this idea, and now we learn for the first time that it is the immediate fate of the affect to be converted into anxiety, no matter what quality of affect it would otherwise have been had it run a normal course. This transformation of affect is, moreover, by far the more important effect of the process of repression. It is not so easy to present to you; for we cannot maintain the existence of unconscious affects in the same sense as that of unconscious ideas. An idea remains up to a point the same whether it is conscious or unconscious; we can indicate something that corresponds to an unconscious idea. But an affect is a process involving a discharge of energy, and it is to be regarded quite differently from an idea; without searching examination and clarification of our hypotheses concerning mental processes,

we cannot tell what corresponds with it in the unconscious—
and that cannot be undertaken here. However, we will preserve the impression we have gained, that the development
of anxiety is closely connected with the unconscious system.

I said that conversion into anxiety, or better, discharge in
the form of anxiety, was the immediate fate of libido which
encounters repression; I must add that it is not the only or
the final fate of it. In the neuroses, processes take place which
are intended to prevent the development of anxiety, and which
succeed in so doing by various means. In the phobias, for instance, two stages in the neurotic process are clearly discernible. The first effects the repressions and conversion of the
libido into anxiety which is then attached to some external
danger. The second consists in building up all those precautions and safeguards by which all contact with this external-
ized danger shall be avoided. Repression is an attempt at
flight on the part of the ego from the libido which it feels to
be dangerous; the phobia may be compared to a fortification
against the outer danger which now stands for the dreaded
libido. The weakness of this defensive system in the phobias
is of course that the fortress which is so well guarded from
without remains exposed to danger from within; projection
externally of danger from libido can never be a very sucessful
measure. In the other neuroses, therefore, other defensive
systems are employed against the possibility of the development of anxiety; this is a very interesting part of the psychology of the neuroses. Unfortunately it would take us too
far afield and also it would require a thorough grounding in
special knowledge of the subject. I will merely add this. I have
already spoken of the 'counter-charges' that are instituted by
the ego upon repression, which must be maintained so that
the repression can persist. It is the task of this counter-charge
to carry out the various forms of defence against the development of anxiety after repression.

To return to the phobias: I may now hope that you realize
how inadequate it is to attempt merely to explain their content, and to take no interest in them apart from their derivation—this or that object or situation which has been made into

a phobia. The content of the phobia has an importance comparable to that of the manifest dream—it is a façade. With all due modifications, it is to be admitted that among the contents of the various phobias many are found which, as Stanley Hall points out, are specially suited by phylogenetic inheritance to become objects of dread. It is even in agreement with this that many of these dreaded things have no connection with danger, except through a *symbolic* relation to it.

Thus we are convinced of the quite central position which the problem of anxiety fills in the psychology of the neuroses. We have received a strong impression of how the development of anxiety is bound up with the fate of the libido and with the unconscious system. There is only one unconnected thread, only one gap in our structure, the fact, which after all can hardly be disputed, that 'objective anxiety' must be regarded as an expression of the ego's instinct for self-perservation.

THE THEORY OF THE LIBIDO: NARCISSISM

WE HAVE REPEATEDLY, AND AGAIN QUITE RECENTLY, REFERRED to the distinction between the sexual and the ego-instincts. First of all, repression showed how they can oppose each other, how the sexual instincts are then apparently brought to submission, and required to procure their satisfaction by circuitous regressive paths, where in their impregnability they obtain compensation for their defeat. Then it appeared that from the outset they each have a different relation to the task-mistress Necessity, so that their developments are different and they acquire different attitudes to the reality-principle. Finally we believe we can observe that the sexual instincts are connected by much closer ties with the affective state of anxiety than are the ego-instincts—a conclusion which in one important point only still seems incomplete. In support of it we may bring forward the further remarkable fact that want of satisfaction of hunger or thirst, the two most elemental of the self-preservative instincts, never results in conversion of them into anxiety, whereas the conversion of unsatisfied libido into anxiety is, as we have heard, a very well-known and frequently observed phenomenon.

Our justification for distinguishing between sexual and ego-instincts can surely not be contested; it is indeed assumed by the existence of the sexual instinct as a special activity in the individual. The only question is what significance is to be attached to this distinction, how radical and decisive we intend to consider it. The answer to this depends upon what we can ascertain about the extent to which the sexual instincts, both in their bodily and their mental manifestations, conduct themselves differently from the other instincts which we set against them; and how important the results arising from these differences are found to be. We have of course no motive for maintaining any difference in the fundamental nature of the two groups of instincts, and, by the way, it would be difficult to apprehend any. They both present themselves to us merely as descriptions of the sources of energy in the individual, and the discussion whether fundamentally they are one, or essentially different, and if one, when they became separated from each other, cannot be carried through on the basis of these concepts alone, but must be grounded on the biological facts underlying them. At present we know too little about this, and even if we knew more it would not be relevant to the task of psycho-analysis.

We should clearly also profit very little by emphasizing the primordial unity of all the instincts, as Jung has done, and describing all the energies which flow from them as 'libido.' We should then be compelled to speak of sexual and asexual libido, since the sexual function is not to be eliminated from the field of mental life by any such device. The name libido, however, remains properly reserved for the instinctual forces of the sexual life, as we have hitherto employed it.

In my opinion, therefore, the question how far the quite justifiable distinction between sexual and self-preservative instincts is to be carried has not much importance for psycho-analysis, nor is psycho-analysis competent to deal with it. From the biological point of view there are certainly various indications that the distinction is important. For the sexual function is the only function of a living organism which extends beyond the individual and secures its connection with its species. It is undeniable that the exercise of this function does not always bring advantage to the individual, as do his other activities, but that for the sake of an exceptionally high degree of pleasure he is involved by this function in dangers which jeopardize his life and often enough exact it. Quite peculiar metabolic processes, different from all others, are probably required in order to preserve a portion of the individual's life as a disposition for posterity. And finally, the individual organism that regards itself as first in importance and its sexuality as a means like any other to its own satisfaction is from a biological point of view only an episode in a series of generations, a short-lived appendage to a germ-plasm which is endowed with virtual immortality, comparable to the temporary holder of an entail that will survive his death.

We are not concerned with such far-reaching considerations, however, in the psychoanalytic elucidation of the neuroses. By means of following up the distinction between the sexual and the ego-instincts we have gained the key to comprehension of the group of transference neuroses. We were able to trace back their origin to a fundamental situation in which the sexual instincts had come into conflict with the self-preservative instincts, or—to express it biologically, though at the same time less exactly—in which the ego in its capacity of independent individual organism had entered into opposition with itself in its other capacity as a member of a series of generations. Such a dissociation perhaps only exists in man, so that, taken all in all, his superiority over the other animals may come down to his capacity for neurosis. The excessive development of his libido and the rich elaboration of his mental life (perhaps directly made possible by it) seem to constitute the conditions which give rise to a conflict of this kind. It is at any rate clear that these are the conditions under which man has progressed so greatly beyond what he has in common with the animals, so that his capacity for neurosis would merely be the obverse of his capacity for cultural development. However, these again are but speculations which distract us from the task in hand.

Our work so far has been conducted on the assumption that the manifestations of the sexual and the ego-instincts can be distinguished from one another. In the transference neuroses this is possible without any difficulty. We called the invest-

ments of energy directed by the ego towards the object of its
sexual desires 'libido,' and all the other investments proceeding from the self-preservative instincts its 'interest'; and by
following up the investments with libido, their transformations, and their final fates, we were able to acquire our first
insight into the workings of the forces in mental life. The
transference neuroses offered the best material for this exploration. The ego, however,—its composition out of various
organizations with their structure and mode of functioning—
remained undiscovered; we were led to believe that analysis
of other neurotic disturbances would be required before light
could be gained on these matters.

The extension of psychoanalytic conceptions on to these
other affections was begun in early days. Already in 1908 K.
Abraham expressed the view after a discussion with me that
the main characteristic of dementia præcox (reckoned as one
of the psychoses) is that in this disease *the investments of objects with libido is lacking.* (*The Psycho-Sexual Differences
between Hysteria and Dementia Præcox.*) But then the question arose: what happens to the libido of dementia patients
when it is diverted from its objects? Abraham did not hesitate
to answer that it is turned back upon the ego, and that *this
reflex reversion of it is the source of the delusions of grandeur
in dementia præcox*. The delusion of grandeur is in every way
comparable to the well-known overestimation of the object in
a love-relationship. Thus we came for the first time to understand a feature of a psychotic affection by bringing it into relation to the normal mode of loving in life.

I will tell you at once that these early views of Abraham's
have been retained in psychoanalysis and have become the
basis of our position regarding the psychoses. We became
slowly accustomed to the conception that the libido, which
we find attached to certain objects and which is the expression
of a desire to gain some satisfaction in these objects, can also
abandon these objects and set the ego itself in their place;
and gradually this view developed itself more and more consistently. The name for this utilization of the libido—NARCIS-
SISM—we borrowed from a perversion described by P. Näcke,

in which an adult individual lavishes upon his own body all the caresses usually expended only upon a sexual object other than himself.

Reflection then at once disclosed that if a fixation of this kind to the subject's own body and his own person can occur it cannot be an entirely exceptional or meaningless phenomenon. On the contrary, it is probable that this *narcissism* is the universal original condition, out of which *object-love* develops later without thereby necessarily effecting a disappearance of the narcissism. One also had to remember the evolution of object-libido, in which to begin with many of the sexual impulses are gratified on the child's own body—as we say, auto-erotically—and that this capacity for auto-erotism accounts for the backwardness of sexuality in learning to conform to the reality-principle. Thus it appeared that auto-erotism was the sexual activity of the narcissistic phase of direction of the libido.

To put it briefly, we formed an idea of the relation between the ego-libido and the object-libido which I can illustrate to you by a comparison taken from zoology. Think of the simplest forms of life consisting of a little mass of only slightly differentiated protoplasmic substances. They extend protrusions which are called pseudopodia into which the protoplasm overflows. They can, however, again withdraw these extensions of themselves and re-form themselves into a mass. We compare this extending of protrusions to the radiation of libido on to the objects, while the greatest volume of libido may yet remain within the ego; we infer that under normal conditions ego-libido can transform itself into object-libido without difficulty and that this can again subsequently be absorbed into the ego.

With the help of these conceptions it is now possible to explain a whole series of mental states, or, to express it more modestly, to describe in terms of the libido-theory conditions that belong to normal life; for instance, the mental attitude pertaining to the conditions of "being in love," of organic illness, and of sleep. Of the condition of sleep we assumed that it is founded upon a withdrawal from the outer world and a concentration upon the wish to sleep. We found that the nocturnal mental activity which is expressed in dreams served the purpose of the wish to sleep, and, moreover, that it was governed exclusively by egoistic motives. In the light of the libido-theory we may carry this further and say that sleep is a condition in which all investments of objects, the libidinal as well as the egoistic, are abandoned and withdrawn again into the ego. Does not this shed a new light upon the recuperation afforded by sleep and upon the nature of fatigue in general? The likeness we see in the condition which the sleeper conjures up again every night to the blissful isolation of the intrauterine existence is thus confirmed and amplified in its mental aspects. In the sleeper the primal state of the libido-distribution is again reproduced, that of absolute narcissism, in which libido and ego-interests dwell together still, united and indistinguishable in the self-sufficient self.

Two observations are in place here. First, how is the concept 'narcissism' distinguished from 'egoism'? In my opinion, narcissism is the libidinal complement of egoism. When one speaks of egoism one is thinking only of the *interests* of the person concerned, narcissism relates also to the satisfaction of his libidinal needs. It is possible to follow up the two separately for a considerable distance as practical motives in life. A man may be absolutely egoistic and yet have strong libidinal attachments to objects, in so far as libidinal satisfaction in an object is a need of his ego: his egoism will then see to it that his desires towards the object involve no injury to his ego. A man may be egoistic and at the same time strongly narcissistic (i.e. feel very little need for objects), and this again either in the form taken by the need for direct sexual satisfaction, or in those higher forms of feeling derived from the sexual needs which are commonly called "love," and as such are contrasted with "sensuality." In all these situations egoism is the self-evident, the constant element, and narcissism the variable one. The antithesis of egoism, "altruism," is not an alternative term for the investment of an object with libido; it is distinct from the latter in its lack of the desire for sexual satisfaction in the object. But when the condition of love is developed to its fullest intensity altruism coincides with the investment of an object with libido. As a rule the sexual object draws to itself a portion of the ego's narcissism, which becomes apparent in what is called the 'sexual overestimation' of the object. If to this is added an altruism directed towards the object and derived from the egoism of the lover, the sexual object becomes supreme; it has entirely swallowed up the ego.

I think you will find it a relief if, after these scientific phantasies, which are after all very dry, I submit to you a poetic description of the 'economic' contrast between the condition of narcissism and that of love in full intensity. I take it from a dialogue between Zuleika and her lover in Goethe's *West-östliche Divan:*—

Zuleika:

The slave, the lord of victories,
The crowd, with single voice, confess
In sense of personal being lies
A child of earth's true happiness.
There's not a life he need refuse
If his true self he does not miss:
There's not a thing he cannot lose
If he remains the man he is.

Hâtem:

So it is held! so well may be!
But down a different track I come
Of all the bliss earth holds for me
I in Zuleika find the sum.
Does she expend her being on me,
Myself grows to myself of cost;
Turns she away, then instantly
I to my very self am lost.
And then with Hâtem all were over;
Though yet I should but change my state
Swift, should she grace some happy lover,
In him I were incorporate.[1]

[1] [Taken, with very slight modifications, from Ernest Dowden's translation.—TR.]

The second observation is an amplification of the theory of dreams. The way in which a dream originates is not explicable unless we assume that what is repressed in the unconscious has acquired a certain independence of the ego, so that it does not subordinate itself to the wish for sleep and maintains its investments, although all the object-investments proceeding from the ego have been withdrawn for the purpose of sleep. Only this makes it possible to understand how it is that this unconscious material can make use of the abrogation or diminution in the activities of the censorship which takes place at night, and that it knows how to mould the day's residue so as to form a forbidden dream-wish from the material to hand in that residue. On the other hand, some of the resistance against the wish to sleep and the withdrawal of libido thereby induced may have its origin in an association already in existence between this residue and the repressed unconscious material. This important dynamic factor must therefore now be incorporated into the conception of dream-formation which we formed in our earlier discussions.

Certain conditions—organic illness, painful accesses of stimulation, an inflammatory condition of an organ—have clearly the effect of loosening the libido from its attachment to its objects. The libido which has thus been withdrawn attaches itself again to the ego in the form of a stronger investment of the diseased region of the body. Indeed, one may venture the assertion that in such conditions the withdrawal of the libido from its objects is more striking than the withdrawal of the egoistic interests from their concerns in the outer world. This seems to lead to a possibility of understanding hypochondria, in which some organ, without being perceptibly diseased, becomes in a very similar way the subject of a solicitude on the part of the ego. I shall, however, resist the temptation to follow this up, or to discuss other situations which become explicable or capable of exposition on this assumption of a return of the object-libido into the ego; for I feel bound to meet two objections which I know have all your attention at the moment. First of all, you want to know why when I discuss sleep, illness, and similar conditions, I insist upon dis-

tinguishing between libido and 'interests,' sexual instincts and
ego-instincts, while the observations are satisfactorily explained by assuming a single uniform energy which is freely
mobile, can invest either object or ego, and can serve the
purposes of the one as well as of the other. Secondly, you will
want to know how I can be so bold as to treat the detachment of the libido from its objects as the origin of a pathological condition, if such a transformation of object-libido into
ego-libido—or into ego-energy in general—is a normal mental
process repeated every day and every night.

The answer is: Your first objection sounds a good one. Examination of the conditions of sleep, illness, and falling in love
would probably never have led to a distinction between ego-
libido and object-libido, or between libido and 'interests.' But
in this you omit to take into account the investigations with
which we started, in the light of which we now regard the
mental situations under discussion. The necessity of distinguishing between libido and 'interests,' between sexual and
self-preservative instincts, has been forced upon us by our insight into the conflict from which the transference neuroses
arise. We have to reckon with this distinction henceforth. The
assumption that object-libido can transform itself into ego-
libido, in other words, that we shall also have to reckon with
an ego-libido, appears to be the only one capable of solving
the riddle of what are called the narcissistic neuroses, e.g.
dementia præcox, or of giving any satisfactory explanation of
their likeness to hysteria and obsessions and differences from
them. We then apply what we have found undeniably proved
in these cases to illness, sleep, and the condition of intense
love. We are at liberty to apply them in any direction and
see where they will take us. The single conclusion which is
not directly based on analytical experience is that libido is
libido and remains so, whether it is attached to objects or to
the ego itself, and is never transformed into egoistic 'interests,'
and vice versa. This statement, however, is another way of
expressing the distinction between sexual instincts and ego-
instincts which we have already critically examined, and

which we shall hold to from heuristic motives until such time as it may prove valueless.

Your second objection too raises a justifiable question, but it is directed to a false issue. The withdrawal of object-libido into the ego is certainly not pathogenic; it is true that it occurs every night before sleep can ensue, and that the process is reversed upon awakening. The protoplasmic animalcule draws in its protrusions and sends them out again at the next opportunity. But it is quite a different matter when a definite, very forcible process compels the withdrawal of the libido from its objects. The libido that has then become narcissistic can no longer find its way back to its objects, and this obstruction in the way of the free movement of the libido certainly does prove pathogenic. It seems that an accumulation of narcissistic libido over and above a certain level becomes intolerable. We might well imagine that it was this that first led to the investment of objects, that the ego was obliged to send forth its libido in order not to fall ill of an excessive accumulation of it. If it were part of our scheme to go more particularly into the disorder of dementia præcox I would show you that the process which detaches the libido from its objects and blocks the way back to them again is closely allied to the process of repression, and is to be regarded as a counterpart of it. In any case you would recognize familiar ground under your feet when you found that the preliminary conditions giving rise to these processes are almost identical, so far as we know at present, with those of repression. The conflict seems to be the same and to be conducted between the same forces. Since the outcome is so different from that of hysteria, for instance, the reason can only lie in some difference in the disposition. The weak point in the libido-development in these patients is found at a different phase of the development; the decisive fixation which, as you will remember, enables the process of symptom-formation to break out is at another point, probably at the stage of primary narcissism, to which dementia præcox finally returns. It is most remarkable that for all the narcissistic neuroses we have to assume fixation-points of the libido at very much earlier phases of development than those found in hysteria or the obsessional neurosis. You have heard, however, that the concepts we have elicited from the study of the transference neuroses also suffice to show us our bearings in the narcissistic neuroses, which are in practice so much more severe. There is a very wide community between them; fundamentally they are phenomena of a single class. You may imagine how hopeless a task it is for anyone to attempt to explain these disorders (which properly belong to psychiatry) without being first equipped with the analytic knowledge of the transference neuroses.

The picture formed by the symptoms of dementia præcox, incidentally a very variable one, is not determined exclusively by the symptoms arising from the forcing of the libido back from the objects and the accumulation of it as narcissism in the ego. Other phenomena occupy a large part of the field, and may be traced to the efforts made by the libido to reach its objects again, which correspond therefore to attempts at restitution and recovery. These are in fact the conspicuous, clamorous symptoms; they exhibit a marked similarity to those of hysteria, or more rarely of the obsessional neurosis; they are nevertheless different in every respect. It seems that in dementia præcox the efforts of the libido to get back to its objects, that is, to the mental idea of its objects, do really succeed in conjuring up something of them, something that at the same time is only the shadow of them—namely, the verbal images, the words, attached to them. This is not the place to discuss this matter further, but in my opinion this reversed procedure on the part of the libido gives us an insight into what constitutes the real difference between a conscious and an unconscious idea.

This has now brought us into the field where the next advances in analytic work are to be expected. Since the time when we resolved upon our formulation of the conception of ego-libido, the narcissistic neuroses have become accessible to us; the task before us was to find the dynamic factors in these disorders, and at the same time to amplify our knowledge of mental life by a comprehension of the ego. The psychology of the ego, at which we are aiming, cannot be founded upon data provided by our own self-perceptions; it must be based, as is that of the libido, upon analysis of the disturbances and disintegrations of the ego. We shall probably think very little of our present knowledge of the fate of the libido, gained from the study of the transference neuroses, when that further, greater work has been achieved. But as yet we have not got very far towards it. The narcissistic neuroses can hardly be approached at all by the method which has availed for the transference neuroses; you shall soon hear why this is. With these patients it always happens that after one has penetrated a little way one comes up against a stone wall which cannot be surmounted. You know that in the transference neuroses, too, barriers of resistance of this kind are met with, but that it is possible bit by bit to pull them down. In the narcissistic neuroses the resistance is insuperable; at the most we can satisfy our curiosity by craning our necks for a glimpse or two at what is going on over the wall. Our technique will therefore have to be replaced by other methods; at present we do not know whether we shall succeed in finding a substitute. There is no lack of material with these patients; they bring forward a great deal, although not in answer to our questions; at present all we can do is to interpret what they say in the light of the understanding gained from the study of the transference neuroses. The agreement between the two forms of disease goes far enough to ensure us a satisfactory start with them. How much we shall be able to achieve by this method remains to be seen.

There are other difficulties, besides this, in the way of our progress. The narcissistic disorders and the psychoses related to them can only be unriddled by observers trained in the analytic study of the transference neuroses. But our psychiatrists do not study psychoanalysis and we psychoanalysts see too little of psychiatric cases. We shall have to develop a breed of psychiatrists who have gone through the training of psychoanalysis as a preparatory science. A beginning in this direction is being made in America, where several of the leading psychiatrists lecture on psychoanalytic doctrines to their students, and where medical superintendents of institutions and asylums endeavour to observe their patients in the light of this theory. But all the same it has sometimes been possible for us here to take a peep over the wall of narcissism, so I will now proceed to tell you what we think we have discovered in this way.

The disease of paranoia, a chronic form of systematic insanity, has a very uncertain position in the attempts at classification made by present-day psychiatry. There is no doubt, however, that it is closely related to dementia præcox; I have in fact proposed that they should both be included under the common designation of *paraphrenia*. The forms taken by paranoia are described according to the content of the delusion, e.g. delusions of grandeur, of persecution, of jealousy, of being loved (erotomania), etc. We do not expect attempts at explanation from psychiatry; as an example, an antiquated and not very fair example, I grant, I will tell you the attempt which was made to derive one of these symptoms from another, by means of a piece of intellectual rationalization: The patient who has a primary tendency to believe himself persecuted draws from this the conclusion that he must necessarily be a very important person and therefore develops a delusion of grandeur. According to our analytic conception, the delusion of grandeur is the direct consequence of the inflation of the ego by the libido withdrawn from the investment of objects, a secondary narcissism ensuing as a return of the original early infantile form. In the case of delusions of persecution, however, we observed things which led us to follow up a certain clue. In the first place we noticed that in the great majority of cases the persecuting person was of the same sex as the persecuted one; this was capable of a harmless explanation, it is true, but in certain cases which were closely studied it appeared that the person of the same sex who had been most beloved while the patient was normal became the persecutor after the disease broke out. A further development of this becomes possible through the well-known paths of association by which a loved person may be replaced by someone else, e.g. the father by masters or persons in author-

ity. From these observations, which were continually corroborated, we drew the conclusion that persecutory paranoia is
the means by which a person defends himself against a homosexual impulse which has become too powerful. The conversion of the affectionate feeling into the hate which, as is
well-known, can seriously endanger the life of the loved and
hated object then corresponds to the conversion of libidinal
impulses into anxiety, which is a regular result of the process
of repression. As an illustration I will quote the last case I
had of this type. A young doctor had to be sent away from
the place where he lived because he had threatened the life of
the son of a university professor there who had previously
been his greatest friend. He imputed superhuman power and
the most devilish intentions to this friend; he was to blame for
all the misfortunes which had occurred in recent years to the
family of the patient and for all his ill-luck in public and in
private. This was not enough, however; the wicked friend and
his father, the professor, had caused the war and brought
the Russians over the border; he had ruined his life in a
thousand ways; our patient was convinced that the death of
this criminal would be the end of all evil in the world. And
yet his old love for him was still so strong that it had paralysed
his hand when he had an opportunity of shooting his enemy
at sight. In the short conversation which I had with the patient
it came to light that this intimate friendship between the
two men went right back to their school-days; on at least one
occasion it had passed beyond the boundaries of friendship,
a night spent together had been the occasion of complete
sexual intercourse. The patient had never developed any of
the feeling towards women that would have been natural at his
age with his attractive personality. He had been engaged to a
handsome, well-connected girl, but she had broken off the
engagement because her lover was so cold. Years after, his
disease broke out at the very moment when he had for the
first time succeeded in giving full sexual gratification to a
woman; as she encircled him in her arms in gratitude and
devotion he suddenly felt a mysterious stab of pain running
like a sharp knife round the crown of his head. Afterwards

he described the sensation as being like that of the incision made at a post-mortem to bare the brain; and as his friend was a pathological anatomist he slowly came to the conclusion that he alone could have sent him this woman as a temptation. Then his eyes began to be opened about the other persecutions of which he had been the victim by the machinations of his former friend.

But how about those cases in which the persecutor is of a different sex from that of the persecuted one, and which appear therefore to contradict our explanation of this disease as a defence against homosexual libido? Some time ago I had an opportunity of examining a case of the kind, and behind the apparent contradiction I was able to elicit a confirmation. A young girl imagined herself persecuted by a man with whom she had twice had intimate relations; actually she had first of all cherished the delusions against a woman who could be recognized to be a mother-substitute. Not until after the second meeting with him did she make the advance of transferring the delusional idea from the woman to the man; so that in this case also the condition that the sex of the persecutor is the same as that of the victim originally held good also. In her complaint to the lawyer and the doctor the patient had not mentioned the previous phase of her delusion and this gave rise to an apparent contradiction of our theory of paranoia.

The homosexual choice of object is originally more closely related to narcissism than the heterosexual; hence, when a strong unwelcome homosexual excitation suffers repudiation, the way back to narcissism is especially easy to find. I have so far had very little opportunity in these lectures of speaking about the fundamental plan on which the course of the love-impulse during life is based, so far as we know it; nor can I supplement it now. I will only select this to tell you: that the choice of object, the step forward in the development of the libido which comes after the narcissistic stage, can proceed according to two types. These are: either *the narcissistic type,* according to which, in place of the ego itself, someone as nearly as possible resembling it is adopted as an object; or *the anaclitic type (Anlehnungstypus)*[1] in which those persons who became prized on account of the satisfactions they rendered to the primal needs in life are chosen as objects by the libido also. A strong libido-fixation on the narcissistic type of object-choice is also found as a trait in the disposition of manifest homosexuals.

You will remember that in the first lecture given this session I described to you a case of delusional jealousy in a woman. Now that we have so nearly reached the end you will certainly want to know how we account for a delusion psychoanalytically. I have less to say about it than you would expect, however. The inaccessibility of delusions to logical arguments and to actual experience is to be explained, as it is with obsessions, by the connection they bear to the unconscious material which is both expressed by, and held in check by, the delusion or the obsession. The differences between the two are based on the topographical and dynamic differences in the two affections.

As with paranoia, so also with melancholia (under which, by the way, very different clinical types are classified), it has been possible to obtain a glimpse into the inner structure of the disorder. We have perceived that the self-reproaches with which these sufferers torment themselves so mercilessly actually relate to another person, to the sexual object they have lost or whom they have ceased to value on account of some fault. From this we concluded that the melancholic has indeed withdrawn his libido from the object, but that by a process which we must call 'narcissistic identification' he has set up the object within the ego itself, projected it on to the ego. I can only give you a descriptive representation of this process, and not one expressed in terms of topography and dynamics. The ego itself is then treated as though it were the abandoned object; it suffers all the revengeful and aggressive treatment which is designed for the object. The suicidal impulses of melancholics also become more intelligible on the supposition that the bitterness felt by the diseased mind con-

[1][This name refers to the *dependence* of the sexual instincts on the self-preservative instincts for their first object, i.e. the suckling mother.—TR.]

cerns the ego itself at the same time as, and equally with, the loved and hated objects. In melancholia, as in the other narcissistic disorders, a feature of the emotional life which, after Bleuler, we are accustomed to call *ambivalence* comes markedly to the fore; by this we mean a directing of antithetical feelings (affectionate and hostile) towards the same person. It is unfortunate that I have not been able to say more about ambivalence in these lectures.

There is also, besides the narcissistic, an hysterical form of identification which has long been known to us. I wish it were possible to make the differences between them clear to you in a few definite statements. I can tell you something of the periodic and cyclic forms of melancholia which will interest you. It is possible in favourable circumstances—I have twice achieved it—to prevent the recurrence of the condition, or of its antithesis, by analytic treatment during the lucid intervals between the attacks. One learns from this that in melancholia and mania as well as other conditions a special kind of solution of a conflict is going on, which in all its pre-requisites agrees with those of the other neuroses. You may imagine how much there remains for psychoanalysis to do in this field.

I also told you that by analysis of the narcissistic disorders we hoped to gain some knowledge of the composition of the ego and of its structure out of various faculties and elements. We have made a beginning towards this at one point. From analysis of the delusion of observation we have come to the conclusion that in the ego there exists a faculty that incessantly watches, criticizes, and compares, and in this way is set against the other part of the ego. In our opinion, therefore, the patient reveals a truth which has not been appreciated as such when he complains that at every step he is spied upon and observed, that his very thought is known and examined. He has erred only in attributing this disagreeable power to something outside himself and foreign to him; he perceives within his ego the rule of a faculty which measures his actual ego and all his activities by an *ego-ideal*, which he has created for himself in the course of his development. We also infer that he created this ideal for the purpose of recovering thereby the self-satisfaction bound up with the primary infantile narcissism, which since those days has suffered so many shocks and mortification. We recognize in this self-criticizing faculty the ego-censorship, the 'conscience'; it is the same censorship as that exercised at night upon dreams, from which the repressions against inadmissible wish-excitations proceed. When this faculty disintegrates in the delusion of being observed, we are able to detect its origin and that it arose out of the influence of parents and those who trained the child, together with his social surroundings, by a process of identification with certain of these persons who were taken as a model.

These are some of the results yielded by the application of psychoanalysis to the narcissistic disorders. They are still not very numerous, and many of them still lack that sharpness of outline which cannot be achieved in a new field until some degree of familiarity has been attained. All of them have been made possible by employing the conception of ego-libido, or narcissistic libido, by means of which we can extend the conclusions established for the transference neuroses on to the narcissistic neuroses. But now you will put the question whether is it possible for us to bring all the disorders of the narcissistic neuroses and of the psychoses into the range of the libido-theory, for us to find the libidinal factor in mental life always and everywhere responsible for the development of disease, and for us never to have to attribute any part in the causation to the same alteration in the functions of the self-preservative instincts. Well now, it seems to me that decision on this point is not very urgent, and above all that the time is not yet ripe for us to make it; we may leave it calmly to be decided by advance in the work of science. I should not be astonished if it should prove that the capacity to induce a pathogenic effect were actually a prerogative of the libidinal impulses, so that the theory of the libido would triumph all along the line from the actual neuroses to the severest psychotic form of individual derangement. For we know it to be characteristic of the libido that it refuses to subordinate itself to reality in life, to necessity. But I consider it extremely probable that the ego-instincts are involved secondarily and that disturbances in their functions may be necessitated by the pathogenic affections of the libido. Nor can I see that the direction taken by our investigations will be invalidated if we should have to recognize that in severe psychosis the ego-instincts themselves are primarily deranged; the future will decide—for you, at least.

Let me return for a moment to anxiety, in order to throw light upon the one obscure point we left there. We said that the relation between anxiety and libido, otherwise so well defined, is with difficulty harmonized with the almost indisputable assumption that objective anxiety in the face of danger is the expression of the self-preservative instincts. But how if the anxiety-affect is provided, not by self-interest on the part of the ego-instincts, but by the ego-libido? The condition of anxiety is after all invariably detrimental; its disadvantage becomes conspicuous when it reaches an intense degree. It then interferes with the action that alone would be expedient and would serve the purposes of self-preservation, whether it be flight or self-defence. Therefore if we ascribe the affective component of objective anxiety to the ego-libido, and the action undertaken to the ego-preservative instincts, every theoretical difficulty will be overcome. You will hardly maintain seriously that we run away *because* we perceive fear? No, we perceive fear *and* we take to flight, out of the common impulse that is roused by the perception of danger. Men who have survived experiences of imminent danger to life tell us that they did not perceive any fear, that they simply acted—for instance, pointed their gun at the oncoming beast—which was undoubtedly the best thing they could do.

TWENTY-SEVENTH LECTURE

TRANSFERENCE

NOW THAT WE ARE COMING TO THE END OF OUR DISCUSSIONS
you will feel a certain expectation which must not be allowed
to mislead you. You are probably thinking that I surely have
not led you through all these complicated mazes of psychoanalysis only to dismiss you at the end without a word about
the therapy, upon which after all the possibility of undertaking psychoanalytic work depends. As a matter of fact I could
not possibly leave out this aspect of it; for some of the phenomena belonging to it will teach you a new fact, without
knowledge of which you would be quite unable to assimilate
properly your understanding of the diseases we have been
studying.

I know you do not expect directions in the technique of
practising analysis for therapeutic purposes; you only want to
know in a general way by what means the psychoanalytic
therapy works and to gain a general idea of what it accom-
plishes. And you have an undeniable right to learn this; nevertheless I am not going to tell you—I am going to insist upon
your finding it out for yourselves.

Think for a moment! You have already learnt everything
essential, from the conditions by which illness is provoked to
all the factors which take effect within the diseased mind.
Where is the opening in all this for therapeutic influence?

First of all there is the hereditary disposition,—we do not often mention it because it is so strongly emphasized in other quarters and we have nothing new to say about it. But do not suppose that we underestimate it; as practitioners we are well aware of its power. In any event we can do nothing to change it; for us also it is a fixed datum in the problem, which sets a limit to our efforts. Next, there is the influence of the experiences of early childhood, which we are accustomed in analysis to rank as very important; they belong to the past, we cannot undo them. Then there is all that unhappiness in life which we have included under 'frustration in reality,' from which all the absence of love in life proceeds—namely, poverty, family strife, mistaken choice in marriage, unfavourable social conditions, and the severity of the demands by which moral convention oppresses the individual. There is indeed a wide opening for a very effective treatment in all this; but it would have to follow the course of the dispensations of Kaiser Joseph in the Viennese legend—the benevolent despotism of a potentate before whose will men bow and difficulties disappear! But who are we that we can exert such beneficence as a therapeutic measure? Poor as we are and without influence socially, with our living to earn by our medical practice, we are not even in a position to extend our efforts to penniless folk, as other physicians with other methods can do; our treatment takes too much time and labour for that. But perhaps you are still clinging on to one of the factors put forward, and believe you see an opening for our influence there. If the conventional restrictions imposed by society have had a part in the privations forced upon the patient, the treatment could give him the courage and even directly advise him to defy these obstacles, and to seize satisfactions and health for himself at the cost of failing to achieve an ideal which, though highly esteemed, is after all often set at naught by the world. Health is to be won by "free living," then. There would be this blot upon analysis, to be sure, that it would not be serving general morality; what it gave to the individual it would take from the rest of the world.

But now, who has given you such a false impression of analysis? It is out of the question that part of the analytic treatment should consist of advice to "live freely"—if for no other reason because we ourselves tell you that a stubborn conflict is going on in the patient between libidinal desires and sexual repression, between sensual and ascetic tendencies. This conflict is not resolved by helping one side to win a victory over the other. It is true we see that in neurotics asceticism has gained the day; the result of which is that the suppressed sexual impulses have found a vent for themselves in the symptoms. If we were to make victory possible to the sensual side instead, the disregarded forces repressing sexuality would have to indemnify themselves by symptoms. Neither of these measures will succeed in ending the inner conflict; one side in either event will remain unsatisfied. There are but few cases in which the conflict is so unstable that a factor like medical advice can have any effect upon it, and these cases do not really require analytic treatment. People who can be so easily influenced by physicians would have found their own way to that solution without this influence. After all, you know that a young man living in abstinence who makes up his mind to illicit sexual intercourse, or an unsatisfied wife who seeks compensation with a lover, does not as a rule wait for the permission of a physician, still less of an analyst, to do so.

In considering this question people usually overlook the essential point of the whole difficulty—namely, that the pathogenic conflict in a neurotic must not be confounded with a normal struggle between conflicting impulses all of which are in the same mental field. It is a battle between two forces of which one has succeeded in coming to the level of the preconscious and conscious part of the mind, while the other has been confined on the unconscious level. That is why the conflict can never have a final outcome one way or the other; the antagonists meet each other as little as the whale and the polar bear in the well-known story. An effective decision can be reached only when they confront each other on the same ground. And, in my opinion, to accomplish this is the sole task of the treatment.

Besides this, I can assure you that you are quite misinformed if you imagine that advice and guidance concerning conduct in life forms an integral part of the analytic method. On the contrary, so far as possible we refrain from playing the part of mentor; we want nothing better than that the patient should find his own solutions for himself. To this end we expect him to postpone all vital decisions affecting his life, such as choice of career, business enterprises, marriage or divorce, during treatment and to execute them only after it has been completed. Now confess that you had imagined something very different. Only with certain very young or quite helpless and defenceless persons is it impossible to keep within such strict limitations as we should wish. With them we have to combine the positions of physician and educator; we are then well aware of our responsibility and act with the necessary caution.

You must not be led away by my eagerness to defend myself against the accusation that in analytic treatment neurotics are encouraged to "live a free life" and conclude from it that we influence them in favour of conventional morality. That is at least as far removed from our purpose as the other. We are not reformers, it is true; we are merely observers; but we cannot avoid observing with critical eyes, and we have found it impossible to give our support to conventional sexual morality or to approve highly of the means by which society attempts to arrange the practical problems of sexuality in life. We can demonstrate with ease that what the world calls its code of morals demands more sacrifices than it is worth, and that its behaviour is neither dictated by honesty nor instituted with wisdom. We do not absolve our patients from listening to these criticisms; we accustom them to an unprejudiced consideration of sexual matters like all other matters; and if after they have become independent by the effect of the treatment they choose some intermediate course between unrestrained sexual licence and unconditional asceticism, our conscience is not burdened whatever the outcome. We say to ourselves that anyone who has successfully undergone the training of learning and recognizing the truth about himself is henceforth strengthened against the dangers of immorality, even if his standard of morality should in some respect deviate from the common one. Incidentally, we must beware of overestimating the importance of abstinence in affecting neurosis; only a minority of pathogenic situations due to frustration and the subsequent accumulation of libido thereby induced can be relieved by the kind of sexual intercourse that is procurable without any difficulty.

So you cannot explain the therapeutic effect of psychoanalysis by supposing that it permits patients free sexual indulgence; you must look round for something else. I think that one of the remarks I made while I was disposing of this conjecture on your part will have put you on the right track. Probably it is the substitution of something conscious for something unconscious, the transformation of the unconscious thoughts into conscious thoughts, that makes our work effective. You are right; that is exactly what it is. By extending the unconscious into consciousness the repressions are raised, the conditions of symptom-formation are abolished, and the pathogenic conflict exchanged for a normal one which must be decided one way or the other. We do nothing for our patients but enable this one mental change to take place in them; the extent to which it is achieved is the extent of the benefit we do them. Where there is no repression or mental process analogous to it to be undone there is nothing for our therapy to do.

The aim of our efforts may be expressed in various formulas —making conscious the unconscious, removing the repressions, filling in the gaps in memory; they all amount to the same thing. But perhaps you are dissatisfied with this declaration; you imagined the recovery of a nervous person rather differently, that after he had been subjected to the laborious process of psychoanalysis he would emerge a different person altogether, and then you hear that the whole thing only amounts to his having a little less that is unconscious and a little more that is conscious in him than before. Well, you probably do not appreciate the importance of an inner change of this kind. A neurotic who has been cured has really become a different person, although at bottom of course he remains the same— that is, he has become his best self, what he would have been under the most favourable conditions. That, however, is a great deal. Then when you hear of all that has to be done, of the tremendous exertion required to carry out this apparently trifling change in his mental life, the significance attached to these differences between the various mental levels will appear more comprehensible to you.

I will digress a moment to enquire whether you know what 'a causal therapy' means? This name is given to a procedure which puts aside the manifestations of a disease and looks for a point of attack in order to eradicate the cause of the illness. Now is psychoanalysis a causal therapy or not? The answer is not a simple one, but it may give us an opportunity to convince ourselves of the futility of such questions. In so far as psychoanalytic therapy does not aim immediately at removing the symptoms it is conducted like a causal therapy. In other respects you may say it is not, for we have followed the causal chain back far beyond the repressions to the instinctive predispositions, their relative intensity in the constitution, and the aberrations in the course of their development. Now suppose that it were possible by some chemical means to affect this mental machinery, to increase or decrease the amount of libido available at any given moment, or to reinforce the strength of one impulse at the expense of another—that would be a causal therapy in the literal sense, and our analysis would be the indispensable preliminary work of reconnoitring the ground. As you know, there is at present no question of any such influence upon the processes of the libido; our mental therapy makes its attack at another point in the concatenation, not quite at the place where we perceive the manifestations to be rooted, but yet comparatively far behind the symptoms themselves, at a place which becomes accessible to us in very remarkable circumstances.

What then have we to do in order to bring what is unconscious in the patient into consciousness? At one time we thought that would be very simple; all we need do would be to identify this unconscious matter and then tell the patient what it was. However, we know already that that was a short-sighted mistake. Our knowledge of what is unconscious in him is not equivalent to his knowledge of it; when we tell him what we know he does not assimilate it *in place of* his own unconscious thoughts, but *alongside* of them, and very little has been changed. We have rather to regard this unconscious material topographically; we have to look for it in his memory at the actual spot where the repression of it originally ensued. This repression must be removed, and then the substitution of conscious thought for unconscious thought can be effected straightaway. How is a repression such as this to be removed? Our work enters upon a second phase here; first, the discovery of the repression, and then the removal of the resistance which maintains this repression.

How can this resistance be got rid of? In the same way: by finding it out and telling the patient about it. The resistance too arises in a repression, either from the very one which we are endeavouring to dispel, or in one that occurred earlier. It is set up by the counter-charge which rose up to repress the repellent impulse. So that we now do just the same as we were trying to do before; we interpret, identify, and inform the patient; but this time we are doing it at the right spot. The counter-charge or the resistance is not part of the unconscious, but of the ego which co-operates with us, and this is so, even if it is not actually conscious. We know that a difficulty arises here in the ambiguity of the word 'unconscious,' on the one hand, as a phenomenon, on the other hand, as a system. That sounds very obscure and difficult; but after all it is only a repetition of what we have said before, is it not? We have come to this point already long ago.—Well then, we expect that this resistance will be abandoned, and the countercharge withdrawn, when we have made the recognition of them possible by our work of interpretation. What are the instinctive propelling forces at our disposal to make this possible? First, the patient's desire for recovery, which impelled him to submit himself to the work in co-operation with us, and secondly, the aid of his intelligence which we reinforce by our interpretation. There is no doubt that it is easier for the patient to recognize the resistance with his intelligence, and to identify the idea in his unconscious which corresponds to it, if we have first given him an idea which rouses his expectations in regard to it. If I say to you: "Look up at the sky and you will see a balloon," you will find it much more quickly than if I merely tell you to look up and see whether you can see anything; a student who looks through a microscope for the first time is told by the instructor what he is to see; otherwise he sees nothing, although it is there and quite visible.

And now for the fact! In quite a number of the various forms of nervous illness, in the hysterias, anxiety-conditions, obsessional neuroses, our hypothesis proves sound. By seeking out the repression in this way, discovering the resistances, indicating the repressed, it is actually possible to accomplish the task, to overcome the resistances, to break down the repression, and to change something unconscious into something conscious. As we do this we get a vivid impression of how, as each individual resistance is being mastered, a violent battle goes on in the soul of the patient—a normal mental struggle between two tendencies on the same ground, between the motives striving to maintain the countercharge and those which are ready to abolish it. The first of these are the old motives which originally erected the repression; among the second are found new ones more recently acquired which it is hoped will decide the conflict in our favour. We have succeeded in revivifying the old battle of the repression again, in bringing the issue, so long ago decided, up for revision again. The new contribution we make to it lies, first of all, in demonstrating that the original solution led to illness and in promising that a different one would pave the way to health, and secondly, in pointing out that the circumstances have all changed immensely since the time of that original repudiation of these impulses. Then, the ego was weak, infantile, and perhaps had reason to shrink with horror from the claims of the libido as being dangerous to it. To-day it is strong and experienced and moreover has a helper at hand in the physician So we may expect to lead the revived conflict through a better outcome than repression; and, as has been said, in hysteria, anxiety-neurosis, and the obsessional neurosis success in the main justifies our claims.

There are other forms of illness, however, with which our therapeutic treatment never is successful, in spite of the similarity of the conditions. In them also there was originally a conflict between ego and libido, leading to repression—although this conflict may be characterized by topographical differences from the conflict of the transference neuroses; in them too it is possible to trace out the point in the patient's life at which the repressions occurred; we apply the same method, are ready to make the same assurances, offer the same assistance by telling the patient what to look out for; and here also the interval in time between the present and the point at which the repressions were established is all in favour of a better outcome of the conflict. And yet we cannot succeed in overcoming one resistance or in removing one of the repressions. These patients, paranoiacs, melancholics, and those suffering from dementia præcox, remain on the whole unaffected, proof against psycho-analytic treatment. What can be the cause of this? It is not due to lack of intelligence; a certain degree of intellectual capacity must naturally be stipulated for analysis, but there is no deficiency in this respect in, for instance, the very quick-witted deductive paranoiac. Nor are any of the other propelling forces regularly absent: melancholics, for instance, in contrast to paranoiacs, experience a very high degree of realization that they are ill and that their sufferings are due to this; but they are not on that account any more accessible to influence. In this we are confronted with a fact that we do not understand, and are therefore called upon to doubt whether we have really understood all the conditions of the success possible with the other neuroses.

When we keep to consideration of hysterical and obsessional neurotics we are very soon confronted with a second fact, for which we were quite unprepared. After the treatment has proceeded for a while we notice that these patients behave in a quite peculiar manner towards ourselves. We thought indeed that we had taken into account all the motive forces affecting the treatment and had reasoned out the situation between ourselves and the patient fully, so that it balanced like a sum in arithmetic; and then after all something seems to slip in which was quite left out of our calculation. This new and unexpected feature is in itself many-sided and complex; I will first of all describe some of its more frequent and simpler forms to you.

We observe then that the patient, who ought to be thinking of nothing but the solution of his own distressing conflicts, begins to develop a particular interest in the person of the physician. Everything connected with this person seems to him more important than his own affairs and to distract him from his illness. Relations with the patient then become for a time very agreeable; he is particularly docile, endeavours to show his gratitude wherever he can, exhibits a fineness of character and other good qualities which we had perhaps not anticipated in him. The analyst thus forms a very good opinion of the patient and values his luck in being able to render assistance to such an admirable personality. If the physician has occasion to see the patient's relatives he hears with satisfaction that this esteem is mutual. The patient at home is never tired of praising the analyst and attributing new virtues to him. "He has quite lost his head over you; he puts implicit trust in you; everything you say is like a revelation to him," say the relatives. Here and there one among this chorus having sharper eyes will say: "It is positively boring the way he never speaks of anything but you: he quotes you all the time."

We will hope that the physician is modest enough to ascribe the patient's estimate of his value to the hopes of recovery which he has been able to offer to him, and to the widening in the patient's intellectual horizon consequent upon the surprising revelations entailed by the treatment and their liberating influence. The analysis too makes splendid progress under these conditions, the patient understands the suggestions offered to him, concentrates upon the tasks appointed by the treatment, the material needed—his recollections and associations—is abundantly available; he astonishes the analyst by the sureness and accuracy of his interpretations, and the latter has only to observe with satisfaction how readily and willingly a sick man will accept all the new psychological ideas that are so hotly contested by the healthy in the world outside. A general improvement in the patient's condition, objectively confirmed on all sides, also accompanies this harmonious relationship in the analysis.

But such fair weather cannot last for ever. There comes a day when it clouds over. There begin to be difficulties in the analysis; the patient says he cannot think of anything more to say. One has an unmistakable impression that he is no longer interested in the work, and that he is casually ignoring the injunction given him to say everything that comes into his mind and to yield to none of the critical objections that occur to him. His behaviour is not dictated by the situation of the treatment; it is as if he had not made an agreement to that effect with the physician; he is obviously preoccupied with something which at the same time he wishes to reserve to himself. This is a situation in which the treatment is in danger. Plainly a very powerful resistance has risen up. What can have happened?

If it is possible to clear up this state of things, the cause of the disturbance is found to consist in certain intense feelings of affection which the patient has transferred on to the physician, not accounted for by the latter's behaviour nor by the relationship involved by the treatment. The form in which this affectionate feeling is expressed and the goal it seeks naturally depend upon the circumstances of the situation between the two persons. If one of them is a young girl and the other still a fairly young man, the impression received is that of normal love; it seems natural that a girl should fall in love with a man with whom she is much alone and can speak of very intimate things, and who is in the position of an adviser with authority —we shall probably overlook the fact that in a neurotic girl some disturbance of the capacity for love is rather to be expected. The farther removed the situation between the two persons is from this supposed example, the more unaccountable it is to find that nevertheless the same kind of feeling comes to light in other cases. It may be still comprehensible when a young woman who is unhappily married seems to be overwhelmed by a serious passion for her physician, if he is still unattached, and that she should be ready to seek a divorce and give herself to him, or, where circumstances would prevent this, to enter into a secret love-affair with him. That sort of thing, indeed, is known to occur outside psychoanalysis. But in this situation girls and women make the most astonishing confessions which reveal a quite peculiar attitude on their part to the therapeutic problem: they had always known that nothing but love would cure them, and from the beginning of the treatment they had expected that this relationship would at last yield them what life had so far denied them. It was only with this hope that they had taken such pains over the analysis and had conquered all their difficulties in disclosing their thoughts. We ourselves can add: 'and had understood so easily all that is usually so hard to accept.' But a confession of this kind astounds us; all our calculations are blown to the winds. Could it be that we have omitted the most important element in the whole problem?

And actually it is so; the more experience we gain the less possible does it become for us to contest this new factor, which alters the whole problem and puts our scientific calculations to shame. The first few times one might think that the analytic treatment had stumbled upon an obstruction in the shape of an accidental occurrence, extraneous to its purpose and unconnected with it in origin. But when it happens that this kind of attachment to the physician regularly evinces itself in every fresh case, under the most unfavourable conditions, and always appears, even in circumstances of a positively grotesque incongruity—in elderly women, in relation to grey-bearded men, even on occasions when our judgement assures us that no temptations exist—then we are compelled to give up the idea of a disturbing accident and to admit that we have to deal with a phenomenon in itself essentially bound up with the nature of the disease.

The new fact which we are thus unwillingly compelled to recognize we call TRANSFERENCE. By this we mean a transference of feelings on to the person of the physician, because we do not believe that the situation in the treatment can account for the origin of such feelings. We are much more disposed to suspect that the whole of this readiness to develop feeling originates in another source; that it was previously formed in the patient, and has seized the opportunity provided by the treatment to transfer itself on to the person of the physician. The transference can express itself as a passionate petitioning for love, or it can take less extreme forms; where a young girl and an elderly man are concerned, instead of the wish to be wife or mistress, a wish to be adopted as a favourite daughter may come to light, the libidinous desire can modify itself and propose itself as a wish for an everlasting, but ideally platonic friendship. Many women understand how to sublimate the transference and to mould it until it acquires a sort of justification for its existence; others have to express it in its crude, original, almost impossible form. But at bottom it is always the same, and its origin in the same source can never be mistaken.

Before we enquire where we are to range this new fact, we will amplify the description of it a little. How is it with our male patients? There at least we might hope to be spared the troublesome element of sex difference and sex attraction. Well, the answer is very much the same as with women. The same attachment to the physician, the same overestimation of his qualities, the same adoption of his interests, the same jealousy against all those connected with him. The sublimated kinds of transference are the forms more frequently met with between man and man, and the directly sexual declaration more rarely, in the same degree to which the manifest homosexuality of the patient is subordinated to the other ways by which this component-instinct can express itself. Also, it is in male patients that the analyst more frequently observes a manifestation of the transference which at the first glance seems to controvert the description of it just given—that is, the hostile or *negative* transference.

First of all, let us realize at once that the transference exists in the patient from the beginning of the treatment, and is for a time the strongest impetus in the work. Nothing is seen of it and one does not need to trouble about it as long as its effect is favourable to the work in which the two persons are co-operating. When it becomes transformed into a resistance, at-

tention must be paid to it; and then it appears that two different and contrasting states of mind have supervened in it and
have altered its attitude to the treatment: first, when the affectionate attraction has become so strong and betrays signs
of its origin in sexual desire so clearly that it was bound to
arouse an inner opposition against itself; and secondly, when
it consists in antagonistic instead of affectionate feeling. The
hostile feelings as a rule appear later than the affectionate and
under cover of them; when both occur simultaneously they
provide a very good exemplification of that ambivalence in
feeling which governs most of our intimate relationships with
other human beings. The hostile feelings therefore indicate an
attachment of feeling quite similar to the affectionate, just as
defiance indicates a similar dependence upon the other person
to that belonging to obedience, though with a reversed prefix.
There can be no doubt that the hostile feelings against the
analyst deserve the name of 'transference,' for the situation in
the treatment certainly gives no adequate occasion for them;
the necessity for regarding the negative transference in this
light is a confirmation of our previous similar view of the positive or affectionate variety

Where the transference springs from, what difficulties it
provides for us, how we can overcome them, and what advantage we can finally derive from it, are questions which can
only be adequately dealt with in a technical exposition of the
analytic method; I can merely touch upon them here. It is out
of the question that we should yield to the demands made by
the patient under the influence of his transference; it would
be nonsensical to reject them unkindly, and still more so, indignantly. The transference is overcome by showing the
patient that his feelings do not originate in the current situation, and do not really concern the person of the physician,
but that he is reproducing something that had happened to
him long ago. In this way we require him to transform his
repetition into *recollection*. Then the transference which,
whether affectionate or hostile, every time seemed the greatest menace to the cure becomes its best instrument, so that
with its help we can unlock the closed doors in the soul. I

should like, however, to say a few words to dispel the unpleasant effects of the shock that this unexpected phenomenon
must have been to you. After all, we must not forget that this
illness of the patient's which we undertake to analyse is not a
finally accomplished, and as it were consolidated thing; but
that it is growing and continuing its development all the time
like a living thing. The beginning of the treatment puts no
stop to this development; but, as soon as the treatment has
taken a hold upon the patient, it appears that the entire pro-
ductivity of the illness henceforward becomes concentrated in
one direction—namely, upon the relationship to the physician.
The transference then becomes comparable to the cambium
layer between the wood and the bark of a tree, from which
proceeds the formation of new tissue and the growth of the
trunk in diameter. As soon as the transference has taken on
this significance the work upon the patient's recollections re-
cedes far into the background. It is then not incorrect to say
that we no longer have to do with the previous illness, but
with a newly created and transformed neurosis which has replaced the earlier one. This new edition of the old disease has
been followed from its inception, one sees it come to light and
grow, and is particularly familiar with it since one is oneself
its central object. All the patient's symptoms have abandoned
their original significance and have adapted themselves to a
new meaning, which is contained in their relationship to the
transference; or else only those symptoms remain which were
capable of being adapted in this way. The conquest of this
new artificially acquired neurosis coincides with the removal
of the illness which existed prior to the treatment, that is, with
accomplishing the therapeutic task. The person who has become normal and free from the influence of repressed instinctive tendencies in his relationship to the physician remains so
in his own life when the physician has again been removed
from it.

The transference has this all-important, absolutely central
significance for the cure in hysteria, anxiety-hysteria, and the
obsessional neurosis, which are in consequence rightly grouped
together as the 'transference neuroses.' Anyone who has

grasped from analytic experience a true impression of the fact
of transference can never again doubt the nature of the suppressed impulses which have manufactured an outlet for
themselves in the symptoms; and he will require no stronger
proof of their libidinal character. We may say that our conviction of the significance of the symptoms as a substitutive
gratification of the libido was only finally and definitely established by evaluating the phenomenon of transference.

Now, however, we are called upon to correct our former
dynamic conception of the process of cure and to bring it into
agreement with the new discovery. When the patient has to
fight out the normal conflict with the resistances which we
have discovered in him by analysis, he requires a powerful
propelling force to influence him towards the decision we aim
at, leading to recovery. Otherwise it might happen that he
would decide for a repetition of the previous outcome, and
allow that which had been raised into consciousness to slip
back again under repression. The outcome in this struggle is
not decided by his intellectual insight—it is neither strong
enough nor free enough to accomplish such a thing—but solely
by his relationship to the physician. In so far as his transference bears the positive sign, it clothes the physician with
authority, transforms itself into faith in his findings and in his
views. Without this kind of transference or with a negative
one, the physician and his arguments would never even be
listened to. Faith repeats the history of its own origin; it is a
derivative of love and at first it needed no arguments. Not until later does it admit them so far as to take them into critical
consideration if they have been offered by someone who is
loved. Without this support arguments have no weight with
the patient, never do have any with most people in life. A
human being is therefore on the whole only accessible to influence, even on the intellectual side, in so far as he is capable
of investing objects with libido; and we have good cause to
recognize, and to fear, in the measure of his narcissism a barrier to his susceptibility to influence, even by the best analytic
technique.

The capacity for the radiation of libido towards other persons in object-investment must, of course, be ascribed to all normal people; the tendency to transference in neurotics, so called, is only an exceptional intensification of a universal characteristic. Now it would be very remarkable if a human character-trait of this importance and universality had never been observed and made use of. And this has really been done. Bernheim, with unerring perspicacity, based the theory of hypnotic manifestations upon the proposition that all human beings are more or less open to suggestion, are 'suggestible.' What he called suggestibility is nothing else but the tendency to transference, rather too narrowly circumscribed so that the negative transference did not come within its scope. But Bernheim could never say what suggestion actually was nor how it arises; it was an axiomatic fact to him and he could give no explanation of its origin. He did not recognize the dependence of 'suggestibility' on sexuality, on the functioning of the libido. And we have to admit that we have only abandoned hypnosis in our methods in order to discover suggestion again in the shape of transference.

But now I will pause and let you take up the thread. I observe that an objection is invading your thoughts with such violence that it would deprive you of all power of attention if it were not given expression. "So now at last you have confessed that you too work with the aid of suggestion like the hypnotists. We have been thinking so all along. But then, what is the use of all these round-about routes by way of past experiences, discovering the unconscious material, interpreting and retranslating the distortions, and the enormous expenditure of time, trouble, and money, when after all the only effective agent is suggestion? Why do you not suggest directly against the symptoms, as others do who are honest hypnotists? And besides, if you are going to make out that by these round-about routes you have made numerous important psychological discoveries, which are concealed in direct suggestion, who is to vouch for their validity? Are not they too the result of suggestion, of unintentional suggestion, that is? Cannot you impress upon the patient what you please and whatever seems good to you in this direction also?"

What you charge me with in this way is exceedingly interesting and must be answered. But I cannot do that to-day; our time is up. Till next time, then. You will see that I shall be answerable to you. To-day I must finish what I began. I promised to explain to you through the factor of the transference why it is that our therapeutic efforts have no success in the narcissistic neuroses.

I can do it in a few words, and you will see how simply the riddle is solved, and how well everything fits together. Experience shows that persons suffering from the narcissistic neuroses have no capacity for transference, or only insufficient remnants of it. They turn from the physician, not in hostility, but in indifference. Therefore they are not to be influenced by him; what he says leaves them cold, makes no impression on them, and therefore the process of cure which can be carried through with others, the revivification of the pathogenic conflict and the overcoming of the resistance due to the repressions, cannot be effected with them. They remain as they are. They have often enough undertaken attempts at recovery on their own account which have led to pathological results; we can do nothing to alter this.

On the basis of our clinical observations of these patients we stated that they must have abandoned the investment of objects with libido and transformed object-libido into ego-libido. By this we differentiated them from the first group of neurotics (hysteria, anxiety, and obsessional neurosis). Their behaviour during the attempt to cure them confirms this suspicion. They produce no transference, and are, therefore, inaccessible to our efforts, not to be cured by us.

TWENTY-EIGHTH LECTURE

THE ANALYTIC THERAPY

YOU KNOW WHAT WE ARE GOING TO DISCUSS TO-DAY. WHEN I admitted that the influence of the psychoanalytic therapy is essentially founded upon transference, i.e. upon suggestion, you asked me why we do not make use of direct suggestion, and you linked this up with a doubt whether, in view of the fact that suggestion plays such a large part, we can still vouch for the objectivity of our psychological discoveries. I promised to give you a comprehensive answer.

Direct suggestion is suggestion delivered directly against the forms taken by the symptoms, a struggle between your authority and the motives underlying the disease. In this struggle you do not trouble yourself about these motives, you only require the patient to suppress the manifestation of them in the form of symptoms. In the main it makes no difference whether you place the patient under hypnosis or not. Bernheim, with his characteristic acuteness, repeatedly stated that suggestion was the essence of the manifestations of hypnotism, and that hypnosis itself was already a result of suggestion, a suggested condition; he preferred to use suggestion in the waking state, which can achieve the same results in hypnosis.

Now which shall I take first, the results of experience or theoretical considerations?

Let us begin with experience. I sought out Bernheim in Nancy in 1889 and became a pupil of his; I translated his book on suggestion into German. For years I made use of hypnotic treatment, first with prohibitory suggestions and later combined with Breuer's system of the fullest inquiry into the patient's life; I can therefore speak from wide experience about the results of the hypnotic or suggestive therapy. According to an old medical saying an ideal therapy should be rapid, reliable and not disagreeable to the patient; Bernheim's method certainly fulfilled two of these requirements. It was much more rapid, that is, incomparably more rapid in its course than the analytic, and it involved the patient in no trouble or discomfort. For the physician it eventually became monotonous; it meant treating every case in the same way, always employing the same ritual to prohibit the existence of the most diverse symptoms, without being able to grasp anything of their meaning or significance. It was a sort of mechanical drudgery—hodman's work—not scientific work; it was reminiscent of magic, conjuring, and hocus-pocus, yet in the patient's interests one had to ignore that. In the third desideratum, however, it failed; it was not reliable in any respect. It could be employed in certain cases only and not in others; with some much could be achieved by it, and with others very little, one never knew why. But worse than its capricious nature was the lack of permanence in the results; after a time, if one heard from the patient again, the old malady had reappeared or had been replaced by another. Then one could begin to hypnotize again. In the background there was the warning of experienced men against robbing the patient of his independence by frequent repetitions of hypnosis, and against accustoming him to this treatment as though it were a narcotic. It is true, on the other hand, that at times everything fell out just as one could wish; one obtained complete and lasting success with little difficulty; but the conditions of this satisfactory outcome remained hidden. In one case, when I had completely removed a severe condition by a short hypnotic treatment, it recurred unchanged after the patient (a woman) had developed ill feeling against me without just cause; then after a reconciliation I was able to effect its disappearance again and this time far more thoroughly; but it reappeared again when she had a second time become hostile to me. Another time I had the following experience; during the treatment of an especially obstinate attack in a patient whom I had several times relieved of nervous symptoms, she suddenly threw her arms round my neck. Whether one wished to do so or not, this kind of thing finally made it imperative to enquire into the problem of the nature and source of one's suggestive authority.

So much for experience; it shows that in abandoning direct suggestion we have given up nothing irreplaceable. Now let us link on to the facts a few comments. The exercise of the hypnotic method makes as little demand for effort on the part of the patient as it does on the physician. The method is in complete harmony with the view of the neuroses generally accepted by the majority of medical men. The practitioner says to the nervous person: "There is nothing the matter with you; it is merely nervousness, therefore a few words from me will scatter all your troubles to the winds in five minutes." But it is contrary to all our beliefs about energy in general that a minimal exertion should be able to remove a heavy load by approaching it directly without the assistance of any suitably devised appliance. In so far as the circumstances are at all comparable, experience shows that this trick cannot be performed successfully with the neuroses. I know, however, that this argument is not unassailable; there are such things as explosions.

In the light of the knowledge we have obtained through psychoanalysis, the difference between hypnotic and psychoanalytic suggestion may be described as follows: The hypnotic therapy endeavours to cover up and as it were to whitewash something going on in the mind, the analytic to lay bare and to remove something. The first works cosmetically, the second surgically. The first employs suggestion to interdict the symptoms; it reinforces the repressions, but otherwise it leaves unchanged all the processes that have led to symptom-formation. Analytic therapy takes hold deeper down nearer the roots of the disease, among the conflicts from which the symptoms proceed; it employs suggestion to change the outcome of these conflicts. Hypnotic therapy allows the patient to remain inactive and unchanged, consequently also helpless in the face of every new incitement to illness. Analytic treatment makes as great demands for efforts on the part of the patient as on the physician, efforts to abolish the inner resistances. The patient's mental life is permanently changed by overcoming these resistances, is lifted to a higher level of development, and remains proof against fresh possibilities of illness. The labour of overcoming the resistances is the essential achievement of the analytic treatment; the patient has to accomplish it and the physician makes it possible for him to do this by suggestions which are in the nature of an *education*. It has been truly said therefore, that psychoanalytic treatment is a kind of *re-education*.

I hope I have now made clear to you the difference between our method of employing suggestion therapeutically and the method which is the only possible one in hypnotic therapy. Since we have traced the influence of suggestion back to the transference, you also understand the striking capriciousness of the effect in hypnotic therapy, and why analytic therapy is within its limits dependable. In employing hypnosis we are entirely dependent upon the condition of the patient's transference and yet we are unable to exercise any influence upon this condition itself. The transference of a patient being hypnotized may be negative, or, as most commonly, ambivalent, or he may have guarded himself against his transference by adopting special attitudes; we gather nothing about all this. In psychoanalysis we work upon the transference itself, dissipate whatever stands in the way of it, and manipulate the instrument which is to do the work. Thus it becomes possible for us to derive entirely new benefits from the power of suggestion; we are able to control it; the patient alone no longer manages his suggestibility according to his own liking, but in so far as he is amenable to its influence at all, we guide his suggestibility.

Now you will say that, regardless of whether the driving

force behind the analysis is called transference or suggestion, the danger still remains that our influence upon the patient may bring the objective certainty of our discoveries into doubt; and that what is an advantage in therapy is harmful in research. This is the objection that has most frequently been raised against psychoanalysis; and it must be admitted that, even though it is unjustified, it cannot be ignored as unreasonable. If it were justified, psycho-analysis after all would be nothing else but a specially well-disguised and particularly effective kind of suggestive treatment; and all its conclusions about the experiences of the patient's past life, mental dynamics, the unconscious, and so on, could be taken very lightly. So our opponents think; the significance of sexual experiences in particular, if not the experiences themselves, we are supposed to have "put into the patient's mind," after having first concocted these conglomerations in our own corrupt minds. These accusations are more satisfactorily refuted by the evidence of experience than by the aid of theory. Anyone who has himself conducted psychoanalyses has been able to convince himself numberless times that it is impossible to suggest things to a patient in this way. There is no difficulty, of course, in making him a disciple of a particular theory, and thus making it possible for him to share some mistaken belief possibly harboured by the physician. He behaves like anyone else in this, like a pupil; but by this one has only influenced his intellect, not his illness. The solving of his conflicts and the overcoming of his resistances succeeds only when what he is told to look for in himself corresponds with what actually does exist in him. Anything that has been inferred wrongly by the physician will disappear in the course of the analysis; it must be withdrawn and replaced by something more correct. One's aim is, by a very careful technique, to prevent temporary successes arising through suggestion; but if they do arise no great harm is done, for we are not content with the first result. We do not consider the analysis completed unless all obscurities in the case are explained, the gaps in memory filled out, and the original occasions of the repressions discovered. When results appear prematurely, one regards them as obstacles rather than as furtherances of the analytic work, and one destroys them again by continually exposing the transference on which they are founded. Fundamentally it is this last feature which distinguishes analytic treatment from that of pure suggestion, and which clears the results of analysis from the suspicion of being the results of suggestion. In every other suggestive treatment the transference is carefully preserved and left intact; in analysis it is itself the object of the treatment and is continually being dissected in all its various forms. At the conclusion of the analysis the transference itself must be dissolved; if success then supervenes and is maintained it is not founded on suggestion, but on the overcoming of the inner resistances effected by the help of suggestion, on the inner change achieved within the patient.

That which probably prevents single effects of suggestion from arising during the treatment is the struggle that is incessantly being waged against the resistances, which know how to transform themselves into a negative (hostile) transference. Nor will we neglect to point to the evidence that a great many of the detailed findings of analysis, which would otherwise be suspected of being produced by suggestion, are confirmed from other, irreproachable sources. We have unimpeachable witnesses on these points, namely, dements and paranoiacs, who are of course quite above any suspicion of being influenced by suggestion. All that these patients relate in the way of phantasies and translations of symbols, which have penetrated through into their consciousness, corresponds faithfully with the results of our investigations into the unconscious of transference neurotics, thus confirming the objective truth of the interpretations made by us which are so often doubted. I do not think you will find yourselves mistaken if you choose to trust analysis in these respects.

We now need to complete our description of the process of recovery by expressing it in terms of the libido theory. The neurotic is incapable of enjoyment or of achievement—the first because his libido is attached to no real object, the last because so much of the energy which would otherwise be at his disposal is expended in maintaining the libido under repression, and in warding off its attempts to assert itself. He would be well if the conflict between his ego and his libido came to an end, and if his ego again had the libido at its disposal. The task of the treatment, therefore, consists in the task of loosening the libido from its previous attachments, which are beyond the reach of the ego, and in making it again serviceable to the ego. Now where is the libido of a neurotic? Easily found: it is attached to the symptoms, which offer it the substitutive satisfaction that is all it can obtain as things are. We must master the symptoms then, dissolve them—just what the patient asks of us. In order to dissolve the symptoms it is necessary to go back to the point at which they originated, to review the conflict from which they proceeded, and with the help of propelling forces which at that time were not available to guide it towards a new solution. This revision of the process of repression can only partially be effected by means of the memory-traces of the processes which led up to repression. The decisive part of the work is carried through by creating— in the relationship to the physician, in "the transference"—new editions of those early conflicts, in which the patient strives to behave as he originally behaved, while one calls upon all the available forces in his soul to bring him to another decision. The transference is thus the battlefield where all the contending forces must meet.

All the libido and the full strength of the opposition against it are concentrated upon the one thing, upon the relationship to the physician; thus it becomes inevitable that the symptoms should be deprived of their libido; in place of the patient's original illness appears the artificially acquired transference, the transference-disorder; in place of a variety of unreal objects of his libido appears the one object, also 'phantastic,' of the person of the physician. This new struggle which arises concerning this object is by means of the analyst's suggestions lifted to the surface, to the higher mental levels, and is there worked out as a normal mental conflict. Since a new repression is thus avoided, the opposition between the ego and the libido comes to an end; unity is restored within the patient's mind. When the libido has been detached from its temporary object in the person of the physician it cannot return to its earlier objects, but is now at the disposal of the ego. The forces opposing us in this struggle during the therapeutic treatment are on the one hand the ego's aversion against certain tendencies on the part of the libido, which had expressed itself in repressing tendencies; and on the other hand the tenacity or 'adhesiveness' of the libido, which does not readily detach itself from objects it has once invested.

The therapeutic work thus falls into two phases; in the first all the libido is forced away from the symptoms into the transference and there concentrated, in the second the battle rages round this new object and the libido is made free from it. The change that is decisive for a successful outcome of this renewed conflict lies in the preclusion of repression, so that the libido cannot again withdraw itself from the ego by a flight into the unconscious. It is made possible by changes in the ego ensuing as a consequence of the analyst's suggestions. At the expense of the unconscious the ego becomes wider by the work of interpretation which brings the unconscious material into consciousness; through education it becomes reconciled to the libido and is made willing to grant it a certain degree of satisfaction; and its horror of the claims of its libido is lessened by the new capacity it acquires to expend a certain amount of the libido in sublimation. The more nearly the course of the treatment corresponds with this ideal description the greater will be the success of the psychoanalytic therapy. Its barriers are found in the lack of mobility in the libido, which resists being released from its objects, and in the rigidity of the patient's narcissism, which will not allow more than a certain degree of object-transference to develop Perhaps the dynamics of the process of recovery will become still clearer if we describe it by saying that, in attracting a part of it to ourselves through transference, we gather in the whole amount of the libido which has been withdrawn from the ego's control.

It is as well here to make clear that the distributions of the libido which ensue during and by means of the analysis afford no direct inference of the nature of its disposition during the previous illness. Given that a case can be successfully cured by establishing and then resolving a powerful father-transference to the person of the physician, it would not follow that the patient had previously suffered in this way from an unconscious attachment of the libido to his father. The father-transference is only the battlefield on which we conquer and take the libido prisoner; the patient's libido has been drawn hither away from other 'positions.' The battlefield does not necessarily constitute one of the enemy's most important strongholds; the defence of the enemy's capital city need not be conducted immediately before its gates. Not until after the transference has been again resolved can one begin to reconstruct in imagination the dispositions of the libido that were represented by the illness.

In the light of the libido theory there is a final word to be said about dreams. The dreams of a neurotic, like his "errors" and his free associations, enable us to find the meaning of the symptoms and to discover the dispositions of the libido. The forms taken by the wish-fulfilment in them show us what are the wish-impulses that have undergone repression, and what are the objects to which the libido has attached itself after withdrawal from the ego. The interpretation of dreams therefore plays a great part in psychoanalytic treatment, and in many cases it is for lengthy periods the most important instrument at work. We already know that the condition of sleep in itself produces a certain relaxation of the repressions. By this diminution in the heavy pressure upon it the repressed desire is able to create for itself a far clearer expression in a dream than can be permitted to it by day in the symptoms. Hence the study of dreams becomes the easiest approach to a knowledge of the repressed unconscious, which is where the libido which has withdrawn from the ego belongs.

The dreams of neurotics, however, differ in no essential from those of normal people; they are indeed perhaps not in any way distinguishable from them. It would be illogical to account for the dreams of neurotics in a way that would not also hold good of the dreams of normal people. We have to conclude therefore that the difference between neurosis and health prevails only by day; it is not sustained in dream-life.

It thus becomes necessary to transfer to healthy persons a number of conclusions arrived at as a result of the connections between the dreams and the symptoms of neurotics. We have to recognize that the healthy man as well possesses those factors in mental life which alone can bring about the formation of a dream or of a symptom, and we must conclude further that the healthy also have instituted repressions and have to expend a certain amount of energy to maintain them; that their unconscious minds too harbour repressed impulses which are still suffused with energy, and that *a part of the libido is in them also withdrawn from the disposal of the ego*. The healthy man too is therefore virtually a neurotic, but the only symptom that he *seems* capable of developing is a dream. To be sure when you subject his waking life also to a critical investigation you discover something that contradicts this specious conclusion; for this apparently healthy life is pervaded by innumerable trivial and practically unimportant symptom-formations.

The difference between nervous health and nervous illness (neurosis) is narrowed down therefore to a practical distinction, and is determined by the practical result—how far the person concerned remains capable of a sufficient degree of capacity for enjoyment and active achievement in life. The difference can probably be traced back to the proportion of the energy which has remained free relative to that of the energy which has been bound by repression, i.e. it is a quantitative and not a qualitative difference. I do not need to remind you that this view provides a theoretical basis for our conviction that the neuroses are essentially amenable to cure, in spite of their being based on a constitutional disposition.

So much, therefore, in the way of knowledge of the characteristics of health may be inferred from the identity of the dreams dreamt by neurotic and by healthy persons. Of dreams themselves, however, a further inference must be drawn—namely, that it is not possible to detach them from their connection with neurotic symptoms; that we are not at liberty to believe that their essential nature is exhausted by compressing them into the formula of 'a translation of thoughts into archaic forms of expression'; and that we are bound to conclude that they disclose dispositions of the libido and objects of desire which are actually in operation and valid at the moment.

We have now come very nearly to the end. Perhaps you are disappointed that under the heading of psychoanalytic therapy I have limited myself to theory, and have told you nothing of the conditions under which the cure is undertaken, or of the results it achieves. I omit both, however: the first, because in fact I never intended to give you a practical training in the exercise of the analytic method; and the last, because I have several motives against it. At the beginning of these discussions I said emphatically that under favourable conditions we achieve cures that are in no way inferior to the most brilliant in other fields of medical therapy; I may perhaps add that these results could be achieved by no other method. If I said more I should be suspected of wishing to drown the depreciatory voices of our opponents by self-advertisement. Medical "colleagues" have, even at public congresses, repeatedly held out a threat to psychoanalysts that by publishing a collection of the failures and harmful effects of analysis they will open the eyes of the injured public to the worthlessness of this method of treatment. Apart from the malicious, denunciatory character of such a measure, however, a collection of that kind would not even be valid evidence upon which a correct estimate of the therapeutic results of analysis might be formed. Analytic therapy, as you know, is still young; it needed many years to elaborate the technique, which could only be done in the course of the work under the influence of increasing experience. On account of the difficulties of imparting instruction in the methods the beginner is thrown much more upon his own resources for development of his capacity than any other kind of specialist, and the results of his early years can never be taken as indicating the full possible achievements of analytic therapy.

Many attempts at treatment made in the beginning of psychoanalysis were failures because they were undertaken with cases altogether unsuited to the procedure, which nowadays we should exclude by following certain indications. These indications, however, could only be discovered by trying. In the beginning we did not know that paranoia and dementia præcox, when fully developed, are not amenable to analysis; we were still justified in trying the method on all kinds of disorders. Most of the failures of those early years, however, were not due to the fault of the physician, or to the unsuitability in the choice of subject, but to unpropitious external conditions. I have spoken only of the inner resistances, those on the part of the patient, which are inevitable and can be overcome. The external resistances which the patient's circumstances and surroundings set up against analysis have little theoretic interest but the greatest practical importance. Psychoanalytic treatment is comparable to a surgical operation and, like that, for its success it has the right to expect to be carried out under the most favourable conditions. You know the preliminary arrangements a surgeon is accustomed to make—a suitable room, a good light, expert assistance, exclusion of the relatives, and so on. Now ask yourselves how many surgical operations would be successful if they had to be conducted in the presence of the patient's entire family poking their noses into the scene of the operation and shrieking aloud at every cut. In psychoanalytic treatment the intervention of the relatives is a positive danger and, moreover, one which we do not know how to deal with. We are armed against the inner resistances of the patient, which we recognize as necessary, but how can we protect ourselves against these outer resistances? It is impossible to get round the relatives by any sort of explanation, nor can one induce them to hold aloof from the whole affair; one can never take them into one's confidence because then we run the danger of losing the patient's trust in us, for he—quite rightly, of course—demands that the man he confides in should take his part. Anyone who knows anything of the dissensions commonly splitting up family life will not be astonished in his capacity of analyst to find that those nearest to the patient frequently show less interest in his recovery than in keeping him as he is When as so often occurs the neurosis is connected with conflicts between different members of a family, the healthy person does not make much of putting his own interest before the patient's recovery. After all, it is not surprising that the husband does not favour a treatment in which, as he correctly supposes, his sins will all come to light; nor do we wonder at this, but then we cannot blame ourselves when our efforts remain fruitless and are prematurely broken off because the husband's resistance is added to that of the sick wife. We had simply undertaken something which, under the existing conditions, it was impossible to carry out.

Instead of describing many cases to you I will tell you of one only, in which I had to suffer for the sake of professional conscientiousness. I took a young girl—many years ago—for analytic treatment; for a considerable time previously she had been unable to go out of doors on account of a dread, nor could she stay at home alone. After much hesitation the patient confessed that her thoughts had been a good deal occupied by some signs of affection that she had noticed by chance between her mother and a well-to-do friend of the family. Very tactlessly—or else very cleverly—she then gave the mother a hint of what had been discussed during the analysis; she did this by altering her behaviour to her mother, by insisting that no one but her mother could protect her against the dread of being alone, and by holding the door against her when she attempted to leave the house. The mother herself had formerly been very nervous, but had been cured years before by a visit to a hydropathic establishment—or, putting it otherwise, we may say she had there made the acquaintance of the man with whom she had established a relationship that had proved satisfying in more than one respect. Made suspicious by her daughter's passionate demands the mother suddenly *understood* what the girl's dread signified. She had become ill in order to make her mother a prisoner and rob her of the freedom necessary for her to maintain her relations with her lover. The mother's decision was instantly taken; she put an end to the harmful treatment. The girl was sent to a home for nervous patients, and for many years was there pointed out as an "unhappy victim of psychoanalysis"; for just as long I was pursued by damaging rumours about the unfortunate results of the treatment. I maintained silence because I supposed myself bound by the rules of professional secrecy. Years later I learned from a colleague who had visited the home and there seen the girl with agoraphobia that the intimacy between the mother and the wealthy man was common knowledge, and that in all probability it was connived at by the husband and father. To this "secret" the girl's cure had been sacrificed.

In the years before the war, when the influx of patients from many countries made me independent of the goodwill or disfavour of my native city, I made it a rule never to take for treatment anyone who was not *sui juris*, independent of others in all the essential relations of life. Every psychoanalyst cannot make these stipulations. Perhaps you will conclude from my warnings about relatives that one should take the patient out of his family circle in the interests of analysis, and restrict this therapy to those living in private institutions. I could not support this suggestion, however; it is far more advantageous for the patients—those who are not in a condition of severe prostration, at least—to remain during the treatment in those circumstances in which they have to struggle with the demands that their ordinary life makes on them. But the relatives ought not to counteract this advantage by their behaviour, and above all should not oppose their hostility to one's professional efforts. But how are you going to induce people who are inaccessible to you to take up this attitude? You will naturally also conclude that the social atmosphere and degree of cultivation of the patient's immediate surroundings have considerable influence upon the prospects of the treatment.

This is a gloomy outlook for the efficacy of psychoanalysis as a therapy, even if we may explain the overwhelming majority of our failures by taking into account these disturbing external factors! Friends of analysis have advised us to counterbalance a collection of failures by drawing up a statistical enumeration of our successes. I have not taken up this suggestion either. I brought forward the argument that statistics would be valueless if the units collated were not alike, and the cases which had been treated were in fact not equivalent in many respects. Further, the period of time that could be reviewed was too short for one to be able to judge of the permanence of the cures; and of many cases it would be impossible to give any account. They were persons who had kept both their illness and their treatment secret, and whose recovery in consequence had similarly to be kept secret. The strongest reason against it, however, lay in the recognition of the fact that in matters of therapy humanity is in the highest degree irrational, so that there is no prospect of influencing it by reasonable arguments. A novelty in therapeutics is either taken up with frenzied enthusiasm, as for instance when Koch first published his results with tuberculin; or else it is regarded with abysmal distrust, as happened for instance with Jenner's vaccination, actually a heaven-sent blessing, but one which still has its implacable opponents. A very evident prejudice against psycho-analysis made itself apparent. When one had cured a very difficult case one would hear: "That is no proof of anything; he would have got well of himself after all this time." And when a patient who had already gone through four cycles of depression and mania came to me in an interval after the melancholia and three weeks later again began to develop an attack of mania, all the members of the family, and also all the high medical authorities who were called in, were convinced that the fresh attack could be nothing but a consequence of the attempted analysis. Against prejudice one can do nothing, as you can now see once more in the prejudices that each group of the nations at war has developed against the other. The most sensible thing to do is to wait and allow them to wear off with the passage of time. A day comes when the same people regard the same things in quite a different light from what they did before; why they thought differently before remains a dark secret.

It is possible that the prejudice against the analytic therapy has already begun to relax. The continual spread of analytic doctrine and the numbers of medical men taking up analytic treatment in many countries seem to point in that direction. As a young man I was caught in just such a storm of indigna-

tion roused in the medical profession by the hypnotic sugges-
tion-treatment, which nowadays is held up in opposition to
psychoanalysis by the "sober-minded." As a therapeutic instrument, however, hypnotism did not bear out the hopes
placed in it; we psychoanalysts may claim to be its rightful
heirs and should not forget how much encouragement and
theoretic enlightenment we owe to it. The harmful effects reported of psychoanalysis are essentially confined to transitory
manifestations of an exacerbation of the conflict, which may
occur when the analysis is clumsily handled, or when it is
broken off suddenly. You have heard an account of what we
do with our patients, and you can form your own judgement
whether our efforts are likely to lead to lasting injury. Misuse
of analysis is possible in various ways: the transference especially, in the hands of an unscrupulous physician, is a dangerous instrument. But no medical remedy is proof against
misuse; if a knife will not cut, neither will it serve a surgeon.

I have now reached the end. It is more than a conventional
formality when I say that I myself am heavily oppressed by
the many defects of the lectures I have delivered before you.
I regret most of all that I have so often promised to return
again in another place to a subject that I had just touched
upon shortly, and that then the context in which I could keep
my word did not offer itself. I undertook to give you an account of a thing that is still unfinished, still developing, and
now my short summary itself has become an incomplete one.
In many places I laid everything ready for drawing a conclusion, and then I did not draw it. But I could not aim at
making you experts in psychoanalysis; I only wished to put
you in the way of some understanding of it, and to arouse
your interest in it.

INDEX